On Freedom and the Will to Adorn

CHERYL A. WALL

On Freedom and the Will to Adorn
The Art of the African American Essay

University of North Carolina Press *Chapel Hill*

This book was published with the assistance of the Anniversary Fund
of the University of North Carolina Press.

Set in Arno by Westchester Publishing Services
Manufactured in the United States of America

The University of North Carolina Press has been a member
of the Green Press Initiative since 2003.

Library of Congress Cataloging-in-Publication Data
Names: Wall, Cheryl A., author.
Title: On freedom and the will to adorn : the art of the
    African American essay / Cheryl A. Wall.
Description: Chapel Hill : University of North Carolina Press, [2018] |
    Includes bibliographical references and index.
Identifiers: LCCN 2018016245| ISBN 9781469646893 (cloth : alk. paper) |
    ISBN 9781469646909 (pbk : alk. paper) | ISBN 9781469646916 (ebook)
Subjects: LCSH: African American authors—History and criticism. |
    Essayists, American. | Essay.
Classification: LCC PS153.N5 W328 2018 | DDC 814.009/896073—dc23
    LC record available at https://lccn.loc.gov/2018016245

Cover illustration by Nathan W. Moehlmann, Goosepen Studio & Press

Portions of chapters 4 and 6 were previously published in a different form. Chapter 4 includes material
from "Stranger at Home: James Baldwin on What It Means to Be an American," in *James Baldwin:
America and Beyond*, edited by Cora Kaplan and Bill Schwarz (Ann Arbor: University of Michigan Press,
2011), 35–52. Chapter 6 includes material from "Living by the Word: June Jordan and Alice Walker's
Quest for a Redemptive Art and Politics," in *Toward an Intellectual History of Black Women*, edited by Mia
Bay et al. (Chapel Hill: University of North Carolina Press, 2015), 233–51. Used here with permission.

For my great-nieces and great-nephew:

Morgan Reid

Marjani Reid

Micah Reid

Mikhel Reid

Contents

Acknowledgments ix

Prologue: Moving from the Margins 1

CHAPTER ONE
On Freedom and the Will to Adorn: The African American Essay 10

CHAPTER TWO
Voices of Thunder: Nineteenth-Century Black Oratory and the
Development of the African American Essay 36

CHAPTER THREE
On Art and Such: Debating Aesthetics during the
Harlem Renaissance 84

CHAPTER FOUR
Stranger at Home: James Baldwin on What It Means to
Be an American 119

CHAPTER FIVE
The Mystery of American Identity: Ralph Ellison 148

CHAPTER SIX
On Women, Rights, and Writing: June Jordan and Alice Walker 176

Epilogue: Essaying in the Digital Age 217

Notes 229

Bibliography 253

Index 263

Acknowledgments

I have incurred many debts in the process of writing this book. Chief among them is the debt I owe to the graduate and undergraduate students at Rutgers who read essays in my courses, shared their opinions, and questioned mine. They have made this a much better book than it would have been without them. I have tried to discharge my debt to my colleagues mainly by citing their books and articles, but some I need to thank by name. For reading all or part of the manuscript, I thank Ryan Kernan, Douglas Jones, Richard Miller, Stéphane Robolin, and Evie Shockley, as well as the anonymous readers at the University of North Carolina Press. I owe a special thank you to Barry Qualls, my most willing and careful reader, who has commented on multiple versions of these pages. I am grateful to Frances Foster for insisting I read writers from the nineteenth century and to Kelly Josephs and Tzarina Prater for giving me confidence enough to write about twenty-first century blogs.

I am grateful to the members of the Towards a Black Women's Intellectual History collective, especially Mia Bay, Farah Jasmine Griffin, Martha Jones, and Barbara Savage, for inviting me to participate in a project that nurtured and challenged my thinking about the essay as a mode of intellectual production for African American women. Over the years that this book has taken shape, I have also benefitted from exchanges with many smart and generous interlocutors, including Elizabeth Alexander, Kathryn Sophia Belle, Daphne Brooks, Thadious Davis, Corinne Field, Douglas Field, Arlette Frund, Jacqueline Goldsby, Mae Henderson, Cora Kaplan, Andrée-Anne Kekeh-dika, Dwight McBride, Jocelyn Moody, Brian Norman, Bill Schwarz, Hortense Spillers, Justine Talley, Mary Helen Washington, Deborah White, and Andréa Williams.

For their sharp questions and insightful comments, I thank audiences at Barnard College, Case Western Reserve University, Cleveland State University, the Caribbean Philosophical Association, the Collegium for African American Research Conference at Université de Paris Diderot, the Collegium of Black Women Philosophers, Emory University, New York University, Northwestern University, Oklahoma City University, Queen Mary University in London, Rutgers University, Universidad de La Laguna in Tenerife, Spain,

Université de Paris VIII, Vincennes-St. Denis, the University of Michigan, Vanderbilt University, and Yale University.

For brilliant conversations and technical expertise, I thank my graduate assistants Brian Becker, Gabrielle Everett, Ariel Martino, Amadi Ozier, Beth Perry, Elliott Souder, and especially Tasia Milton. I thank as well the archivists who assisted me with the research for this project, especially Randall Burkett at the Manuscripts and Research Library at Emory, Steven Fullwood and Miranda Mims at the Schomburg Center for Research in Black Culture, Marilyn Morgan at the Schlesinger Library, and the staff of the Library of Congress.

For permission to reprint previously published material, I thank the University of Michigan Press and the University of North Carolina Press.

This is my second experience working with the editors at the University of North Carolina Press, and I am grateful for the always incisive advice of Mark Simpson-Vos. I am also appreciative of the contributions of Dino Battista, Kristen Bettcher, Iris Oakes, and Jessica Newman. Finally, everything I do depends on the love and encouragement of my family. My daughter Camara and sister Gatsie are my biggest fans. I am blessed that my niece Monique and her husband Paul share their wonderful children with me. It is my joy to dedicate this book to Morgan, Marjani, Micah, and Mikhel Reid.

On Freedom and the Will to Adorn

Prologue

Moving from the Margins

Writing at the Margins, the subtitle of a collection of Toni Morrison's nonfiction, captures exactly the status of the essay in literary studies in general and African American literary studies in particular.[1] Occasional and provisional, essays seem to exist alongside literature's major genres. Many do not seek to claim status as literature; rather, they are written in response to an immediate crisis or concern. In the African American tradition, these concerns are often political, a fact that reflects the efficacy of the essay to raise awareness, analyze situations, and catalyze action. But writers also use the genre to offer analyses of fiction, drama, and poetry, sometimes their own and sometimes not. Many of the most influential works of literary criticism in the tradition are essays. A novelist may write an autobiographical aside or weigh in on a pressing political or social issue. A poet may invoke her precursor and outline a tradition in which she locates her writing. Still, to many readers, essays lack significance in their own right.[2] The aim of this book is to move consideration of the African American essay from the margins to the center.

What is an essay? Readers and critics agree that it is much easier to say what an essay is not, rather than what it is. It is not a philosophical treatise, although it may be the site of philosophical reflection. It is not a systematic argument, although it may make a case for a particular position. It is not reportage, although it may recount events. It is not autobiography, although it may tell parts of the author's life. An essay is not a letter, though some essays that are written for publication assume the guise of private correspondence. James Baldwin's "Letter to My Nephew" is one example; Ta-Nehisi Coates's *Between the World and Me*, putatively addressed to his son, is another. In looking for an affirmative definition, critics may agree that rather than exhausting a subject, the essayist works around and through a specific aspect of it, prompted usually by a particular and often personal encounter with its implications. The hybridity of the form makes it capacious enough to incorporate other genres—short stories, literary and political critique, and memoir. If the formal criteria are vague, the opportunities the form affords are not. The essay offers its creator intellectual freedom—the freedom to work around, with, and through an idea. It is, as its name denotes, a trial or an attempt.

In large part because it is perceived as occasional writing, the essay has achieved little critical currency. Even its practitioners describe the genre in belittling terms: "dispersed meditations," "fragments of my deceits," and "free association artistically controlled" are representative.[3] When a publisher contacted W. E. B. Du Bois asking whether he had material for a book, Du Bois proposed a scholarly study. He remembered the publisher's response: "They asked, however, if I did not have some essays that they might put together and issue immediately, mentioning my articles in the *Atlantic Monthly* and other places. I demurred because volumes of essays always fall so flat . . . . Nevertheless I got together a number of my fugitive pieces."[4] When collected, those fugitive pieces became *The Souls of Black Folk*. Ironically, although Du Bois published foundational works of scholarship, including *The Philadelphia Negro* and *Black Reconstruction*, *Souls* is his most enduring work. Tellingly, he called the pieces in *Souls* chapters rather than essays.[5] Perhaps he did so to signal that the eight previously published pieces were extensively revised, but his decision may reveal some doubt he harbored about the seriousness of the essay form. Many critics have expressed similar doubts.

Consensus exists on one point. Michel de Montaigne, the sixteenth-century French aristocrat, initiated and named the genre. In "Of Practice," he wrote, "What I chiefly portray is my own cogitations, a shapeless subject that does not lend itself to expression in actions. It is all I can do to couch my thoughts in this airy medium of words."[6] For Montaigne, the challenge of the essay was not so much to express his ideas as to convey the experience of thinking itself, to convey the flow, the wanderings of his thoughts. He believed in the integrity of his experience and boasted of his putative lack of erudition. He did not expect his words to produce actions; he hoped only to communicate his thoughts and the process that produced them. Nothing seems less relevant to a tradition of African American writers, many of whose essays are explicitly calls to action. Yet, if many African American essayists reject Montaigne's sense of the essential privacy of the essay, its limitations to the mind of the writer, they retain a desire to make the process of their thinking transparent.

For example, in his introduction to *Nobody Knows My Name*, James Baldwin describes the essays it contains as "a very small part of a private logbook . . . . The questions which one asks oneself begin, at last," he reflected, "to illuminate the world, and become one's key to the experience of others."[7] Baldwin's description is one that Montaigne would have recognized. Writing out of the belief that "what is useful to one may also by accident be useful to another," Montaigne believed that his writing would resonate with readers everywhere.[8]

Like Montaigne, Baldwin wrote essays that are intensely subjective, that give the reader his personal perspective on the world around him. It is hard to imagine that Baldwin, whom the novelist Mary McCarthy once described as a man who had read *everything,* had not read Montaigne.[9] Refusing to rely on the wisdom and writing of the past, Montaigne embraced the "thorny undertaking . . . to follow a movement so wandering as that of our own mind."[10] Baldwin, by contrast, had not only to take into account but actively to struggle against the external world in order to create a space for the brilliant thoughts that tracked across his mind. Although he writes more revealingly about his personal experience than most African American essayists before him, he is never just writing for and about himself. Even when he is recounting experiences that are singularly his own, as, for example, the winter he spent in a remote Swiss village where he was the only black man the villagers had ever seen, he is most often writing about the condition of blacks in the United States of America and beyond. In so doing, Baldwin demonstrates Theodor Adorno's assertion in "The Essay as Form" that "the relationship to experience—and the essay invests experience with as much substance as traditional theory does mere categories—is the relationship to all of history."[11] In "Stranger in the Village," for example, Baldwin famously uses the cathedral at Chartres to emblematize European history; at the same time, he invokes the blues as an emblem for the history of black Americans. The result is an essay that, as Toni Morrison observes, illustrates how one "could go as a stranger in the village and transform the distances between people into intimacy with the whole world."[12] The production of that intimacy, or its semblance, is at the core of Baldwin's art.

Like Baldwin, Ralph Ellison turns to the essay to answer personal questions, in particular, "the question of what was the most desirable agency for defining myself." Written at a time when he still clung to his original ambition to be a musician rather than a writer, the essay allowed him to resolve a "crucial conflict raging deep within." As he describes it, writing the essays that would be collected in *Shadow and Act* "was an acting out, symbolically, of a choice which I dared not acknowledge."[13] Readers are hardly aware of this inner conflict, perhaps because Ellison holds readers at a greater remove than Baldwin does. In his introduction, Ellison predicts, wrongly, that the significance of his early essays would be primarily autobiographical. To that end, he shares recollections of his Oklahoma boyhood and youthful aspirations to become a Renaissance man. Nevertheless, most readers read his essays for their insights into literature and art as well as for their understanding of the democratic culture of the United States as a harbinger of a political and social democracy not yet achieved. If Ellison's essays do not have the semblance of intimacy that Baldwin's do, they convey a similar sense of the immediacy that is characteristic of the genre.

Neither an exploration of philosophical concepts or scientific principles nor a historical compendium, the essay explores its own moment. Adorno embraces the description of the essay as "fragmentary and contingent," rejecting the "customary objection" that this character diminishes the genre's value. He endorses the essay's refusal of the postulate that "totality is a given," which is the basis for the objection in the first place. For African American writers, who enter a discursive arena in which their own history and—before the mid-twentieth century—their humanity was not recognized or acknowledged in philosophy or science, their own experience was the only truth on which they could rely. The essay, "which shakes off the illusion of a simple and fundamentally logical world, an illusion well suited to the defense of the status quo," was an ideal genre with which to combat the illogic of their positionality and the fundamental injustice of that status quo.[14] African American essayists have acknowledged that the truth of their experience was both fragmentary and partial and have offered the understanding they drew from it as contingent. And yet, their writings exemplify another of Adorno's assertions, to wit: "The essay, however, does not try to seek the eternal in the transient and distill it out; it tries to render the transient eternal."[15] That readers return to Baldwin's "Stranger in the Village," to W. E. B. Du Bois's "Of Our Spiritual Strivings," and to Zora Neale Hurston's "How It Feels to Be Colored Me" confirms the success of their renderings.

Although they have written in various genres, African American writers as notable and diverse as W. E. B. Du Bois, James Baldwin, and Alice Walker have done their most influential work in the essay; *The Souls of Black Folk*, *The Fire Next Time*, and *In Search of Our Mothers' Gardens* are landmarks in African American literary history. However, many more writers—including Ralph Ellison, Jessie Fauset, Zora Neale Hurston, James Weldon Johnson, and Richard Wright—are acclaimed essayists, even though they achieved greater fame for their work in other genres. Consequently, critics turn to their essays mainly for the light they shed on the authors' better-known texts. But the focus of this book is on the essay itself. It analyzes its political potency, its legacy of the pulpit and the podium, its utility for aesthetic debates, and the space it offers for personal recollection and philosophical reflection. As it considers the cultural and political work the essay performs, it analyzes its formal strategies and their historical antecedents. Although it is not a history of the genre, it offers a protocol for reading its texts.[16]

For that reason, the illustrative examples include many texts familiar to students of African American literature. While scholars have studied the relationship between, for example, Hurston's essays and her novels and analyzed the continuities and points of contention between Baldwin's and Wright's politics and aesthetic principles, they have paid little attention to the genre in which these arguments are made. This book will study the form as well as the contents of the arguments.

Its compactness and portability have made the essay appealing to writers and thinkers who belong to a community that has been defined and defined itself as perpetually in crisis. They write in the tradition of Ralph Waldo Emerson, who refashioned the essay genre in the United States by making it more outward than inward looking, and who, unlike Montaigne, hoped to move his audience to action.[17] Drawing on traditions of nineteenth-century oratory and extending the autobiographical impulse of the slave narrative, black writers shaped the essay to advance the struggle for freedom above all. So, for example, in *The Souls of Black Folk*, one hears echoes of the orators Henry Highland Garnet and Alexander Crummell. In their use of typographical elements and blazing rhetoric, one sees the imprint of David Walker's *Appeal* on the pages of essays by Amiri Baraka and June Jordan. Just as speeches by Douglass and Garnet responded to the urgent issues of abolition and citizenship in the nineteenth century, essays by Du Bois, Wright, Baldwin, and Patricia Williams respond to the urgent issues of desegregation and citizenship in the twentieth. One sees as well traces of the autobiographical impulse that fueled the narratives by writers such as William Wells Brown and Harriet Jacobs, who also believed that their exceptional personal histories shed light on the experiences of the masses of black Americans. Even the most personal essays in the African American tradition continually engage the subject of freedom.

Starting with Victoria Matthews's "The Value of Race Literature" in 1895 and continuing through the Harlem Renaissance and beyond, the essay became the medium in which debates over aesthetics were waged. Alain Locke in "The New Negro" and "Negro Youth Speaks" (1925) pronounced the manifesto of the movement, one in which the arts became a key front in the battle for equal rights. In his preface to the first edition of *The Book of American Negro Poetry*, published three years earlier, James Weldon Johnson had declared, "The final measure of the greatness of all peoples is the amount and standard of the literature and art they have produced."[18] He went on to make a case for the originality and importance of folklore, spirituals, the cakewalk, and ragtime and to predict that young black artists would distill these forms into fine art. Their creations would uplift the race. Young artists Langston Hughes in "The Negro Artist and the Racial Mountain" and Zora Neale Hurston in "Characteristics of Negro Expression" took exception to the proposition that art should serve ends other than those the artist identified. Their essays are declarations of artistic independence. Both take their lead from the storytellers, the singers of spirituals and blues, whose art inspired and enabled their own. When they drew on traditions of African American musical and oral performances in their texts, they left a distinctive mark on the essay as a genre.

As she studied their art, Hurston deemed one of its key characteristics, "the will to adorn," second only to the penchant for drama that African Americans expressed in their everyday lives. She identified specific contributions that blacks had made to the English language: (1) the use of metaphor and simile, (2) the use of the double descriptive, and (3) the use of verbal nouns. In defiance of then-conventional wisdom that blacks were unable or unwilling to master the master's tongue, Hurston asserted that blacks had changed the way southern white people spoke. But more than linguistic elements, "the will to adorn" expressed an attitude toward language. That attitude encompassed an impulse toward embellishment, an understanding that language did more than convey information, and a commitment to beauty as a cardinal value.

In this book, "the will to adorn" signals first the importance of the essay for aesthetic debates. But it also signals, following Hurston, a way of understanding the genre itself. I want to consider the digressiveness of African American essays as an enactment of the will to adorn, an expression of an attitude toward language. Hurston contends that the will to adorn "arises out of the same impulse as the wearing of jewelry and the making of sculpture."[19] It is the urge to embellish, to make language an expression of beauty. Although the styles change dramatically over time, African American essays share an impulse toward embellishment and display a consciousness that the language they employ is important for its own sake. Even essays that intend to rouse readers to action reflect the sensibility that *how* they make their argument is as illuminating as what the argument becomes. This premise is taken for granted in the study of other literary genres—poems and novels, for example. I contend that one can read essays as well for the pleasure they provide. Readers, like writers, may pause and take delight in the language of the argument, whether or not they find the argument persuasive.

Black writers have used the essay for interventions in social and political debates, whether over slavery and abolitionism, civil rights, feminism, or affirmative action. The dialogic form of the essay which strives to produce the effect of the spontaneous, the tentative, and the open-ended lends itself to exploring complex and contentious issues. When they posit arguments, many essays defer conclusions, or at least remain open to the possibility that other conclusions might be plausible. In either case, they invite readers to join a dialogue, one that is presumed or imagined to continue after the essay ends. To make their case, they might paint verbal portraits of race leaders, artists, and activists, or they might reflect on their own experiences. To be sure, they often advance an argument. However, as Georg Lukács observes, "The essay is a judgment, but the essential, the value-determining thing about it is not the verdict . . . but the process of the judging."[20] It is a process in which the reader participates. So we read Alice Walker's "The Civil Rights Movement: What Good Was It?" not to learn that the movement was valuable, which we already know, but to learn through her use of analysis and irony how to argue its worth.

A hallmark of the form is the window it opens into the writer's mind. Readers watch writers think their way through a topic. As they qualify their thoughts, reject one idea and choose another, writers call attention to the quest for the right word or phrase. The essay offers not only information but the pleasure of the text as well. Unlike scientific or academic writing, but very much like the oration, the essay calls attention to its language and form. A well-turned phrase, an arresting image, and a memorable anecdote are essential tools. Readers may ultimately be drawn more intimately into an engagement with the object that the essayist turns around for their inspection as well as his or her own. The intimacy of that engagement is deepened by the fact that readers encounter the object on the printed page; they may return to the text as often as they desire. This activity is the source of both freedom and satisfaction. Readers may take delight in or courage from words that have inspired them. Or they may argue against viewpoints with which they disagree.[21]

Despite the general critical neglect of the genre, an informal taxonomy of the essay exists. Formal, informal, personal, familiar, critical, and meditative are some of the types. These terms do not work particularly well for the African American tradition. *The Souls of Black Folk*, for example, opens with the highly personal, though hardly informal, essay, "Of Our Spiritual Strivings," which is followed by the formal, impersonal, and authoritative "Of the Dawn of Freedom," the pioneering historical account of Reconstruction in the post–Civil War South. In the essays that follow, the personal and political are mutually constitutive. Contemplations of the aesthetic partake of the political so that, for instance, the sorrow songs are both the "most beautiful expression of human experience born this side the seas" and a searing protest against slavery. To take another example, "In Search of Our Mothers' Gardens" is at once Alice Walker's exploration of her literary lineage and a meditation on her mother's life; it is also a protest against the racism and sexism that thwart the potential of so many black women. Legal theorist and scholar Patricia Williams uses the *Brown v. Board of Education of Topeka* decision as the touchstone for her volume *The Alchemy of Race and Rights*, in which the civil rights movement and its afterlife play a role analogous to that of Reconstruction in *Souls*. But while Williams analyzes cases and deploys legal discourse (several of the essays first appeared in law journals), she invents an "intentionally double-voiced and relational" mode of writing that can encompass meditations on her great-great-grandmother's enslavement as well as her own encounters with racism. These experiences motivate and inform her arguments on jurisprudence.[22]

If the questions the African American essay explores remain strikingly consistent across centuries, the language of the texts markedly changes. Writers enact the will to adorn in different registers. Despite the concerns their essays share, no one would mistake the diction of Amiri Baraka for that of David Walker or June Jordan's for that of Anna Julia Cooper. An analysis of essays by African Americans with reference to these linguistic shifts enables us to answer the second and central question this book raises: what is an African American essay? As with the first question, the answer is elusive. But by focusing on three strategies that writers have used to express the will to adorn—(1) "democratic eloquence," (2) "troubled eloquence," and (3) "vernacular process"—we can analyze how the African American essay does its work.

I borrow "democratic eloquence" from historian Kenneth Cmiel, who uses it to define a distinctively nineteenth-century American prose style, one that is shorn of the flourishes associated with the formal literary diction of the time. I borrow "troubled eloquence" from critic and poet Nathaniel Mackey to think through the innovations that African American writers make to the essay genre. The term speaks to the unexpected turns in their work, the hesitations and improvisations that characterize it. I borrow my third term, "vernacular process," from Ralph Ellison, who defines "the vernacular as a dynamic *process* . . . . In it the styles and techniques of the past are adjusted to the needs of the present, and in its integrative action the high styles of the past are democratized."[23] In his view, jazz musicians are the exemplars of vernacular process, but it applies to writers as well. For Ellison as essayist, the vernacular process enables the discussion of the most serious cultural and philosophical issues, including the meaning of democracy, in colloquial language characterized by wit and verve. Vernacular process describes not only Ellison's own practice as an essayist but that of Hurston and Walker as well.

These terms do not imply a linear progression. Democratic eloquence characterizes both the prose of Maria Stewart in the early nineteenth century and Patricia Williams in the late twentieth century. Similarly, while *The Souls of Black Folk* seems to me to initiate the sound of troubled eloquence in the tradition, it is the key mastered by Baldwin. Hurston's essays enact vernacular process as they celebrate the plenitude of African American culture, yet sometimes seemingly despite themselves, they inscribe a troubled eloquence. The essays collected in *Black Fire*, the signal anthology of the Black Arts movement, edited by Amiri Baraka and Larry Neal, partake of both democratic eloquence and vernacular process. The lines blur, and the terms are intended to be suggestive rather than definitive.

What is certain is the centrality of the essay to the African American literary tradition. Black writers began writing essays in the late eighteenth century. They made the form their own in the nineteenth century both literally, as they circulated their writing in broadsides and pamphlets whose production they controlled, and aesthetically, as they began to incorporate rhetorical devices honed in speeches and orations into written texts. Throughout the twentieth century and into the twenty-first, writers have turned to the essay to advance political causes from the civil rights movement to Black Lives Matter. Writers continue to turn to the essay to contemplate their role as artists and argue for and against the criteria by which the art they produce is judged. They find it to be a genre ideally suited for personal recollections and reflections, which invites readers to engage in a dialogue about their own ideas, feelings, and experiences. *On Freedom and the Will to Adorn* argues that far from marginal, the African American essay is a significant genre in its own right. It deserves the most careful critical consideration.

CHAPTER ONE

On Freedom and the Will to Adorn

The African American Essay

Who were the first persons to get the unusual idea that being free was not only a value to be cherished but the most important thing that someone could possess? The answer, in a word: slaves.

—Orlando Patterson, *Freedom*

The will to adorn is the second most notable characteristic in Negro Expression.

—Zora Neale Hurston, "Characteristics of Negro Expression"

No subject has engaged African American essayists more than freedom. The writing begins with demands that slavery be abolished and appeals to the nation to live out its creed. Whether circulated in newspapers, pamphlets, or broadsides, the earliest examples of the African American essay helped to define what freedom meant to those who were not free and to some of those, black and white, who were. After slavery was abolished, blacks recognized that although they were no longer legally enslaved, they were not yet free. Essayists contemplated the subject of freedom throughout the twentieth century as the struggle for citizenship rights continued. Their conceptions of freedom expanded to encompass gender as well as race. As the essay continued to offer a space in which alternative concepts of freedom could be explored, some writers moved beyond legalistic definitions and began to imagine a freedom centered in the individual rather than the race. Others explored concepts of freedom that originated outside the geographical and psychological borders of the United States.

As black essayists worked around and through ideas of freedom, they worked new variations on the genre of the essay itself. The open-endedness of the form provided its practitioners an artistic freedom. The essay allowed them to stamp the apparent formlessness of the essay with their own artistic signature. For some this meant channeling the voices of the disenfranchised into the official discourse of democracy. Others sounded a troubled eloquence through foregrounding the pain of their individual alienation. Many used the essay to announce and enact the cultural freedom that African Americans achieved even in the face of political oppression. The adorned language that characterized African American oral expressions in genres as diverse as the folktale, the sermon, the courtship ritual, and the toast—and that became crucial elements in the fiction, poetry, and drama—made its mark on the genre of the essay as well.

Through a series of representative examples, this chapter charts these changes, while paying attention to the ways that the essay served as the medium for aesthetic debates among black writers and cultural workers. These debates centered on the relationship between art and politics in general and between aesthetics and ideology in particular. Did the writer speak for him- or herself, or as a representative of the race? What subjects were urgent, what perspectives were valuable, and what was the appropriate language for the African American essay? Should the will to adorn be accentuated or subordinated to political exigencies? The last proved a false choice. As this book will demonstrate, the African American essay is at its best an expression of both the determination to be free *and* the will to adorn.

In his magisterial study, *Freedom in the Making of Western Culture*, Orlando Patterson asks the question, "Who were the first persons to get the unusual idea that being free was not only a value to be cherished but the most important thing that someone could possess?" He gives the answer, "in a word: slaves." In the absence of simple definition of freedom, Patterson offers a tripartite conception: personal freedom, sovereignal freedom, and civic freedom. The first is the most widely accepted understanding of the term: the sense that one is not coerced or restrained by another person in doing something desired; conversely, it is the sense that one can do as one pleases within the limits of that other person's desire. Sovereignal freedom is the power to act as one pleases, regardless of the wishes of others; it is the freedom slave owners possessed in regard to those they enslaved. Civic freedom is "the capacity of adult members of a community to participate in its life and governance."[1] For the first two hundred and fifty years of their history in what became the United States, most people of African descent were denied freedom in all of these dimensions. They did not have the capacity to fulfill their individual desires, while they were subjected to the unchecked powers of their owners to act as *they* pleased. Civic freedom remained a dream deferred, though the examples of their white countrymen kept civic freedom in the forefront of their consciousness.

Those who were free had their own reasons to preserve distinctions between freedom and slavery. Even before the founding of the republic, black people were deployed as evidence in philosophical and political debates over freedom in America. As Toni Morrison observes, "The slave population, it could be assumed, offered itself up as surrogate selves for meditation on problems of human freedom."[2] It could not have been otherwise: the struggle for liberty and equality was contemporaneous with the institutionalization of slavery. As colonial leaders contemplated the rights they deserved as free men, they passed laws such as the Virginia Slave Code of 1705 proscribing the rights of those they enslaved. By the end of the eighteenth century, when freedom had been won for whites—at least those who were male and propertied—slavery was the assumed condition of blacks. At its inception, the nation inscribed the fact of slavery into the Constitution.

Citizenship by definition guaranteed rights that slavery denied. In historian Edmund Morgan's formulation, "the meaning and the guarantee of (white) equality depended on the presence of slaves. White men were 'equal in not being slaves.'"[3] Poor whites willingly accepted the leadership of their wealthy countrymen whom they believed shared their interests as they shared their racial identity. As elite slaveholders like Thomas Jefferson, James Madison, and George Washington led the fight against the tyranny of the English monarchy, they promised a victory for freedom and equality for all included in the national covenant. The identification of whites with freedom and blacks with enslavement calcified. On a more abstract level, as Saidiya Hartman observes, "the entanglement of bondage and liberty shaped the liberal imagination of freedom."[4] Although their participation was seldom acknowledged, blacks in America were not silent in the debates over the meaning of freedom. For them, freedom was after all an urgent practical matter as well as a matter of intense reflection. They were keenly aware that the putatively universal rhetoric of rights and revolution excluded them. They strove nevertheless to assert their membership in the nascent nation this rhetoric defined.

In May 1788, shortly before the Constitution was ratified, a free black who used the pseudonym Othello published "An Essay on Negro Slavery." It called on Americans to abolish a practice "inconsistent with the declared principles of the American Revolution," deplored the effect of the slave trade on Africa, and in a rhetorical turn that would be repeated many times through the nineteenth century, warned that God would punish Americans "with a dreadful attention to justice," if they persisted in countenancing slavery.[5] With this invocation of divine punishment, Othello became one of the first writers to identify slavery as a sin that corrupted the nation's ideals. Adopting a pseudonym that bespeaks a desire to associate with traditions of eloquence, Othello deployed the discourse of Christianity, to which many blacks even in the colonial era laid claim, in order to create a space for himself in the discourse of rights. At the level of abstraction, those rights should have been as available to him as to anyone, just as the supposed promises of Christianity were. But only by prophesying damnation on his fellow believers could Othello claim his discursive space.

Othello's writing is the earliest essay that can be attributed to a black author in the United States. It was published in *American Museum*, a journal that in its first issue, in January 1787, reprinted Thomas Paine's *Common Sense*, the pamphlet that stoked the flames of the revolution. The journal boasted a distinguished roster of contributors including John Adams, Alexander Hamilton, Thomas Jefferson, and George Washington. If their writings set the template for American exceptionalism, "An Essay on Negro Slavery" challenged the emergent nation's sense of rectitude. From its earliest iteration, the African American essay endorsed the democratic ideals the nation professed, while condemning its failure to fulfill them. In their writing, the relationship of African Americans to the nation would remain a complicated allegiance.

Broadsides and pamphlets were among the earliest print media that circulated in the New World, and blacks used them in part to counter the degrading depictions of the race in the dominant society's media. Many pamphlets were printed versions of orations, such as that of Methodist minister John Marrant titled, *A Sermon Preached on the 24th Day of June 1789, Being the Festival of St. John the Baptist, at the Request of the Right Worshipful the Grand Master Prince Hall and the Rest of the Brethren of the African Lodge of the Honorable Society of Free and Accepted Masons in Boston by the Reverend Brother Marrant, Chaplain.*[6] Embedded in its title is the link between churches and fraternal organizations like the African Lodge of North America, popularly known as the Prince Hall Masons in honor of its founder. These groups shared the impulse to document their activities. That impulse animated other pamphleteers, including Richard Allen and Absalom Jones, founders of the African Methodist Episcopal (AME) Church, who published *A Narrative of the Proceedings of the Black People During the Late Awful Calamity in Philadelphia* (1794) documenting the heroic actions of blacks during the yellow fever epidemic that convulsed the city in 1793.

In 1810, another AME leader, Daniel Coker, published *A Dialogue Between a Virginian and an African Minister*, exposing the failure of white Methodists to address the evils of slavery and refute the widespread belief that the Bible justified the institution. After the minister delivers a scriptural exegesis refuting the claim, the (white) Virginian asks where the minister studied divinity. "In the school of Christ," the minister responds. "And I think that is the best place for a gospel minister to take his degrees. But sir, I think you said something about Saint Paul." The use of the dialogue, a genre that dates back to classical Greece and is an important antecedent of the European essay, as well as the speaker's sardonic tone and confident demeanor, anticipates and perhaps influences later abolitionist texts. The African minister assumes a spiritual authority superior to that of the educated white southerner. He has an answer to every query the Virginian raises, whether regarding the economic cost of emancipation or the social costs of intermarriage. A man of reason and uncommon respect, the Virginian is doubtless inspired by Thomas Jefferson. It is the minister, however, who cuts to the heart of the matter, which is "the liberty of a man. The man himself claims it as his own property. He pleads (and I think in truth) that it was originally his own; and he has never forfeited, nor alienated it; and therefore, by the common laws of justice and humanity, it is still his own."[7] Freedom is an inherent right, the property of every man, even men who themselves are considered property.

Pamphlets like *A Dialogue* protesting slavery and advocating freedom circulated in northern cities and towns, often under the aegis of churches and social organizations. Before there were formal antislavery societies, black Americans pioneered a rich tradition of protest writing. Philosophically, they refined concepts of liberty. Politically, they incited resistance to slavery in the South and discrimination in the North. They honed expressions of democratic eloquence that drew from the models of the Declaration of Independence, the Constitution, and the King James Bible.

The ideal of the United States as synonymous with freedom continues to stand at the center of the national mythology. Yet, the history of blacks in slavery has lasted longer than the history of blacks in freedom. If for the nation's founders, freedom presumed its antithesis, the condition of enslavement, for formerly enslaved people, who wrote about their prior and present condition, it was clear that freedom and slavery were not antithetical. Blacks who were legally free did not enjoy the rights of citizenship. As historian Nathan Huggins put it, they were "not really free people in terms of the society, they were black people who were not owned."[8] Consequently, they were not only subjected to discrimination but were frequently required to show proof of their status. In their experience slavery and freedom, as it was obtained for both fugitives and free blacks in the North, existed on a continuum.

In sermons and orations, fugitive slaves and free men and women took to the podium to advocate for abolition and citizenship rights. Their spoken words informed their written texts as their written texts informed their spoken words. Once the texts were printed, they were often read aloud so that those who were illiterate could have access to them. Oratorical strategies left their mark on the written texts of Frederick Douglass, Henry Highland Garnet, Frances E. W. Harper, Maria Stewart, and David Walker. In their texts they achieved a formal but plainspoken prose that I term democratic eloquence.[9] That is, their language was eloquent but not elevated; they blended the conventions of written prose with the speech of ordinary people. They tackled the crucial issues of the day—abolition being the most urgent—in terms that were memorable yet accessible to their audience.

Frederick Douglass exemplifies democratic eloquence. His prose was straightforward and unaffected; he recounted traumatic experiences in a matter-of-fact tone that had the effect of heightening the trauma and deepening the respect for its survivors. At the same time, his ironies eviscerated the oppressors. With a simple vocabulary, measured cadence, and regular syntax—except for those passages whose inversions call attention to themselves—Douglass wrote for a general audience. He employed familiar rhetorical tropes: repetition, parallelisms, and antitheses. A self-educated man, he made few classical allusions, but he made frequent references to the Bible; he rightly assumed that his audience was as familiar with these allusions as he was. He made occasional use of figures of speech and analogies to press his point. While he did not use folk idiom, he did not eschew figurative language—adorned language, if you will—but his figures in the main derived from his experience rather than his reading. Without using folk idiom, he gestured toward black people's penchant for adorned language. Moreover, his invocations of enslaved people in the body of his text narrowed the gap between their experiences and those of his free Northern and British audiences.

Many of the nineteenth-century orators, whom I dub "voices of thunder" in the next chapter, were ministers. Henry Highland Garnet, for example, was a Presbyterian cleric, trained in hermeneutics; he brought the strategies for interpreting biblical texts to the interpretation of political texts and events. As they would be for his twentieth-century descendants, the founding documents of the republic were grist for his mill. Garnet's orations were as intense and dramatic as sermons. Like sermons, they succeeded to the extent that auditors and readers internalized their message. The influence of Protestant thought and worship practices was so pervasive in U.S. black communities that even those speakers who were not ministers assimilated the rhetorical styles of the pulpit. That is, they made frequent use of the repetitions, interjections, and biblical allusions to which their audiences were accustomed. In appropriating these elements for written texts, they participated in a larger movement among nineteenth-century American writers and thinkers. But their use of traditions of African American musical and oral performance sounded a distinctive note.

The incorporation of elements from African American oral culture is perhaps the most visible sign of the innovations the black writers have made in the essay. But it is not the only one. As Nathaniel Mackey observes, critics have been loath to recognize innovations by blacks in literary form rather than content. His term "troubled eloquence" suggests a way to think about these formal contributions. For Mackey, "trouble is a threshold," the entry place into black letters. That trouble is both an external referent and an internal challenge, which makes the term especially useful for a study of essays in which the public and private often overlap. According to Mackey, troubled or "othered" eloquence "registers a need for a new world and a new language to go along with it."[10] In its expression, eloquence takes unexpected form, as for example, the eloquence of hesitation or inarticulateness.

In many respects, W. E. B. Du Bois's essays in *The Souls of Black Folk* partake more of classical literary styles than of the democratic eloquence of Douglass and Harper.[11] But his is a troubled eloquence. Notably, his writings register a historical shift in which freedom becomes aligned as much with individual identity as with a people's collective freedom. In the first essay, "Of Our Spiritual Strivings," he poses a question never imagined by the eminent Victorians Thomas Carlyle and Matthew Arnold, whose essays he admired: "How does it feel to be a problem?" The question acknowledges the trouble at the threshold of his consciousness. He gives a series of answers in different modes—the autobiographical, philosophical, historical, and sociological— but none of the answers is sufficient to answer a question that should never have had the occasion to be asked. Despite his formidable erudition, Du Bois the essayist writes for the general reader, not the specialist. He draws insights from the academic disciplines he has mastered but presents them without scholarly apparatus. His manner recalls another of Theodor Adorno's observations: "In the essay, discrete elements set off against one another come together to form a readable context; the essay erects no scaffolding and no structure. But the elements crystallize as a configuration through their motion. The constellation is a force field, just as every intellectual structure is necessarily transformed into a force field under the essay's gaze."[12]

The force field for Du Bois is the condition of blacks in the post-Reconstruction world, a world which Du Bois both observes and inhabits. He begins his essay with elements of the personal, posing a question that he creates or distills from his own experience. He acknowledges that the question is never phrased in his exact words, but it is implicit in racialized questions white men pose to him, questions he does not deign to answer. "And yet," he allows, "being a problem is a strange experience,—peculiar even for one who has never been anything else, save perhaps in babyhood and in Europe."[13] "Strange" and "peculiar" are recurring adjectives that link the familiar anecdote of the white girl, new in town, who refuses his visiting card to the collective condition of black Americans. Double consciousness is a "peculiar sensation." Trouble begins for Du Bois at the moment when, stunned by the girl's rejection, he recognizes his racial difference. The alienating effects of that difference play out in short recollections of his school days, when his superior intellect allows him to transcend the rejection of his white peers. But the bitterness the rejection engenders leads Du Bois to ask a second question, in a phrase reminiscent of Old Testament prophets, "Why did God make me an outcast and a stranger in mine own house?"[14]

The question has another inescapable echo: the spirituals "Nobody Knows the Trouble I've Seen" and "Lord, How Come Me Here?" express a similar sense of bewilderment and angst. These echoes suggest the profound ways in which the spirituals were both a source and model for Du Bois's troubled eloquence. He borrows much of his imagery from the spirituals. For example, the image of his grieving wife as "a childless mother" seems to invert the aching lyric "sometimes I feel like a motherless child." That line and the phrase that follows, "a long way from home," capture the existential dilemma of enslaved people who found themselves dislocated and dispossessed. For good reason, "home" is one of the most familiar spiritual tropes. But the spirituals express as well existential questions that anticipate and inform those posed by Du Bois. "Lord, how come me here?" reflects a sense of alienation that resonates with "How does it feel to be a problem?" The trouble at the threshold of consciousness that Du Bois represents in his essays clearly had antecedents in the songs of the black and unknown bards who likewise sought to understand their condition in the American wilderness.

No one before him had been more appreciative of the spirituals than Du Bois, for whom they constituted the "singular spiritual heritage of the nation and the greatest gift of the Negro people" (205). But they were also "persistently mistaken and misunderstood," their message "naturally veiled and half articulate" (205, 209). Du Bois discerned in the sorrow songs what other commentators had failed to perceive—that is, a profound critique of the institution of slavery. (Douglass is the great exception; his 1845 *Narrative* is the origin of the phrase "sorrow songs."[15]) For Du Bois, the critique of slavery was the source of the "real poetry and meaning" of the songs, the poetry and meaning that lay beneath "conventional theology and unmeaning rhapsody" (210). The examples he quotes not only protest the exploitation of labor, they inscribe the disruption of family ("mother and child are sung, but seldom father") and emotional exile ("the mountains are well known, but home is unknown") (211). Literally and figuratively, these are instantiations of trouble at the threshold of consciousness. When Du Bois queries how he came to be an outcast and a stranger in his own house, he is emulating the creators of the spirituals by fashioning a question in a biblical mode that conveys an urgent secular critique. Du Bois extends the long-standing identification of enslaved blacks with the biblical Hebrews by creating metaphors in the same key, for example, "Emancipation was the key to a promised land of sweeter beauty than ever stretched before the eyes of wearied Israelites" (7). Three lines from a spiritual—"Shout, O Children!/Shout, you're free!/For God has brought your liberty"—capture the jubilation of emancipation in the freed peoples' "own plaintive cadences" (7). The epigraph to the opening chapter is the first reference to those cadences. The silent bars of "Nobody Knows the Trouble I've Seen" represent the "naturally veiled and half articulate" message of enslaved black folk to the world, as Du Bois explains in "The Sorrow Songs." That explanation comes at the end of *Souls*. By not quoting the lyrics or even giving the title of the song in the beginning, Du Bois suggests how buried the "strange meaning of being black" in America at the dawn of the twentieth century remains for his readers.

As much as Du Bois seeks to invite his readers into the world behind the veil, the epigraphs represent what they cannot hear, indeed, what cannot be said outright. Moreover, the music acts as a bridge that spans the experiential gap between the creators of the spirituals and the cosmopolitan Du Bois. He remembers in "The Sorrow Songs" that even as a child the songs had stirred him strangely. Before he learned their history, he knew them at once "as of me and of mine" (204). In the full knowledge of their history, Du Bois embraces the sorrow songs as his own. By steeping himself in their legacy, he earns the right to speak for those whose silent voices are figured in his text.[16] Their troubled eloquence informs his troubled eloquence.

Zora Neale Hurston's "How It Feels to Be Colored Me" (1928) is a meditation on freedom and racial identity that could not be more different from Du Bois's. Refusing the construction of herself as a problem and rejecting the burdens of history, Hurston's persona is fully engaged with the feelings that the essay's title promises to explore. She claims her right to her subjectivity and her own language; she speaks for no one but herself. Insistently colloquial in her diction and humorous in her tone, the speaker is intent on seeming to have nothing to prove. In sharp contrast to earlier essays in the tradition, Hurston's begins with a joke. "I am colored but I offer nothing in the way of extenuating circumstances except the fact that I am the only Negro in the United States whose grandfather on his mother's side was *not* an Indian chief."[17] To a degree the joke is aimed at the essay's white readers, who might have assumed that black racial identity required some explanation. But the joke is directed at blacks as well, especially those who are eager to claim a Native American heritage in order to claim to be something more than black. Hurston might also be signifying on Du Bois when she writes this. In 1920, he dramatically charted his genealogy in *Darkwater: Voices from within the Veil* that included "a flood of Negro blood, a strain of French, a bit of Dutch, but thank God! no 'Anglo-Saxon.'"[18] In any case, the Native American heritage—here with the intimations of a royal lineage—is a badge of distinction that Hurston's speaker does not need. She is happy to be just who she is—without any mitigating explanations.

"How It Feels to Be Colored Me" uses what Ralph Ellison would define as "vernacular process" to explore its subject. Ellison used the term to describe how "the most refined styles of the past are continually merged with the play-it-by-ear improvisations which we invent in our efforts to control our environment and entertain ourselves."[19] For Ellison the vernacular is not racialized. He points to *The Adventures of Huckleberry Finn* as an example of the vernacular process at work in the novel. The process yields an American novel that is distinguishable from its English antecedents. Mark Twain sets the template, as the language of the first-person narrator/protagonist of *Huckleberry Finn* signals the invention of a democratic style.[20] Of course, Ellison appropriates that style as a novelist, but he does so as an essayist as well. His style as an essayist is consistently digressive, in keeping with the styles and techniques of the past, but their discursive shifts that incorporate a more colloquial prose and insistent allusions to jazz suggest improvisation rather than digression as a formative principle in the enactment of a vernacular process.

Hurston's use of vernacular process unfolds similarly. Her essay is digressive as it moves from childhood recollections to college reminiscences to a scene in a Harlem nightclub. It uses colloquial expressions to convey serious ideas; it tackles with humor some of the same subjects that provoke Du Bois's anguish. Consider how Hurston expresses her understanding that race is a social construction. For Du Bois, the moment of racial recognition occurs when the white girl rebuffs him; it sends him into an emotional tailspin. For her part, Hurston announces forthrightly, "I remember the very day that

I became colored" (826) and begins an account of a childhood that was in its way as idyllic as Du Bois's had been in his New England village before his encounter with his new classmate, except that Eatonville, Florida, was an "exclusively colored town." Ironically, in the all-colored town, Hurston did not feel colored. It is only when she leaves and moves to Jacksonville at age thirteen that she experiences a delayed racial recognition. "I was not Zora of Orange County anymore," she recalls, "I was now a little colored girl. I found out in certain ways. In my heart as well as in the mirror, I became a fast brown—warranted not to rub or run" (827).[21] As she becomes conscious of a fixed racial identity, Hurston's speaker trades in bravado, as for example in her insistence that when she is discriminated against, she feels "merely" astonished that anyone can deny themselves "the pleasure of my company" (829). The performance of bravado in Hurston's essay protects her speaker against the anger and despair that threaten Du Bois's persona.

Hurston's conception of freedom is strictly personal; it has nothing do with history or politics. History would offer only excuses for a speaker who proclaims "slavery is sixty years in the past" (827). While she concedes that it took a "terrible struggle" to make "an American out of a potential slave," she does not regret the cost. Indeed, she declares, shockingly, "Slavery is the price I paid for civilization" (827). To be sure, the essay's "I" has not been enslaved, so has not paid this price. But the end result of a struggle that has been waged on her behalf is her ability to declare herself free. Casting off the burden of history, she can identify herself in the present as an American who is running a race unencumbered. She goes so far as to say she is freer than her white counterpart, because "the game of keeping what one has is never so exciting as the game of getting" (828). The use of metaphors from sports and games creates a discursive space in which politics can be held at bay. The tone is at once ebullient and arch.

That tone derives in part from the essay's rejection of race as an immutable condition. Race is instead a feeling that comes and goes depending on where one is and what one does. In scenes at Barnard and at the nightclub, the speaker feels herself most colored when thrown against a white background. Freedom is the choice to identify or not with a racially defined experience. It thus enables the speaker to make the essay's most famous declaration: "But I am not tragically colored. There is no great sorrow dammed up in my soul, nor lurking behind my eyes. I do not mind at all. I do not belong to the sobbing school of Negro-hood who hold that nature somehow has given them a low-down dirty deal and whose feelings are all hurt about it. Even in the helter-skelter skirmish that is my life, I have seen that the world is to the strong regardless of a little pigmentation more or less. No, I do not weep at the world—I am too busy sharpening my oyster knife"(827).

The speaker separates herself from those who view blackness as a tragedy, a condition that would require explanation and expiation. She does not mind being black; the reference to "nature" suggests that she is further separating herself from those who would essentialize race. Abjuring any identification with weakness, "Zora" is certain that she as an individual is strong and therefore poised to win at the game of life. The image of her sharpening her oyster knife captures the spirit of bravado that pervades the essay. It is also significant that even within the paragraph the essay shifts discursive registers. It opens with a formal, even melodramatic statement. But by the fourth sentence, the diction shifts to the idiomatic "low-down dirty deal" and "helter-skelter skirmish." These phrases anticipate Hurston's observation in "Characteristics of Negro Expression," where one of the elements of the "will to adorn" is the use of the double descriptive. In such linguistic turns, Hurston democratizes the high styles of the past in just the way Ellison describes.

Hurston's conception of freedom as individual represents a crucial turn in the development of the twentieth-century African American essay. Equally important was the decoupling of the idea of freedom from the tenets of the U.S. nation-state. A notable example is "Cuba Libre," the opening essay in LeRoi Jones's collection titled *Home*, which examines the relevance of freedom as defined outside of, and counter to, the U.S. context.[22] On a philosophical level, it considers what civic freedom means, when not defined in terms of electoral politics or capitalism. The essay works on one level as reportage, an account of a trip by a group of black intellectuals to Cuba in 1960. It records interviews with government officials and encounters with Cuban poets and workers—interviews and encounters that are facilitated by the author's fluency in Spanish; it also gives an extended account of the events commemorating the first anniversary of the revolution. On another, personal, level, it is a record of Jones's evolution from an apolitical "beat poet" to a poet for whom art without politics is inconceivable, the poet who finds a home in Harlem and then Newark, where he embraces black nationalism. On all three levels, the essay is constructed as a physical journey from Greenwich Village to Havana and from Havana to the Sierra Maestra mountains, and a metaphysical journey from ignorance to possible enlightenment, and from apathy to potential commitment. While the geographical journey can be mapped, the changes in consciousness remain ineffable.

The essay opens in Jones's Greenwich Village apartment where he is hosting a party. The phone rings and he is invited to join a trip to Cuba, a place where he has never thought of going. He is asked whether, as a poet, he "might like to know what's *really* going on down there."[23] In 1960 Jones has yet to publish a volume of poems, so the invitation is couched in part by an appeal to his vanity. The appeal is enhanced by his inclusion in a group that was to include the prominent black writers James Baldwin, Alice Childress, Langston Hughes, and John Killens—none of whom actually made the trip. But Jones's lack of curiosity about the rest of the world, which he deems typically American, is a much deeper problem than his literary reputation. For him, as for most of his countrymen and -women, Cuba Libre is the name of a cocktail.[24] Given the anti-Communism of the U.S. government and press, Cuba would be the last place Americans would expect to learn about freedom.

The turning point in the essay comes when a young Cuban woman challenges Jones's political bona fides. Jones responds, "I'm a poet . . . what can I do? I write, that's all, I'm not even interested in politics" (147). She accuses him of being "a cowardly bourgeois individualist." Screaming and stomping, a young Mexican poet piles on: "You want to cultivate your soul? Well, we've got millions of starving people to feed, and that moves me enough to make poems out of" (147). Jones does not respond to these indictments, and his silence makes them speak louder.[25] They resonate throughout the remainder of the essay, and perhaps beyond. Jones returns to the United States as a political poet who rejects the ethic of individualism and the aesthetic of art for art's sake.

The remainder of the essay recounts Jones's journey by train, bus, and on foot to the site on the island where the revolution was won. It describes the crowds of impassioned Cubans and their allies from throughout the Americas. (Jones is repeatedly reminded that "American" is not an identity exclusive to citizens of the United States.) The crowd's fervor proves unsettling: "I was ecstatic and frightened. Something I had never seen before, exploding all around me" (148). Buoyed by the experience, Jones ceases to be an observer and becomes a participant. Yet, his revolutionary cries retain a homegrown flavor: "Viva Calle Cuarenta y dos," "Viva Symphony Syd," "Viva Cinco Punto," and "Viva Turhan Bey." Rather than the Cuban revolution, Jones pledges his fealty to Forty-Second Street, a jazz disc jockey, a jazz club, and a Hollywood movie actor.[26] With these linguistic crossings and jazz-inflected soundings— on both the levels of content and form—Jones expands the parameters of the African American essay.

Within a few years after his return to the United States, Jones changed his name to Amiri Baraka, became a black nationalist and later a Marxist who used his writing to try to spark in the black masses of the United States the revolutionary ardor he admired in Cuba. While some of his readers were persuaded that black people in the United States could achieve freedom only through revolution, most of the working-class blacks he hoped to reach were not.

Patricia Williams looks at the subject of freedom through a different lens. She writes as a law professor and as a woman who came of age in the aftermath of the civil rights and Black Power movements. In my reading, *The Alchemy of Race and Rights* (1991) is a bookend with *The Souls of Black Folk*. What Reconstruction was to Du Bois, the *Brown v. Board of Education of Topeka* decision is to Williams: a moment of limitless possibility and devastating disappointment. The post–civil rights moment is the force field in which the essays in *The Alchemy of Race and Rights* unfold. While the specific cases the essays address—Tawana Brawley, Howard Beach, Eleanor Bumpers, Bernhard Goetz—have faded from the headlines, the causes they explore, including affirmative action, police brutality, and racist violence, continue to be the focus of public debates. At the book's core is the continuing struggle to claim and define freedom for African Americans. Like Du Bois, Williams combines political critique with personal reflection and infuses democratic eloquence with troubled eloquence.

In a sign of the social and political progress that African Americans—particularly privileged African Americans—made across the twentieth century, Williams, unlike Du Bois, emphasizes her professional identity, both in the book's subtitle, *Diary of a Law Professor*, and in her use of specialized academic language. Yet she argues that the language of the law is insufficient to her task. What she fashions instead is "an intentionally double-voiced and relational" mode of writing.[27] This mode of writing incorporates the personal as well as the political; it opens up space to represent feelings as well as coolly rational analysis. The analysis is couched in the language of critical theory, feminism, African American history, political science and rhetoric as well as constitutional law. Williams writes for her fellow academics, but her audience extends beyond the academy. In a move that transgresses legal protocols, Williams locates the motive for this new mode of writing in her personal experience. Referring to "persistent perceptions of me as an inherent contradiction"—that is, being perceived as "too black" or "not black enough"—she acknowledges the extent to which both the substance and the style of her writing derive from her personal experience. While the essays are mainly about the jurisprudence of rights, they also address implicitly the question Du Bois posed in 1903, "How does it feel to be a problem?" Like Du Bois, Williams makes it clear that her problematic status derives from those who misperceive who she in fact is.

Tellingly, Williams traces her interest in the law in general and her specialized interest "in the intersection of commerce and the Constitution" to her family history. Her great-great-grandmother was the slave of a Tennessee lawyer, who purchased her when she was eleven and he was thirty-five and impregnated her when she was twelve. Whether pondering the intricacies of the laws that enslaved her ancestor or imagining her ancestor's adolescent feelings, Williams grapples with the legal and affective meanings of freedom. She quotes from a speech she wrote to present to a law school audience. It argues that the Declaration of Independence and the Constitution conceive of freedom on the one hand as "the letter of the law which describes a specific range of rights and precepts," and on the other hand as "the spirit of the law, the symbology of freedom," which is in some ways "utterly meaningless or empty" and at the same time "a vessel to be filled with possibility, with a plurality of autonomous yearnings" (16). Williams's project in her essays is to be attentive to both the letter and the spirit of the law. To explore the latter, she needs to find a genre more pliant than a legal treatise: the essay fulfills her purpose.

The choice is controversial, as the frequent criticism of her colleagues attests. They object to her writing as being too personal and too emotional. When she offers a defense of her approach, she writes like an essayist. "I deliberately sacrifice myself in my writing. I leave no part of myself out, for that is how much I want readers to connect with me. I want them to wonder about the things I wonder about, and to think about some of the things that trouble me" (92). In other words, she invites readers to participate in what Lukács calls the process of judging; she invites them to join her in thinking through complex and contentious issues. She strives to earn their trust even when they disagree with her conclusions: she puts herself on the line. She offers legal definitions and glosses current events in plainspoken prose, but insists on letting her readers know what she is both thinking *and* feeling about the subjects she addresses. The result is a fusion of democratic eloquence and troubled eloquence.

As the preceding discussion demonstrates, the genre of the essay has been crucial for interventions in political debates, whether about abolition, anti-imperialism, or desegregation. It has also been a primary medium for debates about the purpose and form of literature and art. Given the historical context in which they unfolded, these aesthetic debates are closely aligned with questions of freedom as well. Indeed, many of the same writers join both sets of debates. There is, however, a discernible shift in emphasis. Rather than defining what freedom is or how it can be achieved politically, these essays foreground the role art can play in attaining it. Although the emphases shift, the essays continue to reflect patterns of democratic eloquence, troubled eloquence, and vernacular process. Moreover, whatever its subject, the essay provides a space both to define and enact the will to adorn.

"The Value of Race Literature" (1895) by Victoria Earle Matthews initiates the aesthetic debates that recur among black writers across the twentieth century. It is worth noting that Matthews's words were first delivered at a meeting called by African American women to protest attacks on their gender and race. In this political speech, later published as an essay, Matthews queries the purpose of literature, the validity of race as a category, the representation of black subjects in writing by white authors, and the audience for writing by blacks.[28] Decades before Ellison, Baraka, and Morrison, she posits music as a touchstone for literary expression by invoking Antonín Dvořák's assertion that Negro melodies "can be the foundation of a serious and original school of composition to be developed in the United States."[29] In his *New World* symphony, the Czech-born composer would test his claim. By analogy, Matthews suggests that folklore could serve as the foundation of literary art. Most significantly, she calls for an engaged literature. Writing during the period historian Rayford Logan would deem "the nadir of the Negro's status in American society," Matthews argues if literature could not win the war against race prejudice, it could do much to advance the cause.[30]

Anticipating objections to the premise of her essay, Matthews asks whether there was such a thing as a literature demarcated by race, "apart from the general American literature." She quickly notes that a similar question might be asked regarding American literature itself. If a race literature exists, she queries, how might it be defined? She argues that historical conditions had created inevitable differences in "the limitations, characteristics, aspirations, and ambitions" of black Americans that are reflected in their writing. To date, she concedes, their literary achievement is undistinguished, but the array of authors she cites evinces an impressive literary presence. Her definition of literature is capacious and includes history, biography, scientific treatises, sermons, speeches, travel writing and essays, as well as poems and novels. Starting with Phillis Wheatley, she lists dozens of authors with references to their work, including William Wells Brown, Frederick Douglass, Samuel Cornish and John Russwurm (founders of *Freedom Journal*, the first national black newspaper, established in 1827), Frances Watkins Harper, Charlotte Forten Grimké, and historian George Washington Williams. Plainspoken in its eloquence, the roll call supports her argument that a race literature exists and that women as well as men have created it.

Matthews also cites a large number of non-black writers, from Americans Mark Twain and William Dean Howells to the Europeans Alexandre Dumas, Alexander Pushkin, and Ivan Turgenev. Some of these references advance her argument that literature has an instrumental value, while others work mainly to show off her erudition. But while some of the specifics are not always germane, the issues Matthews explored in her essay continue to resonate. Does African American literature exist? If so, do African American writers carry particular responsibilities to their natal communities? What are the criteria by which their writing is judged? Are they obligated to criticize negative images of blacks created by whites? Should they themselves depict only positive images of blacks? What relationship does race literature have to the literature of the dominant society? Who is its audience? Although few of the writers who came to print in the next century had heard of Victoria Matthews, many grappled with the questions she raised.

As they did, they raised the essay to a greater level of prominence. Reflecting with an acute self-consciousness their obligations and frustrations as artists who represented the race—both on the page and in their public personae—writers of the Harlem Renaissance debated questions of aesthetics and politics vigorously. I explore these debates at length in Chapter 3, "On Art and Such." Suffice it to say here that some writers of this period found the burden of race more onerous than others. Langston Hughes famously declared in "The Negro Artist and the Racial Mountain" that artists should pay no heed to what either whites or blacks thought about their work. To the call that artists should mine the raw material of folklore, James Weldon Johnson responded in the affirmative, while Zora Neale Hurston insisted that the folk artist, who was inevitably "the Negro farthest down," was the true artist. To a substantial degree, the essays these writers composed enacted the aesthetic they formulated. Consequently, no one mistakes Hughes for Alain Locke or Jessie Fauset for Hurston. Whether they chose to uplift the race or to dig deeply into the recesses of its culture, the content of their arguments shaped the form of their expression.

Questions over the function of African American literature and the criteria by which it should be judged continued to reverberate. In 1937, Richard Wright published "Blueprint for Negro Literature," an essay that is often read as his literary manifesto. In keeping with its title, the essay is divided into numbered sections, beginning with "1. The Minority Outlook," followed by "2. The Role of Negro Writing: Two Definitions." Other sections take up "The Problem of Nationalism in Negro Writing" and "Subject and Theme." The ninth and final section carries the heading "The Necessity for Collective

Work." But what is interesting formally about "Blueprint" is the way in which its argument exceeds its structural constraints.

Not surprisingly, the essay argues for a social consciousness among black writers that is comparable to the social consciousness of the black working class. Unlike literature that is tethered to a past in which "humble" novels, poems, and plays are figured as "decorous ambassadors who go a-begging to white America," the working class demonstrates a deep social consciousness that needs only to be channeled in a new direction.[31] Significantly, the essay first appeared in *New Challenge*, a second version of a journal cofounded by Dorothy West, which Wright as editor moved to the Left. Its one issue included contributions by Alain Locke and Sterling Brown, among other veterans of the New Negro Renaissance. "Blueprint" declares the end to that chapter in literary history. Writers of the new generation would do well to turn to the folklore that nourishes workers—a folklore that is created by and speaks to blacks in the way that Wright hoped literature could. The essay urges writers at once to affirm and transcend the nationalism of the black community. That nationalism is expressed through folklore, as well as through social institutions. Ironically, in an essay that seems to set forth literary dictates, it refers twice to the fluidity of the culture it urges black writers to embrace. In the same breath that the essay argues for a social realism, it acknowledges that social realism is inadequate. In order to achieve the requisite "complex simplicity," black writers are urged to draw on Eliot, Stein, Joyce, and the full roster of literary modernists. The most compelling necessity for the black writer, however, is a "perspective," "that fixed point in intellectual space where writers stand to view the struggles, hopes, and sufferings of their people," the point that Marxism had provided Wright. Yet, even the enumerated list that constitutes this "Blueprint" does not predict a result. It cannot envision the literature it prescribes. The autonomy of craft, and the force of the imagination, as well as the complexity of the conditions of the lives the black writer strives to represent made the future of black literature impossible to predict.

It was no coincidence that James Baldwin's essay, "Everybody's Protest Novel," critiqued what he considered Wright's failure to achieve the complex simplicity he championed. For Baldwin, Wright's *Native Son* was to the twentieth century what Harriet Beecher Stowe's *Uncle Tom's Cabin* had been to the nineteenth: a one-dimensional sentimental tract. Sentimentality, which Baldwin defined as "the ostentatious parading of excessive and spurious emotion," was their shared failing. The dishonesty of sentimentality for Baldwin was the antithesis of truth, which was not in turn necessarily tied to the ideal of freedom, an individual condition that transcends the political, but which he identified instead as "freedom which cannot be legislated, fulfillment which cannot be charted."[32] This freedom exists in a wholly different realm from that sought by Douglass and Garnet. Baldwin's conception of freedom for the individual rather than the collective could be fruitfully compared to ideas set forth in previously discussed essays by Du Bois and Hurston. But Baldwin is not discussing personal freedom here. He is refracting his concerns through the prism of literature and art.

Although the critique of Wright accounts for the essay's enduring fame, Baldwin's one-time mentor is discussed only in the last paragraph. Rejecting Wright is the final act in Baldwin's effort to clear a space for his own art. Earlier in the essay he dismisses his white contemporaries James Cain and Anita Loos; they, like Wright, are scorned for their failure to create fictions as complex as the realities they purport to represent. Baldwin's use of the modernist keywords "ambiguity" and "paradox" suggest the aesthetic standard to which he aspires. Yet there is little in "Everybody's Protest Novel" to tie Baldwin's aspirations to the art-for-art's-sake tenets conventionally associated with the modernists. Rather, Baldwin hopes to use the literary strategies of modernism in the service of an honest representation of black life. As I will show in Chapter 4, "Stranger at Home: James Baldwin on What It Means to Be an American," his determination to explore the many dimensions of African American experience and his commitment to examining the complexities of his own consciousness produce a "troubled eloquence" discernible in the content and form of his essays.

When in "Everybody's Protest Novel," Baldwin decries the critical tendency to view African American literature in terms of sociology rather than art, he anticipates a recurrent theme in Ellison's essays. In "Autobiographical Note," the preface to *Notes of a Native Son*, Baldwin's first volume of essays, he singles Ellison out for praise. "Mr. Ellison," he writes, "is the first Negro novelist I have ever read to utilize in language, and brilliantly, some of the ambiguity and irony of Negro life."[33] Baldwin, like Ellison, argues that ambiguity and irony are not qualities black writers need to appropriate from white writers: these qualities are inherent in African American life.

In "Brave Words for a Startling Occasion," the presentation he made as he accepted the National Book Award for *Invisible Man* and later published as an essay in *Shadow and Act*, Ralph Ellison elaborates on this theme. He describes the speech he heard around him as he composed his masterwork as "an alive language swirling with over three hundred years of American living, a mixture of the folk, the Biblical, the scientific and the political. Slangy in one stance, academic in another, loaded poetically with imagery at one moment, mathematically bare of imagery in the next."[34] He deployed this language in his essays as well as his fiction. The essays incorporate literary allusions, colloquial expressions, political discourse, and humor. When, in "The World and the Jug," Ellison compares his situation as a writer to both Wright and Baldwin, he asserts that all write not only out of their experience but of their reading and their discipline as writers. Baldwin, Ellison avers, "is not the product of a Negro store-front church but of the library, and the same is true of me."[35] Ellison's statement is partially true and purposely provocative: while Baldwin could not have become the writer he became had he never left the storefront church, he would not have been the writer he was had he never been in one. Quite apart from this Baldwin aside, the goal of Ellison's essay was to intervene in debates about the relationship between race and writing. Was black writing merely a mirror of black life? If so, the writer was an observer who simply transcribed what he or she saw. Or was the writer an artist, who by virtue of his wide reading, discipline, and craft transformed the raw material of life into art? To consider the black writer anything other than an artist was for Ellison a form of racial condescension.

Although Ellison's prose could be knife-sharp, he did not, like Wright, publish blueprints or manifestos. Instead, like Baldwin, he became a prolific essayist. The keywords of his writing—freedom, fluidity, experiment, openness, and diversity—are key terms in most definitions of the essay. As is typical of the genre, Ellison's essays look at the many sides of every subject—turning each subject over, handling it, and arriving at whatever conclusion it reaches in a seemingly unplanned, open-ended, and digressive way. Carefully crafted though they are, his essays sometimes appear to be free improvisations. They adhere to the pattern Adorno describes in "The Essay as Form," where he writes that the essay "thinks in fragments, just as reality is fragmentary, and finds its unity in and through the breaks and not by glossing them over . . . ." (16). The pleasure of Ellison's essays derives in part from his rejection of structural constraints and his embrace of the form's inherent discontinuities.

Larry Neal issued a rebuke to Baldwin and Ellison as he announced a paradigm shift in African American letters in the opening lines of his signature essay: "The Black Arts Movement is radically opposed to any concept of the artist that alienates him from his community. Black Art is the aesthetic and spiritual sister of the Black Power concept."[36] Although Baldwin spent much of the 1960s on the front lines of the civil rights movement, he had left the United States to take up residence in France in 1948. Ellison, who lived at the northern edge of Harlem, was perceived to have joined the white American literary elite. In 1968 when Neal published his essay titled "The Black Arts Movement," neither Baldwin nor Ellison was favorably inclined toward Black Power, though Baldwin later softened his stance. Equally discomfiting for both would have been the imperative that art support an explicit political agenda. Neal argued that Black Arts and Black Power assumed the existence of two Americas—black and white: "The Black artist takes this to mean that his primary duty is to speak to the spiritual and cultural needs of Black people" (257). Baldwin and Ellison recognized no such duty; they cultivated the broadest audiences they could. Indeed, Baldwin addressed his essays in *The Fire Next Time* (1962) specifically to white Americans. Moreover, both paid homage to their white precursors, whom Ellison called his "literary ancestors."[37]

For Neal in 1968, the "destruction of the white thing, the destruction of white ideas and white ways of looking at the world" was paramount. While Neal's language and even more so the language of the illustrative texts he cites are laced with violence, Neal insists that the goal of Black Art is ethical. He argues that black ethics and aesthetics are inextricably bound. Both serve to end the oppression of black America and the Third World. Violence, verbal violence at the least, is required to achieve that goal. For black artists to fulfill their role in the transformation of the social order, they must reject and destroy the "Euro-American cultural sensibility" and replace it with the humane, ethical sensibility of Black Art.

Neal identifies LeRoi Jones, soon to rename himself Amiri Baraka, as the "prime mover and chief designer" of the Black Arts Movement (263). The two men edited the movement's signal anthology *Black Fire*, also in 1968. Both believed that the fusion of ethics and aesthetics they called for in literature had already been achieved in black music. Baraka's landmark study *Blues People: Negro Music in White America* (1963) had implied as much when it argued that black Americans' worldview was expressed through their music, and therefore one could chart the history of black Americans through a study of that music. Baraka proposed a variation of Du Bois's perspective in *Souls*, except that for Baraka blues, not the spiritual, was the definitive black American music. Baraka extended his argument in the highly influential "The Changing Same (R&B and New Black Music)," an essay that exemplifies the more experimental and poetic mode Baraka crafted in the essays he published in the late 1960s and beyond. In contrast to "Cuba Libre," in which Castro's revolutionary rhetoric and praxis were catalysts for the essayist's personal and political transformation, in "The Changing Same," African American music becomes a focus of the essay's arguments and a model for its structure.

Few listeners at the time perceived a close connection between rhythm and blues and free jazz, the more common name for what Baraka dubbed "New Black Music." The audiences were certainly different: most of those who danced to James Brown did not meditate to John Coltrane. Baraka was intent on showing that the music of both men was rooted in religious traditions that could be traced to Africa. Analogously, Baraka asserted, the Miracles of Motown were "spiritual," as was jazz innovator Albert Ayler. The rhythm and blues singers came out of the black church and adhered to what Baraka deemed a "practical" religion, while Coltrane and Ayler aspired to a "mystical" religion. But, he argued, "the differences . . . are artificial, or they are merely indicative of the different places of spirit."[38] Social protest was another binding force, which motivated Charles Mingus's "Fable for Faubus," as well as Stevie Wonder's recording of Bob Dylan's "Blowin' in the Wind."[39] The essay concludes by resolving the oppositions, stating, "the New Black Music and R&B are the same family looking at different things. Or looking at things differently" (211). Overturning the hierarchy that "practical" and "mystical" seem to suggest, the essayist remarks, "James Brown's screams, etc., are more 'radical' than most jazz musicians sound, etc." (210). The judgment reflected Baraka's racialized nationalism: free jazz was less "radical," because it incorporated the influences of European atonal music. Whether Tin Pan Alley, Beethoven, or Schönberg, such influences were "music lessons of a dying people" (194). Many of the black musicians he valorized would have disagreed.

Baraka's own position shifts as he works around his subject. Throughout the essay, he engages in his own brand of vernacular process in language inflected with hip jargon and black urban speech. Describing the blurred lines between gospel music and rhythm and blues, he writes, "in the straight city jamup gospel, echo chambers, strings, electric guitars, all are in evidence, and Jesus is jamup contemporary, with a process and silk suit too, my man" (192). In a sentence, Baraka describes the instrumentation, the dress, the hairstyles, and the *attitude* of gospel quartets. The gospel singer is as much a hipster as the soul man. Indeed, as the biographies of many attest, they were often the same person.[40]

With its frequent use of ellipses, sentence fragments, and interpolations of poetic lines, "The Changing Same" strives to be as affective and experimental as the music it valorizes. For example, Baraka writes of Coltrane, "the music is a way into God. The absolute open expression of everything" (193). At another point in the essay, words are no longer organized into sentences; keywords "Change," "Freedom," "Spirit," and "Essence" invite readers to complete the thoughts the words initiate. Later, an italicized "note" interrupts the prose and serves more as entreaty than analysis: *Let the new people take care of some practical bi-ness and the R&B take care of some new bi-ness and the unity musick, the people-leap, can begin in earnest* (208–9).

The statement inverts the perspectives earlier assigned to the rhythm and blues artists and the jazz musicians. Seeming to echo the closing stanza of Margaret Walker's poem "For My People," which urges a new generation to rise and take control, Baraka urges musicians to sound a new consciousness— "the people-leap"—and inspire the unity that precedes and provokes revolution.

In its riffs on freedom, "The Changing Same" highlights interconnections between the two sections of this chapter. Eschewing any attempt at being systematic or philosophical, it allows for many different kinds of freedom. The civil rights movement aspires to civic freedom, although in a sarcastic reference to the "freedom to be a white man," that is unavailable to all people of color, the essay denigrates the movement's effectiveness. Musicians, whether they play R&B or jazz, are seeking the different and more difficult freedom "to want your own particular hip self" (195). Readers can fill in their own examples, from the camel walk danced by James Brown to the futuristic music performed by Sun Ra and his Arkestra. As Carter Mathes argues, in its "sensory expansion . . . generated through the projection of its innovative sounds," the new music "offered space for imagining radical ideas of black identity."[41] Mathes analyzes the ways that writers, including Baraka and Neal, strived to create similar spaces in their poetry and drama. Baraka strives to achieve comparable spaces in his essay.

Almost all the musicians Baraka invokes in "The Changing Same" are men.[42] By contrast, Alice Walker commands her readers to heed the songs of black women: "Listen to the voices of Bessie Smith, Billie Holiday, Nina Simone, Roberta Flack, and Aretha Franklin . . . and imagine those voices muzzled for life."[43] In "In Search of Our Mothers' Gardens," her most famous essay, Walker contrasts these legendary singers to the "crazy," "Sainted" black mothers and grandmothers who were forbidden to read and write, who lacked the means to paint and to sculpt, and who were consequently driven mad. Walker esteems the creativity of those who survived, who were inspired by the "will to adorn" and who in the process of expressing it achieved a spiritual freedom; their creations expand Walker's definition of art. Moreover, in its digressiveness, "In Search" enacts the "will to adorn" even as it honors it.

"In Search" incorporates literary allusions and analyses and addresses questions to its readers that urge them to think through the essay's arguments; it references historical facts and interjects autobiographical fragments. It catalogs the aspersions routinely cast on ordinary black women and avers that the fate suffered by black women who are frustrated artists is even meaner. It links the critical neglect of Phillis Wheatley's poetry to her physical suffering. When it takes readers to the museum gallery that exhibits a quilt by an anonymous black woman, it invites them implicitly to reflect on the possible circumstances of *her* life, in light of the sickness and impoverishment that marked the end of Wheatley's. It ends by asserting that art by black women is less often found in museums or in books than in their everyday practices of quilting, cooking, and gardening. The poet's mother in her garden is as much an artist as her daughter whose words we are reading. Every digression in the essay pivots back to the question at its heart: "What did it mean for a black woman to be an artist in our grandmothers' time? In our great-grandmother's day? It is a question with an answer cruel enough to stop the blood" (233).

Midway through the writing, Walker introduces the essay's title and then begins its most important digression, a short sketch of her mother's life. Her mother exemplifies "those millions of black women who were not Phillis Wheatley or Lucy Terry" or any of the writers and artists she catalogs. "I found," Walker writes, "while thinking about the far-reaching world of the creative black woman, that often the truest answer to a question that really matters can be found very close" (238). This statement, like those of Baldwin and Patricia Williams previously discussed, is the perspective of an essayist, who uses his or her individual experience to work through issues that resonate far beyond themselves. In this case Walker returns to the question around which her essay pivots and which, truth be told, had rarely been addressed in print before. Her mother's story reinforces the point: Minnie Lou Walker, whom the writer does not name here, is a sharecropper, the mother of eight children, whose life is defined largely by the hard labor she performs. Indeed, "there was never a moment for her to sit down, undisturbed, to unravel her own private thoughts . . . ." (238). Anticipating her reader's puzzlement, Walker interposes another question, "But when, you will ask, did my overworked mother have time to know or care about feeding the creative spirit?"(239).

Rather than answer the question directly, Walker describes the quilt hanging in the Smithsonian made by "an anonymous Black woman in Alabama, a hundred years ago" (239). Its subject is the Crucifixion, which connects the quilter to the crazy saints that open the essay and which reinforces Walker's assertion that spirituality is the basis of art. Averting the question again, Walker returns to Woolf, quoting her famous observation that "Anon, who wrote so many poems without signing them, was often a woman." The anonymous quilter becomes part of a broader tradition of female artists. The essay then returns to the figure of Walker's mother, whose stories, she confides, have enabled her own. She not only includes some of the stories themselves in her published fiction, she incorporates "something of the manner" in which her mother told them: her mother influences the content and the form of her daughter's fiction. Walker thereby claims her biological mother as her literary foremother.

The author's mother is, however, an artist in her own right. The mother's relationship to her garden is the relationship of the artist to her work: "She is involved in work her soul must have. Ordering the universe in the image of her personal conception of Beauty" (241). Her garden is the mother's canvas. As the essay describes it, the essay's title becomes both literal and metaphorical. The garden, "so brilliant with colors, so original in its design," planted on land the family did not own, belongs to the mother. The mother's garden inspires what is arguably the essay's most lyrical passage: "Whatever she planted grew as if by magic, and her fame as a grower of flowers spread over three counties. Because of her creativity with flowers, even my memories of poverty are seen through a screen of blooms—sunflowers, petunias, roses, dahlias, forsythia, spirea, delphiniums, verbena . . . and on and on" (241). Arranged in a metrical pattern and highlighting the internal rhymes among them, the names of the flowers constitute a poem. The paragraph's thesis that poverty does not destroy the creative spirit restates the essay's theme and resonates with one of Hurston's central tenets in "Characteristics of Negro Expression," from which I take the subtitle "the will to adorn." Hurston writes that "there can never be enough of beauty, let alone too much."[44] When Walker ends her sentence—"and on and on"—she captures this sensibility.

In mainly colloquial language, the essay takes up issues of art and aesthetics, asking readers to consider an expansive definition of art that collapses the binary between arts and crafts, folk art and high art. Implicitly, it asks whose interests such distinctions serve. Explicitly, it challenges readers to question who can be considered an artist. By using the metaphor of the garden—a common subject for Western artists, some of whom, like Claude Monet, are celebrated for the gardens they planted as well as for those they painted—the essay reminds us that women and men, blacks and whites, the privileged and the poor are valued differently even when they perform the same activity. Walker's description of her mother is the portrait of an artist, who has achieved a spiritual freedom that is invisible to those who oppress her. It is akin to the freedom that Du Bois heard in the spirituals and that Ellison witnessed in the jam sessions. Moreover, like the jazz musician who to Baraka channeled revolutionary fervor, the mother/artist inculcates in Walker and in her readers the "respect for possibilities," chief among which is the possibility of freedom.

The subject of freedom will resonate throughout this book. In the following chapters, I analyze the sermons and orations of nineteenth-century men and women who laid the foundation for the African American essay. I then chart the debates on art and aesthetics that preoccupied writers during the Harlem Renaissance, before turning to four of the most influential essayists of the twentieth century: James Baldwin, Ralph Ellison, June Jordan, and Alice Walker. They extend some of the arguments of their precursors and deploy similar rhetorical strategies even as they expand definitions both of freedom and of art. In an epilogue, I consider the status of the essay in the twenty-first century as it shifts its medium from print to digital.

CHAPTER TWO

Voices of Thunder

Nineteenth-Century Black Oratory and the Development of the African American Essay

In the name of God we ask, are you men? Where is the blood of your fathers?
Has it all run out of your veins? Awake, awake; millions of voices are calling you!
Your dead fathers speak to you from their graves. Heaven, as with a voice of
thunder, calls on you to rise from the dust.

—Henry Highland Garnet, "An Address to the Slaves of the United States" (1848)

More than a century before James Baldwin electrified the nation and the
world with the publication of *The Fire Next Time* in 1962, African Americans
had marshaled the power of the word in defense of themselves. In their
speeches and pamphlets, their spoken words and written texts, they laid the
foundation for what became the African American essay as we think of it
today. Baldwin followed David Walker and Maria Stewart, free blacks who
lived in Boston in the 1820s, and who wrote jeremiads lamenting the failure of
the nation to live out its creed and prophesying destruction unless it changed
its path. Biblical allusions, metaphors, and rhetorical strategies—especially a
sheath-sharpened irony—are as pervasive in powerful orations of Frederick
Douglass and Henry Highland Garnet as in essays by Baldwin and June Jordan.
In a different register, Frances Watkins Harper voiced appeals for racial uplift
during Reconstruction that resonated with texts popular at the turn of the
twentieth century. Proceedings of literary societies recorded polite debates
about the purpose of literature that gave way to the strident exchanges of the
next century. Even though the stylized "I" so central to essays by W. E. B. Du
Bois, Zora Neale Hurston, and Alice Walker belongs to the autobiographer
rather than the essayist in the nineteenth century, one can discern its signature in the mark the slave narrative left on all forms of African American
prose.

What is most significant about black oratory in terms of its influence on
the development of the essay is its complicated circuit of transmission. Words
were composed to be spoken, published to be read, and then often spoken
aloud again as they were read to audiences who could not read. The line between spoken and written was blurred by nineteenth-century conventions. In

1837, Ralph Waldo Emerson presented "An Oration, Delivered before the Phi Beta Kappa Society," that when retitled "The American Scholar" became one of the best known and most influential American essays. The address was then published the same year in pamphlet form before being retitled and reprinted in *Nature, Addresses and Lectures* in 1849. Henry Highland Garnet's "Address to the Slaves of the United States of America" followed a similar path of publication. However, unlike Emerson, Garnet wrote his speech with a keen understanding that most of those to whom it was directly addressed were illiterate. As had David Walker before him, he wanted this audience to hear his message. Many of those who did could do so because written texts circulated as spoken words. That circulation required literate speakers who were able to hold an audience's attention and were willing to put themselves in harm's way in order to reproduce the message. It also required that the message itself be readily comprehensible. With that goal in mind, early nineteenth-century pamphleteers and orators drew on the rhetorical conventions of African American Protestantism familiar to audiences whose religious faith was foundational to their sense of themselves. Many assumed a prophetic stance in which they channeled the voice of thunder to which Reverend Garnet referred. In so doing they made the case against injustice for themselves and for past and future generations. Extending Garnet's metaphor, I argue that black orators hoped to become voices of thunder, channeling their fathers (and mothers) in order to command the attention of their peers and their oppressors. To that end, they appropriated the rhetoric of the founding documents of the American republic, which they remade into a rhetoric of counterrevolution, and they conveyed with searing honesty the material realities of life in America for blacks, both enslaved and free.

Enforced illiteracy is one of the best known truths about life under slavery, yet a vibrant print culture sprang up in African American communities in the early nineteenth century.[1] It produced an array of genres: pamphlets, newspaper articles, eulogies, sermons, speeches, poems, and autobiographical narratives. Most of these writings were directed toward a black audience and published in newspapers like *Freedom's Journal* (1827–1829), *The Rights of All* (1829), and *The Colored American* (1837–1841) or published by religious denominations, as, for example, the *Christian Recorder*, a publication of the African Methodist Episcopal (AME) Church, or published by the authors themselves. Somewhat later, blacks would find outlets for their work in the abolitionist press, outlets that in the case of Mary Shadd Cary and Frederick Douglass, they themselves created. These writings evince what Ralph Ellison described as the "free-floating literacy" that traditionally existed in black

American communities, even when formal education was proscribed under segregation as well as slavery. Not only were there more literate blacks than conditions would seem to allow, but they read to and for people unable to read themselves.

This practice complicates the ideal of literacy championed in the 1845 *Narrative of the Life of Frederick Douglass*, arguably the most famous representation of the relationship between reading and freedom in the African American tradition. As Elizabeth McHenry argues, scholars' subsequent reliance on the paradigm suggested by Douglass's narrative "fails to take into account the extent to which the spoken word offered many black Americans access to written texts." Her research into nineteenth-century literary societies in black communities revealed memberships that included the literate and illiterate alike. The societies "endorsed a broader notion of oral literacy that did not valorize the power of formal or individualized literacy over communal knowledge."[2] McHenry's concept of "oral literacy" has implications for writers as well as readers. They shared a common set of references, secular as well as sacred, that facilitated comprehension. Moreover, similar formal strategies characterized written as well as oral texts. For example, nineteenth-century black orators relied on repetition, a crucial element in oral texts across cultures. They also employed interjections, parallelisms, and patterns of call and response that narrowed the gap between oral and written modes. Most strikingly, many of them invoked the presence of their illiterate auditors in the texts themselves.

The status of free blacks was only slightly less precarious than that of the enslaved. In the South, they could be called upon to verify their status at any time. If they lacked written documentation, they risked being fined, imprisoned, or sold into slavery. In the North, free blacks agitated for citizenship rights and argued against the tenets of the pseudoscientific racism that held them to be less than human. They also grappled with the impact of racism in their everyday lives. The job market was segregated. As Douglass discovered after he fled slavery, white laborers in Massachusetts routinely refused to work alongside blacks, especially in the skilled trades. Churches were segregated, and often so were schools. Northern blacks struggled for their own human dignity. But they were mindful of the ties of kinship and consciousness that bound them to blacks in slavery. Not surprisingly, many of those who wrote and led were abolitionists. Literate blacks were generally supportive of the movement: indeed, most of the subscribers to William Lloyd Garrison's *The Liberator* were blacks. In 1854, the free-born Watkins Harper described what we might today term her positionality thus: "Identified with a people over whom weary ages of degradation have passed, whatever concerns them, as a race, concerns me."[3] Whether in the South or the North, no concern was more urgent than freedom.[4]

In its inaugural issue, March 16, 1827, *Freedom's Journal's* editors, Samuel E. Cornish and John B. Russwurm, announced, "We wish to plead our own cause. Too long have others spoken for us."[5] The editors were well prepared to speak for themselves. Cornish was a Presbyterian minister who was born free in Delaware in 1795; Russwurm was born free in Jamaica in 1799 and was one of the first blacks to graduate from an American college (Bowdoin, 1826). Although based in New York City, *Freedom's Journal* was the first black newspaper aimed at a national audience. As Cornish and Russwurm wrote in a letter "To Our Patrons," their aim was to correct the misrepresentations of the race in public discourse. Although they were ready to concede the "many instances of vice among us," which they attributed mainly to poverty, they objected to the ways that the actions of individuals were used to malign the entire group. In their dedication to racial uplift, the editors advocated education above all, but promised that "useful knowledge of every kind, and every thing [sic] that relates to Africa, shall find a ready admission to our columns." References to Haiti and South America further evinced their Pan-Africanist perspective. Indeed, Russwurm would emigrate to Liberia shortly after *Freedom's Journal* ended its run in March 1829. Although the editors promised not to be "unmindful of our brethren who are still in the iron fetters of bondage," they never devoted an editorial to the subject of abolition. Their potential readership of "Five Hundred Thousand" was the free black population of the United States, for whom they hoped to create a forum on all "subjects which concern us."[6] In addition to political articles advocating citizenship rights for blacks and articles that recounted historical events, the newspaper printed pieces devoted to self-help and moral uplift, as well as poems and short stories. While the paying subscribers numbered only around 800, the newspaper's circulation in urban communities—among congregations and literary societies as well as among friends and neighbors—meant it reached many more, including those who heard rather than read what was in its pages.

Not coincidentally, David Walker was a steadfast supporter of *Freedom's Journal*. Even before the first issue was published, he held a meeting in his home to consider "giving aid and support" to the paper, an event that the inaugural issue recorded. He then signed on as an agent whose task it was to aid in distribution. A loyal reader of the paper, he would later incorporate its themes into his *Appeal*, particularly the identification of Egypt with Africa and its descendants, the comparative analysis of slavery, the heroic history of

Haiti, and the issue of emigration. Finally, Walker became a contributor to the journal. His articles included "The Necessity of a General Union Among Us" (December 19, 1828), which, like his *Appeal*, was a plea for racial unity.

Both Cornish and Russwurm would start other newspapers: *The Colored American* and *The Rights of All*, respectively. Cornish was also active with the Phoenix Society, one of a number of groups established to encourage reading and writing among black Americans. As Elizabeth McHenry observes, these literary societies varied in size and formal organization. Some set up libraries or reading rooms, some provided instruction for beginning or advanced readers, while others encouraged the dissemination of creative work which they read and discussed corporately. Some also sponsored lectures and oratorical performances.[7] As a consequence, they fostered the creation and dissemination of nineteenth-century African American texts.

Finally, the Negro Convention Movement was a crucial venue for the production of black spoken and written texts. It began in 1830 when delegates from the mid-Atlantic states as well as Maryland and Virginia came together in Philadelphia "to devise ways and means for the bettering of our condition." Samuel Cornish was there, along with businessman and abolitionist James Forten and Richard Allen, at the first of what became a series of meetings that took place over the next thirty years. Douglass and Garnet would eventually play leading roles. According to historians John Hope Franklin and Evelyn Higginbotham, "The importance of national black convention meetings as formal mechanisms for fostering group consciousness and protest cannot be overstated."[8] Key to that consciousness were orations such as "An Address to the Slaves of the United States of America," that subsequently circulated as printed texts and that laid the ground for the African American essay. As Carla Peterson avers, all of these institutions—the press, literary societies, and the convention movement—were central to "the reproduction of African-American social, cultural, and literary knowledge in the nineteenth century."[9]

Given the larger frame that Peterson invokes, it is not surprising that few nineteenth-century black authors identified writing as their vocation. They were instead preachers and spiritual seekers, abolitionists and social reformers, teachers and entrepreneurs. David Walker owned a used-clothing shop in Boston. Maria Stewart worked for years as a domestic in a minister's parsonage before mounting the podium in the cause of citizenship rights for free blacks. After a brief sojourn in the public eye, she retreated to the classroom and the hospital, where she earned her living and carried out a creed of service. In addition to being a minister, Henry Highland Garnet was a newspaper editor and a lecturer on temperance and abolition. Frederick Douglass, the nineteenth century's preeminent black author and leader, was a fugitive slave, ship caulker, abolitionist, orator, autobiographer, newspaper editor, and statesman. Before the Civil War, Frances Watkins Harper traveled through the North winning fame for poems like "The Slave Auction" and "The Slave Mother" and winning converts to the abolitionist cause. After the war, she traveled through the South with messages of uplift for freedmen and women and continued to speak on behalf of temperance and women's suffrage.

Some of Maria Stewart's writings were published as "essays." Others were published as speeches or orations, as were many of the pieces published by her peers. From the lecture circuit, Watkins Harper sent letters to abolitionist and religious newspapers that, like her speeches, were intended for publication. What is most important for my purpose is that all appeared in print. Whether or not these pieces had first been disseminated orally, after they were "read" from the podium, they circulated as written texts. Their dual status as oral and written texts is one of their defining features and one of the most important for the development of the twentieth-century essay.

In antebellum America, whites no less than blacks were enamored of the spoken word; they flocked to speeches the way their descendants attend sporting events and rock concerts. They set their expectations at a high bar. For some, "oratory was among the supreme manifestations of art."[10] In what was dubbed as early as the 1850s "the golden age of American oratory," Henry Clay, John Calhoun, and Daniel Webster had built political careers on the basis of their eloquence at the podium. The lyceum movement started in 1826 to foster popular education brought lecturers to middle-class Americans; these audiences preferred cultural uplift to politics. For other audiences, however, what one scholar calls the "culture of eloquence" was handmaiden to social and cultural reform.[11] They were animated by the belief that words had the power to effect action.

According to Garnet, who reprinted it along with his signature "Address to the Slaves" in 1848, *David Walker's Appeal* was "among the first, and was actually the boldest and most direct appeal in behalf of freedom" made by blacks during the early years of the nineteenth century.[12] The righteousness of its anger and the fever heat of its prose were unrivalled. It assailed the evils of slavery, urged unity and uplift among blacks both free and enslaved, and rebuked those who argued that black repatriation to Africa was the only solution to the problem of race in America. Its call for blacks to take up arms to end slavery incited bravery among blacks who heard it and put fear in the hearts of slaveholders, who quickly banned the publication in the southern United States. Their efforts thwarted Walker's ambitious plan to disseminate his pamphlet through a network of black abolitionists in the South. As he notes in the text itself, most blacks were illiterate, and the slave system enforced their ignorance by law. But he urged that those who could not read his manifesto to "Get some one [*sic*] to read it to them, for it is designed more particularly for them."[13] His wish was granted. One contemporary writer attested, "I have known a small company of individuals patiently listen at one sitting to hear David Walker's 'Appeal to the Free People of Color,' read through."[14] Venues for such readings existed throughout the nation. Even in the South, blacks had organized churches in which they were able surreptitiously to create and share visions of freedom. Black orators in the North spoke openly in support of antislavery resistance. Walker drew on these models for the *Appeal*.[15] Its rhetorical flourishes, especially its unvarnished ironies, repetitions, and interjections ("I say"), as well as its distinctive typography create the semblance of oral performance. Deploying an eclectic range of reference from world history and literature, it locates the struggle of blacks in nineteenth-century America in the broadest historical and geographical contexts. At the same time it is explicitly nationalist in its concerns and in the mode of its address.[16] Walker writes to urge black Americans, his "dearly beloved Brethren and Fellow Citizens," to rise up and revolt against the intolerable condition of slavery.

Yet readers remain conscious of the individual voice of David Walker, who announces in the first sentence that he has himself traveled over "a considerable portion of these United States" and that the convictions he expresses are based on his personal observations. At the end of the text he reasserts the primacy of his experience, as he writes, "I do not speak from hearsay—what I have written, is what I have seen and heard myself" (79). He describes his visit to a camp meeting in South Carolina where "a very great concourse of people . . . collected together to hear the word of God" and heard instead a false gospel of blood and whips rather than of peace (41). He recalls scenes of enslaved people being forced at the behest of their masters to beat their closest kin. He recounts articles he has read from newspapers across the country that convey the horrors of slavery and that, as often as not, quote the slaveholders' own words to indict their actions. He records conversations with people he has met, including the colored bootblack who announced himself content in his situation, and thereby becomes a prime example of the degradation of black people's spirit. By combining a personalized witness with traditions of oral performance, Walker lays the ground for the development of a distinctively "African American" essay.

While it addresses black people in the United States "in particular, and very expressly," *David Walker's Appeal, in Four Articles, Together with A Preamble, to the Colored Citizens of the World, But in Particular, and Very Expressly to Those of the United States of America*, published in three editions in 1829 and 1830, situates them in the larger context of "colored citizens of the world." It attributes the status of "citizen" to black people everywhere, an attribution that the *Appeal* defends and elaborates. In sum, the *Appeal* is a claim that rests on civil and divine authority. It simultaneously delineates that authority and challenges black people to act on it. For those in the United States, the *Appeal* draws its sanction from the nation's founding documents. Organized into a preamble and four articles, it clearly intends to evoke the model of the U.S. Constitution. In its substance, no less than its structure, the Constitution is a key intertext. More important still is the Declaration of Independence, an extended excerpt from which is quoted in the conclusion. Walker meant to be taken seriously, and the structural echo of the Constitution works to heighten the import of the text. But the Declaration of Independence inscribed the permanent ideal to which he believed the nation should aspire.[17]

Throughout the *Appeal*, Walker engages as well with Thomas Jefferson's *Notes on the State of Virginia* in which Jefferson refuses to recognize blacks as human, let alone as citizens. As the author of both the Declaration, which insisted that all men were created equal, and *Notes*, which insisted that blacks were not men, Jefferson embodied the contradiction at the heart of the national identity. To assert their humanity, blacks had to turn to a higher authority. As his allusions to scripture—from Genesis to Revelations—demonstrate, Walker locates that authority in the Bible, which he adamantly believed to be an antislavery document. On the first page of the *Appeal*, he professes himself a Christian, and his civic and spiritual identities remain intertwined.

His explicit address to "his brethren" notwithstanding, Walker also directed his accusation at the nation whose commission of the crime of slavery was irrefutable. The nation was called to account in an international tribunal, indicated by the references to the colored citizens of the world as well as by laudable invocations of the English. As a free black, the North Carolina–born son of an enslaved father and a free mother, whose own legal status even in Boston was tenuous, Walker wrote as one keenly aware of the risks.[18] In one of his characteristic flourishes, he describes his expectation of being "held up to the public as an ignorant, impudent and restless disturber of the public peace," who would perhaps be imprisoned or killed as a result of his brash publication (4). He did in fact die the year after the *Appeal* was published but likely of natural causes.[19] Significantly, while his is a criminal and political complaint, it is also a spiritual entreaty. Slavery was a sin as well as a crime. Walker warned his white countrymen who were "so happy to keep blacks in ignorance and degradation" not to forget "that God rules in the armies of heaven and among the inhabitants of the earth, having his ears continually open to the cries, tears, and groans of his oppressed people."[20] Both in its meaning and its metaphor, this passage and many others like it identify the *Appeal* with traditions of the black sermon. It confidently proclaims the existence of an omnipotent yet anthropomorphic deity that is on the side of the enslaved. It also imparts agency to the enslaved whose "cries, tears, and groans" will move this deity to action on their behalf. Their voices are the source of their power. Walker both invokes and choreographs these voices in his text.

Its unique typography—what scholar Marcy Dinius aptly describes as "a graphic riot of italics, small and full capitals, exclamation points, and pointing index fingers"—gives us a sense of not only how the *Appeal* was meant to be read but how it is to sound.[21] In so doing it blurs the boundaries between the written and oral tradition. The typographical elements chart Walker's vocal modulations, even as they guide the modulations of his readers. Its instructions were particularly germane for those who read the text aloud to their peers. Readers were cued when to raise their voices and when to speed up and slow down; the typography offered a guide to tonal modulation as well by visually conveying the text's verbal ironies. So, for example, as Walker observes that "all the inhabitants of the earth, (except however, the sons of Africa) are called *men*, and of course are, and ought to be free," the reader/speaker adds the requisite emphasis. What follows requires a raised voice and a rapid delivery: "But we, (coloured people) and our children are *brutes!!* and of course are, and *ought to be* SLAVES to the American people and their children forever!! To dig their mines and work their farms; and thus go on enriching them, from one generation to another with our *blood* and our *tears!!!* (9). The disjunction between blacks' sense of themselves and their oppressors' definition of them—"coloured people" and "brutes"—builds into a crescendo of sarcasm and anger. Dinius compares the typographical elements to the dynamic marks on a musical score. They capture the dynamics of Walker's performance and choreograph the performance of others. Even the manicule, or pointing index finger, that is the oddest typographical element in the text, may be read as a stage direction for Walker's readers. Although the ostensible purpose of the manicule was to mark Walker's additions to the second and third editions of the pamphlet, its effect was to point an accusatory finger at whites who oppress black people.[22] This would have been no less true on the speaker's platform than on the page. It is worth noting, too, that the image used as cover art for at least one twentieth-century edition of the *Appeal* features a well-dressed man at a podium whose gesticulations provoke bodily responses from members of his audience, some of whom are bowed down in postures of prayer.[23]

Scholars classify the *Appeal* as a jeremiad, a literary genre named for Jeremiah, the Old Testament prophet who, as Amos, Micah, Hosea, and Isaiah had done before him, lamented the sinfulness of his people and warned them that if they did not repent, they would be destroyed by God's wrath. Walker partakes of this tradition, as he warns both blacks and whites that if they failed to live according to the biblical imperative for justice, they would guarantee their destruction. The historical parallels are suggestive. It fell to the biblical Jeremiah to counsel the Israelites through years of exile after Babylonia had captured Jerusalem. He preached that his people's apostasy had produced their subjugation, yet he prophesized an eventual restoration—a paradise in Canaan that would surpass what had been lost. In post-biblical cultures, jeremiads, also called political sermons, served secular as well as spiritual ends. Sacvan Bercovitch describes the "American jeremiad," the first distinctively American literary genre, as "a ritual designed to join social criticism to spiritual renewal, public to private identity, the shifting 'signs of the times' to certain traditional metaphors, themes, and symbols."[24] Bercovitch dates its beginnings to the Puritans who used biblical typology to understand and cope with the dangers and uncertainties of their lives in the New World.

With its capacity to map historical experience onto biblical narrative, to combine social criticism and spiritual renewal and to reconcile public to private identity, the jeremiad proved attractive to black writers. But, for them, the jeremiad necessarily served a different purpose. It both affirmed and challenged the premise of American exceptionalism, given the evident failure of the nation to act out either its religious mission or its secular creed. At the same time, it also held out the possibility of redemption, which was tied to the abolition of slavery in the nineteenth century and the elimination of segregation in the twentieth. As scholar Wilson Moses observes, in the black jeremiad, authors "revealed a conception of themselves as a chosen people" along with "a clever ability to play on the belief that America as a whole was a chosen nation with a covenantal duty to deal justly with blacks."[25] Moses argues that the black jeremiad is a nineteenth-century genre. I disagree. The genre which *Walker's Appeal* helps to inaugurate continues throughout the twentieth century— with writers including Baldwin, Jordan, and Martin Luther King Jr.—and into the present. As it does, the black jeremiad's address to two chosen peoples—one white and one black, whose destinies are inextricably linked—becomes harder to sustain. Initially, this conception was drawn from a typological understanding of history that was for blacks a strategy both for psychic survival and political liberation. By the late twentieth century, however, the emphasis on the uniqueness of African American experience would prove problematic, as blacks in the United States forged political alliances with people of African descent across the diaspora. Even though Walker wrote with an understanding that blacks in America belonged to a transnational community of black citizens, he referred to a common consciousness rather than a political coalition. The form and the politics of the *Appeal* were stamped by their origin in the United States.

As its original format confirms, the *Appeal* participates in the American tradition of pamphleteering. The similarities extend beyond the format. As did Thomas Paine, the author of the most famous Revolution-era text, *Common Sense*, Walker appreciated the importance of claiming a public voice and using printed texts to build a nation, or in Walker's case, a nation-within-a-nation. Significantly, too, Thomas Paine used slavery as a metaphor for the condition of the colonists, an analogy that those who suffered literal rather than figurative slavery seized upon eagerly. Echoing and contesting the patriots of the Revolution, Walker asks whether the sufferings of white Americans under the British were "one hundredth part as cruel and tyrannical" as those inflicted on blacks who "have never given your fathers the least provocation" (79). As Gene Jarrett notes, "Walker wrote in a nascent tradition of black pamphleteers" as well.[26] In addition to Richard Allen, Absalom Jones, and Daniel Coker, these include James Forten, who published a series of *Letters from a Man of Colour* (1813), and Prince Saunders, who authored "An Address Before the Pennsylvania Augustine Society" (1818). None of their texts circulated as widely or left as deep a historical imprint as the *Appeal*. But they all drew from a common storehouse of oratorical strategies that resonated with the literate and illiterate alike.

Chief among these is repetition, a strategy that is crucial to the power of the *Appeal*. Numerous times it reiterates as self-evident truth that "the colored people of these United States are the most degraded, wretched and abject set of beings that ever lived since the world began" (3). The extremity of their condition serves several rhetorical purposes. The first is simply to intensify the call for amelioration, to "awaken" in blacks (his "afflicted brethren") a spirit of inquiry and resistance. The second is comparative. From its initial iteration, the condition of enslaved blacks in the United States is compared to enslaved populations throughout history: in Egypt, Sparta, and Rome and the contemporary world. Walker drives home the point that slavery in Christian America is worse than in so-called heathen nations. The third purpose is to heighten the contradiction between the nation's democratic principles and its material realities, the contradiction that allows "our miseries and wretchedness in this *Republican Land of Liberty!!!!!*"(5). The repetitions work finally to convey the prophetic warning that God will avenge the oppression of his people; the day of reckoning is close at hand. The warning might be a caution for white Americans, but its purpose is to fortify the spirits of blacks.

Walker writes as a passionate prophet, but he assumes other mantles as well. At the beginning of the preamble, in a familiar conceit, he acknowledges his unworthiness to perform the task he has undertaken. Only the pen of a Josephus or a Plutarch could do it justice, he allows, thereby establishing at once his humility and his erudition. He promulgates a logical argument against the wrong of slavery. The historical references that he marshals in support range from Julius Caesar and Mark Antony to the fall of Constantinople. He is like Josephus a statesman and historian, and like Plutarch a moral philosopher, although he holds these titles without portfolio. Duty compels that he persist. He identifies a threefold duty: to his black brethren, to his country, and to God. As he fulfills that duty, he demonstrates the breadth of his historical and literary knowledge, the depth of his biblical knowledge, and his familiarity with the daily life of black people in the United States.

At its core, the *Appeal* is a brief on behalf of the humanity of blacks. Displacing the power of the slaveholder, it asserts that God is the *master* of the whole human family. It asks those who can to acknowledge that blacks are human—their "improminent" noses and woolly heads notwithstanding—that they love their spouses and children as others do. To those who cannot recognize blacks' humanity, it threatens divine retribution. In the present, the inability of whites to recognize blacks' humanity—and more pointedly, the inability of blacks to embrace their own humanity—results in the degradation and abjection that Walker references repeatedly, often in identical language. Repeated, too, is the interjection "I say," which focuses attention on the presence of a singular voice speaking on behalf of the degraded black collective. Addressing their oppressors, the voice entreats, "I say, if God gives you peace and tranquility, and suffers you thus to go on afflicting us and our children, who have never given you the least provocation,—Would he be to us *a God of justice?*"(8). In one of his more muted figures, Walker offers to "close my remarks on the suburbs, just to enter more fully into the interior of this system of cruelty and oppression" (8). The movement of the text resonates with Du

Bois's invitation to his reader to step within the veil. Here the entry into the interior signals Walker's deeper engagement with slavery in Article I. Unlike Du Bois, however, Walker moves first into biblical typology rather than autobiography or social history.

The Exodus narrative frames Article I, entitled "Our Wretchedness in Consequence of Slavery," a section that like the other articles and the preamble might be read as a proto-essay. "I refer you in the first place," Walker writes, "to the children of Jacob, or of Israel in Egypt" (9). No biblical narrative was as important to nineteenth-century black Americans as Exodus. It allowed them to make sense of their otherwise inexplicable condition by comparing it to that of the Israelites. Moreover, it increased their faith in a similarly providential liberation.[27] Yet Walker does not simply identify enslaved blacks with the biblical Hebrews. He asserts in addition that American blacks resembled Egyptians phenotypically, who, he contends, were less villainous than most of his audience believed. For example, he remarks that Egyptian leaders appointed Joseph and Moses to high office; to Walker, their appointments stand in stark contrast to the situation of blacks in America, where no black holds even the low office of constable or is allowed to serve on a jury. The biblical allusions thus serve a polemical as well as a spiritual purpose. Facts about black life in the United States continue to be introduced in this fashion, as examples of treatment that is worse than the biblical slaves endured. So, for example, when Walker mentions that Pharaoh also arranged for Joseph to marry an Egyptian, he cites the illegality of intermarriage in the United States. Then he reveals something of his mettle: "I would wish, candidly, however, before the Lord, to be understood, that I would not give a *pinch of snuff* to be married to any white person I ever saw in all the days of my life" (11). The reason to mention intermarriage at all, Walker insists with daring irony, is to draw the contrast between the treatment of blacks in Christian America and that of the Hebrews in "heathen" Egypt.

By far the worst thing about slavery in the United States, Walker insists, is the denial of black people's humanity. Above all other Americans, Jefferson personifies this denial. Consequently, *Notes on the State of Virginia* (1782) becomes a key intertext for the *Appeal*. The only full-length book that Jefferson published during his lifetime, *Notes* compiles his observations on the natural history of Virginia as well as some of his most influential statements on the political and legal history of the nation, including his views on constitutional principles such as the separation of church and state, governmental checks and balances, individual liberty, the problem of slavery, and the racial differences that underlay the "peculiar institution." As both the author of the Declaration and the master of the slave plantation at Monticello, Jefferson daily confronted the contradiction that Walker denounced. Jefferson rationalized the contradiction by arguing that the innate inferiority of blacks —"inferior to the whites in the endowments of both body and mind"—suited them for slavery and rendered them unfit for citizenship.[28] At the same time, Jefferson recognized that slavery could not be sustained within U.S. borders over the long term; his preferred solution was that blacks be colonized elsewhere. As Walker foresaw, Jefferson's views—with their pseudoscientific veneer—would shape racist ideology for generations: "Mr. Jefferson's remarks respecting us, have sunk deep into the hearts of millions of whites, and never will be removed this side of eternity" unless blacks resolved to refute his falsehoods at every turn (30).[29]

Walker invokes Jefferson first to underscore his contention that unlike the biblical Hebrews, enslaved blacks in the United States suffer the "*insupportable insult*" that they are "not of the *human family*" (12). He alludes to Jefferson's slander that blacks were descended from orangutans. (Jefferson's slander was of course more specific and more odious, as he charged that male orangutans preferred to mate with black women above the females of their own species.)[30] Addressing his reader, Walker appeals "to every man of feeling—is this not insupportable?" Not finding sufficient recourse on earth, he addresses heaven. But the depth of his own feeling does not dull Walker's gift for irony. He turns Jefferson's reputation on its head: "It is indeed surprising, that a man of such great learning, combined with such excellent natural parts, should speak so of a set of men in chains" (12). Then, before he develops his own argument for "natural rights" for black people, he recounts a parable that illustrates the respective situation of whites and blacks. In the parable, the races are represented by two wild deer, a representation that undermines the hierarchy Jefferson worked so hard to impose. In Walker's story, one deer is placed in an iron cage, while the other is let go. Yet the caged deer is expected to run as fast as his free double. The expectation, Walker makes clear, is foolish. Still, he acknowledges, that pointing to the disparity in the condition of the races does not counter Jefferson's assertion that the inferiority of black people is innate; its outward sign is the "unfortunate" color of blackness. Walker refutes this assertion roundly. In a ringing declaration of race pride, he thanks God for blackness ("as though we are not as thankful to our God, for having made us as it pleased himself, as they [the whites] are for having made them white" [14]).[31] He then appropriates the argument of the Declaration of Independence when he insists on freedom as a "natural right" for blacks and whites equally. A note conveys his appreciation for the difficulty that blacks, enslaved as they are by reason of their color, might have embracing this argument. In some of the text's most straightforward prose, he addresses his brethren directly: "For you must remember that we are men as well as they. God has been pleased to give us two eyes, two hands, two feet, and some sense in our heads as well as they. They have no more right to hold us in slavery than we have to hold them, we have just as much right, in the sight of God, to hold them and their children in slavery and wretchedness as they have to hold us, and no more" (14).

This passage demonstrates Walker's democratic eloquence at its best. The perfectly balanced initial phrase and its repetition ("as well as they") puts blacks and whites on equal rhetorical footing. The enumerated "natural parts" of black men bespeak their humanity as eloquently as those of Jefferson himself. Their rights are equally God-given. The logician in Walker extends the comparison to one which would have impressed all of his readers as extreme. If whites have the right to enslave blacks, then blacks have the right to enslave whites. His seeming expression of humility—"some sense" as opposed to the erudition he attributes to Jefferson—makes the final claim more persuasive. Despite their intellectual limitations, their ignorance enforced by law, blacks could perceive the injustice of their condition and be led to correct it.

In his refutation of Jefferson's slanders, Walker demonstrates the breadth of his own knowledge. Point by point he disputes Jefferson's contention that slavery in antiquity was harsher than in the United States. In response to Jefferson's reference that when a Roman master was murdered, all his slaves in the same house or within hearing were condemned to death (25), Walker echoes Patrick Henry in proclaiming, ". . . had I not rather die, or be put to death, than to be a slave to any tyrant, who takes not only my own, but my wife and children's lives by the inches?" (16). Unstated but understood by his readers was the fact that under U.S. law, families rather than individuals were enslaved, and the status of slave passed from generation to generation. In response to Jefferson's catalog of the enslaved Romans who became great artists, thereby "proving" that race rather than status accounted for the condition of blacks in the United States, Walker contended that "Every body [*sic*] who has read history, knows, that as soon as a slave among the Romans obtained his freedom, he could rise to the greatest eminence in the State, and there was no law instituted to hinder a slave from buying his freedom" (18). His historical references not only demonstrate the breadth of Walker's knowledge, they evince his understanding that for centuries white men had made similar appeals in defense of their own freedom. He deliberately deployed their rhetoric on his own behalf and on behalf of his people. With the confidence inspired by both his knowledge and pride, Walker expressed gratitude to whites who had refuted Jefferson's slanders against blacks but argued that self-respect demanded that blacks speak for themselves. To that end, he urged blacks to buy copies of *Notes on the State of Virginia* for their sons. By reading not only Jefferson's text but the U.S. laws that refuted Jefferson's assertions, blacks could begin to break the intergenerational curse of slavery.

As Article II of the *Appeal*, "Our Wretchedness in Consequence of Ignorance," argues, the condition of blacks derived from the system of slavery itself and from the ignorance that in Walker's view kept blacks from overthrowing it. To a substantial extent, his solutions fit under the rubric of racial uplift; indeed he helped set the template for the rhetoric of reform through the next two centuries. Education is the holy grail. As did many of his contemporaries, Walker gestures toward a golden past in which Africa was a center of learning. Walker draws no distinction between the history of Egypt and of sub-Saharan Africa, when he lays claim to this past: "I say, when I view retrospectively, the renown of that once mighty people, the children of our great progenitor, I am indeed cheered" (22). For Walker, education is inextricably linked to self-respect. He dares black Americans to aspire to a storied legacy and warns that in their ignorance they mistake rudimentary training for knowledge. Yet, even as he advocates the acquisition of literacy and the proper rules of grammar, the consequences of ignorance that he cites are not mainly economic. They are instead racial betrayals: for example, the man who when ordered by the slaveholder whipped his own wife, the woman who aided the escape of the slave driver during a revolt, and the bootblack who gloried in his menial position. In Walker's analysis, only ignorance could explain the complicity of blacks in their own oppression.

Although Walker placed the responsibility for changing their condition on black people, he recognized that the blame for the condition itself lay elsewhere. In the remaining two articles of the *Appeal*, he holds institutions that have the imprimatur of the nation's leaders responsible. The first is the false Christianity of slaveholders that taught slaves to be resigned to their condition: a misinterpretation of the scripture that Walker deems sinful. The second is the propaganda of the American Colonization Society (ACS), an organization established in 1816 and led by such eminent figures as Henry Clay, John Randolph, and Francis Scott Key, that sought to implement Jefferson's ideas about the repatriation of black people. If the debilitating effect of false Christianity was long term, the threat of the ACS was imminent. Indeed, by 1830, the society had settled almost 1,500 blacks in the colony of Liberia in

West Africa.[32] In another indication of the broad acceptance of the ACS program, the capital of Liberia, Monrovia, was named for the U.S. president, James Monroe. As would subsequent black essayists, Walker wrote to address crises that were both existential and immediate.

He understood that his words were not sufficient to the cause. His call for violent revolutionary action, just as the nation's founders had engaged, was the logical endpoint, if the most controversial aspect, of his argument. With a final ironic gesture, he first quotes and then rewrites major portions of the Declaration of Independence to serve his particular purpose. Even in quotation, the opening lines of the Declaration seem to speak directly to the situation that Walker has outlined. He has enumerated the "human events" that make radical action necessary. His quotation ends with another sentence that in this context seems freshly resonant: "But when a long train of abuses and usurpations, pursuing invariably the same object, evinces a design to reduce them under absolute despotism, it is their right, it is their duty to throw off such government, and to provide new guards for their future security" (78). Readers could recognize the larger import of the *Appeal*'s catalog of abuses and usurpations—the exploitation of labor, theft of property, physical beatings, psychological insults, and family disruptions—all of which are designed to render blacks inhuman and unfit not only for citizenship in the U.S. nation but from membership in the human family. Walker reaffirms his earlier contention that tyranny suffered by the American colonists paled in comparison with that suffered by enslaved blacks.

Lest they miss the point, Walker addresses readers directly: "See your declaration, Americans!! Do you understand your own language? Hear your language, proclaimed to the world, July 4, 1776." Then literally appropriating their language to his own cause, he inserts a manicule, a pointing index finger, which turns the most famous lines of the document into an indictment of those who fail to honor them: "We hold these truths to be self evident—that ALL MEN ARE CREATED Equal!! *that they are endowed by their Creator with certain inalienable rights; that among these are life, liberty, and the pursuit of happiness!!*" (78). Again, Walker uses various fonts and series of exclamation points to guide the performance of the text and to amplify its meaning.[33] Significantly, he does not end his engagement with the Declaration with the resounding theme of human equality. Rather, having documented the humanity of black people in his text, he asks his readers to listen again to the sentence quoted above. This time when he adds emphasis to the statement, "it is their *right*. It is their *duty* to throw off such government," the pronoun references are unmistakable (79). Black Americans, both enslaved and "free," have not only the right but the duty to revolt. Even as state and local governments moved quickly to censor *Walker's Appeal*, its influence on black orators and writers could not be suppressed.[34]

In her introduction to her first publication, "Religion and the Pure Principles of Morality, the Sure Foundation on which We Must Build," Maria W. Stewart paid homage to her fellow activist and Boston neighbor, "the most noble, fearless, and undaunted David Walker."[35] She went on to welcome the martyrdom that she believed he had suffered. Like Walker, Stewart wrote out of her own experience (she frequently used the first-person pronoun) and out of her reading, especially of the Bible. Noting that we do not know whether Stewart read the Bible herself or it was read to her, Carla Peterson argues that Stewart lived and studied under conditions that some scholars term "secondary orality in which 'oral' and 'literate' are not so much a dichotomy as a continuum, mutually interactive and illuminating."[36] Like oral literacy, the concept of secondary orality credits the possibility that Stewart knew texts she may not have read. Members of Stewart's audience doubtless had similar experiences. Thus when she quoted scripture extensively at the podium and on the page, it evinced both her knowledge and the knowledge of those who heard her. Some of the allusions she makes affirm the humanity of black people. For example, addressing an audience of blacks, she cites Psalm 8:5: "He hath crowned you with glory and honor; hath made you but a little lower than the angels." Scholar Marilyn Richardson's assessment of Stewart is apt: "Resistance to oppression was, for Stewart, the highest form of obedience to God" (9). The same might be said of David Walker. Walker's rhetoric, no less than his personal example, inspired her. Her words, like his, inscribed an unbreakable connection between the spiritual and political realms. She drew no more distinction between them than between the oral and written traditions in which she voiced her views. Indeed, many of her publications first took the form of speeches. Her written texts retain the characteristic direct address, repetitions, and rhetorical flourishes of the podium. Echoing the *Appeal*, she described the impetus to write "in view of our wretched and degraded situation, and sensible of the gross ignorance that prevails among us" (28). As had Walker (and Anne Bradstreet, the Puritan poet, who was the first woman in the American colonies to publish a book), Stewart cloaked her words in the garment of humility.[37] Specifically, she located the authority to write in the spiritual conversion she underwent the year before.[38]

Two aspects of her authorial persona pose a contrast to Walker's. The first is the insertion of autobiography: in a brief paragraph, she highlights her girlhood status as orphan and her present status as widow. She thereby fore-grounds her gender and class status, along with her race. In words that resonate with Walker's, she addresses her sisters directly: "O, ye daughters of Africa, awake! Awake! Arise! No longer sleep nor slumber, but distinguish yourselves. Show forth to the world that ye are endowed with noble and exalted faculties" (30). But her references to black women are not always so exalted: she seems well acquainted with their day-to-day experience. One of her rhetorical questions ponders, "How long shall the fair daughters of Africa be compelled to bury their minds and talents beneath a load of iron pots and kettles?" (38). In addition to making this a general point here, Stew-art might have been writing back to a specific passage in *Walker's Appeal*, in which he condemned in detail a black woman who betrayed a rebellion against a coffle driver. Her actions impressed Walker as nothing but "servile deceit, combined with the most gross ignorance" (26). As Carla Peterson contends, this female figure "serves as the emblem of black disunity" in the *Appeal*.[39] I would argue that Stewart responds here with a call for unity that centers not on men, as in Walker, but on women. The daughters of Africa could and would distinguish themselves. In further distinction from Walker, although Stewart on occasion assumes the spirit of revolt, she is quicker to associate herself with a spirit of reform. As she avers, "Far be it from me to recommend to you [Afric's sons], either to kill, burn or destroy. But I would strongly recommend to you to improve your talents" (29).

Her less imperative tone notwithstanding, Stewart was a woman of stun-ning personal courage. She garnered no little notoriety when on Septem-ber 21, 1832, she transgressed prevailing gender codes and reportedly became the first woman in U.S. history to deliver a public lecture before "a promiscu-ous audience"—that is, an audience of men and women—at Boston's Franklin Hall, the site of the meetings of the New England Anti-Slavery Society.[40] The speech itself focuses on Stewart's gender, a focus that she achieves by paraphrasing Isaiah 6:8 and proclaiming, "Methinks I heard a spiritual interrogation—'Who shall go forward and take off the reproach that is cast upon the people of color? Shall it be a woman?' And my heart made this reply—'If it is thy will, be it even so, Lord Jesus!'" (45). Her language resem-bles that of the female preachers Jarena Lee and Zilpha Elaw, who were her contemporaries. In answer to the spirit's call, these women also recounted a private wrestling and a public response. They, too, transgressed social codes for women and accepted the call to preach an orthodox gospel.[41] However, the interiority of the spiritual interrogation in Stewart's case led to a more peculiar oration.

In the lecture at Franklin Hall, Stewart does not address the wages of sin or testify at length to her spiritual conversion. She instead addresses the condition of black people, free black women in particular. Acknowledging the horrors of slavery, she hones in on the "little better" conditions endured by northern blacks who are legally free but whose souls are shackled. Her personal witness in this regard is that she has had no access to education ("to the vast field of useful and scientific knowledge") and relies on "moral capability" alone.[42] (Lecturing to a roomful of social reformers, Stewart must have realized that "moral capability" trumped formal education.) Continuing in a personal vein, she refers to women, presumably white, who refuse to hire black girls regardless of their character. She interpolates rhetorical questions that demonstrate the inexplicability of their treatment: "Ah! Why is this cruel and unfeeling distinction?" (46). The questions reinforce the irrationality of prejudice, even as they create an implied pattern of call and response that partakes of traditions of oral performance. The audience is invited to answer with at least a nod at the injustice of the situation. Stewart's textual response is a poetic couplet that echoes the theme if not the artfulness of Phillis Wheatley: "Though black their skins as shades of night/Their hearts are pure, their souls are white" (46).[43] Neither Stewart nor Wheatley could free herself from the racial iconography of the Bible. Stewart's specific references to the material realities of black women's lives were more effective: "spending their lives as house-domestics, washing windows, shaking carpets, brushing boots, or tending upon gentlemen's tables." Stewart follows this catalog by stating her willingness to die "for expressing her sentiments" and by declaring her identity as an American: "for I am a true born American: your blood flows in my veins, and your spirit fires my breast" (46).[44] Her American identity is rooted in freedom and work, nativism and ideology. She lays claim, as a black woman, to the spirit of the Revolution and the founding documents of the republic.

Stewart's attitudes toward her homeland were complex if not contradictory. In one moment, she observes white Americans "thriving in arts and sciences and in polite literature" and whose "highest aim is to excel in political, moral, and religious improvement." As a consequence and despite the fact that they show no concern for black people, they are enjoying the promises of the Bible. Using a passage from Jeremiah, she implores her fellow blacks to stop backsliding and achieve the same promises.[45] While Stewart implies that whites do not deserve their good fortune, given their failure to right injustice, she emphasizes the need of blacks—the audience that she addresses—to repent.[46] Elsewhere she proclaims to America, "I love and admire thy virtues as much as I abhor and detest thy vices" (43). Her writings make plain both the virtues and the vices and the difficulty of balancing her responses to both. In "An Address Delivered at the African Masonic Hall" in 1833, she draws a vivid contrast between white and black Americans. Here she complicates her earlier statement regarding the success and "noble reputation" that white Americans enjoy, when she remarks that "in reality blacks have been their principal foundation and support. We have pursued the shadow, they have obtained the substance; we have performed the labor, they have received the profits; we have planted the vines, they have eaten the fruits of them."[47] Not even Frederick Douglass used parataxis to greater effect.

The power of Stewart's essays depends on their historical and political saliency as well as their rhetorical strategies. Aware of the military service of blacks who fought both in the Revolutionary War and "bravely under the command of Jackson, in defense of liberty," she asks, "But where is the man that has distinguished himself in these modern days by acting wholly in the defense of African rights and liberty?" Then again evoking David Walker, she adds, "There was one; although he sleeps, his memory lives" (57). As did Walker, Stewart implores blacks to fight on their own behalf as they had in the War of Independence and the War of 1812; Stewart's husband had served in the latter.[48] She alludes to Africa as a seat of learning—"the most illustrious men of Greece flocked hither for instruction"—and quotes the scriptural promise that "Ethiopia shall again stretch forth her hands" (58). Yet Stewart does not dwell in idylls of the past. Instead she urges blacks to resist the importuning of the ACS, to invest in schools in the United States, and to sign a petition calling for the abolition of slavery in the District of Columbia. She rues the inability of free blacks to achieve their rights but notes that their condition is beginning to improve. In the spirit of Walker, she prophesizes that a new generation of "the sons and daughters of Africa" will arise and "put down vice and immorality among us." At such time, if the demands of these spiritually worthy blacks are not met, "they will spread horror and devastation around" (63). To ward off this apocalypse, Stewart appeals to her *white* brethren "to awake" and assist black Americans who, she promises, will be loyal ("cling to you more firmly") and who aspire to equality, not superiority.

As her listeners well knew, the scene of horror and devastation that Stewart prophesized had been partially realized in Southampton, Virginia, in the summer of 1831, when Nat Turner led an armed band of blacks in rebellion against their slave masters. Scores of whites were killed, and a larger number of blacks died in the aftermath. The reaction across the South was intense. Militias were organized specifically to punish participants in the revolt and to terrorize blacks in general. Laws were passed prohibiting literacy among blacks, whether enslaved or free, and to disallow public meetings of blacks without white supervision. The reaction spread to the North as well. In both regions, whites accused *Walker's Appeal* of helping to sow the seeds of rebellion. Stewart's address to her brethren and her assurance that blacks wanted nothing more than equality must be read in this context. She recognized the vulnerability of her position and expressed a measure of spiritual fatigue. Yet she found the courage to end her speech on a defiant note. Her words sound her resistance to the program of the ACS and fearlessness in the face of violent reaction to black revolt. By implicitly identifying Africa as "a strange land," even as they call for African rights and liberty, her words enact the paradoxical condition of being a "free" black in the United States of America: "They would drive us to a strange land. But before I go, the bayonet shall pierce me through. African rights and liberty is a subject that ought to fire the breast of every free man of color in these United States, and excite in his bosom a lively, deep, decided, and heartfelt interest" (64).

Stewart's defiance notwithstanding, she was near the end of her brief public career. She delivered what was billed as "Mrs. Stewart's Farewell Address to her Friends in the City of Boston" on September 21, 1833. In substantial measure, the speech was a defense of her political activism. In it she revisits the moment of "spiritual interrogation," and restates what she saw as the divine call on her life: "I believe, that for wise and holy purposes, best known to himself, he hath unloosed my tongue, and put his word into my mouth, in order to confound and put all those to shame that have rose up against me" (67). In acknowledgement of the fact that much of the criticism she has received is based on her gender, she identifies her vocation with the women of the Bible—Deborah, Esther, and Mary Magdalene. She asks: if women were called in biblical times, why not in her own day? She draws on secular authority as well in the form of a book with the unwieldy title *Women, Sketches of the History, Genius, Disposition, Accomplishments, Employments, Customs and Importance of the Fair Sex In All Parts of the World Interspersed With Many Singular and Entertaining Anecdotes By a Friend of the Sex* published by an Englishman named John Adams in 1790. Stewart refers glancingly to historical figures from antiquity through the fifteenth century in order to justify her intervention in the public sphere. Before she takes her leave, she implies that her efforts have not been in vain, for "the mighty work of reformation has begun among this people" (70).

Bitterly, Stewart addresses those blacks who have forced her departure from the podium and from the city of Boston: "It was contempt for my moral and religious opinions in private that drove me thus before a public. Had experience more plainly shown me that it was the nature of man to crush his fellow, I should not have thought it so hard" (70). Now, she avers, the contempt of blacks has driven her back to the private sphere. She questions the usefulness of political discussions, which "sow the seed of discord, and strengthen the cord of prejudice" (72). Instead she resolves to depend on God—though not before she insists for a last time that she was well aware "that if I contended boldly for his cause, I must suffer. Yet, I chose rather to suffer affliction with his people than to enjoy the pleasures of sin for a season" (73–74). With a sizable dose of self-righteousness, she promises to forgive her enemies, bless those who have hated her, and pray for those who have persecuted her. Adhering to her Christian tenets, she imagines that she and her fellow believers would soon be reunited in heaven. In fact, Stewart lived another forty-six years and continued her political work in New York, where she joined a female literary society, in Baltimore, where she taught school, and in Washington, D.C., where she joined the effort to establish Episcopalian churches for blacks, including St. Luke's Church, led by Alexander Crummell. She published two additional volumes of prose, *Productions of Mrs. Maria W. Stewart* (1835) and *Meditations from the Pen of Mrs. Maria W. Stewart* (1879); the latter was published the year she died. No evidence exists that she ever spoke in public again.

Unlike Stewart, Henry Highland Garnet never relinquished his role as orator and race leader. As she had, he determined to burnish the memory of David Walker. "When the history of the emancipation of the bondmen of America shall be written," he averred, "whatever name shall be placed first on the list of heroes, that of the author of the Appeal will not be second."[49] His command to the slaves of the United States—"Let your motto be RESISTANCE! RESISTANCE! RESISTANCE!"—resounded Walker's signal theme and appropriated his favorite typographical features. The response was similar as well. Garnet's fellow activists, led by Frederick Douglass, deemed Garnet's invocation of retaliatory violence dangerous, and the convention failed to approve it.[50] Some of the challenges he laid down to his audience seem directly inspired by Walker. This chapter's epigraph is an example. Garnet and his contemporaries hoped to become voices of thunder, channeling their fathers (and mothers), in order to command the attention of their peers and their oppressors. In his command for his brethren to awake and assert their manhood, Garnet certainly echoes Walker. The genealogical references are more specific than in the *Appeal*, which points to one of the crucial differences in their mode of address. Garnet addressed the "slaves of the United States of America," rather than the "colored citizens of the world." While his immediate audience was made up of free blacks in attendance at the National Negro Convention in Buffalo, New York, in 1843, he spoke to and for a national constituency of the slave and the free, the living and the dead.[51]

Garnet produced a cogent text, appropriate in its length and the simplicity of its syntax to the podium—at least to the podium of nineteenth-century America. The speech lasted an hour.[52] He was a master of metaphor and simile (as above when the heavens speak "as with a voice of thunder"), and his prose was less weighted with biblical quotation than his precursors Walker and Stewart. As they did, he compares the condition of enslaved blacks to the colonists who waged war in order to escape oppression. But intervening history has provided inspiration in the example of those heroic blacks—Denmark Vesey, Nat Turner, Joseph Cinque, and Madison Washington—who led revolts against slavery, and he uses their stories along with repeated invocations of the number "four million," the population of blacks in America, to instill courage in his audience. This repetition is one of several traces of the text's original oratorical mode.

Garnet's opening salutation seems at once to mock his fellow activists who meet regularly at national conventions "to sympathize with each other, and to weep" over the condition of the enslaved and to welcome the enslaved into the circle of concern. He posits their common cause—"nor can we be free while you are enslaved. We therefore write to you as being bound with you" (90). He addresses an audience, then, that is beyond the reach of his speaking voice but not of his written word. In the next sentence he insists that free blacks are not only "bound" by common humanity but by specific ties of kinship. Himself born a slave on a Maryland plantation, Garnet might have spoken from his own experience when he enumerated the "tender relations of parents, wives, husbands, children, brothers, and sisters, and friends" that tied the slave to the free. He then addressed the slaves of the United States "affectionately." The adverb repositions the slaves from victims of oppression to members of a community of kin. When he speaks of the "deep gulf" that slavery has "fixed" between the slave and the free, his words tap into a wellspring of emotion. The use of the alliterative "f" and "s" in the clause that personifies the horror of slavery—"it afflicts and persecutes you with a fierceness which we might not expect to see in the fiends of hell"—intensifies the affective import of his words. Yet Garnet's purpose is not to document the evils of slavery: the nation's sins are too numerous to catalog "in this short address," he observes. He wants only to bring hope to those who suffer from them.

For Garnet as for his contemporaries and descendants, the path toward a hopeful future is charted through the past. In the next several paragraphs, Garnet encapsulates the history of Africans in America, a history that in 1843 stretched back more than 200 years. That history is anomalous in the U.S. nation, for blacks "came not with their own consent, to find an unmolested enjoyment in the blessings of this fruitful soil" (90). Moreover, their first contact with men who called themselves Christians was with slaveholders who "exhibited the worst features of corrupt and sordid hearts" (90). In the moral allegory that Garnet narrates, the slaveholders refused to listen to the voices of "Freedom," "Humanity," "Wisdom," and "Jehovah," all of which inveighed against the injustice of slavery. But for naught: "Its throne is established, and now it reigns triumphantly" (91).

The American Revolution is Garnet's second historical touchstone. He argues that the colonists held England responsible for the existence of slavery in America, but once they gained their independence, instead of ending slavery they "added new links to our chains" (92). Nevertheless, like Walker, Garnet is unstinting in his admiration for the Declaration, "a glorious document" held in reverence by patriots of every nation for its "Godlike sentiments" (92). He admires as well the "burning eloquence" of the republican orators, who, like the here unnamed Patrick Henry, cried "LIBERTY OR DEATH" (92). Such a statement, he contends, "ran from soul to soul like electric fire." Self-consciously standing in the tradition of their eloquence, he claims the legacy of their arguments as well, as he declares the right of blacks to physical resistance. After all, he asserts, "all men cherish the love of Liberty. The nice discerning political economist does not regard the sacred right, more than the untutored African who roams in the wilds of the Congo" (92). Garnet would eventually go to Liberia, but at this point in his life he knew nothing firsthand of Africa. The salient point he makes is that the love of freedom is innate; it does not depend on one's location or education. Elsewhere in his speech, he discusses the ignorance that is imposed on slaves either by law or by custom. He mourns the fact that slaves are unable to read the Bible; worse, slavery makes it impossible for them to follow the Ten Commandments. How can a slave love God more than his master, or keep the Sabbath holy, or love his neighbor as himself? Yet he insists that insofar as freedom and rights are concerned, the slaves' illiteracy is immaterial as is their imperfect religious practice. Their humanity entitles them to freedom and gives them the right to fight for it.

In a rhetorical echo of *Walker's Appeal*, Garnet uses inversion to demonstrate the illogic of defenses of slavery, although he relies on racialized definitions of "heathen" and "civilized" to make his point. He asks what the response would be if a band of heathen men should attempt to enslave a race of Christians and place their children under the influence of some false religion. "Surely," he concludes, "heaven would frown upon the men who would not resist such aggression, even to death" (93). Then he describes the situation that does obtain and offers the same conclusion. Implicit in both suppositions is the critique of Christianity as it is practiced in the southern United States. Garnet argues the case that so-called Christian slaveholders exhibited the "worst features of corrupt and sordid hearts"—they act, that is to say, like heathens. In another charged comparison, he asserts that the slaveholder is as wrong as the "man thief" who stole the ancestors from the coast of Africa. In a subsequent formulation, he refers to the original enslaver as a "soul thief," the agent of evil whom the ancestors had the right to resist. All of these formulations reinforce the idea of slavery as a spiritual crime, a violation that is more serious than a crime against the flesh alone.

As he does numerous times throughout his oration, Garnet addresses the slaves directly: "Brethren, the time has come when you must act for yourselves. It is an old and true saying, that 'if hereditary bondmen would be free, they must themselves strike the blow'" (93). He assures them they have allies abroad: European nations have condemned the slave trade. Still, the slaveholding South is unyielding. But Garnet issues a series of imperatives that will begin to redress the situation. Instead of Walker's manicules, Garnet relies on verbal commands to point the bondsmen to the "more effectual door" that will lead to their liberation. "Look," "Hear," "Remember," "Think" (repeated three times), "Appeal," "Promise," "Point," Tell," "Inform," he exhorts (94). Each command is followed by instructions that move from the visceral ("Remember the stripes your fathers bore") to the abstract ("Inform them that all you desire, is FREEDOM, and that nothing else will suffice"). One imperative directs them to "Think of the undying glory that hangs around the ancient name of Africa," then immediately follows with the caution that they should not forget that they are native-born Americans entitled to the rights that appertain thereto. Garnet shifts between the practical—urging enslaved people to promise that they will work harder if they are paid for their labor—and the apocalyptic—urging them to warn their oppressors of the "righteous retribution of an indignant God." Even without the cues that Walker's typographical elements supplied, readers can sense Garnet's cadence and "hear" the rising crescendos of his voice. After the penultimate instruction to inform their oppressors of their desire for freedom, Garnet intones, "Do this, and forever cease to toil for the heartless tyrants, who give you no other reward but stripes and abuse" (94).

Yet the transcendent promise of freedom is merely a pause in Garnet's oration. It is followed by a realistic assessment of realities on the ground. The wages of resistance are likely to be death. Despite their identification with the biblical Israelites, blacks cannot expect "a grand Exodus from the house of bondage," because "THE PHARAOHS ARE ON BOTH SIDES OF THE BLOOD-RED WATERS" (94–95). By 1843, the hope that Walker had expressed, especially his admiration for British abolitionism, had faded. So too had the utility of the jeremiad. Garnet does not expect providential justice. Instead he perceives the only remaining alternative is to embrace the Revolutionists' cry of liberty or death and struggle. The deprivations of slavery have prepared blacks to accept the hardships of resistance. To inspire his audience to take up the cause of armed revolt, Garnet offers a roll call of black revolutionaries. His praise for these noble men whose memories are cherished, or if they are alive, whose "names are surrounded by a halo of glory" (96) is unstinting. But the soaring rhetoric immediately trends downward.

Perhaps yielding to the disapproval of his fellow conferees, Garnet pulls his punches. In one of the shortest paragraphs in the speech, he advises that a violent revolution would be "INEXPEDIENT" and argues instead for a labor strike, an action that surely would also have been met with swift and violent retribution. Apart from the high odds against success, Garnet asserts that the spirit of the age is opposed to war and bloodshed, a dubious assertion five years before the revolutions that burst across Europe in 1848. He adds that the spirit of the gospel is also opposed. The brevity of its description suggests that Garnet's heart is not in the proposal for nonviolent resistance. Within six sentences he moves from asserting that there are too few blacks to mount a revolution to declaring, "Remember that you are FOUR MILLIONS" (96).

That defiant tone carries to the end. Garnet assures the enslaved that they have the power "to torment the God-cursed slaveholders" until they grant them their freedom. He dares blacks to overcome their reputation for patience and challenges them to act as men, to protect their wives and children, and to honor the legacy of their dead fathers. He insists that "no oppressed people have ever secured their liberty without resistance," an argument that would win more adherents, including Douglass, in the next several years. At this moment Garnet failed to persuade all those in the room, many of whom found his words inexpedient to say the least. Still, the repetition of "LET YOUR MOTTO BE RESISTANCE" fired a refrain outside the conference as the "Address to the Slaves of the United States of America" was published and disseminated.

In the 1840s, Garnet and Douglass vied for leadership in the abolitionist cause. Both enjoyed reputations as powerful orators. In the foreground of his career, Douglass, whose famous *Narrative* would be published two years after Garnet's "Address," was employed chiefly as an agent for the Massachusetts Anti-Slavery Society; he later served in the same capacity for the American Anti-Slavery Society. He was hired after Garrison heard him describe his experiences in slavery in 1841. Garrison's response was impassioned: "As soon as he had taken his seat, filled with hope and admiration, I rose, and declared that Patrick Henry, of revolutionary fame, never made a speech more eloquent in the cause of liberty, than the one we had just listened to from the lips of that hunted fugitive."[53] This "born orator," as James McCune Smith described him, was so powerful at the podium that audiences began to doubt that he could ever have been a slave.[54] He wrote the 1845 *Narrative* in part to prove that the story he told was his own. In that text, Douglass related an early encounter with *The Columbian Orator*, a popular nineteenth-century textbook that sparked his belief in the power of rhetoric. At age twelve, Douglass purchased as his first book a used copy of *The Columbian Orator*, which he read "at every opportunity" and much of which he committed to memory.[55] He credits the book with enabling him to express his feelings about his enslavement. That was not exactly the purpose the author, Caleb Bingham, envisioned, although as a teacher and pioneer of public schools in Massachusetts, he would probably have been sympathetic. Published in 1797, *The Columbian Orator* was designed to cultivate the "rudiments" of the art of oratory and to "diffuse its spirit among the youth of America."[56] In the introduction Bingham set forth guidelines for effective oration, including rules for the voice and gesture. His audience was American boys (he had previously published a textbook for girls), and he argued that what they called pronunciation, the ancients understood as action. Words did not simply sound good, they did things. Bingham recounted how Caesar at the height of his power heard Cicero speak and immediately fell into "such a fit of shivering that he dropped the papers he held in his hand" (7). Such was the power of the spoken word. Douglass could not help being impressed. He read avidly through the excerpts from speeches and plays, dialogues, and poems commending education, temperance, patriotism, freedom, and courage, and condemning slavery and oppression. A poem by David Everett, an associate of Bingham, sounded the last theme: "Still groans the slave beneath his master's rod,/But nature, wrong'd appeals to nature's GOD./The sun frowns angry at th' inhuman sight;/The stars offended redden in the night" (207).[57] *The Columbian Orator's* table of contents lists famous names from English history and letters: John Milton, William Pitt the Elder and Pitt the Younger, and Irish patriot Richard Brinsley Sheridan. But the volume's selections were eclectic: from Socrates's defense before his accusers to orations by Cato and Cicero to George Washington's first speech to the United States Congress to the "Speech of an Indian Chief, of the Stockbridge Tribe to the Massachusetts Congress." All manner of men spoke, most in defense of themselves and on behalf of the cause of liberty.

Douglass was particularly drawn to the fictional "Dialogue Between Master and His Slave," also written by David Everett, in which a slave's words compel the master to grant him his freedom. (We can only speculate whether Douglass read Daniel Coker's "Dialogue," but Everett certainly seems to have done so.) Everett depicts the following situation: despite the master's kind treatment, the slave has run away twice, and the master complains of his ingratitude. The master had, after all, purchased the slave "fairly." The slave points out that he has not given his consent to be bought, to which the master replies that the slave had no consent to give. The slave counters that he had the lost the power, but not the right, to consent. The history the slave recounts—of being kidnapped in his homeland and brought by ship to a new country where he was sold "like a beast in the market"—emblematizes New World slavery (210). To the master's question whether it is possible to hold the slave by any means other than "constraint and severity," the slave responds that it is not (211). Proving his uncommon virtue, the master frees the slave. While the slave observes that the master is "only . . . undoing a wrong," he acknowledges "how few among mankind are capable of sacrificing interest to justice" (211). Then, seizing the last word, the slave warns the master that he is "surrounded by implacable foes, who long for a safe opportunity" to take revenge (211). "Superior forces alone can give you security," he remarks, then concludes, "As soon as that fails, you are at the mercy of the merciless. Such is the social bond between master and slave" (212).

With that conclusion, the slave, who is the beneficiary of the master's goodwill, levels the playing field. He has proven himself to be the master's intellectual equal, as he counters every argument the master puts forward. Even before the dialogue begins, he has demonstrated his courage by twice escaping. As if in return for his liberty, the slave gives the master fair warning: those whom he continues to enslave will at the first opportunity exact their revenge. Then, in one of the dialogue's most remarkable turns, the slave shifts the terrain from the personal to the abstract. The issue is not his own unjust enslavement, it is the injustice of slavery itself. The individual character of men is beside the point. The institution dictates the social bond between master and slave. It is no wonder that Douglass could recite this dialogue until the end of his life. It dramatizes the intellectual equality of masters and slaves. It demonstrates that courage is the province of the slave as well as the master. It is an argument in favor of the power of the spoken word. Yet, if the slave's words win his freedom, the dialogue insists that an individual's freedom is not the goal. The institution itself must be abolished. That was the work that Douglass undertook as soon as he made his own escape from slavery.

As historian David Blight notes, it is impossible to measure the impact of the textbook on the adult Frederick Douglass, who became one of the most masterful orators ever on the American scene. Yet the book's examples of men who spoke their way into history clearly remained in his consciousness. Their rhetoric shifted between the grand style of their classical precursors and democratic eloquence, the formal but plain speech of Americans.[58] Douglass excelled at the latter and was praised for the "easy, graceful, natural style" of his speeches. While they were certainly graceful, there was little "easy" or "natural" about them.[59] Those adjectives respond to their apparent lack of artifice, their resemblance to everyday speech. Douglass learned from the selections that he recited out loud from Bingham's textbook and took to heart Bingham's guidelines concerning cadence, pace, tonal variety, and the use of gesture. But if *The Columbian Orator* provided the only "formal" training in elocution that Douglass acquired, it was hardly his only source of traditions of eloquence.

Although Douglass is rightly known as a harsh critic of Christianity—in his autobiographies the cruelty of slaveholders is measured in direct proportion to their piety—he had strong ties to the African American church. The same year he discovered *The Columbian Orator*, he underwent a religious conversion.[60] He developed a deep attachment to a lay preacher, a free black man whom he calls "Uncle Lawson" (Charles Lawson), and describes as his "spiritual father" and "chief instructor in matters of religion" (232). More literate than his teacher, Douglass often read the Bible to him aloud. He remembered that, "I could teach him '*the letter,*' but he could teach me '*the spirit*'" (232). When, for example, Douglass anguished that he was *a slave for life* (a phrase he repeated to powerful effect in the *Narrative*), Lawson promised: "the Lord can make you free, my dear. All things are possible with him; only have faith in God" (233). Although he would decide that he had to seize freedom through his own actions, Douglass did get a sense of his destiny from Lawson, a belief that his "life was under the guidance of a wisdom higher than my own" (233). From the beginning, Douglass's faith was tested as he observed the conduct of self-professed Christian slaveholders. Their false Christianity became a central theme in his 1845 *Narrative*, so much so that Douglass felt compelled to add an appendix to distinguish between "the Christianity of this land" and "the Christianity of Christ," lest he be charged with heresy.[61]

For a time he persevered in his faith. While still enslaved in Maryland, he attended and later taught a sabbath school. After his escape he resettled in New Bedford, Massachusetts, and joined the New Bedford Zion Methodist Church, which he served as sexton, steward, class leader, and finally lay preacher. Before he spoke to the antislavery society, Douglass had frequently preached to the black congregation at the New Bedford church. After he joined the abolitionist cause, he traded the pulpit for the podium, yet he appreciated the connection between the two. He recognized that the ministers at New Bedford Zion "helped to prepare me for the wider sphere of usefulness which I have since occupied. It was from this Zion church that I went forth to the work of delivering my brethren from bondage, and this new vocation which separated me from New Bedford, . . . separated me also from the calling of a local preacher." He would remain convinced that the American church was "the bulwark of American slavery."[62] Nevertheless, long after he left the church the traditions of the African American sermon left traces on his oratory. His oratory was a multisplendored art, which he performed during the golden age of oratory in the United States. Indeed, he did as much as anyone to produce this golden age.

On the lecture circuit, Douglass addressed the topics of abolitionism, women's rights, and temperance. He was a bold and charismatic speaker, who refused to be reduced to mere "evidence" against slavery, but instead argued with and against the schools of abolitionism and intervened in other contemporary political and social debates. According to scholar Sarah Meer, Douglass became "a lyceum star," giving speeches across the northern United States on such diverse topics as "Self-Made Men," "Santo Domingo," and "Our Composite Ethnology." In 1845, he embarked on a European tour that lasted for almost two years. To Irish audiences, he echoed Sheridan and called for the repeal of that country's union with Great Britain. In Scotland, he protested the Free Church of Scotland's support of proslavery churches in the United States.[63] Whatever the topic, his speeches deployed the rhetorical strategies of repetition, parallelism, irony, and reversal. He relished the ability to turn the pieties of his oppressors against them.[64] The effect of his words and his charismatic presence left an indelible impression. As one of his admirers wrote, "he was more than six feet in height, and his majestic form, as he rose to speak, straight as an arrow, muscular, yet lithe and graceful, his flashing eye, and more than all, his voice, that rivaled Webster's in its richness, and in the depth and sonorousness of its cadences, made up such an ideal of an orator as the listeners never forgot."[65]

Frederick Douglass delivered "What to the Slave Is the Fourth of July?"—his most famous speech—as a lecture on July 5, 1852 in Rochester, New York, before a racially mixed crowd of approximately 600. Historian William McFeely considers it "perhaps the greatest antislavery oration ever."[66] His decision to speak on the day after the national commemoration followed a practice of protest initiated by black abolitionists earlier in the century.[67] By pointedly addressing his "fellow citizens," Douglass introduces immediately the distinction between citizens and noncitizens of the United States. He remarks upon the "considerable distance" between the platform from which he speaks and the plantation from which he escaped. He asks rhetorically whether the "great principles of political freedom and of natural justice" were extended to blacks and whether he was being "called upon" to express gratitude—in his phrase, "bring our humble offering to the national altar"—for blessings that were in fact *not* extended to blacks.[68] Douglass hereby acknowledges the status of the principles of the Declaration of Independence as the sacred text of the nation, a subject to which the address returns time and again. The creed that the principles constitute is the nation's civil religion, a fact that Douglass emphasizes when he compares the Fourth of July celebration to the feast of Passover. As the Jewish festival celebrates the deliverance of the Jews from bondage in Egypt, the national holiday looks back to the "great deliverance" of the U.S. nation.

To prevent his listeners from growing self-satisfied too quickly, he reminds them that at the age of seventy-six years, theirs is a young nation, "still in the impressible stage of her existence" (403). He thus holds out the hope that a mature nation might right its wrongs. It remains no more than a hope. Building an extended metaphor of the river, he notes that while "great streams are not easily turned from channels," they may rise up in wrath and fury only to "gradually flow back to the same old channel." Yet this is not the worst that could happen. Taking an apocalyptic turn, he envisions the river dried up and leaving nothing behind "but the withered branch, and the unsightly rock," images that tell "the sad tale of departed glory" (403).[69] With this warning he throws the onus back onto his fellow citizens. They are charged with the responsibility of saving a nascent nation from itself.

Douglass's initial gesture in the lecture is to suggest that he is not equal to the task of presenting it: "He who could address this audience without a quailing sensation, has stronger nerves than I have. I do not remember ever to have appeared as a speaker before any assembly more shrinkingly, nor with greater distrust of my ability, than I do this day" (403). He goes on to deny that his is the performative apology of the professional lecturer, while at the same time acknowledging that he is a practiced orator, who has frequently spoken from the very same dais of Corinthians Hall. By this time, Douglass had lived in Rochester for four years and knew many people in his audience. As his oration would confirm, he was well prepared to produce "a high sounding exordium," as he interpolated quotations from Shakespeare's *Julius Caesar*, the poems of Henry Wadsworth Longfellow, the writings of William Lloyd Garrison, the Bible, and the nation's founding documents. The stance that he was intimidated by the task before him was a rhetorical conceit, one that drew attention to his own status as former slave and not-yet citizen.

Yet the apology gives him the leeway to lecture the acknowledged heirs of the nation on their history. Couching that history in the traditional trope of fathers and sons, he praises the fathers who initially esteemed the English government but soon resented being treated as children by their rulers. In retrospect, the American fathers were right to rise up against their colonizers, but Douglass notes that the situation was less clear cut during the revolutionary era: "... there was a time when to pronounce against England, and in favor of the cause of the colonies, tried men's souls" (404). The last phrase alludes, of course, to Thomas Paine's *Common Sense* (1776). Douglass is offering a similar brief in "What to the Slave," although it stops short of advocating the armed resistance that Paine (and later David Walker) advanced. He simply praises the "fathers" of the revolution, while observing sardonically of their sons that "the cause of liberty may be stabbed by the men who glory in the deeds of your fathers. But, to proceed ..." (404). As he does so, he draws implicit parallels between the past and the present. Although his argument echoes *Walker's Appeal*, the tone of his address is more measured. He is keenly conscious of his audience, which unlike Walker's, was largely white.[70] He moves from suggesting that initially the founding fathers did the expected rather than the extraordinary when they "petitioned and remonstrated" (404). But as the British became more tyrannical, in the manner of the Egyptian pharaohs, they provoked an exceptional response. The epigram that Douglass coins to describe it might have stirred fear in the hearts of proslavery activists, had they been able to attribute wisdom or humanity to the slave: "Oppression makes a wise man mad" (404). Having perhaps tested his listeners' limit, he adds that the fathers did not go mad, they instead determined on a remedy for their oppression.

He lavishes praise on the Declaration, figuring it as the "ring-bolt to the chain of your nation's destiny." A nautical device, a ring-bolt was used to move merchandise onto ships and particularly to hook the tacks by which the cannon of a ship were managed and secured. No longer is the Declaration simply a sacred text; it has uses that are both practical and martial. The threat of violence is implicit, and if blacks were to become the heirs to the Declaration, the right to revolutionary violence would belong to them as well as to their "fellow citizens." If that is the logical end to Douglass's argument, he does not state it. He pays tribute instead to the fathers of the republic:

> They loved their country better than their own private interests; and, though this is not the highest form of human excellence, all will concede that it is a rare virtue, and that when it is exhibited, it ought to command respect. He who will, intelligently, lay down his life for his country, is a man whom it is not in human nature to despise. Your fathers staked their lives, their fortunes, and their sacred honor, on the cause of their country. In their admiration of liberty, they lost sight of all other interests. (405–406)

With his usual mastery of understatement and irony, Douglass works as much to bury the fathers as to praise them. Their actions do not, after all, achieve the highest form of human excellence. He admits that their actions are worthy of respect, though that seems far less than the admiration that excellence would demand. A similar syntactical restraint calls into question the most honored tenet of revolutionary patriots: that they were willing to lay down their lives for their country. The insertion of the adverb "intelligently" limits the purchase of patriotism and harkens back to the mindlessness of those who would glory in the deeds of the fathers while betraying the cause of liberty in the present. At the close of the paragraph, Douglass criticizes the fathers themselves, who in the pursuit of their own liberty "lost sight of all other interests." Here he stops short of making the full-throated Garrisonian charge that the Constitution was a slaveholding document, but he is clearly pointing to the fact that it failed to abolish slavery. However much the fathers acted out of a sense of sacred honor, their vision was not equal to their sacrifice.

This critical analysis is surrounded by encomiums more traditional for the occasion, and Douglass goes to considerable effort to compare and contrast the greatness of the first generation of national leaders with those who currently hold sway: "How circumspect, exact and proportionate were all their movements! How unlike the politicians of an hour! . . . They seized upon eternal principles, and set a glorious example in their defence. Mark them!" (406). Stating that he need not go into further detail about the history he recounts, he remarks that it is all too well known, taught as it is in schoolrooms, pulpits, and legislative halls. He acknowledges that the language of the history is as familiar "as household words. They form the staple of your national poetry and eloquence" (406). Douglass turns this observation on its head, when he adds that Americans "are remarkably familiar with all facts which make their own favor" (406). His own engagement with this rhetoric of the founding documents is profound but consistently critical. He sees himself both inside and outside of their purview. On the one hand, he insists on his right to speak as a fellow citizen, while on the other, he embraces his responsibility to speak as a representative of those who remain enslaved.

In the second section of the oration, titled "The Present," Douglass speaks explicitly on behalf of those who are excluded from the national creed. He extends the religious symbolism—if the enslaved were included, his voice would help "to swell the hallelujahs of the nation's jubilee" (408). This jubilee is one that the nation had not yet earned, a jubilee that would for the slaves be more than a decade in the future when in fact "the chains of servitude" were removed. To analogize the gap between slave and citizen, Douglass suggests that the slave might lend his voice to the swell of hallelujahs when the dumb spoke eloquently, or, alluding to the Book of Isaiah when the "lame man shall leap as an hart" (35:6). Both figures bring to mind Douglass's 1845 *Narrative* in which he begins his self-representation as a chattel slave who is compared repeatedly to the domestic animals whose status he shares. If, however, he is socially unable to speak initially, when he becomes a man he speaks eloquently. During his agon with the slavebreaker Covey, he resolves to fight and seizing Covey by the throat, he recalls, "I rose." That motion may be associated with the deer's leap as well as with the biblical resurrection.

At present, if the slave is analogized to the crippled man, he has yet to gain the ability to walk. Consequently, Douglass wonders if the invitation to speak on the nation's annual celebration of its commitment to freedom is a mockery. "This Fourth of July," he declares, "is *yours*, not *mine*" (408). Drawing on the rhetorical figure of chiasmus that Douglass used so effectively in the *Narrative* ("You have seen how a man was made a slave; now you shall see how a slave was made a man"), he now says "*You* may rejoice, *I* must mourn." He underscores the delusion of a nation that sees itself as "a new Israel" and warns that it is dangerous to copy the example of a nation whose crimes led to its divinely ordained destruction. He then appropriates the lament of the biblical Israelites and quotes Psalm 137. As a nineteenth-century orator, Douglass could count on his listeners' familiarity with the text. That familiarity helped make his speech comprehensible when heard. However, the associations Douglass draws around the text were not the ones his white auditors expected. Rather than the U.S. nation, the psalm bespeaks for Douglass the situation of the enslaved Africans when it intones, "By the rivers of Babylon, there we sat down. Yea! we wept when we remembered Zion . . . . For there, they that carried us away captive, required of us a song; and they who wasted us required of us mirth, saying, Sing us one of the songs of Zion. How can we sing the Lord's song in a strange land?" (408).

The spirituals were the slave's answer. Their words were suffused with biblical references, which, as we have seen, analogized the scriptural narratives to the slave's circumstances. For Douglass, however, the power of the spirituals did not derive from their words. In his 1845 *Narrative*, Douglas invented the phrase "every tone a testimony" to distill their power. He understood that the tone and the timbre of the slaves' voices conveyed more than they were allowed to verbalize. Through their timbre as well as their words, then, the "sorrow songs," as Douglass called them, expressed the most profound antislavery critique. Although we cannot be sure how Douglass used the timbre of his own voice to similar ends, we can see how Douglass evokes biblical allusion and tonal memory in his speech. A text of exile and hope, Psalm 137 directly inspired several spirituals, including "Lord, How Come Me Here," "Sometimes I Feel Like a Motherless Child . . . a long way from home," and one that took its title from the Bible verse itself. Through the mediation of the biblical text, Douglass inserts the symbolic voices of the slaves into the oration.

Addressing his fellow citizens again, he asks them now to hear "above your national, tumultuous joy, the mournful wail of the millions of slaves" (408). As their voices are figured as a wordless wail, they deepen the anguish articulated in the lyrics of the spirituals. Douglass asks that he himself be cursed—and silenced—if he does not remember them himself. Then, belatedly, he announces his subject: "AMERICAN SLAVERY." Unchained and putatively free, Douglass identifies himself with the "slave's point of view." Moreover, evoking the complex metaphorical associations of blackness, he announces that "the character and conduct of this nation never looked blacker to me than on this Fourth of July." His indictment is pervasive: it covers the past and the present, even as it holds out hope for the future. Most strikingly, in this most famous jeremiad, Douglass associates divine favor not with the nation but with the "crushed and bleeding slave" (408).

Douglass builds his case against slavery by quoting William Lloyd Garrison from the first issue of *The Liberator*: "I will not equivocate; I will not excuse." Then, like Garrison, he begins his own condemnation of America in "the severest language I can command" (409). As he does so, he speculates that the very harshness of their rhetoric puts off those who would prefer a more reasoned approach. But he offers the rejoinder that there is nothing to reason or argue about. "Must I undertake to prove that the slave is a man?" he queries. "That point is conceded already" (409). The argument he goes on to make is that the very laws of slavery concede as much. The slaveholders implicitly concede the humanity of those they enslave. Why else would slaves be punished for the crime of disobedience? Their punishment is ordered on the premise that they understand right from wrong, that they are, in fact, "moral, intellectual, and responsible" beings. As he notes that the statute books of the South are filled with enactments forbidding the teaching of slaves to read and to write, he jests that when such laws are written with regard to animals, he will argue that the slave is not a man.

Having made the case negatively, Douglass makes it positively. Using a series of gerunds, he catalogs the work that enslaved people perform: ploughing, planting, and reaping; erecting houses, constructing bridges, building ships, working in metals of brass, iron, copper, silver and gold; reading, writing, and ciphering. Theirs is a never-ending whir of human activity. He lists occupations, including lawyers, doctors, ministers, poets, authors, editors, orators, and teachers. Three years before Walt Whitman composed *Leaves of Grass*, Douglass offers his own "song," not of himself but of his people. Like Whitman, Douglass takes delight in the tonal variety of lists and in the active movement of his subjects. He represents blacks not only in the South but "digging gold in California" and "capturing the whale in the Pacific" (409). The geographical expanse, no less than the range of occupation, makes his subjects what Albert Murray would later call "omni-Americans."

"Would you have me argue," Douglass addresses his audience at the end of his catalog, "that man is entitled to liberty?" This question goes right to the heart of the Declaration that is the occasion for the speech in the first place. After all, he notes, "you" have already declared it. To debate the question in this context would be, in Douglass's mocking understatement, "to make myself ridiculous, and to offer an insult to your understanding. There is not a man beneath the canopy of heaven that does not know that slavery is wrong *for him*" (410). And, after another paragraph of rhetorical questions that in fact makes the argument that he disdains, he concludes "the time for such argument is past." Rather than argument, the only response to statements condoning slavery is irony, "scorching irony," of the kind that Douglass has laced throughout his address. Before he unleashes it, he insists that the situation calls for fire rather than light, thunder rather than a gentle shower. "We need the storm, the whirlwind, and the earthquake," he continues, for "the feeling of the nation must be quickened; the conscience of the nation must be roused; the propriety of the nation must be startled; the hypocrisy of the nation must be exposed; and its crimes against God and man must be proclaimed and denounced" (410).

Just as Douglass describes black Americans as men acting, he expects his words to produce dramatic action, as the nature metaphors evince. It may well be that the use of the gerund is a nod to Emerson's invocation in "The American Scholar," of "Man Thinking," a scholar who is not dependent on the books of the past, but on his own ability to discern meaning in nature and in the world around him. Douglass is a master of discernment. By this point in the oration, as Douglass builds to the crescendo, he has left the mask of humility far behind. He has utter confidence that his words are equal to the task at hand. He is willing, moreover, to wield the weapon of irony that would in any other situation alienate the patriotic Americans whose fatherland Douglass eviscerates.

Douglass ends this section of the oration by revising the question that began it. The specificity of the adjective "American" and of the pronoun sharpens the question. Then he formulates an answer that inverts all of the expected meanings of the occasion. For good reason, the following paragraph is the most famous passage in the oration.

> What, to the *American* slave, is *your* 4th of July? I answer: a day that reveals to him, more than all other days in the year, the gross injustice and cruelty to which he is the constant victim. To him, your celebration is a sham; your boasted liberty, an unholy license; your national greatness, swelling vanity; your sounds of rejoicing are empty and heartless; your denunciations of tyrants, brass-fronted impudence; your shouts of liberty and equality, hollow mockery; your prayers and hymns, your sermons and thanksgivings, with all your religious parade, and solemnity, are, to him, mere bombast, fraud, deception, impiety, and hypocrisy—a thin veil to cover up crimes which would disgrace a race of savages. There is not a

nation on the earth guilty of practices more shocking and bloody, than
are the people of these United States, at this very hour (410, emphasis
added).

The slave's response to the nation's call, to its very sense of itself, reveals
the lie: the celebration is a sham, liberty is license, greatness is vanity. Douglass's cadence builds momentum. Beginning with the drawn-out monosylla-
ble "sham," followed by a series of short phrases made up of an adjective and
noun, he then formulates more complex phrases that elaborate the nation's
wrongdoing. Significantly, in an oration that depends on the power of words
to achieve justice, Douglass highlights the ways that language can falsify and
deceive. He emphasizes the falsification of the "national eloquence" he had
cited earlier, as he highlights the *empty* sounds, *brass* fronted impudence,
and *hollow* mockery. The vaunted promises of democracy are as the sound
and the fury signifying nothing. Douglass's denunciation is all the more forceful for deploying plain speech, for attacking the failures of U.S. democracy
with the very democratic eloquence through which it initially announced
itself and pressed its exceptionalist claims. No one was more the master of
that eloquence than this former American slave.

The oration ends with two short sections that serve as something of a
coda to the main address. In the "The Internal Slave Trade," Douglass, like
Walker before him, actually quotes the Declaration. Rather than revise it as
Walker had done, he cites Jefferson's own acknowledgement that slavery "is
worse than ages of that which your fathers rose in rebellion to oppose" to
make the case succinctly (411). Then, in the manner of the jeremiad, Douglass concludes with a statement of faith in the future, a belief that the terrible
wrongs he has identified can be righted. "Allow me to say, in conclusion," he
ends, "notwithstanding the dark picture I have this day presented of the state
of the nation, I do not despair of this country" (412). Although the section's
title is "The Constitution," the hope that Douglass identifies is not written
there. Indeed, it is not bound by the nation's borders at all. It resides instead
in "the obvious tendencies of the age," tendencies that were not in fact obvious to most nineteenth-century Americans. To Douglass, these tendencies
signaled a global age and a belief in the teleology of history: "Oceans no longer divide, but link nations together. From Boston to London is now a holiday
excursion. Space is comparatively annihilated. Thoughts expressed on one
side of the Atlantic are distinctly heard on the other" (412). Having spent
several years in England advocating the abolitionist cause, Douglass was personally aware of the exchange of ideas between Britain and the United States.

His sense of living in a time of technological progress also reflects his personal travels and his appreciation for the inventions that were making the world smaller. Strikingly, however, Douglass's prophetic imagination is not limited to the West. He invokes the Pacific Ocean ("far off and almost fabulous"), and the continents of Asia and Africa. The forces of progress are intellectual and moral, as well as technological. The poem with which he concludes, Garrison's "The Triumph of Freedom," envisions the year of jubilee "the wide world o'er." The celebration that would honor that occasion would dwarf the Fourth of July in 1852 or at any other time.

In the words of one admirer, Frances Watkins Harper was adept at "outbursts of eloquent indignation."[71] Although she may now be better known as poet and novelist, she earned her living on the lecture circuit, where she spoke on behalf of abolition, temperance, and women's suffrage. Her career as social reformer and activist spanned almost seventy years. As part of the black abolitionist network, she worked alongside Douglass and Garnet. As a women's rights advocate, she shared the podium with Susan B. Anthony, Lucretia Mott, and Elizabeth Cady Stanton. In the two weeks before John Brown's execution, she sat vigil with his wife. If on the national stage she agitated for suffrage for blacks and women, locally, in Philadelphia, she waged individual acts of civil disobedience in protest of the discrimination she suffered on coaches. Although she performed feats of physical courage, words were her primary weapon. They won her a wide following, which, unlike Maria Stewart, she was able to sustain. One reason may be that although her politics were often radical, in her personal style she conformed to the gender expectations of the day. Observers commented on her "slender and graceful form" as well as her "soft musical voice."[72] While she may not have spoken in a voice of thunder, however, Frances Watkins Harper acknowledged that "my voice is not lacking in strength, as I am aware of, to reach pretty well over the house."[73]

Aware of the effectiveness of her voice, Watkins Harper gave innumerable lectures, sometimes delivering several speeches a day. She frequently recited her poems as part of these oratorical performances. Some of the speeches were subsequently published, as were letters recounting her travels and highlighting her ideas for reform. Watkins Harper wrote these letters for publication in newspapers that supported the causes for which she fought; we may read them as mini-essays. In addition to being an orator and poet, Watkins Harper was a pioneering novelist. *Iola Leroy, or the Shadows Uplifted* (1892) reflects some of Watkins Harper's experiences in what she described in a letter as "the unreconstructed states."[74] Both the novel and the poetry deployed the conventions of nineteenth-century sentimentality; their purpose was to inspire her audience's determination to work for social reform. Her nonfiction makes this aim explicit. Moreover, as Carla Peterson observes, Watkins Harper's poems and lectures "cannot be considered isolated aesthetic objects that exist separately from one another but must be viewed as coextensive not only with each other but with her essays and fiction as well."[75] *Poems on Miscellaneous Subjects*, published in 1854 and reprinted at least twenty times before her death in 1911, includes letters and essays as well as the poetry the title promises. Watkins Harper repeats specific details and phrases in her poems and prose, a usage that suggests a larger point. As had her peers discussed in this chapter, Watkins Harper purposely blurs the lines between the spoken word and written text.[76] In doing so she reached the multiple audiences—black and white, female and male, illiterate and literate—she hoped to address. She understood that the written word extended the power of her voice far beyond the rooms in which spoke.

Born to free black parents in Baltimore in 1825, Frances Ellen Watkins attended a school founded by and named for her uncle. The William Watkins Academy for Negro Youth featured a curriculum that emphasized biblical studies, the classics, and elocution. Reverend Watkins, who raised Frances after she was orphaned at a young age, became his niece's primary role model. In addition to his vocations as teacher and minister, he was a frequent contributor to *The Liberator*. His work as an abolitionist, teacher, and community leader inspired the path that Watkins Harper followed as an adult. The path was difficult. After leaving school at thirteen, she worked as a domestic servant and dressmaker before finding teaching positions in Ohio and Pennsylvania. When, in 1853, Maryland passed a law forbidding free blacks from the North from entering the state, Frances Watkins pledged herself to the antislavery cause. As had her uncle, she combined a commitment to faith and activism in which the written and spoken words were essential tools.[77]

Thought to be the first black woman hired as a paid lecturer, Watkins Harper traveled widely in the 1850s on behalf of the Maine Anti-Slavery Society and the Pennsylvania Anti-Slavery Society. She lectured in every New England state, as well as New York, Ohio, Pennsylvania, and throughout the Midwest. A visit to Canada in September 1856 prompted her to declare that she had "gazed for the first time upon Free Land." Mapping the historical experience of blacks in America, she wrote, "whatever he was in the land of Washington, beneath the shadow of Bunker Hill Monument, or even Plymouth Rock, *here* he becomes a man and a brother."[78] By drawing references to iconic historical sites that invoke ideals of U.S. freedom, the writer emphasizes the failure of those ideals, not only in the present but from the earliest settlements of the English in the New World. The only place that the ideal has been achieved, the only free land, is Canada. In the last phrase of the quotation, Watkins Harper evokes the famous engraving that featured an African man in chains and on his knees, under the inscription, "Am I Not a Man and a Brother?" Introduced by the London-based Society for the Abolition of the Slave Trade in 1787, the slogan and the image circulated widely in the United States before the Civil War. When excerpts of this letter were reprinted in abolitionist publications such as *The National Anti-Slavery Standard* and *The Underground Railroad* by William Still, readers were sure to recognize the allusion.

In a review of one of her speeches in the *Christian Recorder*, a writer drew an analogy between the lecture platform and the pulpit: "she *felt* that she had been ordained to this ministry—for the service of the pulpit is not the only ministry God had appointed."[79] Unlike Jarena Lee, Zilpha Elaw, and Julia Foote, Watkins Harper never sought a ministerial license. As did they, however, she participated in the work of the AME Church throughout her career. Not only did she present many of her lectures in the denomination's churches, she published frequently in its journal, the *Christian Recorder*. Despite these professional affiliations, Watkins Harper was a lifelong member of the Unitarian Church. Peterson argues that "Evangelical Unitarianism enabled Watkins Harper to envision herself as a poet-preacher whose faith in the particular figure of Christ empowered her to promote social engagement in order to achieve the goal of universal harmony."[80] As Ralph Waldo Emerson exemplified, Unitarians were convinced that faith must be rationalized. (By rejecting the divinity of Christ, Emerson took this stance to its logical conclusion and took himself out of the church.[81]) Unitarianism eventually followed Emerson, but in the nineteenth century it was less concerned with debates over Christology and more engaged with the ways that religion could contribute to social betterment. Consequently, "Unitarians argued that individual 'character' must be attended to in order to create moral beings whose duty it would to be to work for social cohesion in a disordered world." Theirs was not a religion based on emotional fervor. Unitarianism was rather more "a form of social work in which 'experimental activity, the use of books, magazines, lectures and voluntary associations,' was of paramount importance. In particular, Unitarians looked to the spoken word in its many forms— preaching, prayer, hymn singing—as an important instrument for evoking those emotions that would elevate moral conscience and bring about social transformation."[82]

Watkins Harper's adoption of this perspective is apparent in her earliest essays, "Christianity" and "The Colored People in America," published in *Poems on Miscellaneous Subjects*. The former never refers to race, while the latter contains only one reference to religion, yet read together they suggest how Watkins Harper's religious and political beliefs were mutually reinforcing. "Christianity," the essay begins, "is a system claiming God for its author, and the welfare of man for its object." In clear and unadorned prose, it draws distinctions among religion and other forms of human expression, including philosophy, science, poetry, and music, then argues that they all work in unity with Christian precepts. Thus, while it draws on conventional Christian iconography in which, for example, Christianity is personified as "she" and the sins of envy and malice are allegorized, it recognizes a place for philosophy and learning. In so doing, it demonstrates that Watkins Harper does not view religion as inimical to knowledge. Art also has a place: literature brings "her elegance, with the toils of the pen, and the labors of the pencil." Here Watkins Harper offers a brief for poetry as well as preaching. To be sure, the language of the essay alludes to the Bible and to popular hymns, such as William Cowper's "There Is a Fountain Filled with Blood." The social reference is nonspecific: "At [Christianity's] approach, fetters have been broken, and men have risen redeemed from dust, and freed from chains."[83] Initially presented as a lecture entitled "The Elevation and Education of Our People," the second essay contains social references that are necessarily more direct. Its opening clause—"Having been placed by a dominant race in circumstances over which we have had no control"—suggests that Watkins Harper regretted that necessity. But she wholeheartedly embraces her identification with the oppressed: "whatever concerns them, as a race, concerns me." An orator's cadences shape the list of grievances: "Born to an inheritance of misery, nurtured in degradation, and cradled in oppression" begins a question that asks how the condition of the race could be other than it is. Moreover, any race subjected to the same oppression would be in the same condition. As had David Walker and Maria Stewart, Watkins Harper enumerates what she sees as the failings of black people and attributes them to the oppression of whites. Were whites in the same situation, they would exhibit the same failings. Indeed, she dramatizes the situation with references to "the bay of the bloodhound," and reversing the association of blacks with animals, she refers to the "scent of the human tiger" tracking the fugitive slaves. The accretion of detail must have added to the effectiveness of this piece in oral performance. In the conclusion, the speaker finds sources of hope in the creation of black institutions: schools, churches, and newspapers will uplift the race.[84] Adherence to the precepts set forth in "Christianity," these essays contend, would ultimately produce the goals for uplift set forth in "The Colored Race in America."

Most of the argument in "The Colored Race" conforms to the positions held by other black abolitionists discussed in this chapter. But Watkins Harper endorsed divergent modes of resistance as well. For example, she supported the Free Produce movement that advocated a boycott of goods produced by slave labor. In "Could We Trace the Record of Every Human Heart," she argued that the basis for slavery was economic, a fact that undermined the strategy of moral suasion. "Instead of listening to the cry of agony," she asserted that slaveholders "listen to the ring of dollars and stoop down to pick up the coin." The existing excerpt of this oration indicates that the audience applauded this line. As did several of her speeches, this one referred both to the Fugitive Slave Act of 1850 and the *Dred Scott* decision of 1857, which declared that blacks had no rights that whites were compelled to respect. But Watkins Harper's knowledge of both a specific incident—the capture of the fugitive Anthony Burns, who was seized in Boston in 1854 and returned to slavery—and of a broader world set the speech apart. The Burns case sparked a riot in Boston that federal troops were called in to quell. Harper assumes her audience's familiarity with the case, which unfolded, as she noted, in proximity to Boston Harbor, "made memorable by the infusion of three-penny taxed tea." Her first rhetorical conceit is to imagine that Burns had been captured elsewhere: on the deck of an Austrian ship, or on an island or colony of Great Britain or France, perhaps in Tunisia or Egypt. In these nations, Burns would be free, while in the United States, the *Dred Scott* decision left blacks without legal redress. Then, in an even bolder turn, she imagines herself a captive in another country and culture: "Had it been my lot to have lived beneath the Crescent instead of the Cross, had injustice and violence been heaped upon my head as a Mohammedan woman, as a member of a common faith, I might have demanded justice and been listened to by the Pasha, the Bey or the Vizier; but when I come here to ask justice, men tell me, 'We have no higher law than the Constitution.'"[85] Assuming this stance, which depends for its effectiveness on the status of Islam as "other" allows Watkins Harper, the citizen outsider, to claim Christian insider status. From that position, she indicts not only the Fugitive Slave Act but American Christianity that allows it to take effect. As a member of the accepted faith, she challenges her fellow believers to act on the tenets of their belief. In doing so, she remained consistent with the first essay, which claimed a superior position for Christianity; here she gives it primacy over the Constitution.

Watkins Harper asserted a similarly complicated positionality when she took the podium at the Eleventh National Woman's Rights Convention held in New York in 1866. The title of her speech was "We Are All Bound Up Together," which celebrated a common humanity, but its substance pointed to the barriers that had to be overcome before such unity could be achieved. Specifically, Watkins Harper had to confront her position as a black person in a movement for women's rights. She began by confiding, "I feel I am something of the novice upon this platform." Unlike Douglass in his Fourth of July speech, she was not performing a ritualized act of humility; rather, she was recognizing a shift in her goals as an activist from abolition to women's rights, from matters of race to matters of gender. As she phrased it, "Born of a race whose inheritance has been outrage and wrong, most of my life has been spent in battling against those wrongs. But I did not feel as keenly as others, that I had these rights, in common with other women, which are now demanded." In order to explain how she had begun to understand her rights as a woman, she referenced her own experience, a rare autobiographical turn in her writing. Watkins had married Fenton Harper, a widower, in Ohio in 1860; he died unexpectedly in 1864, leaving her to fend for their daughter and his three children from a previous marriage. In the lecture, Watkins Harper, fashioning herself "a farmer's wife [who] made butter for the Columbus market," told how she lost everything she owned to her husband's debtors.[86] Whether to state the facts or highlight the gender dynamics of her situation, she avers that she was left with only one thing: a looking-glass. She also gained the understanding that her gender as well as her race left her with few rights that anyone respected. Making common cause with suffragists was a way forward.

It was not a panacea, however. Watkins Harper asserted that she "did not believe that giving the woman the ballot is immediately going to cure all the ills of life." Moreover, she added, she did not believe in the goodness of white women. Instead, she held that women, like men, could be categorized as good, bad, and indifferent. Finally, she addressed the white women who were her audience: "You white women speak here of rights. I speak of wrongs." Comparing herself to the biblical Ishmael, who felt every man's hand against him, she spoke about the discrimination that she experienced on public transportation in Philadelphia. A woman in the audience interjected that "they will not do that here." To which Watkins Harper responded that en route from Washington to Baltimore, she was forced to ride in the smoking car, an indignity to which none of the white women she addressed would have been subjected. Drawing together the two keywords of the essay, she asks her audience, "Are there not wrongs to be righted?" At the end of the speech, therefore, Frances Watkins Harper embodies the complex positionality of a black woman who advocates rights for women but who remains trapped in the wrongs that define the American experience of her race.

From the end of the Civil War until 1871, Watkins Harper redoubled her efforts and broadened the circuit of her travel to advocate for the rights of her people, male and female. From rural Georgia she wrote William Still that "I am almost constantly either traveling or speaking." Although she wondered whether Still would laugh at remarks she heard in response to her lectures, one doubts that she found them funny. "She is a man," some decided, while others averred, "She is not colored, she is painted."[87] I do not think, as Carla Peterson does, that these responses suggest that people inferred that Watkins Harper was an actress and associated with the disrepute of the theater. Rather, I would propose, they thought of her as a minstrel, a white man in blackface, who had the power of words unimaginable for a black woman. The contrast to the "ideal orator" his auditors heard and saw in Frederick Douglass could not be more dramatic. As a black woman, Watkins Harper could never embody that ideal. She persevered.

Seeing the South for the first time, she spent time among the newly freedmen and women whose suffering and determination depressed and inspired her. Her reports of the material conditions in which they lived both on the level of the mundane (she was struck repeatedly by the fact that their cabins lacked windows) and the traumatic (violence was pandemic) indicted both the present and the past, as most freed people continued to live under circumstances similar to those under which they had been enslaved. In many ways, Watkins Harper was witnessing at first hand the realities that she had spent her career protesting. Of course, she was exposing herself to new dangers. In a letter postmarked from Darlington, South Carolina, she wrote, "Things, I believe, are a little more hopeful," before observing that "there's less murdering."[88] She was inspired by the courage with which the former slaves faced the racist terror and relentless poverty that defined their lives under Reconstruction. She was motivated by the signs of progress that were congruent with her long-held beliefs: freedmen and women were buying homes and saving money, finding jobs and pursuing education. She in turn shored up their spirits with messages of uplift. Often there was no money to pay her, and as a matter of principle, she did not charge a fee for the private meetings she held with black women. In a letter from Greenville, Georgia, she offered a reflection that might have resonated with Zora Neale Hurston, who identified beauty as a cardinal value in rural black culture: "Last night my table was adorned with roses, although I did not get one cent for my lecture."[89] Her audiences gave her what they had, and for the most part she responded with grace. In the end, Watkins Harper's experiences in the post-war South sealed her identification with the "colored people of America." She declared with a combination of pride and ruefulness that "I fall and rise with my people."[90]

In the accounts she sent back north, Watkins Harper offered detailed observations of people's lives. Some of the anecdotes she narrated anticipate those in *The Souls of Black Folk*. For example, in a letter posted from Demopolis, Alabama, in 1871, she describes a visit to a former slave, a brick mason, who occupies the house of his former owner. In "Colored Women in America," she argues for the equality of women: they are equal to men in energy and executive ability. The illustrations she cites in support of her argument capture the texture of lived experience. Girls from sixteen to twenty-two iron until midnight so that they can attend school the next day. A mother of seven persuades her husband to buy a home and promises to take in washing to help with the purchase. Two women as partners lease nine acres and a house, then cultivate the land for ten years, "just as a man would have done."[91] These women are the counterparts of the sharecroppers and freeholders whose experiences Du Bois chronicles in the essay "Of the Black Belt" in *Souls*. A less artful (and less egotistical) narrator, Watkins Harper does not make herself the protagonist of her narrative, but she, like Du Bois, possesses an ethnographer's eye.

In its ethnographical turn as well as its interplay of oral and written genres, Watkins Harper's nonfiction points the way toward the twentieth-century African American essay. Committed to the struggle for freedom, she wrote on behalf of the abolitionist cause. But even at the beginning of her career, she addressed a broad range of subjects. Whether the topic was metaphysical— "Christianity" or "Our Greatest Want," a meditation on the human spirit—or devoted to social and political reform—women's rights or the benefits of temperance—Watkins Harper explored it on both the podium and the page. Those who followed her would address a more literate audience, but their essays would betray the influence of the podium as well.

In their voices of thunder, black orators in the nineteenth century advocated freedom for the putatively free blacks who lived mainly in the northern United States as well as for their brothers and sisters enslaved in the southern states. They appropriated the language of the Bible and of the nation's secular creed to advance their arguments. While citizenship rights and abolition were crucial topics, they spoke on behalf of education, moral uplift, temperance, and women's suffrage as well. They drew on traditions of oral performance to set forth their personal perspectives on political and social issues. Theirs was an individual as well as a collective witness. As their spoken words circulated as written texts, they modeled rhetorical strategies that informed the prose of their peers as well as of their literary descendants. In the case of David Walker, even his use of typography would influence those who came after him. But quite apart from the pattern of their prose or their political arguments, their belief in the power of words to intervene in moments of crisis was paramount.

Like the abolitionist movement, the twentieth-century movements for social justice produced prophetic voices who, channeling their mothers and fathers, spoke truth to power. Like their precursors, these writers appropriated the rhetoric of the Declaration of Independence, which they also remade into a rhetoric of counterrevolution. They deployed the rhetorical strategies if not the theology of African American Protestantism, which by then pervaded black secular life. Moreover, some of them, notably June Jordan and Alice Walker, published essays that first took the form of speeches. However, rather than invoking the figurative presence of unlettered blacks, twentieth-century essayists often fashioned a language for their essays through which these vernacular voices could be heard.

In the meantime, the struggle for freedom shifted terrain. In the first three decades of the twentieth century, art became a key battleground. Some artists embraced the opportunity to serve the cause, while others hoped to safeguard their right to individual expression. Most strove to do both, as their essays repeatedly reveal. Like the better-known poems and the fictions, the essays of the Harlem Renaissance deserve our close attention. They too are notable for what they say and how they say it.

CHAPTER THREE

On Art and Such

Debating Aesthetics during the Harlem Renaissance

And nothing will do more to ... raise his status than a demonstration of
intellectual parity of the Negro through the production of literature and art.

—James Weldon Johnson, Preface to the *Book of American Negro Poetry*

We each have our standards of art, and thus are we all interested parties
and so unfit to pass judgment upon the art concepts of others.

—Zora Neale Hurston, "Characteristics of Negro Expression"

Writers of the Harlem Renaissance vigorously debated whether there were
such a thing as Negro art, and if there were, what purpose it served, as well as
what criteria could be formulated to analyze it. Their debates have been well
chronicled by scholars, including Houston Baker, Nathan Huggins, Akasha
Hull, George Hutchinson, David Levering Lewis, and myself. Yet the changes
that the writers worked on the form of the essay—the genre in which these
debates were waged—is an aspect of African American literary history that
remains unexplored. I argue that the form is intricately connected to the substance of these arguments. Whether the intellectual detachment of Alain
Locke, the fiery polemic of Langston Hughes, the acerbic satire of George
Schuyler, or the jagged harmonies of Zora Neale Hurston, these essays both
formulate and enact the aesthetic they promote.

During the 1920s, the arts were more important than ever before on the
national stage. In the aftermath of World War I, the public's interest in political ideology waned. As he often did, F. Scott Fitzgerald both captured the
contemporary mood and overstated the facts when he declared, "It was characteristic of the Jazz Age that it had no interest in politics at all."[1] The introduction of mass culture—radio, film, records—and the wider distribution of
national magazines erased regional differences. The sense of a distinctly
American culture, as opposed to one extended from England, took hold.[2]
Not coincidentally, those who sought to define the culture also constructed
an American literary tradition that included Melville, Thoreau, Whitman,
and Twain, writers who had advanced arguments for an American literary
nationalism in the nineteenth century. In the 1920s, these writers were incorporated into an American literary tradition that had not yet been recognized

by the academy.[3] Rather than academics, essayists such as Randolph Bourne, Van Wyck Brooks, Horace Kallen, and H. L. Mencken assumed the task of explaining America to Americans. The essay was the form their explanations most often took.

For black Americans, just emerging from the period historian Rayford Logan deemed "the nadir of the Negro," a period that saw the tightening of segregation laws and the uptick of racist terror, the shift in national consciousness offered new options. Despite the social changes prompted by the migration of tens of thousands of rural blacks from the South to northern urban centers, blacks had achieved only limited political and economic progress. It was a lack of progress rather than an absence of interest that led black leaders to concentrate on arts rather than politics. The arts became a primary arena in the battle for social justice.[4] Black intellectuals were eager to participate in the definition of American culture; they insisted that the past contributions of blacks to that culture be recognized, and they debated the effectiveness of the art being created in the present as a political instrument. Some of the artists welcomed the opportunity to contribute to the struggle. Others chafed under the burden of representing the race and of writing in order to achieve political ends.

Given its priority, questions about aesthetic criteria—"The Negro in Art: How Shall He Be Portrayed?" was the title of a symposium in *The Crisis* in 1926—acquired new urgency.[5] Magazines edited by blacks and based in New York City provided forums for these discussions, as did key anthologies. *The Crisis* was the official organ of the National Association for the Advancement of Colored People (NAACP) founded by W. E. B. Du Bois in 1910; *Opportunity* served the same function for the National Urban League and was edited by Charles S. Johnson during the heyday of the renaissance. *The Messenger*, affiliated off and on with unions and edited by A. Philip Randolph and Chandler Owen, was published from 1917 to 1928. At the same time, and to a greater degree than ever before, black intellectuals were invited to contribute essays and commentary to mainstream journals such as *American Mercury*, *The Nation*, and the *New Republic*. Whether in essays, columns, or book reviews, most of the writers of the renaissance weighed in on the debates over Negro art. In the process they brought their distinctive styles to the art of the essay. Although this chapter focuses on Locke, Schuyler, Hughes, and Hurston, it reads their essays in the context of these larger conversations.

Locke's 1925 anthology *The New Negro* is the signature volume of the Harlem Renaissance. It includes pieces from almost all of the period's important writers: Countee Cullen and Langston Hughes, Jessie Fauset and Zora Neale

Hurston, Rudolph Fisher and Claude McKay. It crosses generations from the venerated Du Bois and James Weldon Johnson to the eighteen-year-old poet Helene Johnson. Its comprehensive representation of a cultural awakening that incorporates music, drama, folklore, and visual art as well as poetry and fiction shaped the movement's contours definitively. *The New Negro* announces a renaissance that is both national and transnational. Within the U.S. borders, Charles Johnson analyzes the impact of the Great Migration, while Kelly Miller and Robert R. Moton build cases for the importance of the liberal arts tradition of Howard University on the one hand and the Hampton-Tuskegee model, with its commitment to vocational training, on the other. Despite their divergent histories, the models had merged to a considerable degree. The two essays, like the musical epigraph ("O, rise, shine for Thy Light is a-coming") that stands under the dedication ("To the Younger Generation"), betray the strong shadow cast by Du Bois's *The Souls of Black Folk*. Here, however, Du Bois has only the final word. His essay "The Negro Mind Reaches Out," along with W. A. Domingo's "Gift of the Black Tropics," defines the New Negro as a diasporic figure. Surveying the situation of African people around the globe, it resounds the earlier volume's prophecy: the problem of the twentieth century is the problem of the color line.

Locke's title essay opens the volume on a different note. Its analysis defines the terms in which the New Negro Renaissance was understood then and later. It holds that the locus of black American life has shifted from the feudal precincts of the rural South to the modern northern metropolis. In the process of being transplanted, Locke proclaims, black Americans have been transformed. Sixty years after the Emancipation Proclamation declared freedom for the enslaved population of the Confederacy, the essay proclaims the spiritual emancipation of their descendants. They possess a fresh sense of possibility that, the essay intimates, will compel the nation to grant them an improved social and economic status. A New Negro, self-defined and self-respecting, has assumed leadership of the race. As often as not, this leader is an intellectual and an artist. He—and Locke consistently assumes that race leaders will be men—is well suited to the task, for only the artist/intellectual can understand the phenomenon of the New Negro. The leaders of the past, whether the traditional race leader, the philanthropist, or the sociologist, lack the requisite insight. Moreover, given the priority of the arts in the production of social change, the artist's role is now paramount.[6]

In part to illustrate the point, Locke quotes several poems in his essay. Although the essay does not credit Hughes, the first verse cited is his. It begins "We have tomorrow/Bright before us/Like a flame." As the essay's shifting discursive registers reveal, Locke struggles to sustain the optimistic tone Hughes's poem (titled "Youth") achieves. His overwhelming need to emphasize the positive results in rapid transitions between understatement and hyperbole. He refers, for example, to "the buoyancy within" the black community that compensates "for whatever pressure there may be of conditions from without" (4). This understates dramatically the prejudice that continued to buffet blacks, north and south. At the same time, Locke overstates the case when he characterizes the "migrant masses, shifting from countryside to city," as hurdling "several generations of experience at a leap." As many renaissance texts reveal, the migrants preserved many of their southern traditions in their northern communities. But Locke's essay advances its argument and gains its momentum through the disjunctions it represents. Its discursive shifts do not follow a single direction. They can move from hyperbole to understatement as easily as the reverse. Within four sentences, for example, "something like a spiritual emancipation" has shrunk to "only a strange relief and a new vague urge" (4).

Locke's discursive shifts may also measure his difficulty in figuring out how to write as the Harvard-trained Howard University professor of philosophy he was, while appealing to a general audience of mainly northern white liberals. Consequently, the essay moves from the language of classical education (the "three norns who have presided over the Negro problem") to contemporary social science ("the younger generation is vibrant with a new psychology") to popular culture ("the day of 'aunties,' 'uncles,' and 'mammies' is equally gone" (3, 5). These last references seem to elicit a more robust prose, as Locke asserts, "The popular melodrama has about played itself out, and it is time to scrap the fictions, garret the bogeys and settle down to a realistic facing of facts" (5). As appealing as it is to imagine locking away the ghosts of the past, it is harder to believe that they will not return to haunt. In any case, Locke does not sustain the active voice. The next paragraph begins with a dry academic turn: "First we must observe some of the changes which since the traditional lines of opinion were drawn have rendered these quite obsolete" (5). At other points in the essay, the reliance on the passive voice obscures the argument. What is the evidence that "sentimental interest in the Negro has ebbed"? What constituted that interest in the first place? "The Negro is being carefully studied" begs the question: by whom?

This is not to say that Locke cannot turn a phrase. "[T]he Old Negro had long become more of a myth than a man" is resonant. Locke breathes life into a cliché, and comes closest to the democratic eloquence honed by his nineteenth-century precursors, when he declares that the Negro resents "being regarded as a chronic patient for the sociological clinic, the sick man of American democracy" (11). And "Harlem, I grant you, isn't typical—but it is significant, it is prophetic" is not only a memorable line, it represents one of the only times in the essay that Locke speaks in the first person and addresses the reader directly. The effect is to increase credulity on a controversial point. In support of his case, Locke offers a stunning catalog of Harlemites ("the peasant, the student, the business man, the professional man, artist, poet, musician, adventurer and worker, preacher and criminal, exploiter and social outcast") that makes a case for a cosmopolitan community; the list also adds rhythmic variation to Locke's prose. While he declines to argue for a comparable political significance, Locke suggests that culturally, Harlem is as important as Dublin and Prague—one of the prophecies that history has borne out.

The conclusions to which the essay moves remain debatable. That is, of course, one reason "The New Negro" retains its more than merely historical interest. The questions it raises are still not decided. For example, the essay's claim that American Negroes would act as a vanguard for African peoples in their "contact with Twentieth Century civilization" reflects an unwarranted and unsettling sense of superiority to, as well as a bonding with, continental Africans (14). Locke is on firmer ground when he defines the "new internationalism" of black Americans as "an effort to recapture contact with the scattered peoples of African derivation" (15). But the most insistent claim that Locke makes is in favor of the power of art. Tellingly, the culminating declaration is neither accurate nor eloquent. Its tendentiousness seems to reinforce the weakness of its argument: "The especially cultural recognition they win should in turn prove the key to that revaluation of the Negro which must precede or accompany any considerable future betterment of race relationships" (15). "Should," "in turn," "precede or accompany," as well as "considerable" all qualify the assertion that art has the power to produce social change. Through his prose, Locke seems to concede that the prize is not full citizenship rights—as Du Bois sought in *Souls*—but a betterment of race relationships, a prize that is finally as nebulous as the prose that describes it.[7]

"The New Negro" is one of four essays that Locke contributes to his volume. The others take up more specific issues: literature, the spirituals, and the visual arts. The first, "Negro Youth Speaks," addresses the most comprehensive concerns. Its two aims are (1) to promote the work of the young generation of artists and (2) to advance a particular aesthetic. In the opening paragraph, Locke announces the arrival of a new generation of artists, who constitute the "first fruits" of the Negro Renaissance that the volume names and celebrates. Later, Locke points out that older Negro writers, as important as they were, did not achieve the success the younger generation had managed in just the previous three years. That recognition had come from all the key cultural arbiters: publishers, editors, and critics, as well as the general public. Published in mainstream journals, these writers had garnered national and even international acclaim. As befits an essay that serves to introduce the volume's sampling of these writers' work, Locke ends with a roll call of pathbreakers, an enumeration that reaches its climax with "a vivid galaxy of young Negro poets"—McKay, Toomer, Hughes, and Cullen.[8] He then offers a brief characterization of each writer's work.

But the heart of "Negro Youth Speaks" is the definition of the new aesthetic that Locke identifies in their art. Locke contends that "Negro genius today relies upon the race-gift as a vast spiritual endowment from which our best developments have come and must come" (47). The "race-gift" is the legacy of oppression (what Locke calls "social pressure") that has been at once a "material handicap" and "a spiritual advantage" that infuses the lives of ordinary people with "epic depth and lyric intensity" (47). Here again, Locke echoes *Souls*, but he writes with a different purpose. He is not offering a brief for the humanity of blacks; neither is he building a case for their moral character. Instead he asserts that generations of racial oppression have produced the "conditions of a classical art" (47).

The essay's metaphors convey Locke's classical understanding of art. Imaged as "gifts," "arresting visions," and "vibrant prophesies," art is ineffable. Locke is too much the traditionalist to assay a definition. He argues that young artists express sentiments that the masses feel but are not yet able to articulate. He holds that the artists' expression—not unlike Harlem in the title essay—is an augury of the future. Borrowing a Platonic trope, he argues that their visions and prophecies "[forecast] in the mirror of art what we must see and recognize in the streets of reality tomorrow" (47). Thus, New Negro art fashions an ideal that would be realized in a future that is not far off, the future that Hughes's poem foresees.

Expanding on the chronological reference introduced in its title, "Negro Youth Speaks" depicts these artists in the process of outgrowing the "awkward age" of the stilted and self-conscious art, marked by rhetoric and bombast, of an older generation; ironically, the youth—not their elders—are achieving "cultural maturity." In a passage that also extends the observations of the title essay, Locke asserts that the challenge of young Negro artists is not the achievement of formal mastery, but the achievement of "an inner mastery of mood and spirit." Rather than "speaking *for* the Negro," the New Negro artists "speak *as* Negroes" (48, emphasis added). This statement suggests in part that these artists are free from the demands of representing the race. To the (limited) extent that this is true, their art no longer has to carry the burden of polemic. They can be free, as Locke later declared, to create art for art's sake.[9] At the same time, Locke believes that their work would be racialized. They do not speak as artists after all, but as Negroes. This racialization manifests itself in specific themes, genres, and uses of language. A tension develops in the essay between the ineffability of art on the one hand and the concrete manifestation of "racial idiom" on the other.

Locke's essay is surely in conversation with James Weldon Johnson's preface to the first edition of *The Book of American Negro Poetry* (1922), a piece that displaces this tension. Early on, Johnson announces his dual aims: (1) to inform his audience that poetry by Negroes exists and (2) to use that poetry to encourage the social change that Locke also seeks in *The New Negro*. Johnson famously declares that "no people that has produced a great literature and art has ever been looked upon by the world as distinctly inferior."[10] He identifies four "distinctive American products" created by black Americans—folktales, spirituals, the cakewalk, and ragtime—that prove their capacity for artistic greatness. (Although the last two categories may seem time-bound, Johnson's descriptions invite later readers to broaden the categories to popular dance and jazz.) Like Locke, Johnson perceives these arts to be at once racial and national; they are American arts that have gained international recognition. The argument for the race was an argument about the nation.

But following Brent Edwards's lead, I would argue that Johnson's embrace of the popular arts is the key to the difference between the two men's perspectives. Johnson quotes verses of the spirituals—both words and music—as well as fragments of the blues, alongside excerpts from more than a century of literary poetry by black Americans. The inclusion of "Po' Boy Blues" *and* Phillis Wheatley's "Imagination" suggests the capaciousness of the tradition Johnson develops. To be sure, he considers "folk stuff" to be raw material that a serious artist could mine. Consequently, even if "Go Down, Moses" is one of the strongest themes in the musical literature, it still awaits a trained composer who would turn it into a symphony. However, Johnson's autobiographical recollections of his career as a ragtime composer as well as his status as poet and compiler of the anthology reinforce the impression that the lines between folk and formal poetry, low and high culture, can be crossed freely. Indeed, with "The Creation," Johnson became the first, as Edwards observes, "to attempt to transcribe a vernacular form—the folk sermon—into a literary work."[11] Johnson's example suggests that such crossings might be at the core of a New Negro aesthetic.

This is not the aesthetic Locke outlines. Insisting on the distinction between folk and formal art, Locke pays homage to the "matchless" achievement of Negro folk art, while making it clear that the artists he champions have transcended the provincialism of the folk. They are "modern." In their fiction, they pursue "a lusty vigorous realism," the kind of realism that some of their white contemporaries also pursued. Presumably Locke thinks here of writers such as Sherwood Anderson, Edgar Lee Masters, and Carl Sandburg, writers who moved beyond the moralistic imperatives of turn-of-the-century American literature and drew a more truthful portrait of America, warts and all. Locke believed that the realism these homegrown modernists practiced allowed for the depiction of a more honest representation of race. Writers no longer need always draw Negro characters as moral exemplars worthy of white readers' sympathy. They can in fact write from the inside and represent the breadth of Negro character and experience.

In poetry as well as fiction, young Negro writers use the racial idiom. Their distinctive contribution will be made, Locke avers, "in flavor of language, flow of phrase, accent of rhythm in prose, verse and music, color and tone of imagery, idiom and timbre of emotion and symbolism" (51). The examples he cites are notable: for instance, Johnson's "The Creation," a poem that represents the imagery and cadence of the folk preacher without relying on dialect; McKay's novels, imbued with "peasant irony" and something of Aesop, and his poems that add "folk clarity and naïveté to lyric thought"; Toomer's prose that Locke considers a fusion of the "musical folk-lit" and modernism; and Rudolph Fisher's deft borrowing from folk wisdom as well as from such practitioners of the modern short story as de Maupassant and O. Henry. In each instance the writer appropriates folk material and distills it into art. The folk constitute only one source, however; the artist draws as freely on influences ranging from classical mythology to contemporary modernism. These disparate influences enable the alchemy of art. Locke's examples are more than suggestive. They take on the force of prescription. They seem to require that artists be inspired by the folk; they leave little room for the Negro artists uninterested in racialized art. To be fair, Locke acknowledges in "The Legacy of the Ancestral Arts" that "to the individual talent in art one must never dictate." Nevertheless in urging black American painters and sculptors to look to Africa for models, he maintains that "We ought and must have a school of Negro art, a local and a racially representative tradition." Most black artists agreed, but they disputed the specifics of Locke's aesthetic agenda.[12]

The debate is not directly joined in *The New Negro*. As would be expected, most of the literary texts that follow exemplify Locke's aesthetic precepts. Countee Cullen's short lyrics as well as his major poem "Heritage," Johnson's "The Creation," Hughes's poems, which include "The Negro Speaks of Rivers" and "I, Too," short stories by Fisher and Hurston, prose sketches by Toomer and Waldrond, and Richardson's folk play "Compromise" all enact the aesthetic Locke proposes. However, there are exceptions. Poems by Georgia Douglas Johnson and Angelina Grimké reflect none of the racial idiom Locke describes. Anne Spencer's "Lady, Lady," a poetic portrait of a washerwoman, is more attuned to Locke's aesthetic, though uncharacteristic of Spencer's oeuvre; her poems rarely treat racial subjects.[13] Whatever one takes "folk clarity" to signify, it does not characterize McKay's sonnets "Baptism," "White Houses," and "Russian Cathedral."[14]

Locke exerted enough editorial control that most of the contributors who weigh in on matters of aesthetics reiterate his views. William Stanley Braithwaite was a veteran critic and anthologist from Boston, best known for the *Anthology of Magazine Verse and Yearbook* he published annually beginning in 1913 (the last edition came out in 1939) that included work by Robert Frost, Vachel Lindsay, Amy Lowell, and Wallace Stevens as well as Cullen, Hughes, and Johnson. In "The Negro in American Literature," Braithwaite finds evidence in Negro folklore "of an artistic temperament and psychology precious for itself as well as for its potential use." The essay surveys representations of black character in American literature from *Uncle Tom's Cabin* to the present and summarizes the history of literature by blacks.[15] Harvard-educated and a former English professor at Howard University where he organized the drama troupe called the Howard Players, Montgomery Gregory also predicts that the same "racial characteristics" responsible for the greatness of Negro folk music "are destined to express themselves with similar excellence in the kindred art of drama." In "The Drama of Negro Life," he contends that the "pernicious influence" of minstrel traditions had retarded the development of serious Negro drama, which was "still in its infancy" but sure to win recognition in the future. Echoing Locke, Gregory contends that "The only avenue of genuine achievement in American drama for the Negro lies in the development of the rich veins of folk-tradition of the past and in the portrayal of the authentic life of the Negro masses of today."[16]

Poet, novelist, and editor Jessie Fauset deploys the rhetoric of racial gifts ironically. She begins "The Gift of Laughter" by declaring that "The black man bringing gifts, and particularly the gift of laughter, to the American stage, is easily the most anomalous, the most inscrutable figure of the century."[17] The anomaly reflects most broadly the disjuncture between the Negro as "the funny man of America" and the race's tragic history. More specifically, it reflects the loathsome legacy of minstrelsy that Fauset suggests was a camou-flage for white people's knowledge of, and feelings toward, their black country-men. Here Fauset deftly shifts the mask from the black performer to the white spectator. The spectator rather than the actor is playing false. Indeed, it is the black performer in blackface who first dislocates the mask and reveals a more honest portrayal of a condition that in Fauset's view "may be variously deemed hopeless, remarkable, admirable, inspiring, [and] depressing," but never "merely amusing" (162).

Fauset nods to the contributions of the performers Ernest Hogan and George Walker, as well as Weldon Johnson's former partners, Bob Cole and Rosamund Johnson, but the main subject of her essay is the legendary vaudevillian Bert Williams. "The Symbolism of Bert Williams," an earlier ver-sion of the essay, had been published just after the comedian's death in 1922, in *The Crisis*, the journal Fauset served as literary editor. Williams advances Fauset's argument better than the other performers, not only because he was the most successful but because he was born in the West Indies (probably in Antigua, though the essay misidentifies his birthplace as Jamaica) and had aspired to a career in the legitimate theater. Racism thwarted that ambition. Fauset expresses the result with admirable skill: "Consequently, deliberately, as one who desiring to become a great painter but lacking the means for travel and study might take up commercial art, he turned his attention to min-strelsy" (163). The repeated rhythms of the opening adverbs, the subordinate clause that expresses the subordination of Williams's ambition, and the ironi-cal final statement that positions minstrelsy as something to which one would turn his attention—all of the elements of the sentence reinforce the inexora-ble quality of Williams's fate. The analogy at its heart is misleading, however, because it is not a lack of means but the impassable barrier of race that forces Williams to redirect his aspirations. Indeed, Fauset quickly reveals that Wil-liams traveled to London to study under Pietro, a perhaps fictional figure she describes as a master of the art of pantomime. The analogy remains sugges-tive, not least because it anticipates the fictional situation Fauset invents for the protagonist of her 1929 novel *Plum Bun*. More to the point of the essay, since Williams was not born in the U.S. South, he had to learn the stereo-typical speech and mannerisms of the stage Negro.[18] They are not the natural attributes that racist conventional wisdom held them to be. The fact underscores the reality that the stage Negro was, to echo Locke, a myth rather than a man. For Williams, therefore, his gift of laughter was always "tainted with the salt of chagrin and tears" (167).

Unlike Gregory, Fauset contends that popular Broadway comedies such as *Shuffle Along* and *Runnin' Wild* are more than updated minstrel shows. She sees in them "the genius of a new comic art" (166) and compares them to a "riotous farce" she had once seen in Vienna that induced "the same effect of superabundant vitality" (166). The comparison shifts the focus from the still racialized (if threadbare) plots to the theatrical energy of the performances. Taking care to note the contributions of Charles Gilpin and Paul Robeson, actors who excelled at the art of tragedy, Fauset maintains that the laughter that had been the "emotional salvation" of the race could become the core of its contribution to drama. From quite a distant vantage point, Fauset articulates a conclusion similar to the one that Hurston would reach a decade later.

The challenge would remain the terms of the argument. "Emotional salvation," like "racial gifts," is a phrase that belongs more to theology than criticism. The contributors to *The New Negro* struggle to find a vocabulary that defines the cultural difference they want to celebrate. None doubt the existence of "Negro art." What makes the art Negro is the question. In "Jazz at Home," J. A. Rogers classifies jazz as "one part American and three parts American Negro," then describes the music in hyperbolic terms: "a marvel of paradox," "epidemic contagiousness" (like the measles), "joyous revolt," "safety valve for modern . . . society," "hilarity expressing itself through pandemonium; musical fireworks."[19] But the freedom he hears in the music is also license. And Rogers is as often abashed by what he perceives as its excess and lack of control as he is enthralled by its "primitive vigor." Thus, while Rogers's essay, alone in *The New Negro*, at least acknowledges the existence of the music that is arguably the greatest achievement by black American artists in the 1920s, it does so in terms that are critically deficient, sometimes embarrassed, and often embarrassing. He concludes that jazz "has come to stay, and they are wise, who instead of protesting against it, try to lift and divert it into nobler channels" (224).

Locke was deaf to the art of jazz and blues, and he was less than an ardent fan of contemporary theater. He had little to say about these art forms. But he was serious about the visual arts. After earning a B.A. from Harvard in 1907, Locke was awarded a Rhodes scholarship, the first African American to receive one. An article about his studies is aptly titled "A Black Aesthete at Oxford."[20] For the rest of his life, Locke was a regular visitor to museums throughout Europe and the United States. In the late 1920s, he served as a primary consultant to the Harmon Foundation when it organized the first major exhibitions of African American painting and sculpture. It is not surprising, then, that the closest that *The New Negro* comes to a debate about aesthetics is in essays on the visual arts. Locke carves out the greatest disagreement with physician, business magnate, and iconoclastic art collector Albert Barnes, whose "Negro Art and America," is the second essay in *The New Negro*.

Barnes echoes Locke's critical vocabulary and seems to share his perspectives, but he misses several important nuances. Like Locke, Barnes refers repeatedly to the emotional and spiritual endowments of African Americans. He asserts that as a consequence of their "subjection" in "an Anglo-Saxon environment," they were "bound to undergo the soul-stirring experiences which always find their expression in great art."[21] The spirituals—America's only "great music"—are evidence. Barnes then declares that "the renascence of Negro art is one of the events of our age which no seeker for beauty can afford to overlook" (21).

Barnes was undoubtedly a seeker for beauty; he had already established his eponymous foundation in Merion, Pennsylvania; the mansion that long housed the foundation was built the same year as *The New Negro* was published. (It moved to Philadelphia in 2012.) Barnes's tastes were as eclectic as his fortune was deep; he amassed one of the largest collections of Impressionist and post-Impressionist European paintings in the United States as well as an extensive store of African sculptures, which he exhibited for their aesthetic values rather than their ethnographic significance. The illustrations for Locke's essay "The Legacy of the Ancestral Arts," which include pieces from the Sudan, Benin, Dahomey, and the Congo, are from the Barnes Foundation Collection. In many ways, Barnes's theories on art were fiercely nonhierarchical and democratic. In collaboration with John Dewey, Barnes developed an art curriculum for workers that shaped the offerings at the school run by his foundation. He insisted on displaying his collection without regard to chronology or nationality. A single gallery might hold French paintings, African sculptures, hand-wrought iron, and Pennsylvania Dutch furniture. Nevertheless, his essay inscribes racial hierarchy; it relies heavily on the supposed primitivism of Africans and African Americans, people for whom no boundary exists between art and life.

Locke demurs from this view, especially in the essay on the "ancestral arts." It is worth noting that this essay did not appear in the special March 1925 issue of *Survey Graphic*, titled "Harlem—Mecca of the New Negro," that was the precursor for the anthology.[22] "Negro Art and America" did. It stands to reason, then, that Locke wrote "The Legacy of the Ancestral Arts" with Barnes's essay in mind. In "The Negro Spirituals," also written for the book, Locke deems the music both "primitive" and "classic," both "nationally as well as racially characteristic."[23] But in "The Legacy of the Ancestral Arts," he insists that what has been taken to be "primitive" in black American culture does not derive from Africa. The "naïveté," "sentimentalism," "exuberance," and "improvisational spontaneity" that observers identify—and in *The New Negro* honor—in Negro American art bear no relation to African art. Locke chooses the adjectives "rigid, controlled, disciplined, abstract [and] heavily conventionalized" to describe the plastic arts of Africa, which he argues predominate over the music, poetry, and dance that predominate in America (254). Moreover, he contends, black Americans respond to African art with the same sense of alienation and misunderstanding as the average European or white American. Nonetheless, Locke argues that African art can become a "profound and galvanizing influence" on Negro American artists (256).[24]

How does Locke, himself a Negro American, overcome the alienated attitude he describes? The answer lies in his scholarly detachment. He does not write as an enthusiast, like Barnes. Indeed, he strives throughout this essay to eschew the race pride that is a hallmark of the volume overall. His objective stance shines through in his list of the four reasons that black American artists would do well to study African art: (1) its skill and mastery prove that "the Negro is not a cultural foundling without his own inheritance," (2) its example should encourage the development of sculpture, painting, and the decorative arts among black Americans, (3) the impact of African sculpture on contemporary European art should carry over to black Americans—in contradiction of Locke's earlier contention—because they are "blood descendants, bound to it by a sense of direct cultural kinship," and (4) African art teaches the lessons of "a classical background," lessons "of discipline, of style, of technical control," which the New Negro artist should learn (256). The remainder of the essay elaborates on these reasons. As it does, it offers arresting observations on African art ("African artists really see form in three dimensions") and on contrasts between the histories of European and American art (noting the paradox that black figures are more common in European painting than in American). The catalogs of European, Anglo-American, and African American artists establish Locke's erudition.

The metaphors of legacy, endowment, and inheritance bolster his argument that Negro artists have much to gain from a careful study of African art. Yet here he is careful not "to dictate a style to the young Negro artist," but to press the point that African art in its stylized abstraction offers a radical break from the racial stereotypes that distort the representation of the black body in the visual arts, no less than in literature, in the United States. Perhaps most important, the anonymous African artists have achieved the "inner mastery of mood and spirit" that Locke urges for African Americans in "Negro Youth Speaks." Free of the "pressure" of race and racism, African artists speak as artists. As such, they represent a far from attainable ideal, a reality that Locke is loath to acknowledge.

Locke, Fauset, and Johnson were cosmopolitans who spoke several languages and had traveled abroad extensively. Locke was a frequent visitor to Germany and France, Fauset had studied at the Sorbonne and written about her sojourns to London and Algiers, and Johnson had served at the U.S. consulates in Nicaragua and Venezuela. They were also highly conscious of the diasporic reach of African culture. Locke in his study of African art, Fauset in her translations of Haitian poetry, and Johnson whose preface recognized poets of African descent in Europe and throughout the New World all recognized that the artistic aspirations of Negro artists in the United States reverberated among black artists around the globe. But they could not lose sight of the challenges black Americans confronted at home. All argued that the art of the Negro Renaissance was both racial and national. They hoped that its success would lead to a better status for blacks in the United States.

No one mocked their hopes with a more acerbic wit than George Schuyler. With a title steeped in Americana, his essay "The Negro-Art Hokum" ridicules the very idea of a Negro Renaissance. Not surprisingly, his sneering tone succeeded in eliciting impassioned responses, most notably one from Langston Hughes. In Schuyler's view, American Negroes are Americans, pure and simple, and so is their art. Anyone who argues otherwise, particularly the "eager apostles from Greenwich Village, Harlem, and environs," are fooling the public and themselves. Lists of artists (Du Bois, sculptor Meta Warrick Fuller, and painter Henry Ossawa Tanner) and contemporary public figures who have long since been forgotten (Octavus Cohen, Hugh Wiley) work here to heighten the mockery. The African American artists Schuyler cites had been trained in the centers of Western culture: Du Bois at Harvard and in Berlin, Fuller and Tanner in Paris. Their art is "no more 'expressive of the Negro soul,'" than that of Cohen and Wiley, two white dialect writers who specialize in "darky" stories.[25] The tone of ridicule is relentless. Schuyler begins by rejecting the idea of Negro art and ends by rejecting the idea of racial difference. In that latter moment the seriousness of the essay's purpose is clear. But the mockery is the source of its power. Laced with American vernacular expressions, the essay makes itself an example of the American-ness of American Negroes.

During the 1920s, Schuyler was called the "black Mencken," in tribute to his greatest influence, the journalist and editor H. L. Mencken. The noted journalist Walter Lippman called Mencken "the most powerful personal influence on his whole generation of educated people."[26] In the decade before World War I, Mencken gained fame and notoriety for his attacks on the Puritanism that pervaded American culture; he coined the epithet "Bible Belt." His attacks on the ignorance of his fellow Americans—Southerners in particular—and their attacks on him would later catch the attention of Richard Wright, when he worked as a messenger for an optical company in Memphis. "Jarred and shocked by [his] style, the clear, clean sweeping sentences," Wright was equally stunned by Mencken's courage, his willingness to say things that no one else dared. He decided that Mencken used words as weapons; he would do the same.[27] Unbeknown to Wright, Mencken had already befriended numerous black writers, including James Weldon Johnson and Walter White. For Johnson, Mencken's prose was "a mental cocktail, an intellectual electric shock." He urged black people to read him. Many did, faithfully. At least one scholar credits Mencken with a critical role in the Harlem Renaissance.[28] As editor, he solicited articles from Rudolph Fisher, E. Franklin Frazier, Eugene Gordon, and J. A. Rogers, as well as Du Bois, White, Hurston, and Schuyler. During the time Mencken edited *American Mercury*, no black writer's byline appeared more often than George Schuyler's.[29]

Agnostic yet socially conservative, a man of the people who was also something of an aesthete, Mencken courted controversy. He wrote, for example, that "no virtuous man—that is, virtuous in the Y.M.C.A. sense—has ever painted a picture worth looking at, or written a symphony worth hearing or a book worth reading."[30] By the 1920s, he had become the voice of the educated American, who looked down on those Mencken dubbed the "booboisie." He coedited *The Smart Set*, a popular magazine, from 1914 to 1924, and cofounded *American Mercury* with George Jean Nathan, which Mencken edited from 1924 to 1933. An inveterate wordsmith, he published weekly columns for the *Baltimore Sun* as well as more than a score of books. *Prejudices* was the title of six series of essay volumes. Many critics consider Mencken the most important American essayist of his generation. He was a distinctive stylist. His prose enacted a version of the vernacular process Ellison would later define. According to Carl Bode, one of his several biographers, Mencken's "genius for seizing the unexpected and amusing word, for making the irreverent comparison, and for creating a tone that was not acid but alkaline helped to make him the most readable of American essayists."[31]

Mencken championed the importance of American English. From its initial publication in 1919, his pioneering study *The American Language* held that a distinct language had developed in the United States. It reflected the national character in its impatience with propriety and grammatical rules, its resistance to authority, "an extravagant and often grotesque humor," and a love of metaphor.[32] The book was chockablock with examples; charts contrasted American and British English spelling and vocabulary. Over the course of four editions, it documented changes in the language as well as new etymological findings. Mencken scoffed at the failure of scholars to pursue a serious study of the language, noting "in all other countries the everyday speech of the common people ... has the constant attention of philologists" (5). He filled the gap in a wide-ranging volume that recognized that American English incorporated words from Native Americans and European immigrants. New names were coined in response to new conditions, and distance from the mother country preserved words in the New World that were no longer used in the old. He only glancingly considered the contributions of African Americans to the American language, crediting enslaved Africans with "gumbo," "goober," "juba," "voodoo" (usually corrupted to "hoodoo"), and a very few other words. (In her essay "Characteristics of Negro Expression," Hurston would fill in some of Mencken's gaps.) He argued that apart from southern backwaters—doubtless populated mostly by poor blacks—the American language was a national language. Unlike British English, it featured no dialects.

"Hokum" is the kind of word Mencken relished. According to the *Dictionary of American Slang* (1997), it is probably a blend of hocus-pocus and bunkum. Its roots are in the theater, where it denoted obvious or familiar elements of low comedy, melodrama, sentimentality, or the like, designed to appeal strongly to an unsophisticated audience. Buncombe is a synonym and in one of the illustrations it replaces the then-obsolete "bull." Ironically, another illustration quotes from an informant to *American Speech*: "I ... and my father ... learned the word hokum from the Negroes on my grandfather's plantation [in North Carolina] and from those of Southern Maryland. From then it was carried by the old-timed minstrel troupes ... to the stage."[33] It seems unlikely that either Mencken or Schuyler were familiar with this possible etymology. Schuyler doubtless was responding to the second definition of hokum—"claptrap; flattery, falsehoods, nonsense"—when he wrote, "One contemplates the popularity of the Negro-art hokum and murmurs, 'How come?'"[34]

Schuyler answers in ways that are humorous and cutting. For example, "the Aframerican is merely a lampblacked Anglo-Saxon" presents an anachronistic image that conveys the superficiality of racial difference (310). Perhaps Schuyler was aware of Mencken's contention in *American Language* that the noun "Aframerican, which is now very commonly used in the Negro press, is not American, but was devised by Sir Harry Johnston," an Englishman.[35] In any case, by evoking a technology that precedes the electric light, he consigns the emphasis on such differences to the past. At the same time, the phrase works also to imply that black Americans are less "foreign" than the southern and eastern European immigrants who changed the demographics of the U. S. population in the early twentieth century. The rest of the paragraph reinforces this point as it contrasts the Americanization of immigrants over the course of two or three generations to the black American who has been socialized in the culture for 300 years. The racial difference that attracts attention is the difference evoked by a series of stereotypes as enacted by entertainers and athletes such as Bert Williams and Jack Johnson and figures from literature and advertisements such as Uncle Tom and Aunt Jemima. Even worse are the caricatures that depict blacks as "various monstrosities scrawled by the cartoonists" (311). Monstrosities is a strong word. Yet the essay dilutes its anger by invoking stereotypes that are applied to white Americans. They are represented by a composite of Andy Gump, Jim Jeffries, and a cartoon by Rube Goldberg. As the essay makes clear, only a naïf or a fool would confuse these stereotypes with human beings. But how much harm is done if they do? Schuyler argues that stereotypes that demean blacks should be considered equally harmless because they are equally ridiculous.

The essay's central premise it that blacks in America are subject to the same economic and political forces as whites. Their actions and thoughts are necessarily similar. The premise seems self-evidently mistaken. At a time when racial segregation was the law in most of the United States and de facto segregation was practiced everywhere else, the social forces were clearly unequal. As a consequence, so were the economic and political forces. But Schuyler ignores these facts. Instead he offers an extended anecdote to illustrate the premise; the anecdote takes on the tone of a Hollywood comedy. Schuyler, like his peers, thought in terms of the representative man. Whether black or white, the representative American is awakened by "his Connecticut alarm clock," and rises from "his Grand Rapids bed," eats the same breakfast, works at the same mills, mines, factories, and businesses, wears similar clothing, belongs to the same religious denominations, sees the same movies, smokes the same tobacco, and reads the same "puerile" periodicals. He is a middle-class philistine; the author is in every way his superior.

To suggest that the only difference in material conditions between the average white American and the average black is that the latter might ride in rather than own the same make of automobile was to ignore reality. The gap in income, living conditions, and employment opportunities was vast. In Harlem during the 1920s, for example, the average Negro "held some menial or unskilled position which paid low wages." Indeed, during the same decade that Harlem was in vogue, high rents and low salaries produced congested and unsanitary conditions in the community.[36] The conditions that Harlemites had fled in the South were markedly worse. Without question, Schuyler's representative black American is more myth than man.

Of course, Schuyler is not writing as a social scientist. Data are not his concern. Much like Johnson in his preface, Schuyler argues that nationality is a more crucial determinant for art than race. So Samuel Coleridge-Taylor, Edward Wilmot Blyden, and Claude McKay are Englishmen (not an identity that McKay ever seems to have claimed). Pushkin is Russian, and Dumas, father and son, are French. It follows, then, that Dunbar, Chesnutt, and Johnson are American. Earlier in the essay, Schuyler considers the existence of the cultural expressions (spirituals, blues, and jazz) that might contradict his argument. He dismisses them all as "contributions of a caste in a certain section of the country" (310). If Du Bois considered the spirituals "the most beautiful expression of human experience born this side the seas," Schuyler describes them as "slave songs based on Protestant hymns and Biblical texts." The Charleston is "an eccentric dance invented by the gamins around the public market-place in Charleston, South Carolina" (310). Peasants produce these forms of music and dance. And, for peasants, unlike artists, class, not nation, is determinative. Their expressions resemble each other across oceans: "One recalls the remarkable likeness of the minor strains of the Russian mujiks to those of the Southern Negro" (310). As for the United States, "Any group under similar circumstances would have produced something similar" (310). Schuyler earns the epithet "iconoclast" here. He not only argues that blacks were fully assimilated into American culture in 1926, but that even under slavery they were *culturally* the same as whites.

To the extent that he argues for a common humanity rather than a common culture for blacks and whites, Schuyler writes in a long-standing tradition. Interestingly, he quotes the "Negrophobists," specifically Warren G. Harding, the U.S. president who was himself rumored be part black, to make his point. Harding asserted that there are "fundamental, eternal, and inescapable differences" between white and black Americans. Schuyler rightly deems this "nonsense," an "old myth," and the reflection of race hatred. Why then would blacks believe it? Because they have internalized the words of "vociferous scions of slaveholders," pseudoscientists like Madison Grant, author of *The Passing of the Great Race* (1916), and Lothrop Stoddard, author of *The Revolt against Civilization* (1923), and the less literate followers of the Ku Klux Klan. If the white racists argue that the black American (like Mencken, Schuyler refers to the "blackamoor"—more black?—to mock the blacks who accept this view) is "inferior," the blacks who are susceptible to the denigration apply the only slightly less offensive term "peculiar" to themselves. The essayist acknowledges no difference. In the end, Schuyler concedes that his is a minority view. The majority of Americans believe in the immutability of racial difference. However, inviting the enlightened reader to join his superior community, he writes that "such reasoning . . . must be rejected with a loud guffaw by intelligent people" (312).

Schuyler's essay was still in proof when the managing editor of *The Nation*, Freda Kirchwey, sent it to Langston Hughes. Then enrolled at Lincoln University in rural Pennsylvania, Hughes was enjoying the success generated by his first volume of poems, *The Weary Blues*, published earlier in 1926. The title poem was inspired both by life on Harlem's Lenox Avenue and by the folk blues Hughes had heard as a boy in Kansas. It shared pages with "Aunt Sue's Stories," "The Negro Speaks of Rivers," "Song for a Banjo Dance," and "When Sue Wears Red," poems that explored African American history and culture. In other poems, like "Jazzonia," Hughes experimented with form to invent the new genre of jazz poetry. Schuyler's mockery threatened everything that Hughes had achieved. Within a week, his rejoinder was in the mail. Despite his anger, he was able to respond to Kirchwey's request not for a rebuttal to Schuyler but "rather an independent positive statement of the case for a true Negro racial art."[37] Not only Hughes's most notable essay, "The Negro Artist and the Racial Mountain" (1926) is arguably the most enduring statement of its kind.

Hughes's essay is a declaration of independence on behalf of the black artist, a noun that conveys immediately a conception that is more inclusive than "writer." Artists for Hughes include blues singers and jazz musicians, actors and painters. But the category also includes "drylongso folk," or ordinary people. Among the professionals, he singles out Bessie Smith and Paul Robeson, Charles Gilpin and Aaron Douglas as artists whose work is tied to the experiences of everyday folk. He locates the latter in specifically identified black urban communities in Washington and Chicago as well as Harlem. Cultural practices—both secular and sacred—in these communities separate them from the mainstream. Their vernacular language informs the language of the essay. Indeed, although published in *The Nation*, Hughes frequently shifts the mode of address from the representative reader of that journal to the masses of black folk whose lives he is extolling. At such moments these folk are both the essay's subject and its implied audience.

The essay opens with a now familiar anecdote about the young Negro poet who allegedly confided to Hughes that "I want to be a poet—not a Negro poet." As critics have noted, Hughes develops a syllogism that is notable for its lack of logic. He takes the poet to mean that he wants to write like a white poet, "meaning subconsciously 'I would like to be a white poet,' meaning behind that, 'I would like to be white.'" But the logic does not hold. Not wishing to be defined as a Negro poet—a term that was usually intended to marginalize and diminish one's achievements—was not tantamount to wanting to be white. Most of their contemporaries thought Countee Cullen was the young Negro poet Hughes had in mind. In one of several widely quoted articles, Cullen had told a reporter, "If I am going to be a poet at all, I am going to be POET and not NEGRO POET. That is what has hindered the development of artists among us. Their one note has been the concern with their race." He added that he would write about race, but he would not produce propaganda.[38] What seems at first glance to justify Hughes's essay's conclusions is the confidential tone in which they are shared. Hughes adopts a tone of familiarity with readers that seems to let us in on an intimate exchange. The suggestion is that Hughes can draw the inferences into the young poet's subconscious because he shares a personal connection to him. They are not equals. Hughes presents himself as older and wiser when he doubts that "this poet would ever be a great poet" (305).[39]

At bottom, for Hughes, whiteness is less a matter of individual identity than of cultural hegemony. As he defines the "mountain" that confronts the development of "true Negro art in America," it is "this urge within the race toward whiteness, the desire to pour racial individuality into the mold of American standardization, and to be as little Negro and as much American as possible." He chides not only his fellow poets but African Americans in general for their willingness to forfeit a specific racial identity for a nebulous sense of national belonging. This last image satirizes the Taylorist language of "The Negro-Art Hokum," such as the Connecticut alarm clock and the bed made in Grand Rapids. For Hughes, the empty and imitative culture of the black middle class represents "a very high mountain indeed for the would-be racial artist to climb in order to discover himself and his people." "Standard-ization," "empty," and "imitative" are terms that were already commonplaces of social critique in the America of the 1920s. Hughes sees the masses of African Americans—"the low-down folk"—as the antidote to the philistinism of the dominant society. In his enthusiasm, he romanticizes the lives of the urban masses. More problematically, he does not define "racial individuality," a para-doxical term if there ever was one.

The term is repeated later in the essay, but first Hughes returns to the plight of the young poet, who is rendered even more opaque by the refer-ences to his class position. He belongs to the Negro middle class, a status achieved due to his parents' employment as a steward in a white club and as a seamstress, positions that suggest how complicated class positionality was in early twentieth-century black America.[40] Here middle class is contrasted to poor and to rich, and the young poet is neither. In its preoccupation with so-cial positionality, the essay extends a string of vertical metaphors: "high-class," "low-down folks," "overtones and undertones," "undertow," and "the top of the mountain." This continuum not only charts class position; it also indicates the various levels of alienation and authenticity that mark the Negro artist's struggle with the racial mountain. His individual struggle be-comes a more intense version of the situation faced by all African Americans. The most benighted, the "high-class" blacks, are read out of the race: "Nordic manners, Nordic faces, Nordic art (if any), and an Episcopal heaven" (306). Having gone as far upward as one could go, Hughes returns to earth with relief:

> But then there are the low-down folks, the so-called common element, and they are the majority—may the Lord be praised! The people who have their hip of gin on Saturday nights and are not too important to themselves or the community, or too well fed, or too learned to watch the lazy world go round. They live on Seventh Street in Washington or State Street in Chicago and they do not particularly care whether they are like white folks or anybody else. Their joy runs bang! into ecstasy. Their reli-gion soars to a shout. Work maybe a little today, rest a little tomorrow. Play awhile. Sing awhile. O, let's dance! (306)

The apostrophes—"may the Lord be praised!"—heighten the writer's identification with the people he is describing. He may be romanticizing their vices and their suffering, but his invocation of their speech makes it seem as if theirs are his vices and suffering as well. The effort to transcribe their speech acts, as when the exclamation point interrupts the completion of the sentence, calls to mind Hughes's invention of jazz poetry and the transliterations of jazz in his novel *Not Without Laughter*. Here he does more than transcribe speech and describe actions. He brings the figures of the folk into the essay. Who is invited to sing and dance, if not the low-down folks? Whom would they join, if not the writer?

"The Negro Artist and the Racial Mountain" intervenes in an ongoing discussion of black aesthetics. When it refers to the questions that the poet is asked by his own people, it recalls the months-long symposium in *The Crisis* on "The Negro in Art." When it laments the lack of support for African American literature—which results in Charles Chesnutt's novels going out of print and the lack of respect given Paul Laurence Dunbar as a poet—it calls attention to a problem that belongs to the present as well as the past. Despite the "present vogue in things Negro," black artists still find little support. The portrait of the young writer who supports himself by manual labor, who is ignored by the black bourgeoisie until they discover that he has published a book, and then is at once feted and insulted, is a self-portrait. Middle-class black readers want a particular kind of art—one that presents pleasing images of themselves. A writer who declines to comply, like Jean Toomer or like Hughes himself, could find himself *persona non grata*. The slights that Hughes suffered still stung; he would never forgive the disrespect he believed black society women showed his mother.

The key to Hughes's survival as an artist is to identify as closely as possible with the common folk. Jazz provides the key to that identification. In Hughes's words, jazz is "one of the inherent expressions of Negro life in America; the eternal tom-tom beating in the Negro soul." Arguably the first reference to the tom-tom in the history of the essay, it does not work here as it does in some Harlem Renaissance poetry to invoke a distant African past. Jazz is made-in-America; it is also Negro art. The figure of the tom-tom works to suggest how black people's lives are racialized in the United States: tom-tom becomes a modifier for revolt, work (repeated three times), joy, and laughter. Hughes argues that the worldview that undergirds these aspects of black life is expressed most resonantly through jazz. His task as a writer is to find a literary counterpart for the music. Hughes's essay is one of the first articulations of this task, a task that became one of the central impulses of twentieth-century African American literature.

The essay falters in its effort to define the terms of the argument. When the term "racial individuality" reappears, it is followed by two phrases, although it is not clear whether they are intended to modify it. The first phrase invokes the Negro's "heritage of rhythm and warmth," a phrase that veers close to well-worn stereotypes. The second refers to "his incongruous humor," which is then associated with the blues. Hughes offers a variation on the trope of laughing to keep from crying by referring to "ironic laughter mixed with tears" (307). Nowhere in this passage is it clear how one would express one's race and one's individuality simultaneously. However, Hughes's personal example suggests one possibility.

He is the artist who is inspired by specific vernacular forms—spirituals, blues, and jazz—which he goes on to cite in the essay and which become essential elements in his groundbreaking poetry. He invokes the insistent sound of the music: "Let the blare of Negro jazz bands and the bellowing voice of Bessie Smith singing Blues penetrate the closed ears of the colored near-intellectuals." The alliterative "b's" fortify the writer. The sounds of the music become the call to which he responds. But he can do so because the music gives him access to the group's spiritual power. That power is inscribed in the autonomous self-concept that Hughes perceives among ordinary black folk. He ends his essay with one of the most stirring declarations of artistic autonomy in African American letters: "We younger Negro artists who create now intend to express our individual dark-skinned selves without fear or shame. If white people are pleased we are glad. If they are not, it doesn't matter. We know we are beautiful. And ugly too. The tom-tom cries and the tom-tom laughs. If colored people are pleased we are glad. If they are not, their displeasure doesn't matter either. We build our temples for tomorrow, strong as we know how, and we stand on top of the mountain, free within ourselves" (309).

Endlessly quoted, the paragraph gains its force through the simplicity of its phrases and the directness of its declarations. Young Negro artists *intend* to create. That is, they will be artists, no matter what. They will express their "individual dark-skinned selves," a phrase that is both a variation of, and improvement on, "racial individuality." The speaker recognizes that the audience for Negro art, like the implied audience the essay creates, is both black and white. As a function of his determination to respect the complexity of African American life—the beautiful and the ugly, the pain and the joy—the artist anticipates a mixed response to this work. But it is not a response based on race. He expects to please and anger blacks as well as whites. Yet while anticipating his audience's response, he determines to ignore it. He will not be constrained by the expectations of his contemporaries; he will create art for future generations. Those "temples for tomorrow"—that is, the art itself as well as the metaphorical spaces that fuse the artistic and the spiritual—are the antithesis of the racial mountain with which Negro artists contend in the present. In these spaces, artists are indeed free.

"The Negro Artist and the Racial Mountain" restates Locke's claims for the newness of the young generation of African American artists. It insists on their liberation from the burdens of the past: its fear and shame. It reiterates their commitment to a racial art and insists that the sources for that art are in the expressive culture of rural blacks and their urban kin. As crucial as these affirmations are, there is something more important to the development of the African American essay. By foregoing Locke's periodic sentences and elaborate circumlocutions, Hughes's essay ends by becoming, rather than merely announcing, the bracing freshness of the new.

In January 13, 1938, Zora Neale Hurston finished the essay she was writing for "The Negro in Florida," a volume that was prepared for the Federal Writers Project. The essay, "On Art and Such," would not be published for more than four decades, but it provides rare and useful insights into Hurston's understanding of African American literary and artistic traditions and of herself as an artist.[41] She does not mention the Harlem Renaissance here or anywhere in her writings. Given its subject, the omission in this essay seems especially curious. Hurston was, after all, well aware of both the movement's accomplishments and its failings. Within months of moving to New York in January 1925, she won two second prizes in the literary contests sponsored by *Opportunity* magazine and published one of her short stories, "Spunk," in *The New Negro.* She quickly placed several more stories and plays in *Opportunity* and *The Messenger,* then joined the band of young artists who created the legendary literary magazine *Fire!!* This initial success was dazzling but short-lived. Unlike Hughes, Hurston never found a home in Harlem, and she remained an outsider to the New Negro movement. Like Schuyler, she harbored doubts about its political goals and was suspicious of its leaders' motives. Unlike Schuyler, however, she believed in the possibility of a racial art. She believed as well that the aesthetic agenda that the New Negro leaders—"Negrotarians," in her coinage—set forth was another in a long line of obstacles that thwarted the realization of a true Negro art.

In "Art and Such," Hurston judges African Americans' contribution to the arts harshly: "creation is in its stumbling infancy." She is not addressing the legacy of folklore and music, which confirm the existence of "many undreamed-of geniuses."[42] She concentrates instead on those who would call themselves artists and who, only three generations removed from slavery, continue to wrestle with its legacy of enforced silence. Crippling too are the ideological constraints under which they labor. Compelled to write as race leaders, they are unable to think as individuals or to draw a character as anything other than "a tragic unit of the Race" (908). The tradition that gives pride of place to unimaginative "Race Men" silences artists, including Hurston herself, who do not adhere to its dictates. Hurston does not name these men, but when she refers to the misnaming of the spirituals as "Sorrow Songs," she identifies Du Bois as one of her targets. Locke is surely another.[43]

As she highlights the handful of black artists born in Florida, Hurston identifies Brooks Thompson, a woodcarver whose work is a thing "of wondrous beauty." Asked how he achieved it, Thompson states, "The feeling just came and I did it" (909). Hurston wants to create a free space for writers who can do in words what this unheralded artist has done in his medium. When describing the interior of the house Thompson decorated with his carvings, Hurston notes that "Without ever having known anything about African Art, he has achieved something very close to African concepts . . . ." Not surprisingly, Hurston posits a racial art that owes more to culture than to politics. Although she offers no explanation for the transmission of this artistic tradition, she had previously identified African survivals in the folklore and music she documented in a decade of fieldwork. The storytellers and singers whose words and music she transcribed knew no more of African traditions than Thompson.

In "Art and Such," Hurston insists that the pressure on blacks to conform to political dictates stymies creativity. The paucity of artists is proof. She cites one painter, one sculptor (Augusta Savage, whose subjects are racial, but whose work Hurston considers free of propaganda), one musician, and two writers—James Weldon Johnson and Hurston herself. Hurston's argument with the formal tradition she inherits is that it constrains "feeling that just comes." She seeks at once to replicate the freedom of the folk artist and to achieve the self reflexivity of the formal artist. Writing in the third person about her own work, Hurston cites as defining qualities its "objective point of view" and its language, which gave "verisimilitude to the narrative by stewing the subject in its own juice" (910). "Objective" is Hurston's way of expressing her commitment to artistic freedom. It marks her refusal to advance the race leader's political agenda and asserts that her refusal has made her a better writer.

In a series of essays published during the 1930s, Hurston reflected on her own artistic practices, even as she made the artistic practices of African diasporic communities a central focus of her ethnographic research. These essays reflect the wealth of metaphor and simile, the angularity, asymmetry, and originality that Hurston famously enumerates as "Characteristics of Negro Expression." No less than her fiction, they are "stewed in the juice" of their subjects. We observe in them the discursive juxtapositions that create in prose the jagged harmonies Hurston heard in the spirituals, as well as the music's polyphonic effect. At the same time, the essays demonstrate Hurston's critical reflection. They set forth her conceptions of beauty and art; they define and enact an aesthetic that lies at the core of her literary legacy.

"Jagged harmony" is the term that Hurston invents in "Spirituals and Neo-Spirituals" to convey the defining quality of the spirituals, which she contends "are not really just songs. They are unceasing variations around a theme." In her analysis, "The harmony of the true spiritual is not regular. The dissonances are important and not to be ironed out by the trained musician. The various parts break in at any old time. Falsetto often takes the place of regular voices for short periods. Keys change. Moreover, each singing of the piece is a new creation."[44] This analysis draws sharp distinctions between European American and African American music, beginning with their different understanding of harmony. In the former, harmony is defined as the combination of musical notes, either simultaneous or successive, so as to produce a pleasing effect. But when modified by the adjective "jagged," harmony loses its sense of order and its pleasing tones. Harmony becomes instead a theme around which variations are spun—variations that are as often as not "dissonant," that break in and break order at any time, that accommodate and invite ceaseless improvisation.

I want to appropriate "jagged harmonies" as a critical term for reading Hurston's essays. Rather than consistent and orderly wholes, they are variations around a theme—variations that are as often as not dissonant. "Characteristics of Negro Expression" was published originally as field notes; each section of the essay announces a variation on the ideas introduced in the opening paragraph. Within paragraphs in all of her essays, the tone of the prose may shift suddenly, as though a new voice breaks through the order. In "Folklore and Music," for example, a paragraph begins, "Folklore is the arts of the people before they find out that there is any such thing as art, and they make it out of whatever they find at hand," a statement so often repeated that it has acquired the force of received wisdom (876).[45] It is hard not to be taken aback by what comes next in the text: "Way back there when Hell wasn't no bigger than Maitland, man found out something about the laws of sound" (876). To my ear, this is one of those odd discursive juxtapositions that echo the jagged harmonies of the spirituals. The lyrics of the spirituals can shift instantly from the humorous to the transcendent and back again. "Scandalize My Name" and "Sit Down, Sister" come to mind. But the tonal shifts here come close to music.

The edges of Hurston's essays are jagged—sometimes literally. In addition to regular paragraphs, material is sometimes presented typographically with deep indentations and acute projections. As often as not, these essays end abruptly. Although fixed on the page, the absence of formal endings creates the semblance of continuation. The jagged harmonies constitute a sequence of performative moments rather than the presentation of a sustained thesis. The absence of a sustained argument is, as I have demonstrated throughout this book, a hallmark of the essay. Like those of her peers, Hurston's pieces partake of a dialogic form which strives to produce the effect of the spontaneous, the tentative, and the open-ended. But they differ in their premises, and more strikingly, in their presentation. Attending to their jagged harmonies, readers may hear and comprehend the difference.

Retrospectively, critics have used these pieces, especially "Characteristics of Negro Expression," to provide a protocol for reading Hurston's novels.[46] But we have paid inadequate attention to the formal qualities of the essays themselves. "Characteristics" is suggestive formally as well as substantively. In the stories it recounts, "Characteristics" reflects the drama to which Hurston gives priority among the elements of African American expression. The essay contains much evidence of the "will to adorn." Indeed, its profusion of metaphor and simile exist not only in the examples that are offered to support that observation but throughout the essay itself.

Drama and language are necessarily linked, as Hurston finds drama in the very words that African Americans speak. They are, she asserts, "action words," words that paint concrete pictures rather than convey abstract ideas. By way of illustration, Hurston offers the first simile in an essay that spills over with figures: "Language is like money," she writes (830). Black Americans are barterers, whose words embody their meaning. By contrast, white Americans' relationship to language is like the relationship of paper money to the items they purchase. On another level altogether, white literary artists use language like checks; their words stand in a purely abstract relation to their meaning. As she elaborates her argument, Hurston relies on the binary opposition of primitive and civilized, which substantially undermines its validity for readers today. However, as Lynda Hill notes, Hurston "displays essentialist ideas of her time while illustrating the contradictions implicit in racialist conceptions of culture."[47] Like her peers, Hurston refers to *the* Negro, which encourages readings of her work as essentialist. However, within the essay, intraracial differences are foregrounded in terms of class and gender. Geography is always a factor in Hurston's analysis as well; some of her observations are clearly specific to rural black southerners. In addition to its skillful deployment of the ironies that derive from those contradictions, "Characteristics" defers objections to its argument by the effectiveness of its address. Not only does it engage readers through its deployment of metaphor, it addresses them directly ("Who has not observed?") and indirectly ("Anyone watching Negro dancers . . .") (831, 834). In other words, the essay asks its readers to puzzle out its argument and to confirm the validity of its claims.

In the section on "angularity," for example, the essay asserts the resistance to the straight line in black vernacular culture—objects are set off at angles and dancing bodies assume angular postures. I would speculate that these are the spatial and kinetic complements to jagged harmonies. Earlier in the essay, the irregular margins in the lists of metaphors, similes, and "double descriptives" constitute jagged lines. The layout on the page also partakes of angularity. Asymmetry is another element that Hurston states is present in various modes of expression, including literature. She cites blues couplets attributed to Langston Hughes to inform the theoretical claim that the "presence of rhythm and lack of symmetry are paradoxical, but there they are" (835). In other words, the steadiness of the beat is interrupted by what later theorists call the "break" or the "cut" in the line.[48] Identifying "a rhythm of segments," Hurston argues that "each unit has a rhythm of its own, but when the whole is assembled, it is lacking in symmetry" (835). This asymmetry characterizes the essay, which is constructed in segments of varying lengths, each with its own rhythm.

Early on the essay rejects the "conventional standards" of art that obscure black people's contributions. Once the blinders imposed by those standards are removed, art is visible everywhere one looks: in the improvised performances of daily life, in the language ("the American Negro has done wonders to the English language"), in music, dance, and storytelling (831). Moreover, the essay declares, "Negro folklore is not a thing of the past. It is still in the making" (836). It then quotes two folktales: "Why de Porpoise's Tail is on Crosswise" and "Rockefeller and Ford." The former belongs to the storehouse of animal tales, but the latter is evidence of the contemporaneity of folklore. It also extends the argument with which the essay begins—that the Negro appropriates everything for his own use and through that process achieves originality. In the story the two capitalists square off: they "was woofing at each other." Rockefeller brags that he can build a solid gold road around the world. Ford replies that if he likes it, he would buy it and put one of his "tin lizzies" on it. The storytellers recognize no social distance between themselves and their subjects. They are empowered to mock the titans' pride and ambition. If Rockefeller has a godlike plan to build not streets of gold, as the spirituals imaged heaven, but a golden road that girdles the globe, Ford would bring him down to earth by purchasing his dream and then driving one of his mass-produced cars on it. The storyteller signifies on the hubris of both of his subjects.

As in *Mules and Men,* the folktales in Hurston's essays create the effect of polyphony; many voices speak. These include informants from Hurston's fieldwork, who not only tell stories but give opinions on gender relations; their voices also speak/sing the lyrics from the jook. The form of the essay invites the reader to participate as well. Consider the multiple examples and lists that occur in "Characteristics." These allow spaces for the reader to enter the text, to affirm his or her independent knowledge of the metaphors, or to provide his or her own examples of, say, double descriptives or verbal nouns. After readers have added their own evidence to Hurston's more modest claims, they are better inclined to accept her more controversial ones, as for example the Negro dancer compared to the white is the better artist, because "his dancing is realistic suggestion, and that is about all a great artist can do" (836). Or, "Musically speaking, the Jook is the most important place in America" (841). Or, "To those who want to institute the Negro theatre, let me say it is already established" (845). The truth value of these opinions is debatable, which seems to be the point. Readers are welcome to talk back.

The essay responds both to Hurston's New Negro contemporaries and to long-standing stereotypes about race and culture. It takes on the canard that the Negro lacks originality by asserting that originality is difficult to prove for any group. Then using Shakespeare as her example, Hurston suggests that the artist demonstrates genius in his "treatment of borrowed material" (838). Responding to arguments like Schuyler's that the Negro is like any other American, Hurston stakes her claim for originality by emphasizing the impact that blacks have had on American culture: "While he lives and moves in the midst of a white civilization, everything that he touches is re-interpreted for his own use. He has modified the language, mode of food preparation, practice of medicine, and most certainly the religion of his new country" (838). In this statement Hurston anticipates an agenda for research that has occupied scholars of Black Studies for the last forty years. But she ends the statement with references to Rudolph Valentino and Paul Whiteman that belong to her own time and that speak directly to the readers for whom she wrote.

As though in recognition of readers' probable resistance to her arguments, Hurston follows the section on originality with one on mimicry, two characteristics that would seem to be antithetical. "The Negro, the world over, is famous as a mimic," she declares without fear of contradiction (838). Rather than challenging conventional wisdom, she now seeks to confirm and clarify it. She emphasizes that the love for mimicry is not born of feelings of inferiority: the mimic does not copy because he feels he cannot create, he copies for the love of it. Taking a page from Hughes, she does make an exception for middle-class Negroes, who allegedly suffer from inhibiting insecurities. She then pays Hughes tribute by stating that this group does not consider him a poet because "he writes of the man in the ditch, who is more numerous and real among us than any other" (839). Such statements open both writers to the charge of racial romanticism. Ditchdiggers may have outnumbered white-collar workers, but they were hardly more real. The specific examples that follow alleviate the charge somewhat. Pulling from her ethnographic notes, Hurston recounts a scene from the field and then gives a list of dances that are based on animal imitations: the buzzard lope, walking the dog, the pig's hind legs, and so forth. The more particular her observations are, the more valid they seem. Rather than romanticizing, she is reporting. In addition, if readers find a list incomplete, they are invited, implicitly, to add their own examples.

Her experience in the field makes Hurston's insights into the form of African American religious expressive traditions particularly compelling. "Spiritual and Neo-Spirituals," like "Characteristics," was originally published in Nancy Cunard's 500-page 1934 anthology, *Negro*. Hurston begins by drawing a controversial distinction between spirituals, defined as the collective musical expression sung by believers in worship, and neo-spirituals, the written compositions based on spirituals that were performed by soloists, quartets, and choirs in concert halls in the 1920s and subsequently. "Highly flavored with Bach and Brahms, and Gregorian chants," these compositions were, in her estimation, far inferior to the originals. Hurston declares that true spirituals have never been performed to any audience anywhere. By her definition, such a performance would be impossible: no audience could exist in a performance in which everyone participated. Critics such as Hazel Carby and Paul Gilroy have taken Hurston to task because of this apparent investment in authenticity. Her perspective turns, in Gilroy's words, "on an image of the authentic folk as custodians of an essentially invariant, anti-historical notion of black particularity to which they alone somehow maintain privileged access."[49] Her stance threatens to freeze folk expression in time.

Hurston in fact acknowledges the value of the neo-spirituals arranged by Harry T. Burleigh, Rosamond Johnson, Lawrence Brown, Nathaniel Dett, Hall Johnson, and John Work, yet she proclaims, "But let no one imagine that they are the songs of the people, as sung by them" (871). Her primary concern *is* for the anonymous musicians who kept other traditions of black sacred music alive in their communities rather than on stage or on record. Yet her stance is never simplistic. While she claims a privileged access to the material, she does not write as if folk expression has calcified. Although she does not introduce a third term, she seems aware that traditional spirituals and neo-spirituals are not the sum of black sacred music. Her use of the first term is broad: "Like the folk-tales, the spirituals are being made and forgotten every day" (869). Some of these current ballads, as she calls them, are printed and sold after the services. She refers to a recent popular song that a congregation in New Orleans has retitled "He's a Mind Regulator." The title evokes a floating lyric in black sacred music, one that gives its name to a gospel song that enjoyed decades of popularity throughout the twentieth century.[50] Far from a static form, gospel music—the genre that Hurston does not name—was created in churches in the 1920s and 1930s and continues to reinvent itself in the present.[51]

Neo-spirituals, by contrast, are sung neither by nor for the folk. Through her reference to Bach and Brahms, Hurston implies that their artistic roots are European. That baldly overstates the case, but it allows Hurston to get on with the major work of the essay: its effort to identify the "standards" by which rural black Southerners judge the art they create, or at the least to substantiate the claim that "We each have our standards of art, and thus are we all interested parties and so unfit to pass judgment upon the art concepts of others."[52] In her contrast of European and Negro music, Hurston observes that Negro singing and formal speech are "breathy," while "European singing is considered good when each syllable floats out on a column of air, seeming not to have any mechanics at all. Breathing must be hidden" (871). The parable of two houses she tells to explain this contrast reflects her understanding of cultural difference, and, most profoundly, of different conceptions of beauty. Beauty for the European is a well-painted house, an object of smooth surfaces that conceals its scaffolding as well as the labor that produced it. For the Negro, the beauty of the object lies in the disclosure of the labor that went into its making—just as the singer makes audible his breaths. The beams of the house are left exposed and then decorated with "beautiful grotesques." This oxymoron anticipates her description of Brook Thompson's carvings. But, more important, it hearkens back to the opening of "Characteristics of Negro Expression," where Hurston describes a home she visited in Mobile in which a room was crowded with overstuffed furniture, its walls papered with Sunday supplements of the local newspaper and decorated with seven calendars and three wall pockets, one of which was finished with a lace doily. Every surface of the room was adorned. Hurston characterizes the effect as "grotesque," but if that is what she sees, it is not what she perceives. Contemplating the meaning of decorating a decoration, she concludes, "The feeling back of such an act is that there can never be enough of beauty, let alone too much" (834).

In "Spirituals and Neo-Spirituals," the quest for beauty manifests itself in the essay's reflection on the meaning of the prayer ritual in southern black churches. Hurston asserts that black people regard all religious expression as art, by which she seems to mean that they hold in high esteem those who are able to express their faith artfully. They place the highest value on the beauty of religious expression. In Hurston's view, that beauty is undeniable and profound. She does not hesitate to declare, "Nothing outside of the Old Testament is as rich in figure as a Negro prayer. Some instances are unsurpassed anywhere in literature" (873).[53] Having provided this point of comparison with which her all of her readers are familiar, she presents details of the practice to which those outside the community she depicts would not be privy. While, for example, the prayer may strike the outsider as extemporaneous, such a view is in error. Hurston insists that the prayer follows a formal pattern. As ritual, it is introduced by a hymn. The "prayer artist" is then compelled to create a dramatic setting, by calling attention to the physical situation he shares with his auditors. The interpolation of all or parts of the Lord's Prayer is required, as are the pauses in which the congregation is invited to interject a response. During what Hurston designates the *accelerando* passage, however, the audience takes no part. The prayer artist creates his individual petition. Lest the reader doubt the quality of the artistic performance, Hurston introduces another comparison that challenges any sense of artistic hierarchy the reader may harbor. A response from the audience during this passage "would be like applauding in the middle of a solo at the Metropolitan." As the performance reaches its climax, the artist "adorns" the prayer. Listeners sit in rapt attention: "nobody wants to miss a syllable" (873).

Rather than quoting examples here, as she does for instance in *Mules and Men*, Hurston invents a figure of her own. It partakes of the tentativeness that I attribute to the essay and dares the knowledgeable reader to invent a better figure. It extends moreover the musical metaphors on which the essay has relied, and it offers in conclusion an inscription of the spirit of the worship/artistic experience as a whole. "The best figure that I can think of," Hurston writes, "is that the prayer is an obligato over and above the harmony of the assembly" (874). Her humility is misplaced. The figure not only illuminates the function of the prayer ritual; it theorizes Hurston's concept of the individual artist's relationship to the group. According to the Oxford English Dictionary (OED), "obligato" is a musical figure essential to the completeness of a composition. It is an accompaniment that whether sung or played on an instrument has an independent value. Hurston's metaphor fuses the musical figure that alludes to the elements of performance she describes with the idea of religious duty or obligation. The prayer affirms the spirit of harmony, here meaning the spirit of one accord, the goal of religious worship. "Assembly" denotes a gathering of persons for religious worship or a congregation. As it rises above the assembly, the voice of the artist is distinct from, yet dependent on, the collective.

The metaphor sheds light on Hurston's impatience with the singers of neo-spirituals. It is due less to their proper diction and formal attire or even the relative lack of improvisation in their performances than it is to the absence of the congregation that could affirm their value. Hurston's conception of the artist's role partakes of traditions of West African performance in which the performer is one with the audience. Yet the prayer artist retains a significant degree of individuality, which is heightened when his voice is heard against the sustained response of the congregation. In this regard the prayer artist is in a privileged position. It contrasts sharply to the self-representation of Hurston as artist in "How It Feels to Be Colored Me," the child Zora "speaking pieces" and alienated from her neighbors, or the adult Zora in the New World cabaret, whose racial identity stands out against a white background but whose individual voice is muted in a pattern that evokes slavery's legacy. At the conclusion of "Spirituals and Neo-Spirituals," Hurston sets forth an ideal that she as a writer did not—indeed, could not—achieve. Although she was both the conduit of collective memory and a singular talent, the assembly that was her audience too rarely affirmed her song.

Hurston expresses metaphorically a central dilemma for New Negro artists—the absence of a supportive audience. If it were true, as Walt Whitman proclaimed, that "without great audiences we cannot have great poets," the writers of the Harlem Renaissance were in trouble from the start. In 1928, James Weldon Johnson published an essay on "The Dilemma of the Negro Author" in *American Mercury*, a dilemma he described as "the problem of the double audience."[54] On the one hand, the white American audience expected to encounter familiar racial stereotypes in writing by blacks. That was hardly surprising, since according to Johnson more than 99 percent of the material "written about the Negro in the United States in three centuries" conformed to one of these. Whites were unwilling to overcome their prejudices and engage stories about middle-class blacks, black heroes, or black people in love.[55] In addition, whites rejected black artists who contradicted their expectations. For that reason they had rejected Roland Hayes's performances of European art songs and insisted that he sing spirituals. Black audiences posed the other horn of the dilemma, because they wanted to see only heroic images of themselves. Anything less than complimentary was taboo. And, while Johnson expressed understanding of this desire, the result was to take "the solid ground from under the feet of the Negro writer and leave him suspended" (44). The solution was to fuse the two audiences, but that solution was far off—so far off that Johnson lost his customary eloquence as he tried to describe it. He refers twice to the absence of "a way out." In the end the struggle to achieve a common audience becomes "a third horn" of the Negro writer's dilemma.

In "Negro Artists and the Negro," Wallace Thurman loses his temper. Published in the *New Republic* on August 31, 1927, the essay rants against the failure of black audiences to support black artists. Taking a page from Schuyler, Thurman, who was a journalist and editor and soon-to-be playwright and novelist, mocks the attention paid to the "Negro art fad."[56] But unlike Schuyler's, Thurman's impatience does not arise from the *idea* of Negro art; he is disappointed in the artist's failure to achieve its potential. He expresses little surprise that whites have moved on to something else; instead his ire is directed at blacks who were torn between pride in members of the group achieving recognition and dismay that what they were recognized for was not wholly respectable. "The Negro artist," he concludes, "will receive little aid from his own people unless he spends his time spouting sociological jeremiads or exhausts his talent in building rosy castles around Negro society" (111).

As a consequence, Thurman asserts, the New Negro artist experienced a quick rise, but an equally swift fall. His first example is Hughes. If *The Weary Blues* raised eyebrows, Hughes's second volume, *Fine Clothes to the Jew* (1927), provoked righteous indignation. Thurman quotes one of its most controversial poems that begins "Put on yo' red silk stockings/Black gal" and evokes images of prostitution and miscegenation. It is little wonder that the black establishment was not pleased. Thurman's second example hits even closer to home. He quotes the angriest attack on *Fire!! A Quarterly Devoted to the Younger Negro Artists*, without disclosing that he was the journal's editor. The reviewer's attack, "I have just tossed the first issue of *Fire*—into the fire, and watched the cackling flames leap and snarl as though they were trying to swallow some repulsive dose," seems wildly extreme, especially when contrasted to Thurman's explication of the journal's aesthetic. Like Hughes's poetry, *Fire!!* "was experimental and purely artistic in intention and conception" (109). Rather than the bourgeoisie, the magazine's contributors turned to the proletariat for characters and material. "Proletariat" is a more ideologically specific word than Thurman's peers used, but he sounds much like Hughes when he refers to "people who still retained some individual race qualities and who were not totally white American in every respect save color or skin" (109).

The phrase "individual race qualities," like "racial individuality," sounds paradoxical, though Thurman seems to refer to those individuals—who constitute the masses or proletariat—who are culturally black. The rub, of course, was that the masses did not buy books. Blacks who did, mainly the bourgeoisie, preferred the same kind of art as their white counterparts. As Thurman acknowledged, those whites protested the work of writers such as Dreiser, Anderson, and Sandburg, whose representations failed to endorse their readers' high opinions of themselves. Like Johnson, Thurman does concede the extra difficulty that bourgeois blacks face, because they are so vulnerable to what whites think of them. However, the backhanded compliment he uses to press the point would have done little to win favor with the group: "The American scene dictates that the American Negro must be what he ain't" (111). The reality was that the vast majority of blacks were neither middle class nor book buyers, but the writers of the Harlem Renaissance had reason to pretend they were. Thurman offers a critical survey of the work that resulted; he is, as always, unstinting in his judgment of his peers.

Having begun on a note of ridicule, the essay ends on a note of hope. Within a very few years, the "Negro art 'renaissance'" had reached a state of near sanity." The outsized optimism of "The New Negro" and "Negro Youth Speaks" was gone. Thurman takes a more realistic measure: "Genius is a rare quality in this world, and there is no reason why it should be more ubiquitous among Blacks than Whites" (113). Locke would have doubtless concurred. He might also have concluded that he had won the argument that he had engaged. It was not, after all, that there were *more* black geniuses than white, but that the term "black genius" was not an oxymoron.

If that argument had been settled, the questions it generated about the existence of a racial art, the importance of cultural differences, the definition of aesthetic standards, and the identity of the audience for whom the black artist should create would continue to reverberate throughout the twentieth century. Each succeeding generation would be compelled to respond. The answers that James Baldwin, Ralph Ellison, Amiri Baraka, and Alice Walker devised owe much to the essays on art and such that their predecessors published in the 1920s and 1930s. Whether or not these later writers embraced or rejected Locke's intellectual detachment, Hughes's fiery polemic, Schuyler's acerbic satire, or Hurston's jagged harmonies, they contended with their example. Along with their peers, these pioneers had demonstrated that they could not only use the essay as a medium for aesthetic debates, they could create essays that enacted the aesthetic they proposed.

CHAPTER FOUR

Stranger at Home

James Baldwin on What It Means to Be an American

"It is a complex fate to be an American," Henry James observed, and the principal discovery an American writer makes in Europe is just how complex this fate is. America's history, her aspirations, her peculiar triumphs, her even more peculiar defeats, and her position in the world—yesterday and today—are all so stubbornly profound and stubbornly unique that the very word "America" remains a new, almost completely undefined and extremely controversial proper noun.

—James Baldwin, "The Discovery of What It Means to Be an American"

If I had-a my way, I'd tear this building down.

—Spiritual

My title alludes of course to two of Baldwin's most famous essays, "Stranger in the Village" and "The Discovery of What It Means to Be an American." In the former, the last essay in *Notes of a Native Son* and one of his most eloquent meditations on identity, Baldwin reflects on a sojourn in a Swiss village where by virtue of phenotype and culture, he is a stranger. Against that white landscape to the accompaniment of Bessie Smith's blues, he begins to recreate and embrace the life he had known as a child at home. Reflecting on his native land, however, he claims the status of citizen, not stranger. The second allusion is to "The Discovery of What It Means to Be an American," published in the *New York Times Book Review* in 1959, and the lead essay of his second volume, *Nobody Knows My Name*. Baldwin posed the question of what it means to be an American repeatedly across his career. During the 1950s, his answers frequently deploy a rhetorical approach that I call "strategic American exceptionalism." As the first epigraph above confirms, despite the fact that he writes always to resist the "myth of America" to which Americans "cling so desperately" (139), Baldwin's rhetoric could resonate with that of numerous pro-U.S. Cold War intellectuals.

By the time he wrote *No Name in the Street* (1972), Baldwin recognized the error, the futility of adopting this rhetorical strategy. As he so often did, he turned to the repository of the past. "If I had-a my way, I'd tear this building down" is an epigraph to "Take Me to the Water," the extended essay that opens *No Name in the Street*.[1] Always conscious of the ways that people of the world were dominated by U.S. political and economic power, he records in his essays the process by which that consciousness grew keener as the events of the 1960s played out in Africa and Asia as well as in the United States. In *No Name in the Street*, he maps some of the journeys he has taken and finds himself, more profoundly than ever before, a stranger at home.

Baldwin's career was launched on the cusp of the Cold War. Its politics necessarily shaped the reception of his work and doubtless the work itself. In and out of the academy, U.S. intellectuals were proposing ever grander versions of the uniqueness of the United States. Such ideas could be traced back to John Winthrop's "city on the hill," through Emerson and Whitman to scholars Lewis Mumford and F. O. Matthiessen in the 1920s and 1930s. But during the 1950s scholars enshrined the tenet of American exceptionalism in journals, academic monographs, and in the new discipline of American Studies. As Michael Denning has written, "American studies which had taken shape in the early years of the Cold War, had become—despite the intentions of some of its intellectual founders—a part of what might be called 'the American ideology' of the age of three worlds: the deep sense of the exceptionalism of this 'people of plenty,' the unquestioned virtue of democracy and 'the American way of life,' and the sense that the world was entering an American century."[2] I do not quarrel with Denning's observation that in comparison to American Studies, British cultural studies, which was a contemporary development, has been more influential because, in part, it asked the question "What is culture?" rather than "What is an American?" I would insist, however, that for Baldwin the latter question was productive, not least because, as his characterization of America as "an extremely controversial proper noun" confirms, Baldwin's view of America always implied a critique.[3] His texts contravene the representations of Americans as "people of plenty" and dispute the legitimacy of U.S. democracy. Always cosmopolitan, Baldwin answers the question in light of his experiences in a larger world. But he claims the uniqueness of his American identity consciously and with a particular purpose.

What I call Baldwin's strategic American exceptionalism is analogous to what Gayatri Spivak defines in another context as "a *strategic* use of positivist essentialism in a scrupulously visible political interest."[4] That is, like the scholars of Subaltern Studies who adopt strategic essentialism, Baldwin makes a purposeful and strategic use of American exceptionalism to advance the scrupulously visible political interest of African Americans, indeed, of Americans in general. He adopts this rhetoric partly in order to be heard, but also because it conforms to his belief in the democratic ideals set forth in the founding documents of the United States.

In the tradition of African American intellectuals from the early nine-teenth century forward, Baldwin affirms the nation's democratic principles. From David Walker's *Appeal* to Frederick Douglass in "What to the Slave Is the Fourth of July?" to Anna Julia Cooper's *A Voice from the South* to Martin Luther King Jr.'s "Letter from Birmingham Jail," black activist intellectuals have used the oppression of African Americans to indict and shame a nation whose actions contradict its principles.

Yet, while Baldwin extends this genealogy and affirms the democratic ide-als enunciated in the letters of the republic, he repudiates in particular the myths and illusions of the American exceptionalism proposed by American Studies scholars. In "Nobody Knows My Name," he asserts that the American dream has become the American illusion that material prosperity makes America the envy of the world.[5] He has no use for the myth of the American Adam, who in his innocence takes dominion over all he surveys. He rejects the long-standing dichotomy of American innocence and European experi-ence, by arguing that the failure of his countrymen is the failure to acknowl-edge the burden of their own bloody history.[6] He mocks the myth of America as a classless society, when he contends that "it is easier to cut across social and occupational lines" in Europe.[7]

What *is* unique about the United States in Baldwin's view is the presence of black people and the challenge that their presence poses to Americans' sense of the nation and of themselves. This concern does not reflect a provin-cial point of view. Baldwin was always aware of the connections between Eu-rope and the United States and noted that the principles of democracy of which Americans were so proud were in fact the legacy of European thinkers. The larger question that the American experience raises is whether such a thing as a multiracial democracy is possible. Though he writes in "Stranger in the Village" that "one of the things that distinguishes Americans from other people is that no other people has ever been so deeply involved in the lives of black men and vice versa," the implications were not for Americans alone (129). He ends the essay with one of his most prophetic declarations—"This world is white no longer, and it will never be white again"—a declaration that fore-tells not only the emergence of postcolonial nations but the emergence of a multiracial Europe.[8]

What sets Baldwin's critique further apart is that the political indictment of the failure of the United States to live out its own political creed is just his starting point; his argument with America is ultimately personal. In "Notes for a Hypothetical Novel," he contends, "But to try and find out what Ameri-cans mean is almost impossible because there are so many things they do not want to face. And not only the Negro thing which is simply the most obvious and perhaps the simplest example, but on the level of private life which is after all where we have to get to in order to write about anything and also the level we have to get to in order to live, it seems to me that the myth, the illusion, that this is a free country, for example, is disastrous."[9] The fixation on race prevents whites from confronting their individual fears; they hide behind the nation's myths. Baldwin was committed to deconstructing these myths and redefining what it means to be an American. But he was equally committed to figuring out what his personal responsibility as an American was.

Indeed, unlike most black writers before him, Baldwin was as rigorous in judging his individual stance as a moral agent as he was the morality of the nation state. He calculated the cost of white supremacy in starkly personal terms. Without the veil of fiction, few other black writers had been as willing to lay bare family secrets or the secrets of their own hearts, the self- hatred as well as the love. Baldwin's purpose was hardly to write advertisements for himself, though his example enabled his white peers, including Norman Mailer, to write more explicitly out of their personal experiences than American writers before them had done. Baldwin sought rather to explore the nexus between his individual experiences and social reality. The tour de force title essay "Notes of a Native Son" set the standard for his art, as it mapped the despair and rage of Harlem alongside the mental map of Baldwin's grief and rage over the death of his father. It initiates the "troubled eloquence" that would become his signature.

To borrow Theodor Adorno's terms, Baldwin's essays think in fragments, "just as reality is fragmentary" and find "their unity in and through the breaks."[10] The social reality that Baldwin addressed grew more fragmentary over the course of his career. As he responded to it, Baldwin stretched the form of the essay. His early essays are more tightly structured: they reach conclusions that are never predictable, yet always seem both earned and apt. As he takes up more rancorous and more explicitly political questions, the style of the essays grows looser and more expansive. "Letter from a Region in My Mind," the longer essay of *The Fire Next Time*, runs 20,000 words. The two parts of *No Name in the Street* constitute a book. Yet despite their length, the sensibility that animates these writings is consistent with the earlier pieces. The larger the topic, the more the questions open out to other questions. The range of response widens. Voices other than Baldwin's speak. But, in part, because these essays always begin "with the questions one asks oneself," they retain the semblance of private truth-telling that accounts for so much of their power.[11]

The hybridity of the essay makes it capacious enough to incorporate other genres. A fiction writer, Baldwin frequently interpolates stories in his essays. Some of his most memorable—the story of the purloined bed sheet and of the dinner at the home of Elijah Muhammad, for example—are told in essays. Such stories bump up against literary and political critique, memoir and reportage. "In the essay," Adorno asserts, "discrete elements set off against one another come together to form a readable context; the essay erects no scaffolding and no structure. But the elements crystallize as a configuration through their motion. The constellation is a force field, just as every intellectual structure is necessarily transformed into a force field under the essay's gaze."[12] The intellectual structure of Americanness is a recurrent force field in Baldwin's essays.

Even at the level of the sentence Baldwin qualifies, complicates, and recalibrates his ideas. His periodic sentences allow him to draw ever finer distinctions between histories, experiences, and individuals. In "A Question of Identity," for example, he invokes the American past. "The truth about that past is not that it is too brief, or too superficial, but only that we, having turned our faces so resolutely away from it, have never demanded from it what it has to give."[13] Or, to take another example, as he writes of love in "Notes of a Native Son," "one is absolutely forced to make perpetual qualifications and one's own reactions are always canceling each other out."[14] These elegant sentences invite comparison to Henry James, a comparison Baldwin encouraged. The title *Notes of a Native Son* invokes the title of James's childhood memoir, *Notes on a Son and Brother*, as well as Richard Wright's novel. In *No Name in the Street*, Baldwin credits James with having taught him how to survive in Paris (377).[15] Beyond the transatlantic themes and survival lessons, however, the more important legacy that Baldwin inherits from James is the valorization of individual experience and the premium to be placed on interiority. Moreover, as a homosexual, Baldwin, like James, was acutely conscious of the ways that codes of masculinity stunted the development of American men's interior lives.[16] His prose—with its layered elaborations of feelings as well as ideas—repudiates a conception of manhood as well as a conception of literary style, specifically the hardboiled style popularized in the 1940s by James Cain and Raymond Chandler as well as by Wright. In "Preservation of Innocence," the second essay that Baldwin published after moving to Paris, he wrote a defense of homosexuality that used the misogyny of Cain's and Chandler's fiction to argue that the debasement of the homosexual indicated American culture's debasement of sexuality in general.[17]

Baldwin's essays also express and enact the "will to adorn." His earliest pieces argue for a revised literary aesthetic. When he weighs the consequences of Wright's decision to limit the narrative perspective in *Native Son* to the disfigured consciousness of the protagonist, Bigger Thomas, Baldwin argues that it cuts away a "necessary dimension," that is the "relationship that Negroes bear to one another, that depth of involvement and unspoken recognition of shared experience which creates a way of life."[18] As many critics have noted, the catalog of elements that make up that way of life, or culture, echoes the famous catalog of elements that James identified as lacking in American life.[19] Even as he deploys negation—"no tradition, no field of manners, no possibility of ritual or intercourse," Baldwin emphasizes presence rather than absence in his contemplation of Negro life. In his essays as well as his fiction, he desires to inscribe that presence in the literary text.

Significantly "Many Thousands Gone," the essay in which Baldwin makes this critique, opens with an assertion that he would amplify frequently in his writing:

> It is only in his music, which Americans are able to admire because a protective sentimentality limits their understanding of it, that the Negro has been able to tell his story. It is a story which otherwise has yet to be told and which no American is prepared to hear. As is the inevitable result of things unsaid, we find ourselves until today oppressed with a dangerous and reverberating silence; and the story is told, compulsively, in symbols and signs, in hieroglyphics; it is revealed in Negro speech and in that of the white majority and in their different frames of reference (19).

Baldwin's belief that the truth of black people's history in America had been best conveyed through music rather than words was not original. One traces it back to W. E. B. Du Bois in *The Souls of Black Folk*, who held that the "sorrow songs," "the most beautiful expression of human experience born this side the seas," documented the unwritten history of slavery. The silent bars of music that serve as epigraphs to the essays in *Souls* may be read as hieroglyphs that stand in for the voices that cannot speak through Du Bois's text. Sensual and abstract, these signs withhold as much as they convey. In his 1845 *Narrative*, Douglass anticipated Du Bois as well as Baldwin when he asserted that "the mere hearing of those songs would do more to impress some minds with the horrible character of slavery, than the reading of whole volumes of philosophy on the subject could do.... Every tone was a testimony against slavery, and a prayer to God for deliverance from chains." Douglass professed to have been shocked later to discover that white Northerners thought the slaves' music was "happy."[20] More than a century later, Baldwin responded to the same willful misunderstanding. He borrowed his title from the spiritual,

"No More Auction Block," that is at once a declaration of resistance and a lament "for the many thousands gone." For Baldwin black music is a metaphor
for the unspeakable: what cannot be said both because it is too painful or too
dangerous to express in words and because no one could hear or understand
the words if they could be found. One of Baldwin's goals is to fashion a prose
that can speak across this silence.

He frequently interpolates lines from the storehouse of spirituals and
blues to deepen his meaning and to adorn his prose. As he pointed out in his
speeches, for black Americans spirituals and sermons "had less to do with the
Old Testament than they had to do with our daily life," an observation that
would have resonated with Zora Neale Hurston, who emphasized the drama
of everyday life that was the bedrock of African American expressive culture.[21] As he famously wrote about the performances of the storefront church,
"there is no drama like that drama." For her part, Hurston identified the will
to adorn with the profusion of metaphor, a rhetorical excess that bespeaks
"the feeling that there can never be enough of beauty, let alone too much."[22]
Baldwin shares that penchant for rhetorical excess. Even in the blues, where
the rhetorical mode is more often understatement, the function of the language is to call attention to itself, to perform its state of controlled despair.
But as drawn as he was to the poetic profundity of these oral texts, Baldwin
claimed a range of literary precursors, several of whom would supply the "different frames of reference" that both white and black readers could decode.

Sussing out his influences in the introduction to *Notes of a Native Son*,
Baldwin omits James but identifies the "King James Bible, the rhetoric of the
store-front church, something ironic and violent and perpetually understated
in Negro speech—and something of Dickens' love for bravura."[23] Baldwin's
essays move across these discursive registers—the transcendent rhetoric of
the pulpit, the biting irony of the blues, a complex pattern of figures that recalls James, bravura storytelling that is Dickensian—to produce a style so rich
and distinctive that the Irish novelist Colm Tóibín deems him "the most eloquent man in the America of his time."[24]

Baldwin begins "The Discovery of What It Means to Be an American"
with a quotation from James. He concludes with the statement, "the interior
life is a real life, and the intangible dreams of people have a tangible effect on
the world" (142), a statement that James would have endorsed. Baldwin
shapes his expression of interiority with a prose style that looks back to the
King James Bible as well as to James. But his understanding of the "tangible"
effects of dreams is both his inheritance—that is, the legacy of his racialized
history in the United States, as expressed through the visionary rhetoric of

African American sermons and the laconic ironies of the blues—and the birthright that is his by virtue of being human.[25] The conflict and complementarity between his inheritance and his birthright combine to produce Baldwin's "troubled eloquence."

On the one hand, "Stranger in the Village" holds open the possibility, however distant, of Baldwin individually and of black Americans collectively achieving the status of American citizens. At the same time, the essay uses the words "stranger," "awe," and "wonder" as riffs to sound variations on the theme of the existential homelessness of the African American subject. These strong words name Baldwin's alienation. They sit uneasily next to subjunctive formulations and other expressions of tentativeness ("I suppose," "I am told," "possibly," "presumably") that invite the reader to identify with that alienation. Baldwin has no status apart from stranger. Even as he wears an African face—which the Swiss use to place him—Baldwin recognizes that it is his Americanness that renders him without a place either in Europe or at home. He introduces the idea in the opening paragraph, when he posits that only his status as an American makes it impossible for him to have imagined a place where no one had ever seen a black man. As the essay unfolds, he works through the implications of what his status as a stranger means to the people of the village and more profoundly what his status as a stranger means to him. It ends by reflecting on the ways that his status renders a judgment on his countrymen.

Baldwin's blackness threatens to negate the fact that his experience of the world far exceeds that of the villagers. He is, after all, an American who has traveled to Europe, whereas the Swiss have never left their isolated hamlet. He lists the institutions the village lacks ("no movie house, no bank, no library, no theater") and enumerates the few technological inventions that constitute its purchase on modernity ("very few radios, one jeep, one station wagon" and the one typewriter that he has brought with him). Even the village's modest reputation as a sort of "lesser Lourdes" identifies it with a premodern past. Yet, its residents have the power to render Baldwin an object of curiosity—not unlike the pilgrims who seek the village's healing water.

Of course, Baldwin's only disability is his color. Frequent references to "awe" "astonishment," and "phenomenon" are all occasioned by his race. He becomes "a living wonder" due to his hair and skin color. He recognizes that the power of his physical presence to evoke fear, dread, and amazement prevents him from being perceived as human. What makes Baldwin unable to dismiss the villagers' response as ignorance is the way it resonates with his experience in America. Although it carries no malice and is meant as simple description, "*Neger*" in the village of Loèche-aux-Bains sounds too much like "Nigger" on the streets of New York City. In both places Baldwin is treated as a "stranger," although he insists that he cannot actually be a stranger in America.

"Stranger" denotes historically "one who belongs to another country, a foreigner," now chiefly "one who resides or comes to a country to which he is a foreigner, an alien" (OED). In the village Baldwin is also, according to another definition, a guest or visitor who is in his case the friend of the son of a woman who owns a home there. Moreover, he is, according to a further definition, "an unknown person; a person whom one has not seen before." This meaning is complicated by Baldwin's acknowledgment that he remains as much a stranger during his second extended sojourn in the village as he was during the first. Familiarity does nothing to close the social distance between him and the household of his host. Even though the villagers all know his name, he remains an outsider. Their preoccupation with his hair and phenotype points toward another definition, one that captures the situation of African Americans on both sides of the Atlantic: "a person not of one's kin; more fully *stranger in the blood*" (OED).

Not only do the stares and physical touching confirm Baldwin's status as stranger in the village, so does his response to the annual Lenten ritual of "buying" supposedly pagan Africans in order to ensure their Christian conversion. Two villagers play the role of the Africans by blackening their faces; the blue eyes that stare out of their blackened faces heighten the social distance between the Europeans and their black American guest. Baldwin, whose account of the ritual begins with the passive construction "I am told," soon begins to describe a situation he has not witnessed. He feels compelled to identify with the African "natives," to whom he is racially bound. As he ponders that identification, he imagines the Europeans who first arrived as "strangers" in African villages who take the Africans' "astonishment as tribute." The Europeans never doubt their superiority to their African hosts.

Baldwin does not query whether or not the Africans might have taken their equality for granted, especially since they would have been unacquainted with the centuries of Western civilization that he argues undergird the Europeans' belief in their supremacy. Instead he lists the names on which this belief depends—Dante, Shakespeare, Michelangelo, Da Vinci, Rembrandt—as if their very invocation proves the point.[26] Like James Weldon Johnson before him, Baldwin assumes that the power of culture is preeminent. Economic and military might do not figure in the equation. In Baldwin's imagining, Africans had no names to counter the weight of European civilization.[27] He never considers the possibility that Africans might have had their own sources of cultural capital. For at the moment that Baldwin imagines his identification with Africans, he writes out of his profound sense of personal estrangement, both in Europe and at home. It is surely his projection that the villagers "move with an authority which I shall never have," that they "cannot be, from the point of view of power, strangers anywhere in the world" (121). Although he attributes that authority to their cultural inheritance and political power, the passage turns more on Baldwin's sense of his own lack of authority. That lack stems from his experience in the United States, where he has been treated as a *stranger in the blood* by those to whom he is in fact kin.

This treatment is the source of the rage the essay explores. The rage is directed at the stereotypes that whites invent in order to preserve their distance from blacks. The rage is directed at the history of slavery, which has rendered the African American "unique among the black men of the world in that his past was taken from him" (124). Baldwin's appropriation of the thesis associated with E. Franklin Frazier that black Americans were completely severed from any past in Africa may also account for his disinclination to imagine in any depth the response of Africans in their initial encounter with Europeans. For Baldwin, the identity of African Americans is tied not to an African past but to the history of their ancestors' enslavement in the United States. Saidiya Hartman's observation is suggestive here: "The most universal definition of the slave is a stranger. Torn from kin and community, exiled from one's country, dishonored and violated, the slave defines the position of the outsider. She is the perpetual outcast, the coerced migrant, the foreigner, the shamefaced child in the lineage."[28] Hartman writes as well that "stranger is the placeholder for the missing, the mark of the passage, the scar between native and citizen" (8). This last offers the most compelling connection to Baldwin's essay, a text that Hartman invokes but does not discuss. For as Baldwin rejects the identification with the African "native" whose soul is at risk, he embraces the status of citizen that his countrymen continue to withhold.

The essay's rage is directed finally at the relationship between whites and blacks in the United States: a relationship that white Americans insist is marked by unfamiliarity and otherness. By contrast, American blacks are certain that they know whites better than whites know themselves. Ultimately, Baldwin insists that the difference between *Neger* and nigger is the difference between unfamiliarity or strangeness on the one hand and contempt on the other. Emerging from behind his own mask of blackness in the essay, Baldwin is the figure he describes as the human being who "begins to make himself felt" and who at that moment "cannot escape a certain awful wonder as to what kind of human being it is" (123). In other words, he turns the sense of wonder that has objectified him in the eyes of the Swiss and to a considerable extent in his own eyes onto his newly realized self.

Almost from the beginning of the essay until the end, Baldwin seems hesitant to draw conclusions from the experiences he recounts. In the first paragraph he suggests that his Americanness clouded his perception: "It did not occur to me—possibly because I am an American—that there could be people anywhere who had never seen a Negro" (117). As the essay develops, it recounts experiences that restore Baldwin's individual perception and ultimately yield insight into the U.S. nation's condition. But, in part, because those insights are both personally painful and politically controversial, the essayist seems loath to express them. In the next to the last paragraph, he offers judgments that are substantively damning but stated with a restraint that seems almost tantamount to regret: "I do not think, for example, that it is too much to suggest that the American vision of the world," which is characterized by a willful innocence and a Manichean morality, "owes a great deal to the battle waged by Americans to maintain between themselves and black men a human separation which could not be bridged" (128). The innocence that is in other readings at the heart of an American vision characterized by its sense of its own exceptionalism is here the seed of its potential destruction. The essay moves out of its subjunctive mood at the end, when it restates as fact the possibility broached here. Finally, it shifts to a more positive conclusion that, as the result of America's interracial history, this nation among all nations is best prepared to lead the way to a multiracial future.

No single event could have sharpened Baldwin's sense of himself as a black *American* or troubled his notion of a hierarchical relation between Europeans and Africans more profoundly than the September 1956 Congress of Negro-African Writers and Artists (*Le Congrès des Ecrivains et Artistes Noirs*). Under the shadow of the Cold War, the conference followed in the wake of Bandung, the first conference of nonaligned nations, held in Indonesia in April 1955. At Bandung, leaders of what became known as the Third World sought to position themselves in neither the Western sphere, led by the United States, nor the Eastern sphere, led by the Soviet Union. Now African and Africa diaspora intellectuals assembled to debate the prospects for freedom as the era of colonial rule came to an end. (Ghana would become the first African nation to achieve its independence from Britain in 1957.) Baldwin was keenly aware of the ironies of a meeting focused on the challenges and problems of mainly colonized black folk taking place in the imperial city of Paris, the site of the power that subjugated many of those gathered in the halls of the Sorbonne;

the French government kept a close watch on the proceedings. He was aware as well of the paradoxical situation of the black Americans, who though nominally "free," lived under a strict system of segregation in the United States.

When he described the conference in "Princes and Powers," published in *Encounter* the following year, Baldwin made it clear that his role was as observer, not participant. While impressed by the African and West Indian intellectuals assembled—including Aimé Césaire, Alioune Diop, George Lamming, Jean Price-Mars, and Léopold Senghor—he did not identify with them or with their concerns.[29] Nor did he associate himself with the black American intellectuals present—neither the official U.S. delegation including Horace Bond (father of Julian), Mercer Cook, and John Davis, or the self-appointed Richard Wright, who gave one of the major speeches.[30] (The U.S. State Department refused to issue Du Bois a passport.) Wright's advocacy of a "third way" might have appealed to Baldwin had someone other than his nemesis expressed it and had Wright been better able to refine his terms. Baldwin stood apart, defining himself against this stellar array of black male intellectuals—no women spoke—who were his potential peers.[31]

Baldwin had earlier reflected on the interactions between black Americans and Africans in Paris in "Encounter on the Seine: Black Meets Brown." That essay emphasizes the alienation black Americans experienced in Europe; few in number to begin with, they isolated themselves from each other. But the gap between them is nothing compared to the "gulf of three hundred years" that separates the American Negro and the African. This alienation is "too vast to be conquered in an evening's good-will, too heavy and too double-edged ever to be trapped in speech."[32] Encountering the African in Europe, Baldwin asserts, persuades the black American that he is "a hybrid." Not only is his racial ancestry mixed, so too is his cultural heritage. Baldwin then revises Du Bois, who represents his persona in *Souls* as "bone of the bone and flesh of the flesh" of black folk. In Baldwin's rephrasing, the black American is bone of the bone and flesh of the flesh of white Americans: "they have loved and hated and obsessed and feared each other and his blood is in their soil. Therefore he cannot deny them, nor can they ever be divorced" (89). In contrast to "Encounter on the Seine," "Princes and Powers" suggests that black Americans and Africans *can* bridge the alleged gulf that separates them. Over the days of the conference, they communicate despite the lack of a common language. The essay reveals Baldwin's simultaneous attraction and resistance to forging a common purpose.

From the beginning of the essay Baldwin underscores the exceptionalism of the black American. He contends, "The American Negro is possibly the only man of color who can speak of the West with real authority, whose experience, painful as it is, also proves the vitality of the so transgressed Western ideals" (146). As in "Stranger in the Village," Baldwin seems unable to conceive of an authority that is not derived from Western culture. Neither does he question the worth of Western ideals; he protests the fact that they have not been realized. Presumably, no one is more aware of the gap between the ideals and the reality than the black American, and consequently no one is a more fervent advocate for them. This can only be inferred, however, since the passage does not name the specific ideals at issue. As the essay gradually reveals, individual freedom is foremost among them.

This priority underlies his criticism of the Du Bois controversy. Baldwin laments the fact that Du Bois in a message to the Congress not only protests his unjust treatment by the U.S. government, he urges the conferees to adopt the example of the U.S.S.R. In Baldwin's view, the injustice of Du Bois's situation gives his words undue sway and undermines the influence of the U.S. delegation. Baldwin argues that black Americans were born into a society that is both open and free—not free of racism, but free of the weight of tradition. Both Europeans and Africans labor under that weight. Moreover, Africans bear the psychological brunt of having been invaded and needing to overthrow "the machinery of the oppressor." Black Americans, by contrast, want that machinery to work for them. Although Baldwin would later reject this formulation, here it anchors his endorsement of those elusive Western ideals. Notably, while conference speakers like Lamming use "we" to refer to Africans, the "we" with which Baldwin identifies in "Princes and Power" is always Americans—whites and/or blacks.

Yet even as Baldwin constructs this "we," he positions himself outside it. His disaffiliation with Wright is telling. Wright asserts that there is "a painful contradiction in being at once a Westerner and a black man." He argues, in terms that echo the rationale for both Bandung and the Congress of Negro-African Writers and Artists, for a third point of view. That view acknowledges the interconnectedness among religion, tradition, and imperialism in Western history, but in what Wright perceives as an unintended consequence, Europeans brought the Enlightenment to Africa. Colonialism was in fact "liberating" for Africans because "it smashed old traditions and destroyed old gods" (163). With characteristic understatement, Baldwin judges Wright's conclusion that "'what was good for Europe was good for all mankind'... a tactless way of phrasing a debatable idea" (164). Baldwin also parries a few more satirical thrusts, as when he reports that Wright announced having written his paper on his farm in Normandy and recounts Wright's surprise that the conferees did not share his view of the benefits of colonialism. In both instances, Wright reveals how far out of touch he is with those he would persuade. But Baldwin's real argument with his one-time mentor is that, for Baldwin, Europe is not the post-Enlightenment society it appears. It remains trapped in its own history. Old traditions and gods live on in Swiss villages and in Harlem ghettoes. For better and worse, they continue to structure the lives of those who adhere to them. For Wright, such traditions belong to the past. The future belongs to the African and Asian elites who should seize power for their emerging nations and exercise it as they see fit. When they secure their peoples' freedom, Wright avers, these leaders will relinquish their power. Baldwin is skeptical: princes do not surrender power.

Despite his skepticism of many of the ideas expressed, Baldwin remains fascinated by the conference proceedings. He responds to a lecture on the tonal structure of Youriba [*sic*] poetry, because the speaker conveys his deep love of his subject. Even though Baldwin feels as distant from the world that gave rise to Senghor's Négritude as from the Yoruba, he responds to the aesthetic that Senghor expressed: "It was the esthetic which attracted me, the idea that the work of art expresses, contains, and is itself a part of that energy which is life" (150). Attractive though it is, this is not Baldwin's aesthetic. Rather than communal traditions in which stories are passed down orally, the literary modernism which is Baldwin's mode is individualistic and private: a solitary writer communicating to a solitary reader on the page. The jam session is the only Western counterpart to the "social art" that Senghor valorizes. Even then Baldwin is quick to point to "the ghastly isolation of the jazz musician" (151). The artist in the West, black or white, is an individual. As Baldwin continues to reflect on the position of the artist, he acknowledges a troubling divide between himself as a black American artist and his African peer. If, on its face, he accepts Senghor's argument that indigenous West African cultures are more cohesive and in that regard healthier, he "suspect[s], necessarily, a much lower level of tolerance for the maverick, the dissenter, the man who steals the fire" (151). He might have added the homosexual to this list. The freedom and openness Baldwin invoked earlier in the essay are here connected to an individual freedom that is central to his identity as an artist and as a man.[33]

Among the key topics the conference took up is the question of culture. What is culture? Or, more specifically, do people of African descent share a common culture or a common consciousness? In his career to this point, Baldwin had not been particularly drawn to the first question. He might well have been familiar with the second. It was not new. Alain Locke had posed a variation of it in "The New Negro," where he concluded that blacks shared "a common condition rather than a common consciousness."[34] The question had been debated at the Pan-African Congresses Du Bois helped to organize in 1919, 1921, 1923, and 1927.[35] In 1956, Baldwin comes down on the side of a common consciousness born of a history of oppression. He considers opposing viewpoints, though it seems clear that he finds all of them unpersuasive and many of them uninteresting. One objection crystallizes around the assertion that an analysis of Wright's classic text *Black Boy* "would undoubtedly reveal the African heritage to which it owed its existence" (154). Initially Baldwin dismisses the assertion as unimportant in the same way that asserting that an analysis of *A Tale of Two Cities* would "reveal its debt to Aeschylus" would be, though this aside trivializes the claim as well. "And yet," the phrase that opens the next paragraph, complicates the argument. Such claims are never raised about European literature because Europeans are never forced to prove that they have a literature or a culture. The debate itself exemplifies the oppression of African people. But on a more personal note, Baldwin does not wish to cede his identification with *Black Boy* as "one of the major American autobiographies" and while he acknowledges that "there was undoubtedly something African in all American Negroes, the great question of what this was, and how it had survived, remained wide open" (154). This question would be joined, fiercely, in the next decade.

Of the congress speakers, Césaire and Lamming most captivate Baldwin.[36] They each cut a riveting figure. Césaire has the air of a schoolteacher until he begins to speak, when he reveals "the grace and patience of a jungle cat" and an intelligence "of a very penetrating and demagogic order" (155). Césaire holds the crowded room enthralled. By contrast, Lamming "is tall, raw-boned, untidy, and intense, and one of his real distinctions is his refusal to be intimidated by the fact that he is a genuine writer" (160). Presumably Baldwin has in mind *In the Castle of My Skin*, Lamming's classic novel that was published in 1953. Lamming is the first speaker of the conference to have his remarks cut short; the meeting was running long, and a time limit was newly enforced.

Césaire takes on the relation between colonization and culture. He argues that "all cultures have . . . an economic, social, and political base, and no culture can continue to live if its political destiny is not in its own hands" (155). Colonialism set out to destroy every element of indigenous cultures (languages, customs, tribes, and lives) that resisted its power. Despite the rhetoric of European humanism, the colonizers replaced nothing, for to do so would have meant sharing economic, social, and political power which they had no intention of doing. Indigenous cultures had begun to rot under the pressure of imperialism, but Césaire declares that they had not been destroyed. To thunderous applause he concludes, "We find ourselves today in cultural chaos. And this is our role: to liberate the forces which, alone, can organize from this chaos a new synthesis which will be the reconciliation—*et dépassement*—of the old and the new. We are here to proclaim the right of our people to speak, to let our people, black people, make their grand entrance on the great stage of history" (157).

Baldwin's response is more measured than the crowd's. He is concerned with the question that Césaire does not raise, to wit, what kind of black men has colonialism produced. In other words, he wants Césaire to probe his own identity, much as he himself is doing. (Césaire's failure to do so leaves him open to the charge of demagoguery in Baldwin's view.) Baldwin formulates the situation of African intellectuals in terms not unlike those he uses in "Stranger in the Village." Here he speaks of black intellectuals: "for they were all, now, whether they liked it or not, related to Europe, stained by European visions and standards, and their relation to themselves, and to each other, and to their past had changed" (157). So intent is Baldwin on making the case that one of the great if unintended results of the colonial experience is creating men like Césaire that he misreads the scene that unfolds at the conclusion of the speech. Baldwin argues that the men who throng around him fail to acknowledge Césaire's difference from them. In fact all of the people in the room are men like Césaire—he is not unusual in this company. It is Baldwin who stands apart.

When Lamming observes that the word "Negro" means black—and nothing more—he makes room for Baldwin. Throughout the essay Baldwin queries the assumption of a unitary blackness. Lamming comments, rightly, on the "great variety of heritages, experiences, and points of view which the conference had brought together under the heading of this single noun" (160). He not only recognizes this variety, he embraces it. He points out that while African writers like Amos Tutuola draw on indigenous oral traditions, the novels they write are in English. Yet, these novels signify something to those who are familiar with those traditions that they cannot signify to the English. Baldwin teases out the implications of this idea to conclude that "the great wealth of the Negro experience lay precisely in its double-edgedness . . . . All Negroes were held in a state of supreme tension between the difficult, dangerous relationship in which they stood to the white world and the relationship, not a whit less painful or dangerous, in which they stood to each other" (161). To a degree this is an extension of Du Bois's concept of double consciousness. But now the black figure stands not only before a white world that looks on in "amused contempt and pity," he stands in and out of a transnational black world that offers both kinship and suspicion.

When time is called, Lamming ends with an epigram that one would expect Baldwin to admire, at least for its rhetorical economy, "If silence was the only common language, politics, for Negroes, was the only common ground" (162). Yet Baldwin does not engage the political project. Instead he reports the confusion that ensues as if to confirm that no shared culture exists. A subcommittee assigned to develop a "cultural inventory" cannot do so in the time allotted. The document they belatedly produce is forceful in its assertion that black cultures around the world have been "systematically misunderstood, underestimated, sometimes destroyed" and in its call for "the revival, the rehabilitation, and the development of these cultures as the first step toward their integration in the active cultural life of the world" (166). But like most words produced by a committee, these are destined to die on the page.

The energy of the conference dissipates. Baldwin paints a Parisian street scene at the conclusion that is a bookend to the one that opens the essay. Working-class people go about their daily business and cope with a bread strike. None of the scenes that play out at the conference alters their lives. Despite the intellectual brilliance of the papers and the intensity of the debates, the conference is even less likely to change the lives of blacks at home in Africa, America, and the Caribbean. At least in the short term, it has been ineffectual.

Perhaps for that reason, Baldwin's sense of himself and of black Americans continues to resonate throughout "Princes and Powers." He thinks of the "we" that constitutes black Americans as "the connecting link between Africa and the West, the most real and certainly the most shocking of all African contributions to Western cultural life . . . . [O]ur relation to the mysterious continent of Africa would not be clarified until we had found some means of saying, to ourselves and to the world, more about the mysterious American continent than had ever been said before" (148). His determination to follow his own path is admirable. So too is his willingness to listen and to engage the perspectives of his peers. In 1957, Baldwin's response to these perspectives was to sharpen his sense of himself as an American. However, in years to come he would adapt some of the ideas that were debated at the Sorbonne to an American situation that less and less seemed unique.

The civil rights movement brought Baldwin home. By 1963, he was on the front lines of the struggle, traveling through the South under the auspices of the Congress for Racial Equality (CORE) and making regular appearances on television and radio. He was also at the height of his fame as a writer. His incendiary novel *Another Country* was published in 1962. Despite mixed reviews, it became a national bestseller. Its scenes of interracial and homosexual sex guaranteed the sales. Many readers missed the ethical argument that was at its core. That argument was distilled in an essay, "Letter from a Region in My Mind," commissioned by the *New Yorker*. In 1963, the essay was republished as "Down at the Cross: Letter from a Region in My Mind" along with "My Dungeon Shook: Letter to My Nephew on the One Hundredth Anniversary of the Emancipation," in another bestseller, *The Fire Next Time*.

Its fierce indictments notwithstanding, *The Fire Next Time* is Baldwin's most hopeful volume. It sounds an alarm to his countrymen that he believes at least a few of them can hear. He reveals aspects of black people's lives—the beauty of their poetry and music, the desperation of their faith, and the bonds of their love—through which they achieve a measure of freedom. While Baldwin, not unlike Du Bois in *Souls*, is revealing aspects of black life that have remained hidden from whites, he does not suggest that they have salvific power. Nonetheless they can serve as a model for the new ethic that Baldwin hopes progressive Americans can formulate.

Like literary letters from the biblical Solomon in the book of Proverbs to Benjamin Franklin's *Autobiography*, "My Dungeon Shook" is fashioned as a private document intended for a public audience. It marks the centenary of the Emancipation Proclamation, which is not the occasion it might have been because it is premature to celebrate freedom that had not yet been achieved. Equally important, the correspondence between uncle and nephew—a relationship that worries the patriarchal line—illuminates the personal dimension of the civil rights struggle. Baldwin writes his fifteen-year-old nephew and namesake to share lessons from his family story and the national history. Consequently, he can remark on the nephew's resemblance to his father and grandfather, rail against the society that seeks to constrain the nephew's ambitions as it had his father's, and draw strength from the achievements of past generations.

The letter anticipates the apocalyptic imagery and tone of the second and more famous essay in *The Fire Next Time* when it asks the nephew and the reader over his shoulder to imagine a morning when the sun was shining and "all the stars aflame" (294). For Baldwin, this has in effect been the response of white Americans to the movement of black men out of their place. Yet Baldwin cautions his nephew against despair and urges him to accept his white countrymen and to claim his American home. In doing so he revises the meaning of the terms "acceptance" and "integration," as they were popularly understood in 1963. Blacks need to accept whites, not vice versa, and integration, rather than requiring that blacks become the equals of whites, means requiring whites to see themselves as they are. Blacks, who in Baldwin's view occupy an uncontested moral high ground, have no choice but to assist whites in their unwanted quest for self-knowledge, which will in turn liberate whites and blacks alike. Baldwin recognizes that this liberation is a long way off (maybe another hundred years) but asks his nephew and all the young blacks the nephew represents to take hope from the examples of their forebears, who "in the teeth of the most terrifying odds, achieved an unassailable and monumental dignity" (294).

One of the tensions in the volume as a whole is the insistence on the uniqueness of the African American experience—particularly what Du Bois would have called black Americans' "spiritual gifts"—and an increasing skepticism concerning the nation's exceptionalism. Baldwin insists that there is in black American life "a zest and a joy and a capacity for facing and surviving disaster that are very moving and very rare" (310). These qualities pervade black sacred and secular life; Baldwin found them equally in the church and on the avenue, in gospel music and in blues and jazz. They grow out of a radically different attitude among black Americans toward sensuality and toward death. In a recurrent theme, Baldwin held that white Americans "are terrified of sensuality" and do not understand it. He supplies a definition: "To be sensual, I think, is to respect and rejoice in the force of life, of life itself, and to be *present* in all that one does, from the effort of loving to the breaking of bread" (311). Audre Lorde would press a similar point in her essay "The Uses of the Erotic." As in the blues, the embrace of sensuality for Baldwin is twinned with an acceptance of the reality of death. This acceptance mandates Baldwin's essentially tragic sensibility, a sensibility that is fundamentally at odds with the mindless optimism that he attributes to his countrymen. He understands, however, that the reluctance of Americans to accept the reality of death is not in fact exceptional. In language that pulses with the sermonic cadences he learned in the pulpit, he writes, "Life is tragic simply because the earth turns and the sun inexorably rises and sets, and one day, for each of us, the sun will go down for the last, last time." He avers, "Perhaps the whole root of our trouble, the human trouble, is that we will all sacrifice the beauty of our lives, will imprison ourselves in totems, taboos, crosses, blood sacrifices, steeples, mosques, races, armies, flags, nations, in order to deny the fact of death, which is the only fact we have" (339). Rather than denying death, one ought to live life with such intensity and purpose that one earns one's death. Baldwin's attitudes toward sensuality and death stem from a radical belief in the sanctity of individual experience, and the ethic that he ultimately fashions is rooted in that belief. It requires "a transcendence of the realities of color, of nations, and of altars" (333). In order to achieve it, however, Baldwin suggests he had first to go *down* at the cross—that is, he has to delve into the very realities he hopes to transcend.

"Down at the Cross: Letter from a Region in My Mind" begins with the most compelling of the several accounts Baldwin wrote of the religious crisis he underwent as a teenager. In sharp and vivid vignettes, he brings to life the Harlem avenues he walked as a youth; his traumatic encounters with the pimps, police, and preachers who surveilled his movements; and, most dramatically, his conversion experience: "It was the strangest sensation I have ever had in my life—up to that time and since." One of the pleasures of the text is the immediacy with which Baldwin recounts this moment. Tellingly, it is a moment he was not altogether *in*. "One moment I was on my feet," clapping, singing, and simultaneously working out the plot of a play he is writing. The next moment he was on the floor with "all the vertical saints above me" (304). The language captures the visceral power of the experience even as it cast doubts on its meaning. Another source of textual pleasure is the wicked irony with which Baldwin looks back on his younger, freshly "saved" self: "I rushed home from school, to the church, to the altar, to be alone there, to commune with Jesus, my dearest Friend, who would never fail me, who knew all the secrets of my heart. Perhaps He did, but I didn't, and the bargain we struck, actually, down there at the foot of the cross, was that He would never let me find out" (306).

This self-knowing tone, the confidential posture, and the modulated prose are familiar to readers of Baldwin's earlier essays. But *Fire* has more passages of high-flown oratory and sermonic fury than those pieces. Many of these passages are written in the service of a scathing critique of Christianity—not only in terms of the individual hypocrisy it requires or of the practice of the black American church to mask racial resentment in biblical rhetoric (according to Baldwin, the sinners on their way to hell are always white), but in terms of the religion's imperialist history: "It is not too much to say that whoever wishes to become a truly moral human being (and let us not ask whether or not this is possible; I think we must *believe* that it is possible) must first divorce himself from all the prohibitions, crimes, and hypocrisies of the Christian church. If the concept of God has any validity or any use, it can only be to make us larger, freer, and more loving. If God cannot do this, then it is time we got rid of Him" (314).

Baldwin recognizes how subversive an idea this is. It would be so at any time in American history but is particularly subversive at the height of the civil rights movement, based as it was largely in southern black churches. This is not to say that members of more free-thinking organizations such as the Student Nonviolent Coordinating Committee (SNCC) would have rejected this line of thought. Indeed, the passage looks forward to the emergence of a Black Power movement that also rejected the hypocrisy and conservatism of the church. Notably, the revolutionary tenor of the passage is juxtaposed against a relatively benign portrait of the Nation of Islam, a group that was as frequently demonized in the popular press as the Christian church was revered.

Despite the claim that "the American Negro has the great advantage of having never believed that collection of myths to which white Americans cling," Baldwin is keenly aware that the weight of white supremacy has made blacks vulnerable to the sway of the counter-myth of black separatism (344). The scene in Elijah Muhammad's home conjures an almost idyllic atmosphere. Well-dressed young men "very much at ease, and very imposing" sit across the room from women who hold babies and talk among themselves (322). One knows in retrospect that Muhammad was not the benign spiritual patriarch Baldwin assumes; several of these babies were doubtless his biological children. Here, however, Baldwin suffuses the scene with an otherworldly glow. Confident black masculinity and virtuous black femininity are in perfect symmetry.[37] When Baldwin leaves Muhammad's presence, with a mixture of admiration and ruefulness, he allows his readers to understand how all but irresistible the prophet's lure would be to black men less cosmopolitan, less self-possessed, and less intellectually free than he—that is, how all but irresistible it might be to any black man other than James Baldwin.

Baldwin understands the appeal of black separatism, but he rejects it totally. He does so partly because, as he confides in that same self-knowing tone, he leaves the meeting to "have a drink with several white devils on the other side of town" (331). He has friends whom he will not betray on the altar of race loyalty. His skilled narration allows readers to see him hesitate to reveal this fact to his hosts and then to concede part of the hosts' argument when he realizes that a street address alone identifies its residents as white or black. The separatism to which the Nation of Islam aspires is, to a significant extent, already a social reality. Baldwin understands the desire to seize the political and economic power that would shift the meaning of this reality, that would transform a system of segregation under which blacks were victims to a system of separatism in which they became agents of their own destiny. But that vision is not just fantastic or flawed: it is false. As Baldwin implores, "For the sake of one's children, in order to minimize the bill that *they* must pay, one must be careful not to take refuge in any delusion—and the value placed on the color of the skin is always and everywhere and forever a delusion" (346).

Given this imperative, Baldwin's invocations of a racially specific American exceptionalism need to be placed in context. As Eddie Glaude remarks, Baldwin understands both "how appeals to blackness were warranted in a country so fundamentally committed to white supremacy" and how limited such appeals were both instrumentally and inherently.[38] His racial exceptionalism looks to the past rather than the future. Yes, "the American Negro is a unique creation; he has no counterpart anywhere, and no predecessors" (334). But this uniqueness is a function of history, rather than of any intrinsic racial attributes. And the lessons of that particular history can liberate blacks and whites alike. The survival of America—the survival of both its black and white citizens—requires a disavowal of exceptionalist rhetoric and a rejection of the social institutions that have nurtured it. What blacks and whites must strive toward instead is an ethic of freedom and love that transcends race, nation, and creed. That ethic requires a cessation of the fear that animates both the Christian church and the Nation of Islam. It demands a self-acceptance so profound that it enables the recognition of the value of each individual. It constitutes the way out of the American racial nightmare and the way to forestall the fire next time.

For a brief moment in the early 1960s, Baldwin had reason to believe that African Americans were on the brink of claiming both their inheritance as Americans and their birthright as human beings. But the mountaintop experience of the civil rights movement passed quickly. By the middle of the decade, Baldwin was distressed by conditions in the United States. Writing from his home in Istanbul, he pleaded with family and friends to send information about conflicts within the movement; he conveyed deep concern about the welfare of his family and the repercussions on them of his activism. He also expressed the desire to conduct a lecture tour in the United States, but given the fractured state of the movement, Baldwin worried that he would be unable to find an organization to sponsor it. Nevertheless, he considered it his duty to return to the struggle's front lines. He felt compelled to suggest new directions for the movement, especially in light of the state response to the increasing violence in the South and the North. He believed that black urban communities in particular were virtually under siege. The movement needed to clarify its goals; otherwise the movement might settle for the limited victories it was in the government's interest to grant. Black people, no less than whites, needed to be reminded of what they were fighting for: not integration into a burning house, as he had written and rejected in *The Fire Next Time*, but a reconstructed nation in which its principles would be one with its actions.[39]

Almost a decade passed between the publication of *The Fire Next Time* (1963) and Baldwin's next book of essays, *No Name in the Street* (1972), a book that in its author's words, had been "much delayed by trials, assassinations, funerals, and despair."[40] Its two extended essays, "Take Me to the Water" and "To Be Baptized," are deeply autobiographical, structurally innovative, and intricately connected. They represent both a personal and a political crisis. Baldwin had given up serving his countrymen as Jeremiah and taken on the mantle of Job.[41] He turned from the urgent importuning of those "relatively conscious whites and those relatively conscious blacks" to avert "the fire next time" and, like Job, offered a series of lamentations on the past and the present. His politics had changed; his prose had shifted to a minor key: "The mind is a strange and terrible vehicle, moving according to rigorous rules of its own; and my own mind, after I had left Atlanta, began to move backward in time, to places, people, and events I thought I had forgotten. Sorrow drove it there, I think, sorrow, and a certain kind of bewilderment, triggered, perhaps, by something which happened to me in connection with Martin's funeral."[42]

The metaphor illuminates not only the author's mind, but the genre of the essay. Its looping trajectory pays no heed to chronology or geography; it moves backward and forward in space as well as time. It follows a logic of its own that this passage suggests reflects rules that are no less rigorous for being undefined. It insists on its own autonomy. The trigger for the interior journey in this case is an incident that transpired in private and seems to have only a tangential connection to the public events that are the essay's explicit concern. In the aftermath of the assassinations of Martin, Malcolm, and Medgar, Baldwin reflects on the national and international situation. But he does so through reconsidering his own individual past positions and actions. For the reader of Baldwin's earlier essays, "Take Me to the Water" revisits scenes from his growing up in Harlem to his sojourns in Paris and the American South, to the lecture platforms of the civil rights movement. But the tone has changed. Baldwin's eloquence has grown more troubled. As he puts it, "something has altered in me, something has gone away"; he seems to look back both in anger and sorrow at the road he has traveled (357).

If the trigger for this interior journey is a visit that Baldwin pays to an old friend and his family in the Bronx, the emblem of what he would elsewhere call the price of the ticket is a suit. In a bravura telling that shifts abruptly from dramatic exaggeration to understated irony, Baldwin describes how he told a newspaper columnist that he would never again wear the black suit that he wore to share the stage with Dr. King at Carnegie Hall shortly before King's assassination, and wore again to King's funeral. After the column appears, the wife of a friend who had grown up with Baldwin and was "just his size" calls to say that if Baldwin cannot wear the suit, she hopes he will give it to her husband. Baldwin, the bicoastal celebrity, travels to the Bronx by limousine and begins en route to suffer pangs of guilt. Just as signs of celebrity are evoked throughout the first part of the essay, the adjective "guilty" now recurs five times in one paragraph. Entering the friend's apartment, Baldwin recognizes himself as a stranger in a home where he had once been kin. He condescends to those he has in fact left behind; with little justification he concludes that they have not changed in the intervening years. Acknowledging class divisions that he cannot overcome, he recognizes that his friend, a postal worker, needs a suit and cannot afford Baldwin's "elegant despair."

As it evokes moments in earlier essays, "Take Me to the Water" becomes a critique of its author, a series of judgments on Baldwin's judgments. On the defensive, Baldwin argues with his friend's stepdaughter over William Styron's *Confessions of Nat Turner*, which the girl condemns without having read. His friend stands apart from this exchange, embarrassed. Baldwin's gloss on the moment ("I always think that this is a terrible thing to happen to a man, especially in his own house, and I am always terribly humiliated for the man to whom it happens. Then, of course, you get angry at the man for allowing it to happen" [362]) echoes inexorably the moment in "Notes of a Native Son" in which the white schoolteacher's presence in the Baldwin home confronts his father with "a wholly unprecedented and frightening situation" (68). Here Baldwin reenacts the role of the white schoolteacher as he embarrasses a father in front of his child. The reader discerns how class, no less than race, can produce a "frightening situation" between people. In this instance, the chasm that opens up is especially disconcerting because of the closeness the men, both born poor and black, once shared. The situation continues to deteriorate as Baldwin hectors his friend, who supports the war in Vietnam, for his reactionary political beliefs. Baldwin's rage gets the better of him, and he utters expletives that rupture the prose as starkly as they do the scene. In this moment, Baldwin experiences a crisis of empathy and kinship as well as of language.

Tellingly, the expletive comes in response to the friend's attempt to tell Baldwin what "we," meaning Americans, are trying to do in Vietnam. Throughout his first three volumes of essays Baldwin had famously used this pronoun to claim his citizenship in the U.S. nation. As he once explained, he had done so to avoid assuming the stance of victim. He "shifted the point of view to 'we.' Who is the 'we'? I'm talking about we, the American people."[43] Of course, Baldwin had also insisted that because he "love[d] America more than any other country in the world, and exactly for that reason, [he] insisted on the right to criticize her perpetually."[44] Consequently, here he responds with fury to his friend's assertion of common cause sans critique. "What motherfucking *we*? You stand up, motherfucker, and I'll kick you in the ass!" (364). The reunion stumbles to an end.

On the surface Baldwin has cast himself forever out of the fold by his language. Although his fiction can be deliciously profane, no precedent for this utterance exists in Baldwin's essays. Critics who dismiss *No Name in the Street* because of its anger point to passages like this one.[45] But it is not the specific words, it is the failure of language in general that is at issue here. Earlier in the essay, Baldwin worries needlessly that his friends, members of what was once his church family, would be appalled by his worldly habits. When he arrives, he finds that they have thoughtfully provided an ashtray and a bottle of whiskey. He describes himself to himself as "an aging, lonely, sexually dubious, politically outrageous, unspeakably erratic freak" (363). And the reader is stunned by the writer's willingness to reveal such vulnerability, even abjection. Baldwin then quickly clears psychic space for himself and perhaps for the reader as well by juxtaposing the multiple changes in his own identity to the psychological stasis that defines his friend. Baldwin angrily concludes, "nothing seemed to have touched this man" (363). Surely, nothing he says reaches his friend. Failing to communicate with him, he curses him.

This scene becomes the catalyst that enables Baldwin to reconsider his relation to the masses of black Americans from whom he feels alienated by reason of class, culture, politics, and sexual identity. The last is particularly salient. Including homosexuality in the discussion of identity and civil rights, as Magdalena J. Zaborowska reminds us, "verged on speaking the unspeakable and violating a communal taboo."[46] Yet Baldwin does so throughout *No Name in the Street*. For example, he recollects his first journey South when he was groped by a white man and analyzes the sexual dis-ease that motivates southern racism. He discusses the wrongful incarceration of his friend, Tony Maynard, and analyzes the sexual dis-ease that motivates homosexual rape in prisons. Homophobia in the black community had led to the exclusion of Baldwin and Bayard Rustin from the podium at the 1963 March on Washington. It had given Eldridge Cleaver license to attack Baldwin in his bestseller

Soul on Ice, an attack that Baldwin answered with much more grace than it deserved in *No Name.* Baldwin understood that homophobia was hardly peculiar to black Americans—it was a national disorder—however, it became excruciatingly painful when it was manifested in his natal community.

In a manner characteristic of the essay, a private exchange becomes the ground that enables Baldwin to reconsider his relation to the larger society, in this case specifically his relation as a world-famous black writer to the masses of African Americans and as an African American to the dispossessed peoples of the world (beginning here with the Vietnamese), as well as to his white countrymen. As the rest of the essay loops backward and forward in time, the central question it asks is for whom the sacrifices of the sixties have been made. The bloody suit is finally the martyr's robe, the emblem of suffering and shame. It rightly belongs not to Baldwin or even to King, but to the many thousands gone. The essay struggles to hold at bay the despair that would overwhelm Baldwin were he forced even to consider the possibility that those sacrifices had been made in vain.

Baldwin's situation in *No Name in the Street* calls to mind W. E. B. Du Bois's meditation "Of Alexander Crummell" in *The Souls of Black Folk.* There Crummell, a nineteenth-century free black clergyman who traveled to Britain and Liberia advocating racial justice and eventually founded the American Negro Academy, becomes representative of all black intellectuals who are threatened with the temptations of hate, despair, and doubt. For Du Bois, the triumph of Crummell's life is that he transcended these temptations, temptations with which Du Bois, who places the essay on Crummell just after the elegy for his infant son, still wrestled. For Du Bois, "the tragedy of the age" and of his homeland is that few white Americans had ever heard of Crummell. Baldwin occupies the inverse position. Many of his countrymen know his name, but few understand him or, more vexing, themselves. Rather than simply condemn their ignorance, Baldwin strives to identify failures of his own understanding. And, as he meditates on his own life, he struggles against the temptations of which Du Bois warned.

A transition that reflects on the passage of time and the nonlinearity of history introduces more autobiographical narratives in which Baldwin reflects on his ability and inability to read the situations he was in accurately. If, on the one hand, he anticipated the Algerian revolt based on his observations of Algerians in Paris, on the other hand, seeing Paris from the perspective of an American framework led him to misperceive the relative standing of Arabs and Africans in the metropole. In retrospect, he realizes that in fact the Arabs, who far outnumbered the darker-skinned Africans, were more feared and more exploited. He concedes that he "was also a member of the American colony, and we were, in general, slow to pick up on what was going on around us" (375). Even as his American passport offers protection, his American perspective distorts his vision. That vision restored, he draws an extended comparison between the rise of McCarthyism in the United States and anti-Arab racism in France during the 1950s.

Baldwin returns again and again in *No Name in the Street* to contemplate the relationship of African Americans to a transnational community of the dispossessed and their shared relationship to the West. In so doing, he gives up on strategic American exceptionalism; it has proved its ineffectiveness. Revising the famous passage in "Stranger in the Village," he asserts that "the South African coal miner, or the African digging for roots in the bush, or the Algerian mason working in Paris, not only have no reason to bow down before Shakespeare, or Descartes, or Westminster Abbey, or the cathedral at Chartres: they have, once these monuments intrude on their attention, no honorable access to them." The Baldwin of the early essays was himself a pilgrim to the sacred sites of Western culture and a devoted student of its texts. Now, to bow down before these monuments is to accept that "history's arrogant and unjust judgment of [the dispossessed]" (381). In "Stranger in the Village," by contrast, Baldwin had expressed the hope that what he, as an interloper, saw in the history of the West—imaged by the gargoyles adorning Europe's majestic cathedrals—could awaken his white readers to the inextricability of good and evil in general and to the evil from which they benefit in particular. No such hope survives in *No Name in the Street.*

At times Baldwin gives into despair. He has learned retrospectively that *Encounter*, the magazine that published his essay "Princes and Powers," was a CIA front. He wonders how else his idealism has been exploited and to what extent he has been "the Great Black Hope of the Great White Father."[47] Despite having articulated his positions in a fashion both scrupulously honest and meticulously precise, he recognizes that he has been used.

The possibilities of history are not foreclosed. As he recounts his travels through the U.S. South, where, he recalls, "though I was a stranger, I was home," Baldwin reintroduces readers to the still unsung heroes of the civil rights movement. But his purpose is less to celebrate their valor than to suggest how difficult and how private the choice for nonviolence was and is. One anecdote he shares relates the experience of a black grocer in the South, a voting rights activist. After sitting night after night with his sons, armed and ready to protect his business, the man decides one day that this is no way to live. He gives up his arms—not because his enemies have put down theirs but in order to preserve his sense of who he is. Preserving that sense of oneself as a moral agent constitutes one challenge Baldwin lays down in *No Name in the Street*.

But he does not end there. The second part of the text, "To Be Baptized," moves across time and space with sometimes dizzying rapidity as it memorializes the dead and confronts the living. Baldwin recollects his friendship with Malcolm X and the wariness that preceded it, the news of Malcolm's murder, the doomed effort to bring his story to film, Baldwin's distant relationship with King, the news of King's murder, Baldwin's years-long struggle to free his falsely accused friend Tony Maynard from prison, his meetings with Huey Newton and other members of the Black Panthers, and the broad opposition to the "racist war" in Vietnam. With each narrative the complexities of the current moment multiply. The stories intersect: news of King's death reaches Baldwin in Hollywood where he is talking to the actor Billy Dee Williams, his choice to play Malcolm on film. That memory triggers the memory of hearing the news of Evers's murder as Baldwin travels in Puerto Rico and of Malcolm's death as Baldwin and his sister eat in a London restaurant. The shifts of location reinforce the sense of dislocation, a personal dislocation that mirrors a national—indeed, a global—crisis.

Resolving that crisis requires not just a renewed sense of moral agency but a new set of "economic arrangements," that do not condemn the majority of the world's people to poverty. Resolving that crisis compels revised concepts of empathy and kinship that bind human beings regardless of race. In the meantime, black people respond to the present disarray as best they can. By 1972, blacks in the United States had begun calling themselves Afro-Americans, which Baldwin deems a "wedding . . . of two confusions, an arbitrary linking of two undefined and currently undefinable proper nouns"—Africa, because it is not yet free to define itself, and America, which continues to pose "a profound and dangerous . . . mystery" (472–73). In the last paragraph of *No Name in the Street*, a volume that maps an ever-widening crisis, Baldwin turns back to the community from which he came. He reflects on what it means to be an Afro-American:

> To be an Afro-American, or an American black, is to be in the situation, intolerably exaggerated, of all those who have ever found themselves part of a civilization which they could in no wise honorably defend—which they were compelled, indeed, endlessly to attack and condemn—and who yet spoke out of the most passionate love, hoping to make the kingdom new, to make it honorable and worthy of life . . . . One would much rather

be at home among one's compatriots than be mocked and detested by them. And there is a level on which the mockery of the people, even their hatred, is moving because it is so blind: it is terrible to watch people cling to their captivity and insist on their own destruction. I think black people have always felt this about America and Americans, and have always seen, spinning above the thoughtless American head, the shape of the wrath to come. (474)

These words evince Baldwin's continued resistance to despair and his determination to continue ringing that bell in the night that might yet save Americans from themselves. He continued despite the eclipsed possibility of transcendent unity that he has envisioned in *The Fire Next Time*. He continued even though the moral certitude of the movement was gone and even though Afro-Americans, tempted by the romanticized identities proffered by black nationalists, did not always take on the harder task of working though the complex and contradictory meanings of the terms on either side of the hyphen. Although he wavered, Baldwin never lost the faith that by getting the words right, pushing them until they revealed the complexities of ever more complex realities, insisting that we use language not to evade but to confront the toughest questions, both political and personal, *we*—that is, not just Americans but human beings—just might manage to survive. In the meantime, as the wrath of history still threatens, we have no choice but to keep the faith: "hoping to make the kingdom anew, to make it honorable and worthy of life."

CHAPTER FIVE

The Mystery of American Identity
Ralph Ellison

I began to learn that the American novel had long concerned itself with the puzzle of the one-and-the-many; the mystery of how each of us, despite his origin in diverse regions, with our diverse racial, cultural, religious backgrounds, speaking his own diverse idiom of the American in his own accent, is, nevertheless, American.

—Ralph Ellison, "Hidden Name and Complex Fate"

Whether offering definitions of the blues ("an autobiographical chronicle of personal catastrophe expressed lyrically"), or arguing that all Americans, black and white, wear a mask, or contending that the "attitude of tragic responsibility" expressed in the great nineteenth-century American novels disappeared in their modernist descendants, or positing that "perhaps the mystery of American cultural identity . . . arises out of our persistent attempts to reduce our cultural diversity to an easily recognizable unity," Ralph Ellison's essays are touchstones in American literary criticism and cultural theory.[1] The first collection, *Shadow and Act* (1964), was initially hailed as "brilliant" and "absolutely important" and has only grown in critical estimation since. Ellison biographer Arnold Rampersad ranks its influence on black intellectuals as second only to *The Souls of Black Folk*.[2] A second volume of essays, *Going to the Territory*, earned only slightly less effusive praise when it was published in 1986. To reviewer Louis Menand its essays constituted "the articulation of an enormously valuable view of American culture."[3] To a significant degree, both volumes define the terms for still ongoing debates regarding nineteenth- and twentieth-century American fiction, modernist aesthetics, and race and American culture. If novelist Paule Marshall embraces *Shadow and Act* as the "black writer's bible," scholar John Wright deems Ellison's essays "not as an adjunct to *Invisible Man*, but as its creative coequal and intellectual point of origin."[4]

Although the achievement of *Invisible Man*—a novel that became canonical upon its publication in 1952—created an audience for Ellison's nonfiction, he had begun to publish essays years before. The pieces that he contributed to *New Masses* in the late 1930s reflect first his commitment to Leftist orthodoxy and then his questioning of it. As managing editor of *Negro Quarterly* in 1942 and 1943, he began to fashion more independent views, especially regarding the role of the black writer and the dilemmas that black Americans faced as they weighed their support for World War II. In essays written after the war, Ellison began to adopt the critical positions that he would maintain for the rest of his life.

"Twentieth-Century Fiction and the Black Mask of Humanity," which he wrote in 1946, although it was not published until 1953, introduced a theme that would become a mainstay. The great nineteenth-century American writers—Ralph Waldo Emerson, Herman Melville, Henry David Thoreau, and, above all, Mark Twain—engaged the crucial moral themes animated by slavery. As a consequence of history, race was central to their literary imaginations. Several of these writers not only invented complex black characters, they used those characters to represent the human condition. By contrast, most early twentieth-century American writers either trafficked in racial stereotypes or depicted no black characters at all. Ellison challenged his peers to match their precursors' example. In 1952, his own novel met that challenge.

In the wake of the publication of *Invisible Man*, Ellison became a critic to be reckoned with. In "Change the Joke and Slip the Yoke" and "The World and the Jug," Ellison famously defends his novel against what he saw as the misreadings and simplifications of Stanley Hyman and Irving Howe, respectively. More broadly, in both these pieces Ellison formulates and advances his literary aesthetic. Rejecting the protocols of protest, he claims for himself a literary freedom that black writers before him had been denied. But these essays were never simply about his singular novel. They argued for a revised understanding of American culture. If Ellison rejected Stanley Edgar Hyman's argument in "Change the Joke" that *Invisible Man* was the literary equivalent of a trickster tale, Ellison maintained that the influence of Negro folklore and speech pervaded not only his novel but the nation writ large. At a time when most of his intellectual peers considered jazz as entertainment, if they considered it at all, Ellison argued that the music was American art at its finest. In terms of music, dance, folklore, and speech, African American culture was foundational to American culture. Culturally, Ellison believed that the United States had achieved the goal stated in its motto. The many had become one, and they had done so while preserving their "diverse racial, cultural, religious backgrounds." American culture was a singular mystery that Americans needed to unlock in order to achieve the democracy they proclaimed.

Thus, Ellison, like James Baldwin, confronts the question of American identity, but he recasts it in terms of culture rather than of the individual and answers in a comedic rather than tragic register. In the essay "An Extravagance of Laughter," Ellison alludes explicitly to the question posed by Henry James with which Baldwin wrestled. Ellison thinks back to the time shortly after he arrived in New York City from Tuskegee. He remarks that he was "learning something of the truth of what Henry James meant by the arduousness of being an American."[5] The comment is embedded in an anecdote about a black man and a white woman vying for a seat on the subway. New to the North with a deep sense of segregation's strictures regarding race and gender, Ellison is startled by the scene. The white woman wins the seat, "though only by a hip and a hair" (618). Though Ellison half expects a riot to break out, "the crowd of passengers simply looked on and laughed" (618). He recounts the incident with the same blend of the serious and the comic that characterizes the essay as a whole.[6] Through the distance humor provides, the question of identity becomes broader and less personal.

Later in the essay, he ponders the serious work humor does. Borrowing from Kenneth Burke, he writes, "Comedy should enable us to be observers of ourselves while acting. Its ultimate end would not be passiveness but maximum consciousness. [It should allow] one to 'transcend' himself by noting his own foibles . . . [and should] provide a rationale for locating the irrational and non-rational."[7] If African Americans are at the center of what James describes as the national joke, they develop a consciousness that their white compatriots often lack. They are keenly aware that the racial attitudes that would define them are irrational, yet they have the capacity, perhaps akin to what W. E. B. Du Bois designated "second sight," to survive them.

Ellison believes that American identity remains undefined, but, unlike Baldwin, he is at peace with the fact. In "Twentieth-Century Fiction and the Black Mask of Humanity," he writes, "For despite the impact of the American idea upon the world, the 'American' himself has not (fortunately for the United States, its minorities, and perhaps for the world) been finally defined."[8] Ellison argues that an American identity "equal to the greatness of the land" will be achieved through "a democratic process" that will in fact make one out of the many. Writing in the year before the *Brown v. Board of Education* Supreme Court decision that cracked the foundation of legal segregation, Ellison recognized that any definition of American identity that then existed necessarily excluded blacks and other minorities. When he refers to "this struggle between Americans as to what the American is to be," he alludes undoubtedly to the civil rights movement, which, although just on the cusp of visibility to the majority of Americans, had in fact been under way for decades.[9] Its victories were still in the future. In the meantime, no credible definition of "an American" could be framed. That when it was, it would be equal to the "greatness of the land," suggests how susceptible Ellison was to ideas of American exceptionalism. In contrast to Baldwin who, after it ceased to serve a strategic purpose, gave up on the idea that the U.S. nation was unique, Ellison sustained his belief that American culture was singular.

Like his nineteenth-century precursors, Ellison often first presented his essays as lectures. He first delivered "Hidden Name and Complex Fate: A Writer's Experience in the United States," as a lecture at the Library of Congress in January 1964. Blending autobiography and literary criticism, Ellison considers the role and responsibility of the American writer. He begins by invoking Hemingway ("not by way of inviting far-fetched comparisons," although that would be the inevitable effect) and by refusing the audience's presumptions that he would speak of racial oppression ("to avoid boring you by emphasizing those details of racial hardship which for some forty years now have been evoked whenever writers of my cultural background have essayed their experiences in public").[10] The introduction serves at once to place him in what was then the highest pantheon of American writers and to acknowledge his racial difference, albeit by insisting that his readers could not predict what the effect of that would be. By subordinating the importance of Hemingway's experience—the quality of the art was primary—Ellison was able to put his own racialized experience in perspective. The essay becomes one of Ellison's key statements on the importance of form. Although the form it addresses is the novel, "Hidden Name and Complex Fate" reveals Ellison's approach to the essay as well.

With a wide range of references, including Thomas Mann, André Gide, and the Tar Baby, and quotations from W. H. Auden and an anonymous Negro preacher, the essay recounts anecdotes of names from a two-year-old learning to say hers to a young Ralph Waldo Ellison mocked because of his, and the origins of the wealth of nicknames assigned to people in his neighborhood. It offers a detailed narrative of Ellison's coming-of-age in Oklahoma City that includes one of the most lyrical catalogs in all of his writing of the cultural forces that "claimed him" in his youth:

> So, long before I thought of writing, I was claimed by weather, by speech
> rhythms, by Negro voices and their different idioms, by husky male
> voices and by the high shrill singing voices of certain Negro women, by
> music, by tight spaces and by wide spaces in which the eyes could wander, by death, by newly born babies, by manners of various kinds, company manners and street manners, the manners of white society and

those of our own high society, and by interracial manners, by street fights, circuses and minstrel shows, by vaudeville and moving pictures, by prize fights and foot races, baseball games and football matches. By spring floods and blizzards, catalpa worms and jack rabbits, honeysuckle and snapdragons (which smelled like old cigar butts), by sunflowers and holly-hocks, raw sugar cane and baked yams, pigs' feet, chili and blue haw ice cream. (200–201)

The catalog embraces the natural and the manmade, the sensory and the existential, folk culture and popular entertainment. Human voices are as much a part of the climate as the weather. Spring floods and blizzards signal different seasons but similar threats. The list suggests how categories blur, that snapdragons smell like cigar butts, and raw sugar cane is as delectable as baked yams. It shifts between experiences in which the child participated—foot races and baseball games—and those he could only have observed—prize fights and vaudeville. Despite the legal constraints of segregation, the catalog includes white society as well as black, and it acknowledges class differences on both sides of the color line. Even the names of the flowers denote the range of experience, as they convey both foreboding (snapdragons) and delight (honeysuckle). But the pleasure of the list derives chiefly from its linguistic variety: the alliteration ("husky" and "high," "shrill, singing"), assonance ("pigs' feet, chili"), repetition ("manners"), and novelty ("blue haw ice cream").

Bracketing this evocative list are the writers that Ellison "claimed" as a boy in public school—Shaw, de Maupassant, as well as Emerson, Melville, and Twain—and the writers he "claimed" as a student at Tuskegee—Ezra Pound, Ford Madox Ford, Sherwood Anderson, Gertrude Stein, Hemingway and F. Scott Fitzgerald, and most of all, the T. S. Eliot of *The Wasteland*. In short, Ellison embraced the whole of modern Western literature as his heritage. Through his reading, he writes, "the details of my background became transformed. I heard undertones in remembered conversations which had escaped me before, local customs took on more universal meaning, values which I hadn't understood were revealed" (203). He implies that that meaning enlarged his understanding, so that the segregated world that would have seemed limiting, if not tragic, imbued him with a sense of possibilities.

Through what he would later name a vernacular process, Ellison weaves together these narratives of culture and literature, individual experience and communal life into an essay that is memorable for its form as well as its content. He shifts discursive registers fluidly. For example, he encapsulates his boyhood self in the colloquial phrase "a small brown nubbin of a boy carrying around such a heavy moniker" (195). Then, generalizing about the preconditions of the craft of writing, he remarks, "writers absorb into their consciousness much that has no special value until much later, and often much which is of no special value even then, perhaps, beyond the fact that it throbs with affect and mystery and in it 'time and pain and royalty in the blood' are suspended in imagery" (200). The grand pronouncement seems suited to the elegant periodic sentence that conveys it, but it is followed by the catalog quoted above that ends with "contests between fire-and-brimstone preachers and by presiding elders who got 'laughing-happy' when moved by the spirit of God" (201). At first glance, the actions of the latter seem to have little to do with the "affect and mystery" that the pronouncement introduces. But on reflection, they demonstrate the same impulse that aspires to the divine while remaining rooted, inexorably and comically, in the human. If the fire-and-brimstone preachers have little connection to the "time and pain and royalty in the blood," an unattributed quotation that sounds vaguely Shakespearean, they end up by representing the trace of the past that signifies for the writer in the maturity of his present.

Circling back to where he began, Ellison announces what he brought to the novel as he learned "to add the wonderful resources of Negro American speech and idiom, and to bring into range as fully and eloquently as possible the complex reality of the American experience as it shaped and was shaped by the lives of my own people" (208). Ellison states this as both obligation and achievement, but its fulfillment has required that he not simply engage in what he terms "stylized recitals" of racial grievance, but that he plumb the depths of both the particular culture into which he was born and the national culture: "the puzzle of the one-and-the-many; the mystery of how each of us, despite his origin in diverse regions, with our diverse racial, cultural, religious backgrounds, speaking his own diverse idiom of the American in his own accent, is, nevertheless, American" (190, 207). In an essay that twice deploys the adjective "sacred," once to refer to the nation's founding documents and once to the value and validity of one's own experience, Ellison insists on the inextricability of his personal story and the nation's history. Having mastered the form of the essay, he has been able to "possess and express" the meaning of both in "Hidden Name and Complex Fate."

Like Baldwin's, Ellison's late essays grow more digressive, but unlike Baldwin's they do not become more pessimistic. Indeed, the essays collected in

Going to the Territory are the most insistent and elaborate articulations of his belief in the uniqueness of American culture. It is significant that although he occasionally referred to the United States, Ellison's usual term of reference was to America. As Hortense Spillers observes, *America* for Ellison signifies more than the existence of a nation designated the United States. "To get the right emphasis," Spillers contends, "we would need to recall the Democratic sublime of Whitman and Emerson and the sweeping 'architectonics' of Hart Crane and William Carlos Williams."[11] If Jim Crow had not shaken Ellison's faith in *America*, it is perhaps understandable that Vietnam and Watergate would leave it intact. For many members of the generation that came of age in the 1960s and 1970s, Ellison's faith was difficult, if not impossible, to comprehend. His defense of the war seemed reactionary. Yet his premise that the culture is the creation of blacks as much as of whites has progressive implications. Extending an argument that goes back to the eighteenth century, he argues that blacks are profoundly American, that America could not exist were it not for them. If Du Bois praised the gifts that blacks brought to America, Ellison asserts, in effect, that those gifts made America what it is.

In "What America Would Be Like Without Blacks," he observes that the "fantastic vision of a lily-white America appeared as early as 1713" with the suggestion that enslaved blacks be freed and returned to Africa.[12] A century later, he notes, the American Colonization Society was formed to implement the vision, and white Americans as distinguished as Thomas Jefferson and Abraham Lincoln embraced the fantasy. For Ellison the vision bespeaks not only racism but the moral fatigue that whites then and now experience in the face of the seemingly never-to-be resolved problem of race in the United States. Yet, Ellison suggests, what is "ultimately intriguing" about the fantasy is "the fact that no one who entertains it seems ever to have considered what the nation would have become had Africans *not* been brought to the New World, and had their descendants not played such a complex and confounding role in the creation of American history and culture" (580).

Deliberately, Ellison shifts the lens of his critique to U.S. popular culture, because "on this level the melting pot did indeed melt" (580). Whether movies, television, baseball, jazz, football, or drum-majoretting, U.S. culture represents the blending of many cultures. Not only had segregation failed to exclude blacks from the cultural mainstream, Ellison insists, "Negro Americans are, in fact, one of its major tributaries" (580). Ellison suggests that the social reality in which the black/white binary is consistently, if inaccurately, highlighted blinds Americans to the pluralistic culture they share. In one of the essay's several sly turns, he avers that "most American whites are culturally part Negro American without ever realizing it" (580). The adverb "culturally" is the key term. As it identifies the ground on which Ellison makes his case, it also alludes to generations of jokes that mocked whites' racial anxiety. Despite the vigilance with which they were policed, the nation's bloodlines were not pure; a "nigger in the woodpile" often lurked unawares. The phrase belongs to the storehouse of African American jokes and lies. With this allusive echo, Ellison invokes the group's collective understanding of the pervasive presence of blacks in U.S. life and history, a presence that was biological as well as cultural. But that history is not Ellison's concern.

Instead, anticipating political theorist Benedict Anderson and others, Ellison states that the nation is the product of its language, which he describes as "a colloquial speech that began emerging long before the British colonials and Africans were transformed into Americans" (581). The first formal iteration of this speech is what I deem "democratic eloquence." It is the language of Othello, Maria Stewart, and Frederick Douglass. But Ellison is less interested in the written language than in speech. In describing the sound of the spoken language, he pinpoints its tonality which, he avers, derives in large measure from the "timbre of the African voice and the listening habits of the African ear" (581). Although he never cites Zora Neale Hurston, Ellison's observation is congruent with her assertion in "Characteristics of Negro Expression" that "the American Negro has done wonders to the English language." She, too, hones in on the tonal qualities by noting how blacks had "softened and toned down strongly consonanted words." Her conclusion anticipates Ellison as well when she asserts that "no one listening to a Southern white man talk" could deny the influence of blacks on his speech.[13]

More than observations about language link Hurston and Ellison as essayists. As I discuss in the introduction, Hurston's meditation on racial identity, "How It Feels to Be Colored Me," begins with a joke, and the humor threaded throughout highlights the absurdity of racial categories. It is the "me" that fascinates Hurston's persona, who is most herself when unburdened by the concept of race. Similarly, Ellison's play-it-by-ear improvisations in "What America Would Be Like Without Blacks" are primarily in the comic register. The essay cites historical facts, comments on the current political scene—as when it takes a swipe at Daniel Patrick Moynihan's infamous call for "benign neglect" of the problem of race as a strategy for achieving its solution—and offers serious cultural analysis. At the same time, it interpolates jokes at the expense of the privileged: "So there is a *de'z* and *do'z* of slave speech sounding beneath our most polished Harvard accents, and if there is such a thing as a Yale accent, there is a Negro wail in it—doubtless introduced by Old Yalie John C. Calhoun, who probably got it from his mammy" (581).

While Ellison signifies on the racial, class, and regional stratifications that undermine the achievement of political democracy, it is his comments on language that are most striking. Notwithstanding the social stratifications, the sounds of rural black southern speech resonate in the nation's most prestigious academic institutions. These institutions were complicit in the history of slavery, both directly as a result of investments in the southern economy and indirectly as they educated members of the nation's elite, including wealthy southerners like John C. Calhoun (1782–1850). A leader of the proslavery movement, the South Carolinian served as U.S. congressman, senator, and vice president. Calhoun authored the doctrine of nullification that argued that individual states could nullify federal legislation; the doctrine became the basis for the South's secession from the Union. Despite Calhoun's northern education and his long tenure in the nation's capital, he could not leave behind the sounds of the speech he learned from the black women who raised him. The "wail" is Ellison's approximation of the timbre of African speech. It sounds in the corridors of the nation's most powerful institutions.

The essay goes on to argue that the American literary tradition constitutes the vernacular process writ large when it gives a roll call of nineteenth-century writers beginning with Mark Twain. Ellison anticipates scholar Shelley Fisher Fishkin's argument in *Was Huck Black? Mark Twain and African American Voices* (1992) that the distinctive literary language of Twain's masterpiece was derived in large part from the speech of the author's black childhood friend. Without the specific biographical reference, Ellison asserts, more broadly, that the black man is the "co-creator of the language that Mark Twain raised to the level of literary eloquence" (581). Then, inverting Henry James's famous catalog of the traditions missing from American life, traditions essential to the work of the novelist, Ellison enumerates the contributions of "Negro American style" to that life, traditions that were indispensable to Ellison's work as a novelist: "our jokes, tall tales, even our sports would be lacking in the sudden turns, shocks and swift changes of pace (all jazz-shaped) that serve to remind us that the world is ever unexplored" (582).

To be sure, these traditions inform the style of *Invisible Man*, as Ellison explained in "Hidden Name and Complex Fate." However, the list has larger implications. The catalog might be understood as a late twentieth-century updating of what W. E. B. Du Bois termed the "gifts of the Negro" in *The Souls of Black Folk*, gifts of story and song, sweat and brawn and spirit. Hurston and James Weldon Johnson had earlier added secular expressions to the sacred songs that Du Bois valorized. But Ellison does more than extend the list to include elements of popular culture in his own time, he writes in a vernacular style that is their literary counterpart. His essay is replete with jokes, shocks, and swift changes of pace, as it argues that it is the potential of American democracy that has yet to be explored.

"What America Would Be Like Without Blacks" was written for a popular audience. Published in *Time* magazine (April 6, 1970), it appeared at a time when the civil rights movement was in eclipse and the proponents of Black Power were ascendant. It conveyed the urgent need Ellison felt to remind both blacks and whites that blacks had been and continued to be central to the definition of American culture and therefore to American democracy: "they symbolized both its most stringent testing and the possibility of its greatest freedom" (584). In Ellison's view, blacks, especially, forget this legacy at their peril. In longer essays, written for more sophisticated readers and published in journals such as the *American Scholar, Contemporary Literature,* and *Harper's* magazine, Ellison played extended variations on these themes.

These familiar quotations from his essays encapsulate his perspectives:

"What moves a writer to eloquence is less meaningful than what he makes of it. How much, by the way, do we know of Sophocles' wounds?"[14]
"American democracy is not only a political collectivity of individuals, but, culturally, a collectivity of styles, tastes, and traditions."[15]
"Cut off my legs, and call me Shorty!"[16]

The first speaks to the relationship of the writer's experience to his art, and the second to Ellison's often-stated assertion that the United States had achieved culturally the democracy it had failed to achieve politically. But that last sentence sounds more like something we would expect to read in fiction than in an essay.[17] It is an example of the vernacular process that Ellison enacts in the essay, a process that puts as distinctive a stamp on that form as the changes he wrought in the novel.

In the essay "Going to the Territory," Ellison offers a definition of vernacular process that he applies to American culture, but that also helps us understand the form and structure of his essays. He defines vernacular not as popular speech but as a dynamic *process*, in which "the styles and techniques of the past are adjusted to the needs of the present, and in its integrative action the high styles of the past are democratized" (608). As essayists have always done, Ellison uses his personal experience to reflect and comment on historical and cultural questions. Moreover, Ellison's style as an essayist is, in keeping with the styles and techniques of the past, consistently digressive and richly allusive. But in its discursive shifts that incorporate a more colloquial prose and in its jazz-like riffs, his style enacts a vernacular process in which, as he explains it, "the most refined styles of the past are continually merged with . . . play-it-by-eye-and-by-ear improvisations." It is that process that allows Ellison to move fluidly from Sophocles to signifying.

Vernacular process is also emblematic of the democratic culture, the collectivity of styles, tastes, and traditions that Ellison celebrates throughout his writing. With his affirmation of the centrality of black traditions to American culture, Ellison joins a line of black writers from Du Bois to Alain Locke to James Weldon Johnson and Zora Neale Hurston who celebrate the contributions blacks have made to the United States. Ellison is often in dialogue with these writers, especially Du Bois, and although he never acknowledges her, Hurston as well. As I have demonstrated in an earlier discussion, Hurston's essays enact a "vernacular process" before Ellison coins the term. In any case, the comparisons that scholars make between *The Souls of Black Folk* and *Shadow and Act* are often valid. But Du Bois, in what I call his troubled eloquence, writes in a minor key, emphasizing the tragic dimensions of African American history.

Ellison comes from a different place. In "The World and the Jug," his critical agon with Irving Howe, he asserts that being a Negro American is a "discipline" that "has to do with a special perspective on the national ideals and the national conduct, and with a tragi*comic* attitude toward the universe" (emphasis added).[18] His essays overflow with incident and opinion. They are filled with references to other writers, especially those he deems his "literary ancestors" (Malraux, Dostoevsky, and Faulkner as well as Eliot and Hemingway) and to social and cultural theorists, including Kenneth Burke and Constance Rourke. The plenitude out of which he writes produces "the shocks and swift changes of pace (all jazz-shaped)" that characterize the Ellisonian essay. Comic rather than tragic, often exuberant but never elegiac, Ellison's essays are products of the vernacular process that he names and defines.

The insistent yet unfulfilled quest for freedom by Americans in general and African Americans in particular is embedded in the title of the essay "Going to the Territory." It evokes the fictive territory for which Huck Finn lights out, the historical Indian territory to which Bessie Smith referred when she sang, "Goin' to the Nation, Going to the Terr'tor," and which was a sanctuary for fugitive slaves, and the Oklahoma territory, which gained statehood shortly before Ellison was born. The essay was originally presented as one of two lectures given at the Ralph Ellison Festival held at Brown University in 1979, an event that celebrated the author and his work. The event also included the unveiling of the portrait of Inman Page, the first black graduate of Brown (class of 1877), who late in life served as the superintendent of schools for Negroes in Oklahoma City and principal of Douglass High School, from which Ellison graduated in 1932. Page awarded Ellison his high school diploma, and Page's daughter, Zelia Breaux, introduced Ellison to the discipline of music.

The "lines of destiny" that led to Ellison and Page being honored together so long and far away from the place where they had known each other prompts Ellison to reflect on the "sheer unexpectedness of life in these United States."[19] (While it may have been true in the eighteenth and nineteenth centuries that life unfolded more unexpectedly in the United States than in the traditional societies of Europe and Africa, by the late twentieth century, life unfolded unexpectedly everywhere.) He concludes that had he known more about Page's life and understood more about his own, he might have predicted the unexpected. What is true for the individual experience is true for the nation's history. The essay reflects on both and marks the points at which they intersect.

At the unveiling, Ellison presented "Portrait of Inman Page: A Dedication Speech," which he published as a companion piece, a lead-in, if you will, to "Going to the Territory." He uses the speech both to exalt his mentor—a figure associated in his memory with wisdom and biblical eloquence—and to mock his boyhood self, a child who could not imagine achieving, let alone surpassing, the status of his mentor. The speech turns on a series of juxtapositions that ultimately overturn the initial hierarchy between teacher and pupil and presents the possibilities for overturning the social and political hierarchies to which it explicitly and implicitly alludes. Born in slavery, Page seemed hardly destined to earn a degree at an Ivy League university. But the unexpected became possible as a consequence of the historical fact of Reconstruction and of the exceptional culture of the United States which Ellison describes as "a composite, pluralistic culture-of-cultures . . . all of its diverse elements have been to some extent inspirited by those ideals which were enshrined during the founding of this nation" (588). Those ideals sent graduates of Brown to teach freed men and women in the South; they sent Inman Page to the Oklahoma territory where he imparted the ideals of his New England education to Ellison. This chain of causes and effects across generations is Ellison's rebuttal to the "glib talk" of a "white culture" and "a black culture" in the United States" (587). Anything but separatists, black men like Page and the whites who taught him transmitted particularly American ideals to students like Ellison. These same ideals in turn motivate his art. Consequently, the "interplay, both intentional and accidental, between certain American ideals and institutions and their human agents" produced this occasion of dual honoring (586).

Years before, Ellison and Page had been caught in an even more unlikely embrace. Ellison recounts the details, as he draws out a central theme of the essay. Humor has the power to smash hierarchies and to reveal hidden connections among people in disparate circumstances. While joking with his schoolmates during the obligatory chapel service, Ellison throws a punch that misses its target and lands on Dr. Page. The principal grabs Ellison, and Ellison grabs the ropes of the stage curtain until he loses his grip and the two fall to the floor, with Ellison landing on top. "Still in command," the principal roars. "What do you think you're doing, boy?" Stating the obvious while denying culpability, Ellison responds, "We fell, Mister Page! Mister Page, we *fell!*" (589). Outwardly, Page maintains the mantle of authority, but under his breath, he chuckles. More than the physical fall, the chuckle closes the distance between the man and boy. In the moment, the principal's quiet laugh is rendered inaudible by the raucous laughter that shakes the room. Yet Ellison's story—and it is this anecdote that makes the essay memorable—turns less on the spectacle that their action creates and more on the private joke that he and Page share. Their pratfall closes what Ellison had deemed the unbridgeable, "fixed hierarchal distance ... dictated by age, accomplishment and authority" (585). Dr. Page observes himself in the act and achieves what Kenneth Burke would deem "maximum consciousness." Ellison achieves the same retrospectively. In the spirit of the genre, Ellison's private experience becomes the touchstone for the larger issues the essay addresses.

Clearly revised and expanded, the published version of "Going to the Territory" meanders through considerations of geography, history, biography, music, and culture in order to explore, if not unlock, "the mystery of American identity," the making of one out of many, which is its thematic core. The essay riffs on related motifs such as "the unconscious logic of the democratic process," "the underground logic of the democratic process," and "the random workings of the democratic impulse" (596, 597). Unlike political ideologies, these terms cannot be pinned down: they point to processes that are unconscious, hidden, and random. They result in seemingly inexplicable occurrences like the one that occasions this writing. They are, in this regard, well suited for exploration in the essay. Ellison's essays look at many sides of every subject—turning each subject over, handling it, and arriving at whatever conclusion it reaches in a seemingly unplanned, open-ended, and digressive way. Carefully crafted though they are, his essays appear to be improvisations. They adhere to the pattern Adorno describes in "The Essay as Form," where he writes, "the essay thinks in fragments, just as reality is fragmentary, and finds its unity in and through the breaks and not by glossing them over."[20]

Explicitly concerned with form, "Going to the Territory" identifies jazz as a musical analogue for the impulse that informs Ellison's approach to the essay. The essay is constructed as variations around a theme; the digressions are akin to the jazz artist's improvisations, which take the theme as a foundation but take flight around it. Moreover, the writer, like the jazzman, participates in a dynamic vernacular process characterized by play-it-by-ear improvisations. Finally, jazz, an indispensable element of democratic culture, becomes an analogue for American democracy. In jazz each player contributes his distinctive part to an improvised performance that constitutes a new creation. In the U.S. democracy, citizens bring their distinctive experiences to a nation that is continuously in the process of creation. For reasons that I discuss below, the analogy may not hold in political terms, but it is richly suggestive and artistically generative. "Going to the Territory" is proof of that.

The essay's title invokes geography, and Ellison soon cites, as he often did, the axiom of Heraclitus that geography is fate. In "Remembering Richard Wright," for example, the axiom helps to explain the dissimilarities between Ellison and his one-time mentor and longtime rival. But in "Going to the Territory," the axiom offers a way of understanding the nexus between Ellison and Page. A common impulse drew two generations of African Americans, including Page and Ellison's parents, to Oklahoma. Blacks' understanding of geography as fate predates that migration; according to Ellison it derives from the fact of the Mason-Dixon Line, the historical boundary between slavery and freedom. (Typically, Ellison does not consider any history that predates Africans' arrival in the United States.) Living south of the line meant slavery; living north of the line held out at least the possibility of freedom. Freedom was the ideal that inspired post-Reconstruction blacks to move west where they founded institutions like Langston University, of which Page had been president, and Douglass High School where he became principal in his seventies. So committed is Ellison to his own axiomatic belief that "territory" is synonymous with freedom that he seems to miss the horror inherent in one of the digressive narratives he interpolates in the essay.

Professor Johnson Chesnut Whittaker was Page's predecessor as principal.[21] Born into slavery, Whittaker was the son of a woman who was a personal servant of the famous diarist Mary Boykin Chesnut. Although Ellison does not mention the possibility—he describes Whittaker as "a white black man"—Whittaker may well have been one of the children Chesnut lamented, the son of an enslaved woman, fathered by his master, and reared on the plantation in full view of the master's wife. Ellison is more interested in Whittaker's career at West Point and notes that only the events of Reconstruction made such a career possible. They do not ensure its success. Whittaker's career ends abruptly, after his fellow cadets, having discovered his racial background, tie Whittaker to a cot and notch his ear. No longer the physically perfect human specimen West Point requires, Whittaker is forced to leave the academy. This is at least the story Ellison's mother passes down. Ellison tells his readers that no official record of the incident exists and concludes that the "Army's loss" was the "Territory's gain" (602). He says nothing about the man's mutilation; neither does he mark the irony that as a "white *black* man," Whittaker could never have been a physically perfect human specimen according to the West Point definition. Acknowledging neither the incident's tragic or ironic dimension, Ellison simply moves on.[22]

For Ellison, Oklahoma provides a geographical imaginary that did not exist along a North/South axis. It was an imaginary, much like Hurston's Florida, that was shadowed but not burdened by slavery and its tragic legacy.[23] Black people were able to invent new identities, as when, for example, Hurston's father became the mayor of Eatonville. As he remarked in the preface to *Shadow and Act*, Ellison and his childhood friends considered themselves "Renaissance men" and inhabitants of a frontier that was theirs to claim. At the same time, however, they could not imagine that a man who loomed as large in their lives as Inman Page could be known in the larger white world represented by an institution like Brown University.

True enough, white Americans had not heard of Page or Whittaker. Their history, like that of blacks collectively, remained largely "unwritten." Ellison gestures to Du Bois in this regard when, invoking one of Du Bois's signal ideas as well as one of his signature tropes, he writes that "once in a while the veil which shrouds the details of our unwritten history is thrown back, and not only do the deserving find belated recognition, but sometimes marvelous interconnections between the past and the present spring to light" (593). For the most part, however, that history remained veiled, even into the last quarter of the twentieth century. White Americans did not know black Americans' history, let alone the ways that that history intersected with their own. For their part, black Americans, even including one as knowledgeable as Ellison, could still be surprised by interconnections because they did not know their own history thoroughly enough. Nevertheless, Ellison's tone and perspective in 1980 are fundamentally different from Du Bois's in 1903. If Inman Page is as little known as Alexander Crummell, Ellison's tribute to his mentor is as exultant as Du Bois's tribute to his is elegiac. For Ellison, unlike Du Bois—and unlike Baldwin, for that matter—the history of blacks in America, whether veiled or visible, is not tragic. It is profoundly hopeful.

Achieving this conclusion requires intellectual and technical dexterity. What many black essayists find tragic, Ellison finds "discouraging." Moreover, he allows that Americans are fortunate that so much of their history remains unrecorded, "for if it were, we might become so chagrined by the discrepancies which exist between our democratic ideas and our social reality that we would soon lose heart" (594). Some of what is missing owes to the "sheer rush and density of events," some is the result of Americans' short attention span. Moreover, the fact of "a supposedly classless society" obscures the significance of individuals such as Inman Page, who do not belong to a guild or estate that would make their importance evident. However, Ellison also recognizes that many of the omissions and distortions in the official record are deliberate. He echoes Douglass when he remarks that "Americans can be notoriously elective in the exercise of historical memory" and adept at creating myths that favor their self-image. But his observation, while ironic, lacks Douglass's edge. Alongside their officially sanctioned myths, Ellison avers, Americans' unwritten history lives on—"chaotic and full of contradictions." Though unacknowledged, this history propels the nation's politics. Borrowing again from Kenneth Burke, Ellison argues, "American democracy is a most dramatic form of social organization" (595). Ellison was deeply influenced by Burke's ideas, especially his contention that human beings develop rituals to manage life's risks and complexities. Their cultural creations— folklore and literature, myths and religions, music and dance—were all symbolic "equipment for living."[24] They are designed to impose order on the chaos of life, although as Ellison's comment acknowledges, they cannot fully succeed in doing so.

I contend that Hurston, if not Ellison's source, is, like Burke, his precursor. Without mentioning her name, Ellison revises her assertion in "Characteristics of Negro Expression" that everything the Negro does is acted out. He argues instead that everything the American does is acted out. Through symbolic conflicts such as Reconstruction, one side of every debate imprints its views on the nation. If the South lost the actual war, it won the symbolic battle that followed. The misconception of U.S. identity that resulted continues more than a century later to have consequences—among them is to render the contributions of blacks invisible, even as it rendered black people hypervisible. Viewing the violence of the lynch mob through a Burkean lens, Ellison argued that for Southern whites lynching was "one of the leading symbolic and ritualistic means of asserting their dominance." Symbolic action could take positive or negative form. As Donald Pease notes, "insofar as it prescribed an attitude, a symbolic action contained the recipe for a potential change in attitude."[25] That potential fuels the optimism of Ellison's vision.

As the essay moves beyond the stories of Page, Whittaker, and Ellison, that vision and its stakes become clear. "Going to the Territory" is a grand statement of Ellison's concept of democracy and his understanding of the "mystery of American identity," the alchemy which makes one out of many. Considering Ellison's views in that broad context, Adam Bradley contends that Ellison is "not denying the pernicious effects of racism in America but rather asserting in the face of them his faith in American pluralism, not as the best way for American democracy, but as the only sustainable means."[26] If that ideal has not been achieved in the U.S. economy or its politics, Ellison asserts, it has been achieved in art and culture. Fittingly, his first example is *Invisible Man,* which had occasioned several of the most influential essays in *Shadow and Act.* More than three decades after its publication, Ellison is less concerned about shaping its critical reception than he had been earlier. He does not offer an analysis or a defense, neither does he account for the influences that inform the novel. Rather, he avers that his novel "had become a lens through which readers of widely differing backgrounds were able to see elements of their own experience brought to a unifying focus" (598). The novel is a site of democratic action that allows its readers to retain the specificity of their experiences while seeing them in the context of a larger, unified whole.

Invisible Man is not, however, the essay's main example. In another shift, the essay turns its attention to jazz, for Ellison the quintessentially American music and an exemplary site of democratic action. This essay embeds this shift in the biographical nexus with which it opens, when it introduces Zelia N. Breaux, Inman Page's daughter, Ellison's music teacher and "second mother." This move is reminiscent of "The Little Man at Chehaw Station," which positions classical pianist and Tuskegee professor Hazel Harrison as the one who prepares Ellison by precept as well as example to pursue his dream of becoming a composer. Harrison had studied in Europe; a manuscript inscribed to her by Prokofiev sits atop the Steinway in her Alabama studio. Ellison notes that to "anyone who possessed a conventional notion of cultural and hierarchal order, its presence in such a setting would have been as incongruous as a Gutenberg Bible on the altar of a black sharecropper's church."[27] While Harrison certainly represents a level of artistic excellence to which Ellison aspires, her status as artist is undermined by Ellison's insistence on placing her in maternal relation to him. Although her career lacked the international scope of Harrison's, Breaux played a similar role in Ellison's childhood. She introduced him to the "basic discipline required of the artist" (605) and to a cultural heritage that fused high and low, black and white, American and European. Breaux's professional commitments were diverse: she taught her elementary pupils to dance the Maypole, trained older students in classical musical theory, organized the high school marching band, and ran the Aldridge Theater (named after the black Shakespearean actor Ira Aldridge), which featured drama, vaudeville, blues, and jazz. She helped Ellison understand he was heir to the totality of Western culture, of which she and he both deemed African American culture a part. In an aside, Ellison acknowledges that Breaux discouraged her students from playing jazz, putting her in the category of those he elsewhere deems "the respectable Negroes" in his hometown, who regarded jazz "as a backward low-class form of expression."[28] For her student, of course, jazz becomes the art that best exemplifies democratic culture. If the maternal Breaux introduces "basic discipline," Ellison must defy her rules in order to discover the jazzmen who become his exemplars.[29] In this instance, too, Ellison marginalizes his female mentor. Neither Harrison nor Breaux rise to the level of the literary ancestors or cultural exemplars Ellison valorizes.

By contrast, his embrace of the musicians who play the Aldridge and other Oklahoma City venues is unqualified. They are at once "practitioners of a vernacular style" and "unreconstructed elitists when it comes to maintaining the highest standard of the music which expresses their sense of the American experience" (609). In other words, they compel a standard of excellence from those who would join them on the bandstand; indeed they are notoriously quick to shame anyone who does not make the cut. For Ellison, they are in the tradition of Twain, who creates a literary language out of regional American speech. Charlie Christian, Jimmy Rushing, and Lester Young, three of the jazzmen Ellison celebrates in *Shadow and Act*, create jazz out of the folk blues and seculars they knew from childhood, along with the popular ballads, Tin Pan Alley tunes, and any other musical forms they chose to appropriate. As Ellison is careful to clarify, by "vernacular" he does not mean only expressions of the folk, but the process by which American artists fuse low and high traditions. Like Twain, the musicians enact a process that captures "that which is essentially American in our folkways and manners" (609).

In the middle section of *Shadow and Act*, Ellison writes at length about jazz musicians' dedication to their craft, the hours of daily practice (woodshedding) required to hone it, and the sartorial excellence that was part of the aesthetic of their performance. In "Living with Music," he maintains that "their driving motivation was neither money nor fame, but the will to achieve the most eloquent expression of idea-emotions through the technical mastery of their instruments."[30] Drawing his examples from the jazzmen who played around Oklahoma City during his childhood and did not achieve popular success, Ellison judged these musicians consummate artists. Significantly, he did so at a time when most of his intellectual peers considered jazz entertainment.

As Ellison defines it in "The Charlie Christian Story," "Jazz is an art of individual assertion within and against the group. Each true jazz moment (as distinct from the uninspired commercial performance) springs from a contest in which each artist challenges all the rest; each solo flight, or improvisation, represents (like the successive canvases of a painter) a definition of his identity as individual, as member of the collectivity and as a link in the chain of tradition."[31] While Ellison acknowledges the role of the jazz musician in the group, his definition highlights the role of the musician against the group. In this agonistic relationship, the artist who prevails is the one who challenges the group and defines himself against its pull. He does so each time he plays a solo and makes an individual statement in the context of the group's expression. While he remains a member of the collectivity and a link in the chain of tradition, his success derives from the challenge.

Although Ellison was fond of it, the analogy between the jazz player's relationship to the band and the citizen's relationship to a democratic state is problematic. Citizens need not find themselves in agonistic relationship with the nation, particularly if they understand themselves to be and are understood to be full-fledged members of the group. The analogy seems to work better for those whose citizenship status is in doubt as has certainly been the case for African Americans. It works better yet to conceptualize the role of the artist in society, whose vision is realized as a consequence of his or her antagonistic cooperation with the group—a group from which the artist chooses to stand apart. "Antagonistic cooperation" defines the artist's relation to the group more aptly than the citizen's.

I take issue as well with Ellison's use of jazz as an analogue for democracy. Jazz and the excellence it demands may be emblematic of "democratic culture," but that culture is not synonymous with democracy. Ellison glosses over the difference by asserting that "democracy" is the term for "social perfection (or a perfect society)" and thus represents the fulfillment of excellence. Indeed, perfection is achieved through what sounds very much like artistic composition: "a process of refinement, elimination and integration in which form and function become aesthetically one" (608). One can apply this description to the creation of jazz, the novel, and even to the essay, but it seems harder to apply it to the establishment of democracy. This is not to say that the insistence on excellence does not have aesthetic and moral value, but its political value seems less clear. Excellence is not a criterion for citizenship, which is a birthright, after all. The jazz ensemble seems less apt a symbol of social organization than, say, a community chorus, in which all are welcome no matter how more or less talented. Even the tuneless get to remain on the stage, though they might be asked to sing softly or just mouth the words.

The published essay "Going to the Territory" differs markedly from the talk that Ralph Ellison presented at Brown on September 19, 1979. Toward the end of his life, Ellison often spoke without notes, although he continued to make copious notes before appearances. This seems to have been the case at Brown. In any event a comparison of a transcription of the untitled remarks he presented and the published essay illuminates the connection between oral and written texts, between oratory and the essay that is a central concern of this book.[32] As one would expect, the published text is substantially longer and less repetitive than the spoken one; its terms are refined, facts checked, and misspellings corrected. But it is also less personal and less defensive than the speech that Ellison delivered. After long feeling besieged by attacks from younger black writers who disagreed with his politics and having been heckled on other campuses by black students who had not read his work, Ellison was taken aback by the warm reception he received at Brown.[33] Stating that he felt "rebuked" for every time that he doubted the possibility of communicating his vision, he thanked that audience for affirming that possibility "with their gracious smiles." He then let down his guard.

First, he admitted that he was not "with it." His ideas derived from an earlier time, and his experiences were totally unlike those of the young people in the audience. Indeed, he frequently stopped to clarify his intentions, as when he states, "but what I'm trying to set up for you . . ." He then recounted his experiences in quite personal terms. He remembered meeting Ma Rainey and Ida Cox in Mrs. Breaux's office as well as Oscar Micheaux, the pioneering novelist and filmmaker and the first black writer Ellison ever encountered. He told the story of dancing the Maypole, insisting, "We did not think it was ridiculous." Most poignantly, he stumbled over his explanation of Mrs. Breaux as a second mother: "I had a mother and I loved her very much, but she didn't teach and sometimes I didn't like her, and you know . . . Mrs. [Breaux] was an agent of a broader culture." The idea of a second mother fits into a cultural pattern of fictive kin well known among African Americans, yet the sixty-five-year-old Ellison seems to feel discomfited by what could be read as an act of disloyalty to his mother. He then arguably makes things worse by explaining that Mrs. Breaux was his mother's social superior whose wider world Ellison very much wanted to enter. Speaking more candidly about his early life than was his custom, Ellison also seemed more attuned to the tragic dimensions of history. For example, he refers to the period after Reconstruction as "the reimposition of a system in some ways worse than slavery." He notes that the Whittaker case was in fact a *cause célèbre*, which resulted in the firing of the superintendent of West Point.

Strikingly, the speech takes several stabs at defining "vernacular process," though none of them achieves the clarity of the published essay. For example, when remarking on the eloquence of Dr. Page and others in the Negro community, people who could make the language of the King James Bible and of Shakespeare resound in the spirits of those, many with "backgrounds in slavery," who heard them speak it, Ellison grapples with the meaning and method of the interaction. He reflects that "there had to be a give, there had to be a melting and not in the interest of degrading the best of the high style, rather to Americanize it, to transform it, to make it more suitable for communication with the democracy." In other words, literary eloquence had to be democratized; it had to be made available to all who would appreciate it. On the basis of his experience, Ellison vouches that "all" included the direct descendants of enslaved blacks, who found ways to make this literary eloquence part of their own expression. Ellison insists that "the American style *is* the vernacular style," but allowed that the term needed redefining. He asserts that vernacular did not mean merely popular speech or the speech of the slave, but "vernacular as an approach to the ongoing and rapidly changing American spirit whereby we can take the most refined of styles, the most elevated of styles, not only in language, but in architecture, in music and so on, and familiarize it, adjust it, give it democratic dimensions." As he revised the speech, "approach" became "dynamic process" a term that conveys the motive energy that it connotes. Neither static nor willed, the vernacular process is the writer's inevitable response to a culture that is constantly in flux. When the essay went into print, Ellison retreated behind the mask of cultural critic. But traces of the oral performance remain in the written text.

The shocks and swift changes of pace that characterized the sixties tested Ellison's belief in U.S. culture. At times he was dismayed by what he considered the ahistorical political posturing, and he was angered by his personal rejection by the younger generation of blacks. Although he had kept his distance from the civil rights movement—he had insisted to Irving Howe that "no Negroes are beating down my door, putting pressure on me to join the Negro Freedom Movement," because they understood that he was "enlisted for the duration" and also recognized "a certain division of labor among the members of the tribe"—he was troubled by the backlash to the social progress the movement had achieved.[34] Changes in the nation's musical culture appalled him. He had no patience for jazz that was not dance music; he was not a fan of Charlie Parker, and loathed the free jazz that inspired Amiri Baraka. To his ears, rock and soul music were close to abominations. Always known for his sartorial elegance, he could only laugh at the inversions of race and class epitomized by the popularity of jeans on Ivy League college campuses.

In the essays collected in *Going to the Territory*, Ellison frequently looks to the past in order to understand an increasingly alienating present. Yet he holds fast to his belief in American exceptionalism and cautions against dismissing what he insists on referring to as "the mystery of American identity." Today, outside the precincts of U.S. electoral politics, the idea of American exceptionalism has been discredited. Not only has the nation failed to live out its creed at home, it has acted imperially abroad. Moreover, in terms of its culture, the United States is no longer unique in its heterogeneity. What Ellison thought was unique to the United States may be better understood as processes of modernity. For that reason, his ideas about democratic culture and cultural hybridity remain generative. The issues of cultural adaption and exchange which so engaged Ellison are central to discussions of diaspora and transnationalism. Ellison the man would have doubtless resisted these discussions, but his ideas inform them nevertheless.[35] Most importantly, Ellison's late essays continue to challenge and provoke us.

First delivered as a commencement address at the Curtis Institute of Philadelphia in 1975, "The Little Man at Chehaw Station: The American Artist and His Audience" might be read as Ellison's effort, following "The Wasteland," to shore against his ruins.[36] Rather than the high culture of Europe that Eliot felt had been trashed by the First World War, Ellison was determined to preserve the democratic culture of the United States that he felt was threatened by racial chauvinism among whites and blacks in the last quarter of the twentieth century. Yet it might also be read as a brief for a vernacular process that continues to produce unexpected results, results that Ellison does not so much embrace as report. The young man who seems to represent the narrative present is more laughable than laudable, although Ellison insists that he epitomizes the potential for self-invention that Ellison had long celebrated.

I disagree. But I would argue that in the "little man" Ellison finds his most effective figure for the citizen, one who is both a shaper and a judge of a culture that often excludes him.

In its ideas and references, "The Little Man at Chehaw Station" ranges as widely as "Going to the Territory," but its digressions unfold in three discrete scenes. Two are from Ellison's past: one recounts a conversation with Hazel Harrison at Tuskegee and the other describes an encounter that Ellison had with black workingmen who moonlighted as extras at the Metropolitan Opera. In between these two narratives is an extended description of a young man, "a light-skinned blue-eyed Afro-American featured individual," who makes a spectacular appearance in Ellison's Upper West Side Manhattan neighborhood at a time fairly contemporaneous with the essay's writing. All three moments explore the "mystery of American cultural identity," a phrase that runs like a riff throughout the piece. The structure reinforces the idea that heterogeneity, appropriation, and adaptation have always defined the culture of the United States. Nevertheless, this idea takes Ellison, who both participates in and observes the two retrospective scenes and just observes in the present, by surprise every time. His persona invites readers to share his surprise and adopt his conclusions as their own.

The essay opens with a young Ellison seeking solace from Hazel Harrison after he has performed a trumpet solo that his teachers found lacking in the requisite technique. Harrison fails to offer the succor he expects. She responds instead, "But, baby, . . . in this country you must always prepare yourself to play your very best wherever you are, and on all occasions." The reason, she explains, is that even in the waiting room at Chehaw Station, the whistle stop that served the Tuskegee campus, "there'll always be a little man behind the stove." The man who, contravening one's expectations, will "know the *music*, and the *tradition*, and the standards of *musicianship* required for whatever you set out to perform!"[37] The essay takes the reader inside the "cramped waiting room" of Chehaw Station and evokes, without referring directly to, the realities of Jim Crow. Ellison avers that "a connoisseur might hear the haunting, blues-echoing, train-whistle rhapsodies blared by fast express trains as they thundered past, but the classics? Not a chance!" (491). Although the essay's language belies its critical investments—the fact of a blues "connoisseur" and "train-whistle-rhapsodies" undermine the idea of cultural hierarchy—the young Ellison has yet to learn that lesson. He is indignant that instead of sympathy, the maternal Harrison has given him a riddle. But, like the grandfather's riddle in *Invisible Man*, the riddle of the little man locks itself in the narrator/essayist's memory.

Eventually, the little man becomes identified with Harrison, the first African American to perform with a European orchestra, who, though, stuck in the Alabama backwater, is the exemplar of musicianship.[38] The little man is identified even more explicitly with the New York City workingmen who are at the center of the essay's third narrative. Again, personifying the naïf, Ellison describes himself as an employee of the Federal Writers Project, canvassing for signatures on a petition, when in the basement of a tenement building he overhears a loud, profane argument about the merits of two operatic sopranos. Certain in his identification of the voices as belonging to black laborers, he is mystified that they are both knowledgeable and passionate about a subject of which conventional wisdom decrees they should be ignorant. When he asks how they learned about opera, one responds, "At the Metropolitan Opera, just like I told you. Strip us fellows down and give us some costumes and we make the finest damn bunch of Egyptians you ever seen. Hell, we been down there wearing leopard skins and carrying spears or waving things like palm leafs and ostrich-tail fans for *years!*" (519).

The statement signifies on the august cultural institution's ignorance of both ancient Egyptians and contemporary black Americans, even as it reveals the speaker's cunning ability to profit from both. For Ellison, the men's skill in fashioning whatever identity the situation calls for confirms their Americanness. He chastises himself for being taken in by the American joke, as he calls it, which centers on the "incongruities of race, economic status and culture." It should not be surprising that "the men were products of both past *and* present; were both coal heavers *and* Met extras; were both workingmen *and* opera buffs" (519). Analogously, they were four little men behind the stove at Chehaw Station, who know the music, the tradition, and the requisite standards of musicianship. Ellison concludes, "Seen in the clear, pluralistic, melting-pot light of American cultural possibility, there was no contradiction" (519).

If the mystery of the coal heavers is solved, the mystery of the little man remains. It elicits the extended digressions characteristic of the Ellisonian essay. For example, "being quintessentially American," the little man "enjoys the joke, the confounding of hierarchal expectations, fostered by his mask: that cultural incongruity through which he, like Brer Rabbit, is able to convert even the most decorous of audiences into his own brier patch and temper the chilliest of classics to his own vernacular taste" (496). Never named or described, the little man has no individual history but is emblematic of the national history. He is the representative man, who belongs to the line of representative men celebrated by Emerson and Whitman. By inserting Hazel Harrison, Ellison makes it clear that the representative "man" could be a woman. The figure could also, of course, be black. Although Ellison does not directly identify the little man's race, his race is implicit in Harrison's riddle. In the trickster tradition, the little man is able to outwit those who would deny the complexity of his humanity. At moments in the essay, the little man is identified with Ellison himself, the artist who transmutes his experiences in segregated Oklahoma into a modernist classic, and the thinker whose ideas could be transformational to the nation's understanding of itself. Ellison's stance in this essay is less embattled but still congruent with that he assumes in "The World and the Jug" and "Change the Joke and Slip the Yoke." He is a thinker who is not taken as seriously as he deserves to be, because even those he respects confine him to an intellectual ghetto.

Ellison refuses to be confined. Referring to the Declaration of Independence, the Constitution, and the Bill of Rights, he avers, "We stand, as we say, united in the name of these sacred principles. But indeed it is in the name of these principles that we ceaselessly contend, affirming our ideals even as we do them violence" (501). This paradox of affirmation and betrayal, evoked so often in essays by African Americans, leads Ellison to the larger mystery that his essay explores. The disjuncture between the principles and the reality is the disjuncture between the ideal and the human. In the end, Ellison understands *America* as an abstract ideal. He explains that "principles in action are enactments of ideals grounded in a vision of perfection that transcends the limitations of death and dying. By arousing in the believer a sense of the dis-relation between the ideal and the actual, between the perfect word and the errant flesh, they partake of mystery" (503). Although he does not invoke it, Ellison's language is reminiscent of Kenneth Burke's description of "democracy" as "a god-term." By shifting the grounds of engagement from the secular to the sacred, Ellison returns us to the theological definitions of "mystery," which according to the OED denote a mystical presence, religious truth known only from divine revelation, religious ordinance, or an incident in the life of Christ. This is a necessarily discomfiting moment for those of us who consider the nation a secular entity. But it is not where the essay rests. Rather, it identifies "the most agonizing mystery sponsored by the democratic ideal," as "our unity-in-diversity, our oneness-in-manyness." On a pragmatic level, Americans "cooperate across this mystery," while on a deeper level, "the problem of identity that it poses often goads us to symbolic acts of disaffiliation" (505). As a consequence, Ellison argues, we take refuge in our natal racial, cultural, and religious affiliations. The result is the "blood magic and blood thinking," that he finds "rampant" in the America of the 1970s (505).

Ellison never identifies the proponents of Black Power and the Black Arts Movement as his antagonists, but they haunt the essay. Ellison found what he called "the ideology of blackness" as false and dangerous as the leftist ideology of his youth, an ideology that was pilloried in *Invisible Man*.[39] Even though Black Power was well past its heyday in 1978, Ellison continued to scoff at the idea of "a black culture" or "a white culture" and insisted as he always had that American culture was a tapestry whose threads could not be unwoven. In his view, those who fought for Black Power failed to see the victory that black Americans had already won. From his antagonists' perspective, Ellison failed to see the material realities that they struggled to change. Indeed, the more Ellison evoked abstract ideals, the less respect he earned from younger blacks. He returned the favor in the middle section of "The Little Man at Chehaw Station."

Wearing an Afro and a dashiki, riding boots, and a black Homburg, a blue-eyed black man "disrupts the peace" on Riverside Drive. He emerges from "a new blue Volkswagen Beetle decked out with a Rolls-Royce radiator" (505). The outward confusion would seem to mirror an inward one. The essayist opines that the car "might well have been loaded with Marxist tracts and Molotov cocktails," but its occupant is no revolutionary. He is instead a figure of narcissistic self-regard. Leaving his car, he sets the timer on his expensive camera so he can pose for a series of self-portraits. He never speaks. Unlike the coal heavers, he betrays neither a cultivated sensibility nor vernacular wisdom. He can only make a spectacle of himself.[40] If he is intended to mock the Black Power radicals, his author has changed the joke. For, as Ellison emphasizes, the young man is not simply black; rather, he represents an amalgam of races and hence the heritage of his country. After inviting readers to laugh *at* rather than *with* the young man, Ellison insists that the young man was "exercising an American freedom and was a product of the melting pot and the conscious or unconscious comedy it brews" (507). This statement attempts to associate the young man with the writer's oft-stated values, but the effort seems strained. The young man seems instead to evoke Ellison's unease with the historical moment of the sixties and seventies. Tellingly, one thing that distinguishes this young man from the other figures of the "little man" that the essay introduces is that he is an unwitting figure of comedy. By contrast, the little man behind the stove, Hazel Harrison, the coal heavers, and Ellison himself are all in on the joke.

Ellison is serious in his attack on those who reject the idea of the melting pot, including those whites who have benefitted from it themselves. He

argues that the idea was "never so simplistic or abstract" as its mockers pretend. Indeed, he asserts that few Americans of any group—and here he is certainly speaking of himself—had wanted "to lose [the group's] sense of its unique
past, not even when that past lay clouded in slavery" (508, 509). Ellison was
certainly unwilling to let go of that past. But that refusal would seem to contradict the tenor of the melting pot metaphor. Ellison's general position was
more in line with the cultural pluralism proposed by Alain Locke.[41] Here Ellison seems backed into a defense of the melting pot, because it was the object of his antagonists' attack. More convincingly, he acknowledges that
American culture is the result of "a process of cultural appropriation (and
misappropriation)," though he does not pause to reflect on the historical in-
equities it entailed. The end is what matters: it is through this process, a vernacular process, "that Englishmen, Europeans, Africans, and Asians *became*
Americans" (510, emphasis in original). His inclusion of Asians, for perhaps
the first time, affirms the continuing relevance of Ellison's cultural pluralism.
He wrote with an awareness of the nation's growing diversity, a diversity that
has increased exponentially since. This increasing heterogeneity has proven
as unsettling for many Americans as the young man on Riverside Drive is for
Ellison. Ellison does not deny the challenge and empathizes with the impulse
to avoid it. Then, characteristically, he embraces the chaos and contradiction:

> So perhaps we shy from confronting our cultural wholeness because it of-
> fers no easily recognizable points of rest, no facile certainties as to who,
> what or where (culturally or historically) we are. Instead, the whole is
> always in cacophonic motion. Constantly changing its mode, it appears as
> a vortex of discordant ways of living and tastes, values and traditions, a
> whirlpool of odds and ends in which the past courses in uneasy juxtaposi-
> tion with those bright, futuristic principles to which we, as a nation, are
> politically committed .... Deep down, the American condition is a state
> of unease (504).

The passage revises the familiar critique of the gap between the nation's
principles and its realities. Rather than Baldwin's fire next time, Ellison envisions the present as a whirlpool, an eddy, a vortex that threatens but does not
destroy. The constant motion and the cacophony of sounds make it difficult
to apprehend the cultural wholeness that Ellison believes in but which the
nation's history obscures. In this image, the founding principles evoke not the
past of broken promises but a future in which those promises could be realized. For the present, Americans have no option but to accept the "unease"
that is the American condition. Three decades after "The Little Man at Che-

haw Station" was written, that "unease" describes the global condition. No "facile certainties" define the identity of Americans or anyone else, although the compulsion to cling to natal racial, cultural, and religious affiliations is ever present. The discordant ways of living and tastes, values and traditions clash ever more viciously at the political level, although they sometimes achieve striking juxtapositions culturally. No single creed, sacred or secular, holds out a salvific promise. But the process of cultural adaption and exchange, enacted on a transnational stage, may be a cause for cautious optimism.

Nowhere in Ellison's essays do the names Alice Walker or June Jordan appear. Apart from Hazel Harrison and Zelia Breaux, Mahalia Jackson and Bessie Smith, black women artists are mainly invisible in his writing, even though by the time that "The Little Man at Chehaw Station" was published, a renaissance among African American women writers was rounding out its first decade. In crucial revisions of the tradition that Ellison bequeathed, Walker and Jordan reinsert their black female precursors into a literary history that excluded them. They make their own gendered as well as racialized experiences central to their writing. Yet, even as they reject Ellison's arguments and rely on a divergent set of allusions, they enact a vernacular process, a mode of fusing high and low styles, which he might have recognized.

CHAPTER SIX

On Women, Rights, and Writing

June Jordan and Alice Walker

My life seems to be an increasing revelation of the intimate face of universal struggle. You begin with your family and the kids on the block, and next you open your eyes to what you call your people and that leads you into land reform into Black English into Angola leads you back to your own bed where you lie by yourself, wondering if you deserve to be peaceful, or trusted or desired or left to the freedom of your own unfaltering heart. And the scale shrinks to the size of your skull: your own interior cage.

—June Jordan, "Civil Wars"

The truest and most enduring impulse I have is simply to write.

—Alice Walker, "The Unglamorous but Worthwhile Duties of the Black Revolutionary Artist, or of the Black Writer Who Simply Works and Writes"

Across three and a half decades, June Jordan and Alice Walker became prolific writers, friends, and sisters-in-struggle for civil rights, women's rights, and world peace. They corresponded, lectured together, and blurbed each other's books. Committed though they were to their politics, they were equally dedicated to their art. Their papers, recently opened to scholars, document these twinned commitments. The archives contain multiple handwritten and typed drafts of their writings, numerous invitations, open letters, and flyers from movement activists, as well as voluminous correspondence with devoted readers seeking encouragement and advice. Among the many genres in which they wrote, Walker's and Jordan's essays, in particular, chart their lifelong quest for a redemptive art and politics. Redemption here means the opportunity to seize the possibilities of a freer, more hopeful future, as well as coming to terms with a painful, oppressive past. The oppression they highlight is both racial and gendered. Their essays honor the heroism—and the artistry—of their foremothers even as they posit new definitions of womanhood.

Scrolling through the table of contents of *In Search of Our Mothers' Gardens*, readers perceive how redemptive both art and politics can be. Titles include "Saving the Life That Is Your Own: The Importance of Models in the Artist's Life," "If the Present Looks Like the Past, What Does the Future Look Like?" and "Only Justice Can Stop a Curse." Later volumes include *Living by the Word* (1988), *Anything We Love Can Be Saved* (1997) and *We Are the Ones We Have Been Waiting For: Light in a Time of Darkness* (2006). Jordan's titles are similarly resonant. She put her readers *on call* with a volume of political essays in 1985, identified *technical difficulties* in a volume subtitled *African American Notes on the State of the Union* in 1992, and insisted on the need for *affirmative acts* in 1998. More poignantly, in a challenge to readers to take up her mantle, she titled her posthumously published volume of essays *Some of Us Did Not Die* (2002).[1]

The vision in these texts is congruent with that of a roster of African American secular prophets from Maria Stewart and Frederick Douglass to Martin Luther King Jr. and James Baldwin who have called on their fellow citizens to redeem the promise of American democracy so deeply stained by the legacy of slavery and segregation.[2] Through the force of their words, they have forged communities of readers—across lines of race, gender, and class— that model the egalitarian ideal that they envision in their oratory and prose. This ideal animates Baldwin's call at the end of *The Fire Next Time* for the few "relatively conscious whites" and "relatively conscious blacks" to come together and avert the impending disaster."[3] Sophie Heywood, a character in Toni Cade Bambara's novel *The Salt Eaters*, puts it bluntly: "There is a world to be redeemed .... And it'll take the cooperation of all righteous folks."[4] The concept of a redemptive politics resonates with the genealogy of African American literary tradition generally and with the historical conditions that shaped the lives and work of Jordan and Walker specifically, as well as with their individual political commitments.

Born in Harlem to Jamaican immigrant parents, June Jordan (1936–2002) grew up in Brooklyn. She attended an elite boarding school for girls in Massachusetts before enrolling at Barnard College in 1954, the year that the *Brown v. Board of Education* Supreme Court decision heralded the eventual demise of segregation in the United States. Her early essays map her coming of age against the backdrop of the series of movements for social change that ensued, movements that she would eventually help shape. Alice Walker (1944–), the daughter of Georgia sharecroppers, left home in 1961 to attend Spelman College, the historically black college for women in Atlanta, just as the movement for civil rights took flight. Six years later, after graduating from Sarah Lawrence College, she would publish her first essay, "The Civil Rights Movement: What Good Was It?" Her answer begins with the transformation that it had effected in her own life. As with Jordan, one cause led to another, and it was inevitable that the woman from Bed-Stuy and the woman from rural Georgia would meet and make common cause.

They met first at Sarah Lawrence in 1972; Jordan was on the faculty, and Walker gave the convocation address, in which she declared that it was "a wonderful time to be a black woman" because of a past that boasted a rich literary legacy (which she was beginning to uncover) and because of the full freedom the future promised. Several months later, Jordan traveled to Mississippi where she interviewed Walker and her then-husband, Mel Leventhal, a white civil rights lawyer, as well as legendary freedom fighters Fannie Lou Hamer and Aaron Henry. In the published article Jordan introduced Walker as "the distinguished poet and novelist" and as "a gentle elegant person."[5]

By then, their respective careers were already in full throttle; they lived by the word literally and figuratively. Jordan would eventually publish more than twenty-five books, including multiple volumes of poetry, five children's books, three plays, a novel, and a memoir, before losing her battle with breast cancer in 2002. Her first essay was published in *The Nation* in 1967, and she would produce five books of essays, beginning with *Civil Wars* in 1981. By the time Jordan published *Affirmative Acts* in 1998, Toni Morrison had deemed her our "premiere black woman essayist."[6] For her part, few late twentieth-century essayists have been more widely read than Alice Walker. Published in journals and magazines, especially *Ms.*, Walker's earliest essays circulated among audiences devoted to political activism and intellectual inquiry. As they were reprinted in textbooks for undergraduate courses, not only in literature and women's studies but also in composition, Walker's essays reached audiences far beyond their initial readership. Her first essay collection, *In Search of Our Mothers' Gardens: Womanist Prose* (1983), has never gone out of print. With the publication of *The Color Purple* in 1982, Walker found her greatest fame as a novelist, but she continues to publish in many genres, including poetry, short stories, and children's books. At the time of this writing, she has more than thirty books to her credit.

Morrison's imprimatur notwithstanding, and despite the strength of their prose and their record of publication, Jordan and Walker have not achieved canonical status. Indeed, their writing has suffered critical neglect at best and scorn at worst. Variously dismissed as didactic, politically correct, sentimental, and "New Age," their work carries much less status than, say, Baldwin's.[7] Yet, I argue that their essays extend the genealogy of their more eminent precursors, while questioning and complicating the assumptions that those precursors held. Not surprisingly, in light of the sheer volume of their writing, its quality can be uneven. In some instances, the urgent need to intervene in a political emergency outweighs the desire to refine their prose. Sometimes the essays retain, for good as well as ill, the extemporaneous quality of the podium where they were first presented. But more often than not, their prose demonstrates the precision that comes from painstaking revision.

Publishing in various venues, but most often in *The Progressive* (Jordan) and *Ms.* (Walker), they use the essay to work through their political positions, to define themselves as black women, and to formulate aesthetic principles that serve them in all the genres in which they write. Their writing in fact exemplifies the importance of the essay as a medium for black women's intellectual production. Moreover, I argue, they revise the genre of the essay itself. For example, Jordan's poems sometimes become structural elements in her essays, while in other cases she uses the poetry as a model for her prose. The title "The Difficult Miracle of Black Poetry in America, or Something like a Sonnet for Phillis Wheatley," signals one attempt to blend genres. Throughout her career, Black English is not only a subject that Jordan writes about, it is one she writes through. Walker occasionally interjects poems into her essays as well, but the genre she draws on more often is fiction; the stories that she interpolates sometimes advance and at other times complicate the essays' arguments. Walker's essays imprint themselves on readers' memories due to the lucidity and cadence of the prose, their rich humor, and trenchant irony. They shift discursive registers with ease; vernacular voices speak as eloquently in the essays as in Walker's fiction.

Notably, both women came to political consciousness during the civil rights movement. As it struggled for the rights of African Americans to full U.S. citizenship, the movement redefined the ideal of "we the people" inscribed in the Constitution. The rhetoric of rights advanced the issues of equal access to education, public accommodation, and the vote. But the work of redefining the "we" was the essence of the "revolution" that these activists engaged. It was also the work that contemporary essayists, especially James Baldwin, embraced. Jordan and Walker pursue the implications of the redefinition of national belonging and expand it to include people left out of the social compact for reasons of gender, class, ethnicity, and sexual preference. They protest against the often unreported violence against women and children. They take the dictum that Martin Luther King Jr. asserts in "Letter from Birmingham Jail" that "injustice anywhere is a threat to justice everywhere" and apply it to a world that by the end of the twentieth century had become even smaller than King imagined. But their initial response to the movement is spurred by their realization that women were rendered invisible in the public discourse. They begin to change that. While Jordan writes about Mrs. Hamer, Walker extols the heroism of Mrs. Winsom Hudson, an activist in Harmony, Mississippi, one of an unsung army of female activists.[8] Most strikingly, in a gesture that seems inevitable only in hindsight, they place their own mothers at the center of their political critique.

Jordan often writes out of the tradition of the African American jeremiad—extending a line that runs from David Walker's *Appeal* to Douglass's "What to the Slave Is the Fourth of July?" to King's "Letter." Similarly, Jordan warns the nation to live up to its creed before the "civil wars" that were unfolding up-ended the republic; significantly for Jordan, civil wars not only threaten the public peace but the intimate bonds between men and women and between women. Eventually, and in her view, inexorably, Jordan's perspective broadens to encompass global wars that threaten to annihilate the planet. As she puts it, "My life seems to be an increasing revelation of the intimate face of universal struggle. You begin with your family and the kids on the block, and next you open your eyes to what you call your people and that leads you into land reform into Black English into Angola leads you back to your own bed where you lie by yourself, wondering if you deserve to be peaceful, or trusted or desired or left to the freedom of your own unfaltering heart. And the scale shrinks to the size of your skull: your own interior cage."[9]

No matter how large the subject, Jordan's lens is always personal, her voice is embodied, and singular. Not only is the personal political, the political is personal. The face of universal struggle is intimate; it begins with her lovers and kin, then her neighbors, and her people writ large, until the distance collapses between Bed-Stuy and Angola, as it does between intimate relationships and the struggle for land reform in Mississippi and Africa alike. This is possible because the writer's perspective is shaped by her personal experience, intellect, and desire. She is ever conscious of her particular identity as a woman of African descent living in the United States. While she does not argue that her identity itself grants her special insight, she insists that the history she carries, the experiences of her parents and forebears, bequeath a consciousness of struggle and an imperative to become a moral witness.

Walker is also concerned with reciprocity between the personal and the political, yet she writes with a different emphasis. The metaphor in the title of her first volume of essays contrasts tellingly with "civil wars"; her journey is "in search of our mother's gardens." As an essayist, Walker is perhaps most often lauded for her recuperation of her literary foremothers, especially Zora Neale Hurston, and for her definition of more inclusive traditions of art; she is also a political thinker. She originated "womanism," a concept that in distinguishing itself from feminism insists first of all on the right of black women to define their lives in their own terms. To declare oneself a "black feminist" is implicitly to assume a minority position in someone else's discourse; it is to ignore as well the history of resistance among African American women. Drawn from the black folk expression "womanish," womanism asserts the value of black women's culture and women's love for other women, even as it is "committed to the survival and wholeness of entire people, male *and* female."[10]

Signaling her right to change her own words, Walker appropriates dictionary form to define four meanings of "womanist." She defines the word first by establishing what it is not. Its antonyms include "'girlish,' i.e., frivolous, irresponsible, not serious." A womanist is a black feminist or feminist of color, presumably a new phenomenon in the world. But Walker's definition immediately connects the new to the old. The etymology of her word ("From *womanish*") establishes its derivation from black vernacular speech, as do the illustrations of usage that follow. Walker refers specifically to "the black folk expression of mothers to female children, 'you acting womanish,' i.e., like a woman." Like any good lexicographer, she notes the occasions on which the word might be used by these women, to wit, in response to "outrageous, audacious, courageous or *willful* behavior." The entry goes on to note that the expression from which womanist is derived is "interchangeable" with another black folk expression: "You trying to be grown." The first entry concludes with synonyms for Walker's neologism: "Responsible. In charge. *Serious*."[11]

Additional meanings for "womanist" denote what one does, including loving other women, sexually and/or nonsexually; appreciating and preferring women's culture; sometimes loving individual men, sexually and/or nonsexually; and being "committed to survival and wholeness of entire people, male *and* female" (xi). Here, too, the definition insists that despite the introduction of political and sexual dimensions that the users of "womanish" would not recognize, the concept is traditional in African American history and culture. A statement to illustrate the denotation of "traditionally capable" reads, "'Mama, I'm walking to Canada and I'm taking you and a bunch of slaves with me.' Reply: 'It wouldn't be the first time.'" The third definition enumerates those things that the womanist loves: music, dance, the moon, "the Spirit," love, food, roundness, struggle, "the Folk," and most profoundly, herself. The final meaning is represented as an analogy: "Womanist is to feminist as purple to lavender," which may just denote that its adherent is a deeper shade, or a woman of color. If, on the other hand, it implies that womanism is deeper than feminism, it signifies a troubling essentialism.

Walker's essays explore the implications of all the definition she sets forth in the front matter of *In Search*. Hurston, "funny, irreverent . . . good-looking,

[and] sexy," is surely the term's exemplar. Walker emphasizes Hurston's independent sense of self: "She would go anywhere she had to go: Harlem, Jamaica, Haiti, Bermuda, to find out anything she simply had to know. She loved to give parties. Loved to dance." Hurston's *joie de vivre* is as central to her self-definition as her intellectual commitment, her determination to find out what she had to know and her capacity to find the wherewithal to go where she had to go. Not only was she able to travel outside the United States, she was willing to transgress social norms in pursuit of knowledge. Walker refers to a time when Hurston sold hot dogs in Washington, D.C., in order to record black people's speech. It is fair to say that Hurston represents a new kind of intellectual in the African American tradition. That this essay is subtitled "A Cautionary Tale and a Partisan View" is appropriate; during her lifetime, Hurston's originality earned her more detractors than admirers. But to her partisan Walker, Hurston embodies the individual autonomy and cultural rootedness that womanism celebrates. Her dress combined African tradition (she wrapped her head in scarves) and modern American style (she wore slacks in the 1920s). Walker describes the image she thinks captures Hurston's persona precisely: "I have a photograph of her in pants, boots, and broadbrim that was given to me by her brother Everette. She has her foot up on the running board of a car—presumably hers, and bright red—and looks racy."[12] Offered as a parenthetical aside, almost a confidence, the statement highlights the personal nature of Walker's relationship with Hurston. If not kin herself, she is a good friend of the family. In that persona, she is perhaps allowed a Hurstonian "lie." Any photograph of a car with a running board would have to have been in black and white.[13]

As crucial as the figure of Hurston was to the definition of womanism, it played an equally key role in Walker's development as an essayist. In the 1970s, Hurston was an elusive figure; not even the most basic facts of her biography had been established. In sharp contrast to the triumphalism of Walker's 1990 address, "Anything We Love Can Be Saved: The Resurrection of Zora Neale Hurston and Her Work," the early essays introduced an author who was "in search" of her foremothers generally and "looking for Zora" in particular.[14] The tentativeness of the quest melded with the form. Walker drew on time-honored conventions: foregrounding her own questing persona, deploying quotations from a range of authorities whose positions contradicted each other, all the while moving toward a conclusion that was at once a personal epiphany and a truth that belonged equally to the writer and her reader. But Walker's essays bore her distinctive imprint: the authorities she cited included university professors and unlettered workers. Moreover,

Walker and her southern informants were gifted storytellers, who believed that wisdom was couched in laughter as often as in lofty pronouncement.

In "Looking for Zora," Walker draws a sharp distinction between the substantive if unacknowledged achievement of Hurston the writer and the slippery identity of Hurston the woman. The epigraph to the essay is one of several quotations cited from Robert Hemenway, who was then writing his highly regarded biography. Beginning with the lamentable end of Hurston's life, Hemenway asserts that in the 1970s she was "one of the most significant unread writers in America."[15] In an understated but orchestrated series of observations, Walker demonstrates Hurston's writerly significance. Recounting her aerial view of Hurston's hometown, Walker identifies landmarks from descriptions she has read in Hurston's writing. On the ground, Walker "knows" the landscape from Hurston's books. When a young Eatonville resident directs Walker to the town elder, Mathilda Moseley, Walker recognizes her from the folktale she tells in *Mules and Men*. Much like the narrator in that volume, Mrs. Moseley, a spry eighty-two-year-old, drives into Walker's text. Even when she fails to remember the facts that Walker wants to uncover, her pride, irrepressible spirit, and performance of an autonomous self ("I was so free I had to pinch myself sometimes to tell if I was a married woman" [98]) call Hurston's protagonists to mind. Hurston's acuity as a writer is confirmed.

But her identity remains impossible to pin down. Walker continues on her quest, mapping a journey from Hurston's childhood home in Eatonville to the site of her burial in Fort Pierce, Florida. She weighs the conflicting evidence offered by the many "witnesses" who speak through the essay, including Hurston's neighbors, physician, and undertaker. Their recollections are supplemented by quotations from authorities that include a Yale librarian, Hurston's literary peers Arna Bontemps and Langston Hughes, Walker's students, and Hurston herself.[16] They can agree on nothing—neither where she lived nor why she died or how she looked—let alone on the politics of her ethnographic practice or the aesthetics of her fiction. Rather than offering proof of a particular thesis, these contradictory opinions highlight how difficult it is to come to any conclusion. Looking for Zora is an ongoing project.[17]

In the essay, Walker's gift for storytelling brings her closest to capturing her subject. Paradoxically, the capture occurs as she discovers what she believes is Hurston's grave. The story is by now familiar, but the narrative's structure reveals much about Walker's practice as an essayist. First, she creates vivid characters. Three figures approach the cemetery: the white researcher, Charlotte Hunt, who greeted Walker upon her arrival in Florida, and who possesses more facts about Hurston's life than Walker does; Rosalee, a shy, uneducated, young black woman, who has never heard of Hurston but whose boss at the funeral home compels her participation; and the intrepid Walker, who becomes the protagonist in a mock heroic quest, one that shifts between the laughter and tears that Richard Wright found so objectionable in Hurston's fiction.[18] The quest culminates in a reassessment of Hurston's significance, both literary and biographical, as well as in Walker's rededication to her art.

Secondly, Walker imbues locations with symbolic meaning. The pilgrims arrive at the Garden of the Heavenly Rest, whose name could not be less apt. Nothing is tended. Graves are unmarked, and weeds grow waist-high. The scene evokes rage rather than rest. But one has to see it to react to it; the cemetery has almost disappeared from public consciousness. It is a "Negro" cemetery, where in the current dispensation, no new bodies are buried. Walker observes that it resembles most Negro cemeteries in the South; she is not surprised by the neglect, only by its extent. The "Garden" takes on symbolic weight as a remnant of a segregated past, a past that even black people are content, if not eager, to leave behind. In this sense, the cemetery becomes another one of the mothers' gardens figured in the volume's title, a site of history and memory that needs to be reclaimed.

This search first takes a comic turn, another characteristic of Walker's work. The humor derives from biblical and literary allusions, references to popular culture, and vernacular speech, as well as the absurdity of the situation. With a nod to Genesis, the three women profess to be afraid to enter the garden, because they are afraid of snakes. Charlotte is the first to peel away from the group. Instead of plunging into the weeds, she stands "resolutely near the road," insisting that being "from these parts," she "knows what's out there" (104). Walker takes the cue and channeling Hollywood westerns responds, "'Shit,' I say, my whole life and the people I love flashing melodramatically before my eyes" (104). Rosalee, who has been standing out of the frame, now moves center stage. The two black women will finish the quest. Reclaiming Hurston becomes a racialized mission; it also becomes one that depends more on intuitive ways of knowing than on facts. In the process, the essay takes risks similar to those inherent in Hurston's ethnographic project. In the end, Walker's willingness to assume these risks constitutes an important way in which she honors Hurston's example.

The comedy deepens as Walker, out of desperation, decides to call Zora by name. Rosalee answers with an irreverence that might be called Hurstonian:

"Zora!" I yell, as loud as I can (causing Rosalee to jump). "Are you out here?"

"If she is, I sho hope she don't answer you. If she do, I'm gone."

"Zora!" I call again. "I'm here. Are you?"

"If she is," grumbles Rosalee, "I hope she'll keep it to herself."

"Zora!" Then I start fussing with her. "I hope you don't think I'm going to stand out here all day, with these snakes watching me and ants having a field day. In fact, I'm going to call you just one or two more times." On a clump of dried grass, near a small bushy tree, my eye falls on one of the largest bugs I have ever seen. It is on its back, and is as large as three of my fingers. I walk toward it, and yell "Zo-ra!" and my foot sinks into a hole. I look down. I am standing in a sunken rectangle that is about six feet long and about three or four feet wide. I look up to see where the two gates are.

"Well," I say, "this is the center, or approximately anyhow. It's also the only sunken spot we've found. Doesn't this look like a grave to you?"

"For the sake of not going no farther through these bushes," Rosalee growls, "yes, it do."

"Wait a minute," I say, "I have to look around some more to be sure this is the only spot that resembles a grave. But you don't have to come."

Rosalee smiles—a grin, really—beautiful and tough.

"Naw," she says, "I feels sorry for you. If one of these snakes got ahold of you out here by yourself I'd feel *real* bad." She laughs. "I done come this far, I'll go on with you.

"Thank you, Rosalee," I say. "Zora thanks you too."

"Just as long as she don't try to tell me in person," she says, and together we walk down the field. (105–6)

The story is a comic tour de force. Its humor is sharpened by the narrator's awareness of her own artifice and by Rosalee's role as a comic foil. If drama is the prime "characteristic of Negro expression," Walker wholly embraces it. She lets the reader in on the joke by exaggerating the putative danger and mocking her fears. As the scene unfolds, Rosalee reveals that she, too, has "sufficient poise for drama" and joins in this "impromptu ceremony."[19] Possessed of a quick wit and cutting sense of humor, she goes toe to toe with Walker. Her language is steeped in what Hurston termed "Negro idiom." As the exchange continues, however, she sounds uncomfortably like a black sidekick in old movies, who is controlled by her fear rather than being in control of it. The representation veers close to the line of racial stereotype. To be sure, the razor's edge between stereotype and honest portrayal is one familiar to readers of Hurston's writing. Walker's willingness to go there is surprising, unsettling, and, ultimately, rewarding.

From the beginning of the essay, Walker introduces herself to everyone she meets as Hurston's niece, a lie she admits is unnecessary to solicit information but one altogether central to her understanding of herself as Hurston's literary heir and spiritual legatee. Hence Walker addresses Hurston familiarly, calling her by her first name, fussing with her, and insisting on a response. In one register, the reply comes through the voice and persona of Rosalee, whose sharp rejoinders are reminiscent of the characters that people Hurston's fiction. In another register, the reply comes from Hurston, who in effect speaks from the grave. The scene fuses the mundane and the spiritual, as it collapses the distance between the living and the dead. Here, too, Walker tips a hand to Hurston, whose informants in *Mules and Men* and *Tell My Horse* believed the boundary between the two to be porous. The belief animates scenes in Hurston's fiction as well, and the representations can as easily be comic as transcendent.[20]

The quick transitions from the mundane to the spiritual, the comic to the transcendent are omnipresent in African American expressive culture. Preachers and blues singers can move an audience from laughter to tears in an instant. As I argued earlier, the "jagged harmonies" of Hurston's own essays exemplify this attribute. Walker mines rich humor from her journey in "Looking for Zora," but she expresses her conclusion in prose that shifts seamlessly from the colloquial to the commanding:

> There are times—and finding Zora Hurston's grave was one of them—when normal responses of grief, horror, and so on do not make sense because they bear no real relation to the depth of emotion one feels. It was impossible for me to cry when I saw the field of weeds where Zora is. Partly this is because I have come to know Zora through her books and she was not a teary sort of person herself; but partly, too, it is because there is a point at which even grief feels absurd. And at this point, laughter gushes up to retrieve sanity.
>
> It is only later, when the pain is not so direct a threat to one's own existence, that what was learned in that moment of comical lunacy is understood. Such moments rob us of both youth and vanity. But perhaps they are also times when greater disciplines are born. (115–16)

Walker embeds her response to Hurston's neglect in the broadest possible frame of reference: "there are times." She invites readers to reflect on those moments in their own lives when "normal responses" were inadequate to the occasion. Then shifting to the first person, she reminds her readers that she has not described herself weeping, although she must realize that her words have elicited tears from many of them. Fittingly, the conclusion of the essay is introduced by Hurston's famous declaration that she did not belong to the "sobbing school of Negrohood" (115).[21] Walker refuses to relegate her to a status that, against heavy odds, she declined. Indeed, Walker speaks with an appreciation for the circumstances of Hurston's life as well as of her death while acknowledging the porous boundary between the two (Zora in "the field of weeds" *is*), when she insists that "there is a point at which even grief feels absurd." In a refiguring of the blues lyric, "I have to laugh to keep from crying," Walker insists that, unbidden, "laughter gushes up to retrieve sanity." With this phrase, she forces us to reconsider that razor's edge between stereotype and honest portrayal, to reassess the cultural work and psychological function that laughter performs.[22] The final moment in the essay is contemplative. It states what has been learned and what must be acted on in the future.

I would take nothing away from this magisterial conclusion. Nevertheless, I would argue that the signal moment in "Looking for Zora" occurs in the narrative of Walker's discovery of Hurston's grave. Whether or not it is her grave is unknowable, of course, and the monument that Walker erects is not the headstone she buys but the essay she writes. For Walker, the quest ends in "a greater discipline" and evinces her determination not only to honor Hurston's life but to avoid her fate (116). But the quest transforms Rosalee as well. The homely indifferent girl becomes a beautiful, tough young woman, who is as bold and audacious as the protagonists Hurston celebrated. Having begun the adventure never having heard of Zora Neale Hurston, she ends it by being one of Hurston's spiritual kin. Hurston's legacy is open then to those who would partake of it, even though, in the essay's present, people even in Eatonville do not know who she was.[23] Hurston is, Walker contends, the aunt of all black people, and she suggests that in redeeming her life we come into a fuller understanding of our own. She invites her readers, in other words, to continue to look for Zora.

Like other women whose stories Walker records, Rosalee and Mathilda Moseley become exemplars of womanism. Hurston does not stand alone. She is aligned with the nineteenth-century mystic Rebecca Cox Jackson, an itinerant minister who was dismissed from first the African American Episcopal Church and then from the Shakers because she insisted on following only the command of the spirit. Other womanist exemplars include dozens of black women writers and artists, from Phillis Wheatley to Nella Larsen and Bessie Smith, whom Walker celebrates, the women in Jackson, Mississippi, who in Walker's classroom begin to write their autobiographies, as well as Walker's female kin, her mother and aunts who refused to accept the limitations imposed on them by reasons of race and gender. Some of the stories she tells, as of the "crazy saints" in "In Search of Our Mothers' Gardens," recount women who are beaten down or driven into madness. The women who survive are those who love themselves regardless. Walker's ideas on female autonomy have been generative for social thinkers and theologians, some of whom advocate positions more nationalistic and religious than Walker herself advances.[24] While Walker's coinage has its adherents, history has not borne out the hesitation that inspired it. Black women have defined black feminism proudly, defiantly, and wholly in their own terms.

Indeed, Jordan produced her own black feminist credo, "Where Is the Love?" in 1978. It, too, contends that black feminism is about self-love, self-respect, and self-determination. With its title borrowed from a hit recording by Roberta Flack and Donny Hathaway and its publication in *Essence*, a popular magazine geared to middle-class black women, "Where Is the Love?" appealed to a readership beyond activists and intellectuals. It argued that black feminism is rooted not only in the twin oppressions of race and gender; it is rooted in love. Aligning herself with freedom fighters like Mrs. Hamer and identifying with women and people of color throughout the world, Jordan stakes out her position: "And it is here, in this extreme, inviolable coincidence of my status as a Black feminist, my status as someone twice stigmatized, my status as a Black woman who is twice kin to the despised majority of all the human life that there is, it is here, in that extremity, that I stand in a struggle against suicide. And it is here in this extremity, that I ask, of myself, and of any one who would call me *sister, Where is the love?"* (143).

Jordan embraces the marginality of her position; its very extremity compels and rewards her stance. The sisterhood challenge opens outward to white women and to black men, as well as inward to other black women, as well as to the author herself. The black feminist Jordan claims to be has the moral responsibility to love and respect women who are not like her and, "without fear, to love and respect all men who are willing and able, without fear, to love and respect me" (143). The syntactical structures reinforce the reciprocity of the claims and echo the overlapping call and response of Flack and Hathaway's duet. The credo rejects demands allegedly predicated on the "Good of The People" that are in fact based on concepts of manhood, family, or nationalism and require women's subjugation. In pointing to the female majority, it declares that "We *are* the people" (144). The constitutional echo is deliberate and familiar, for as Jordan remarks in the essay "Black People and the Law: A Tribute to William Kunstler": "No one has ever trusted the founding words of the founding legal documents that defined this republic independent of England more than the Black people of these United States." Given their vulnerability under the law, blacks believed that the circumstances of their lives could be changed profoundly if the law were changed.[25] Even when she grew skeptical of the sentiment, Jordan continued to deploy the rhetoric.

Originally presented at the National Black Writers Conference at Howard University, "Where Is the Love?" put feminism front and center in black intellectual debates. As Jordan reconstructs the event in an author's note in *Civil Wars*, the standing-room-only crowd had come armed for battle. She recognizes that for many in the audience black feminism was synonymous with lesbianism, which allows them to reject it out of hand. Jordan treads carefully, as she refuses to adopt the language of heteronormativity. Instead she adopts a stance that might be called "Baldwinian." She insists that "whatever sexuality anyone elects for his or her pursuit is not my business, nor the business of the state" (144). She defines love as "a steady-state deep caring and respect for every other human being, a love that can only derive from a secure and positive self-love" (144). Couching her intervention in the language of love worked both to defuse the immediate conflict and to reframe the larger challenge. She deems her effort a success. As she concludes, she had hoped to carve out a space in which "we, Black panelists and audience together, would work out a way to deal, even if we didn't want to deal. And that's what happened" (141).[26]

If, like Jordan, Walker demonstrates a sustained engagement with progressive politics, Jordan, like Walker, participates concurrently in the reclamation of African American women's literary history. "Where Is the Love?" ends with a tribute to Georgia Douglas Johnson, the Harlem Renaissance poet. After Walker urged her to read *Their Eyes Were Watching God*, Jordan wrote "Notes Toward a Black Balancing of Love and Hatred"—an essay published the same year as the title essay "In Search of Our Mothers' Gardens"—to argue for the importance of affirmation as well as protest to African American literature and laud the legacies of both Hurston and Richard Wright. In sharp contrast to Hurston and Wright, Walker and Jordan supported each other; they read and commented on each other's writing. In her acknowledgements to *In Search*, Walker thanks her "friend June Jordan" for sharing her thoughts on some of the pieces. In the rest of this chapter, I put the essays of these two remarkable writers in conversation, highlighting their resonances as well as their crosscurrents and discontinuities.

In 1975, Jordan and Walker jointly presented the inaugural Reid Lectures, a series devoted to women's experiences, at Barnard, which published their presentations "Notes of a Barnard Dropout" and "Saving the Life That Is Your Own: The Importance of Models in the Artist's Life," respectively, in booklet form. Jordan included her piece as an essay in *Civil Wars*, and after reworking it extensively used it as the opening essay of her final 2002 collection, *Some of Us Did Not Die*. "Saving the Life" is the lead essay of *In Search*.

Jordan begins "Notes of a Barnard Dropout" by promising to share—or in fact "to try" to share—with her audience her "perspective on things," an innocuous enough promise that is immediately darkened by the announcement that "you could probably characterize my worldview as apocalyptic—or, let's just say that I believe that, as Aretha sings the song, A CHANGE IS GONNA COME."[27] The familiar mode of address stems in part from the fact that these "Notes" first took the form of a speech. Yet "Notes" is essayistic in its tentativeness and in its assertion that its perspective is personal. The use of the subjunctive reinforces the tentative quality, except that there is nothing tentative about apocalypse. The reference to Franklin's recording of the classic Sam Cooke song forces the audience to revise its understanding of a recording they had likely heard on the radio and to consider the possibility that Jordan's perspective is not merely personal but collective. By putting the song's title in caps, she heightens its prophetic signification. She also deploys a strategy that dates back to David Walker, who used it to achieve a similar end.

By the third of three brief paragraphs, Jordan establishes a dialectic between the apocalypse that widespread social injustice portends and the optimism that "life itself compels" (95). Enumerating injustices, Jordan includes the local and the global, the macro (the unequal treatment of women around the world) and the micro (she calls for a "tax strike" to protest the unequal treatment of New York City by the federal government). After laying out her worldview, she proposes to explain how she developed it. It quickly becomes apparent that the social dialectic mirrors the binaries of her life: a working-class childhood and an elite education. The inability of that education to connect the high-flown ideas of the college classroom to the harsh material realities of her neighborhood or even to suggest how academic knowledge might *change* those realities causes her eventually to drop out. Jordan is sometimes wry about the lessons of a liberal arts education—Barnard taught her the difference between an Ionian and a Corinthian column—and sometimes appreciative of its benefits: courses in sociology taught her a new way to think about things, and Barry Ulanov, "a great teacher," challenged her to do things differently. His assignments asked her to make connections between disparate texts and to write about whatever topic she chose without using any forms of the verbs *to be* or *to have*. Despite his pedagogical talent, not even Ulanov, a scholar of jazz as well as of religion and psychology, could illuminate the political value of her education or show her how to connect it to the pain of her personal experience.

In the end, the passion that fuels the essay's rage does not center on abstract arguments about the purpose of education or on the urgent need for social justice, but on the image of Jordan's mother and her nightly ritual of emptying the furnace and carrying heavy pails of ashes up the stairs. This onerous unpaid labor was in addition to the work that she did as a private duty nurse. Her husband required it as the price that she must pay for witnessing his humiliation; despite his hard work, the family remained poor. After introducing this fact, Jordan shares the recollections of her college experiences. Then, at the essay's turning point, she expresses her desire for an apocalypse, a revolution, which would redeem her mother's sacrifices. As the audience fades from her view, she addresses the mother directly and intimately. The last four paragraphs of the essay might be read as prose poems; each begins "Ah, Momma," but the punctuation of the address changes to signal the tonal shifts in the daughter's voice.[28]

Jordan first evokes the memory of the mother in her "little room," a space off the kitchen where the mother's uniforms were stored along with her costume jewelry. To the child, that jewelry had shone like the real thing, though in retrospect she realizes that even the space itself was more a closet than a room and the "secondhand mirror blurred the person" (101). Nothing was seen clearly; yet one moment stands out: the mother's whispered confidence that she had wanted to become an artist. The next "Ah, Momma!" conveys the mature daughter's understanding of what the mother has lost, even though at the time both referred to her desire as "a wish," and the daughter's response was "almost terrified amazement." The tension between the diminutive "wish," and the intense emotions it provoked ("terrified amazement") represents another site of disconnection. The third "Ah Momma:" introduces a contrast between the "little room" and the kitchen it adjoins. The former is the holder of the mother's secrets, her jewelry, her perfumes, and the photographs of an old boyfriend, but it does not allow her to come to self. The kitchen is even less hospitable. It contains no secrets, which, given the daughter's inability to "know" the mother, deepens the mystery about her. In a gesture familiar from fiction, the mother covers her hair: under her nurse's cap when she goes to work and under a head rag at home. The mother's "wild and heavy, beautiful hair" symbolizes the self that she is never able to assert. The next "Ah, Momma," introduces a coded scene of discovery—"it was where I found you, hidden away"; the little room is revealed in subsequent writings to be the site of the mother's death, a suicide. What is represented here is an epiphany: the moment when Jordan determines to prove that she is in fact worthy to be her mother's daughter. The essay's last line is "Ah, Momma, I am still trying" (102). As affecting as this moment is, the essay asks that we read it in context. The daughter's personal determination cannot redeem the mother's sacrifice; to do so will require collective political action.

It is worth noting that Jordan had been in the audience at Radcliffe on May 5, 1972, when Walker read "In Search of Our Mothers' Gardens" for the first time at a symposium on "The Black Woman: Myths and Realities." She had consoled and encouraged Walker when a black woman at a subsequent panel criticized Walker for giving emotional support to her mother rather than to black men. Jordan angrily exclaimed, "But why shouldn't you carry your mother; she carried *you*, didn't she?" The response quelled Walker's tears. Had "In Search of Our Mothers' Gardens," arguably the most influential of Walker's essays, not been published in *Ms.* the year before, it would have been the ideal companion piece for "Notes of a Barnard Dropout."[29]

"Saving the Life That Is Your Own" resonates as well. Like Jordan, Walker reflects, indirectly, on her relationship to Western tradition; she argues that making connections produces the larger perspective necessary to apprehend the whole story—"the one American story." She honors the example of her mother and ties the mother's example to her own literary practice. But the dissimilarities in these two essays are as revealing as these thematic similarities. "Saving the Life" interpolates a series of narratives—from the life of Vincent Van Gogh, to Walker's experiences at college and on the lecture circuit, to her effort to write a story about voodoo, to the family legend about the "crazy Walker aunt," to her proud mother's account of being humiliated during the Depression when a white woman accused her of being too well dressed to deserve government surplus food. These disparate narratives move together to illuminate Walker's situation as a black woman writer in a society where inhabiting those three identities is anomalous. The essay's moves seem spontaneous, as if one thought led necessarily to the next, but that willed randomness is a measure of the writer's craft. An artful essay creates the impression that the reader along with the writer achieves its conclusions. By the time the reader reaches the apostrophes to "Zora," late in "Saving the Life," it seems foreordained that Hurston would be the model that saves Walker's literary life.

The essay begins with an unlikely reference to a letter Vincent Van Gogh wrote to his friend Émile Bernard, six months before the painter committed suicide. Writing from the asylum in Arles, he laments the general state of the world and of his specific predicament: he was an artist who felt keenly the absence of models for his work. Then in the very next sentence he confirms that he continues to work anyway: "But on the other hand, there are beautiful spots here. I have just done five size 30 canvases, olive trees."[30] For Walker, his words exemplify the way an artist thinks: despite the lack of an understanding and appreciative audience, the artist lives for his work. Walker was thirty-one years old in 1975; she had published two books of poetry, *Once* (1968) and *Revolutionary Petunias* (1973), the novel *The Third Life of Grange Copeland* (1970), a book of short stories, *In Love and Trouble: Stories of Black Women* (1973), and a juvenile biography, *Langston Hughes: American Poet* (1973). These achievements notwithstanding, to compare herself to one of the masters of Western art is more than a little audacious.

As the essay unfolds, however, it becomes clear that audacity is both a necessity and a birthright. Walker rues the inability of readers to resist dividing black American and white American writers; then she hypothesizes a difference: blacks, writing out of a tradition that began with the slave narrative, valorize struggle in their literature, while whites explore defeat. Quick though she is to acknowledge that her generalization is not tenable, she uses it to frame a comparison of Kate Chopin's *The Awakening* and Hurston's *Their Eyes Were Watching God*. Today's college students would be surprised to learn that only one person in Walker's audience had heard of Hurston, though they would see in the essay how Walker's efforts helped to change that. Walker interjects a short poem, "I love the way Janie Crawford left her husbands," which underscores the novel's theme of freedom and self-possession.

On the one hand, "Saving the Life" is the record of a writer reading. Walker refers to fifteen fiction writers in the essay, among them Charlotte and Emily Brontë, Colette, Camara Laye, Gabriel García Márquez, and Flannery O'Connor; her title alludes to one of O'Connor's famous stories, "The Life You Save May Be Your Own." Like Hurston's, much of this writing did not show up on the syllabi of courses at either Spelman or Sarah Lawrence. After graduating from the latter, Walker enters what she calls a "college of books."[31] Even as this reading enlarged her perspective, it did not satisfy her thirst for models. But as the essay records the process of the writer writing, it explains how that thirst is quenched. Significantly, the process begins with Walker listening to her mother's story, which in repeated tellings always ends with her nemesis growing old and crippled. To the mother this is divine retribution, but the daughter hears in the story the possibilities for fiction. In order to impart agency to the victim in her story "The Revenge of Hannah Kemhuff," Walker gives her protagonist access to voodoo as a weapon of resistance. In one of several versions she has offered for her discovery of Hurston, here she describes how in doing her research on voodoo, she came across Hurston's name in a footnote.

The first black anthropologist to conduct fieldwork on voodoo, or as she preferred, "hoodoo," Hurston provided the information that Walker needed to complete her story. While her contemporaries often used the terms hoodoo and voodoo interchangeably, Hurston used hoodoo to refer to African-derived spiritual beliefs and practices followed by black southerners in the United States, which she documented in her *Mules and Men*; she used voodoo to refer to the more systematic belief system, which she later studied in Haiti and documented in *Tell My Horse*. In part because she took black people's beliefs and values seriously, even and especially those that were most likely to elicit scorn from outsiders and shame from blacks themselves, Hurston also became the model who affirmed Walker's choice of vocation. Hurston, who was fond of the Black English word "bodacious" (bold + audacious), offers Walker a literary legacy as well as a model for living a free life that is marked by unwavering dedication to one's work. As is typical of Walker's early essays, Hurston's example is tied to the example of Walker's mother and of other women in her family ("the crazy Walker aunt"). About the prize-winning story that fictionalizes her mother's experience, Walker remarks, "In that story I gathered up the historical and psychological threads of the life my ancestors lived, and in the writing of it I felt joy and strength and my own continuity" (13). The larger perspective then connects the literary with Walker's lived experience and personal history. Rather than alienating her from her family in the Western tradition of the male artistic genius, her art—like the essay itself—weaves together its disparate threads.

For both Walker and Jordan, writing is a way of participating in political struggle. In "The Unglamorous but Worthwhile Duties of the Black Revolutionary Artist, or of the Black Writer Who Simply Works and Writes," Walker concedes that her "truest and most enduring impulse . . . is simply to write." Even as she does so, she is keenly aware that "our people are waiting" (133). Devoting herself solely to her art is not an option. She cites teaching remedial reading and preserving the legacy of literary precursors as work the black

writer must do. In unpublished notes for a speech titled "The Essay as a Political Contemporary Form," Jordan expresses her sense of obligation in terms
of the writing itself. Her understanding of the genre and its requirements
clarifies the stakes for all of the essays discussed in this chapter, particularly
her own "Civil Wars."

In Jordan's view, the political essay is an argument and a method of persuasion as well as an art. As an intervention in the political arena in which conflicting ideas compete, it serves the goals of democracy. That is, it offers a
nonviolent means of conflict resolution. Notably, it requires that writers address their readers, who might be political antagonists or indifferent onlookers, directly. The ability to engage in political debate is essential for citizenship;
likewise respect for one's fellow citizens is a cardinal value in a democratic
state. Far from being consigned to the dustbin of history, Jordan argues, essays
appear everywhere in contemporary society—in feature articles, editorials,
fellowship and grant applications, legal briefs, and reviews. Consequently, everyone ought to be able to write them. I am reminded that at Berkeley, where she
taught for more than fifteen years, Jordan led an initiative called "Poetry for
the People," that likewise testified to her belief that art was not for the elite.

The second section of the talk addresses the structure of the political essay. Its method of persuasion might include elements that are "unarguable,"
as in autobiography; "disarming," as in assertions of guilt; and "devious," as in
the deployment of irony, such as "apparently condemning a man but, actually,
setting him up to praise him." In contrast, the essay might employ a "decep-
tively straightforward" approach by appealing to the authority of scholarship
and research (i.e., "the facts"). Or it might assume an "adversarial and/or
quasi-logical" posture, as, for example, "My opponent says/does, but I say/
do" and point-by-point rebuttal, or "the authority of caution." Although Jordan
does not define this last term, I take it to mean the urge to resist having the
final word, the willingness to leave matters open in case more information
comes to light. The "authority of caution" is the authority the essayist exerts.
Jordan adds a final note, "*Art*, yes, but also: The chief enemy of good writing
is insincerity—George Orwell." At the top of the three sheets of yellow-lined
paper, Jordan lists Orwell and Joan Didion as recommended reading.[32]

The disarming argument of "Civil Wars" is that personal integrity and social justice sometimes demand acts of incivility. Moving from general observation to the specific tensions between Jordan and a white female friend to an
account of the 1980 Miami riots that were sparked by the murder of a black
man by the police, the essayist insists that honesty should trump politeness
and violence is the appropriate antidote to violence. In sum, "the courtesies

of order, of ruly forms pursued from a heart of rage or terror or grief defame the truth of every human crisis."[33] Despite the pain attendant to working through these crises, Jordan holds out the hope that the end of these civil wars might be something that looks like love. To make her point, she incorporates elements from the outline referenced above: autobiography, quotations from authorities, appeals to the quasi-logical and to the authority of caution.

"Civil Wars" opens with a scene immediately familiar to most readers—a familiarity reinforced by the use of the second person pronoun. "You" recognize the situation in which you sit politely in a group rather than disrupt the proceeding and get at a truth. Then after stating the thesis—that courtesy "defames" truth—Jordan appeals to an unlikely authority. She quotes from the nineteenth-century English essayist William Hazlitt's "On the Pleasure of Hating." Reading the "panegyric" to hatred as an adolescent, Jordan recalls, she was "shocked awake." "Civil Wars" means to provoke an analogous response in its audience. Yet to narrow the distance between her teenaged self, reveling in forbidden emotion, and her skeptical, perhaps indifferent, and probably well-mannered reader, Jordan concedes that she herself "is frequently polite." She admits that "I go to meetings and sit, properly, in one chair. I write letters to Washington. It's been a long time since I actually hit anybody at all" (180).

Jordan introduces her friend, Frances Fox Piven, as "a brilliant and radical humanitarian," antiracist activist, scholar, and mother.[34] The women have much in common. What divides them are their conflicting views on gay rights—a priority for Jordan who has come out as bisexual and which Piven sees as a digression from civil rights—as well as on Mideast politics and the discord between blacks and Jews in New York. Their sharp disagreements have fractured their friendship. "Civil Wars" recounts a lunch during which their attempt to confront their differences only widens the rift between them. Jordan's article on the murder of Victor Rhodes, a young black Brooklynite, by members of an orthodox Jewish community has outraged Piven, who considers it anti-Semitic. Jordan is stunned by the charge. The atmosphere is heavy with recriminations and hurt.

"And then," the essay announces, "the good news of Miami burst upon America" (182). The terrain shifts from North to South, private to public, thought to action. The shifts are no less jarring than the assertion that riots are "good news." They end "a whole lot of silence." Redirecting her attention, Jordan exults in the uprising. She catalogs the missing signs of order: no leaders, no organization, no spokesman, no agenda, no meetings, no negotiations. Then she summarizes the meaning of the event: "A violated people reacted with violence. An extremity of want, an extremity of neglect, an extremity of racial oppression had been met, at last, with an appropriate, extreme reaction: an outcry and a reaching for vengeance, a wreaking of havoc, in return for wrecked lives, a mutilation of passers-by in return for generations mutilated by contempt and by the immutable mutilations of poverty. Miami was completely impolite" (182–83).

Oppressed people's right to retaliatory violence is a recurrent theme in Jordan's writing—from the portrait of Fannie Lou Hamer's mother in the juvenile biography to Jordan's self-portrait in her memoir *Soldier*.[35] According to her "quasi-logical" reasoning in "Civil Wars," the response to oppression ought to be commensurate to the oppression itself. Through the deft use of alliteration, assonance, and parallelism, the scales are verbally balanced: the violated and violence, extremity of neglect and extreme reaction, wreaking of havoc and wrecked lives. The alliteration (mutilation, mutilated, immutable, and mutilations) represents Jordan at her most oracular. She represents the violence done in the everyday lives of poor blacks—whose poverty has inflicted "immutable mutilations"—as far more destructive than the harm done in the transitory actions of a riot. At the paragraph's end, having achieved an emotional climax, Jordan lowers the temperature and returns to the central argument of the essay with a final alliterative move: "*M*iami was completely *im*polite" (emphasis added).

Jordan wants Miami to represent both historical continuity ("not without precedent") and something new. Unlike urban rebellions in the 1960s, the Miami riots reached beyond black neighborhoods. In Jordan's view, the violence was turned outward toward the community's oppressors rather than inward on itself. The rioters were immune to the blandishments of professional leaders; as Jordan observes approvingly, "there was no tolerance left for airplane leadership," referring to those who were once summoned to put out literal and figurative fires. "When this house caught on fire," she contends, "everybody was home" (184). In a provocation that resonates with Hazlitt's, she describes Miami as "anarchy in the best sense: it was pure" (184). Moreover, it was an act of love—for the murdered and for all Miami blacks. People who lived through the riot might not agree. Historians who document the event reach different conclusions. "Civil Wars" is not an eyewitness account of the Miami riots. Instead the riots occasion larger reflections on violence, history, and the obligation of every citizen to be his or her own leader. Neither race nor gender is determinative.

In her notes on the political essay, Jordan does not define the "authority of caution." But the term is useful in reading the conclusion of "Civil Wars." After a long estrangement, Jordan calls Piven after reading her book *Poor*

People's Movements: Why They Succeed, How They Fail. Jordan explains her decision to call Piven in terms of a *feeling*, rather than a position or ideology, to wit: "What the hell; friendship is not a tragedy; we can be polite" (188). The verbal shrug, the putative devaluation of the relationship, and the recourse to the politeness that the essay has forsworn do not gainsay the moment's significance. Negotiating a truce between friends is every bit as important as negotiating between races or nations, and this truce is no less treacherous to achieve. "To talk" is the essay's last word and final promise, yet it strikes a cautionary note.

Walker's aptly titled essay "Lulls" belongs to the same historical period as "Civil Wars," a period of political disorganization and inactivity. Structured as a series of vignettes, "Lulls" becomes a meditation on the progressive movements' deferred dreams. Returning to Atlanta for the commemoration of King's birthday, not yet a national holiday, Walker joins a march for jobs. Even the marchers have lost the fervor for the cause; the only singer able to infuse the movement anthem "We Shall Overcome" with the "old righteous energy" is a bystander unmistakably strung out on drugs.[36] Rather than the memories of movement victories, the scene stirs thoughts of the relentless efforts by the CIA and FBI to assassinate King's character and undermine the movement. In the wake of his murder, the movement seems almost to have died. Walker's musing on the ineffectiveness of demonstrations anticipates Jordan's, but the tone is conversational: "Marching is such a drag once you realize that every time you're out here ruining your feet, your President and congressmen are off skiing somewhere" (182). What redeems the rally for Walker is her long-lost cousin's voice. Their embrace counters the disillusionment that both women experience. Thus, "Lulls" begins where "Civil Wars" ends, with the hope invested in personal relationships rather than political action.

Surprised that her Ivy League educated cousin has joined the clergy, Walker is unconvinced by her explanation that the church has more power than any other institution in the black community. Worse yet, her cousin explains that the aunts, whose stories "about the old days when each of them had been able to fish and hunt and trap, to shoot 'straight as a man'" Walker cherishes, have relinquished their independence in order to live as much like the white ladies they envied as possible (184). This news renders Walker speechless. Understandably. The aunts' example is at the core of womanism; it buoys Walker's belief that many black women reveled in their autonomy well in advance of the advent of second-wave feminism. Her aunts' regression is discouraging; it registers as an unintended consequence of racial progress.

As Walker contacts friends from her hometown, she wonders whether the price paid for integration has been worth the sacrifice. Joe, who has moved from Eatonton to Boston and then to Atlanta, has nothing good to say about the North, where he could only find menial work and where "Black people . . . have so little unity they won't even get together for a riot" (186). But Joe is an unreliable source; he is so scarred by racism that he calls his young sons "niggers." Walker remembers that she had earlier found his use of the word so hurtful that she stopped seeing him. As the essay recounts the present conversation, Walker's anger is the catalyst for both her cousin and Joe's silent wife to speak. They remark other examples of black self-hatred—including the mocking humor directed at black women on television—and lament the fact that even though they can now live anywhere, they have yet to find a home.

At the time Walker is living in Brooklyn. She boasts to her former neighbors in Jackson, Mississippi, about the trees, the rose garden, and friends who are "so civil and generous and *clean* they are nobody's idea of what New Yorkers are like" (194). The reader later wonders, reluctantly, about the racial identity of these neighbors, for, when asked to name the worst thing that has happened to her in New York, Walker takes a while to respond, then admits that for the first time in her life, she is afraid of other black people. By contrast, in Eatonton, she had felt at ease even with black men on the chain gang. The picture she paints is bleak: "The bonds of black kinship—so sturdy, so resilient—have finally been broken in the cities of the North. There is no mutual caring, no trust. Even the rhetoric of revolutionary peoplehood is hissed out threateningly. The endearment 'sister' is easily replaced with 'bitch.'" Walker describes her "fear" as "part grief," and concludes that "if I were ever attacked or robbed by another black person I doubt I'd recover" (194–95).

Whether or not she overstates the case, Walker opens up a difficult set of questions. Her premise is that the bonds of racial kinship are valuable. They enabled the survival of blacks in the segregated South, where blacks had no choice but to assume that a white face denoted a potential threat. By the same token, black faces signaled refuge. Prisoners depended on the kindness of their fellow blacks; there was no such thing as a black stranger. Implicitly, the essay asks whether these attachments have outlived their usefulness. The answer is unclear. Walker visits her daughter's first teacher in Jackson, where she and her white husband lived in defiance of the law, and remembers that it was there "that the culture and curriculum matched serenely, where Rebecca learned to sing 'Ain't Gonna Let Nobody Turn Me 'Round' as readily as 'You

Are My Sunshine,' where she could hear the story of Harriet Tubman read to her and see Harriet herself in her teacher's face" (196).

As do many blacks who came of age under the regime of segregation, Walker expresses some nostalgia for it. She would seem here, in Jordan's formulation, to take refuge in race and gender. But I think that something more is at work in the reference to her child's teacher. How does self-hatred heal? How does one inculcate a healthy sense of self in black children? Might the lessons of history—from both generations past (Tubman) and the recent past (emblematized in the spiritual the civil rights movement revived)—serve as a balm? Walker seems aware of the intellectual tightrope she walks here, as she gives up the possibility of objective truth by accepting as fact that history's lessons carry a different resonance depending on who teaches them.

What the essay opens up for its readers is a place to have these knotty conversations. All of the vignettes in "Lulls" raise issues that gnaw at thoughtful readers. What comes after protests and demonstrations? Does a "black community" exist? If so, who constitutes it? Who are its leaders? Does the materially comfortable but socially segregated life available to some blacks in postmovement Atlanta represent progress? How does class signify? What does the reverse migration of black people back to the South mean? Are the schools and streets of the North more dangerous for the physical and psychological health of black children than the rural backwaters their parents left behind? All of the answers are tentative. None are easy. All raise as many questions as they resolve. Yet, through her command of the essay form, Walker invites readers to puzzle the issues out with her and welcomes them to share in the understandings that she does achieve. In the end, those understandings belong to writer and reader alike.

Much like Baldwin, Jordan pens numerous essays that might be located in the force field deemed "America." These pieces insist on the one hand that the United States live out its creed at home, and, on the other, that the nation end its hegemony abroad. These dual impulses inspire her to weigh in on the political issues of the day—from the Jesse Jackson campaigns to the Los Angeles riots, the trials of O. J. Simpson and Mike Tyson, the Clarence Thomas–Anita Hill hearings, and the Million Man March. As we have seen, forms of the word "democracy" are omnipresent in Jordan's writing, and she frequently invokes the letters of the republic. To be sure, she takes a revisionist position toward them, asserting that "democracy was never the goal of the Founding Fathers."[37] In contrast, "We the People" perfected the Constitution, a living document, over time. She consistently refers to exemplary Americans, including Douglass, Hamer, King, and Whitman, who led these efforts. Democratic ideals, disfigured by slavery and segregation in the past are sullied in the present by corporate capitalism and greed. In the post-civil rights movement era, she sees democratic ideals taking root abroad—in Lebanon, Nicaragua, South Africa—places where U.S. military and economic power thwart their growth.

Jordan, also like Baldwin, insists on her right to criticize the country that is her home, although she stops short of declaring that she does so out of love. In that regard, she differentiates her skeptical perspective from her parents' full-throated patriotism. An example is "For My American Family: A Belated Tribute to a Legacy of Gifted Intelligence and Guts," which expresses love of family, rather than of country. However, rather than dismiss her family's viewpoint, she works hard to understand it. In large measure, their views derive from the fact that they are immigrants. The heart of Jordan's political intervention is her brief on their behalf: "It is a sad thing to consider that this country has given the least to those who have loved it the most. I am the daughter of West Indian immigrants. And perhaps there are other Americans as believing and as grateful and as loyal, but I doubt it. In general, the very word *immigrant* connotes somebody white, while *alien* denotes everybody else. But hundreds and hundreds of thousands of Americans are hardworking, naturalized Black citizens whose trust in the democratic promise of the mainland has never been reckoned with, fully, or truly reciprocated." [38] Although Paule Marshall and Audre Lorde had written of their immigrant parents before this essay was published, blacks were not associated with the immigrant experience in the public imagination. Significantly, "For My American Family" was commissioned for a special section of *New York Newsday*, published on July 4, 1986. Its title reflects that provenance. Like Douglass on the same occasion a century and three decades before, it pleads that African Americans be recognized as citizens.

The soul of Jordan's essay is a series of sketches of her family, whose lives she traces back to their impoverished childhoods in rural Jamaica. They reinvent themselves as Americans: the prideful father, an autodidact, camera buff, and responsible citizen, who is the first on the block to request improvements from municipal agencies; the mother who affixes a Franklin Delano Roosevelt decal to Jordan's baby carriage and who roots for Joe Louis and Jackie Robinson; and the aunt whose extracurricular activity while a high school student in New Jersey is domestic service and who becomes a New York City school principal. They love America. Their U.S.-born daughter and niece marvels at their journey. When she visits her mother's birthplace, which in 1974 lacks electricity, she wonders how her parents had ever heard of the

United States. To this degree, hers is a typical second generation immigrant story. Race makes it different, as the categories of immigrant and alien denote. Mindful of the struggle to build a life here, she understands, if she does not accept, her relatives' unwillingness to call out racism when they encounter it.[39] The cost of bitterness is too high. Concluding the essay is a paean to Bed-Stuy, a neighborhood that is culturally rich and diverse in the occupations and preoccupations of its residents. The aromas of rice and peas and curried lamb mix with pigs' feet and collard greens. The sounds of boogie-woogie and blues vie with Chopin. The America Jordan embraces is black America. Far from a ghetto, Bed-Stuy constitutes a cultural democracy—not, as Ellison imagines, a fusion of Negro and white elements, but as a multiethnic black community.

"Waking Up in the Middle of Some American Dreams" is set in the Hamptons, which of course signify whiteness and wealth, the antithesis of Bed-Stuy. The essay appears just after "My American Family" in *Technical Difficulties*, which is fitting because the pieces juxtapose ideas of community and success. Through its intersectional lens, "Waking Up" focuses as well on the dangerous myth of American individualism. The essay begins with a stanza from "Poem on a New Year's Eve" that proclaims the poet's determination to define beauty for herself. Rather than the still landscape, "the ocean at the hushpoint of the shore," beauty requires movement and the sound of another's laugh.[40] Yet, when given the opportunity to live in solitude, the poet welcomes it. Where better to hone her craft than in this "privacy paradise," one in which a renowned painter is a none-too-close neighbor? He represents the ideal that the essay undermines, the solitary artist whose work is his life. The painter's regular bouts of public drunkenness evidence the resulting imbalance. If the danger to the male artist comes from within, the female artist is vulnerable to violence from without. While living at her "rented pseudo-Walden Pond," Jordan is raped. Her attacker "had overpowered the supposed protection of my privacy, he had violated the boundaries of my single self" (14). Sexual violence is not, however, the subject of the essay. Strikingly and surprisingly, the attack occasions Jordan's meditation on privacy, solitude, and the artist's responsibility to others.

Even when she poses the comparison as a question, for Jordan to compare her egotistical impulse as an artist to her attacker's brutality is jarring. She asks if his conduct is "entirely different from my own, supposing that nothing mattered as much as my artistic impulse, the one that ruled my friends and my family and my neighbors out of my usual universe" (14). Despite the admission that she does not see her son and rarely uses the telephone, that seems too much of a stretch. Psychological withdrawal registers on a different scale than the violence of a physical attack. More persuasive is her comparison to the painter. It leads to the central assertion of the essay: "what jeopardized his and my safety, and our happiness, was the absence of connections between us and the absence of a sharing, a dependency between the two of us and other people who would care about us, because we care about them" (15). Such dependency is the genesis of community. As Jordan argues, the specifically American ideal of rugged individualism mitigates against its development, as do tropes of the wilderness and the frontier. Moreover, the cherished emphasis on each one as different or special works against identifying either common cause or shared responsibility. Insisting on one's uniqueness makes one less likely to recognize similarities between us, let alone to assume responsibility for the other. Consequently, Jordan rejects the singular identity of artist and claims instead her ordinariness. As she invites her audience to join her in eschewing the status of the autonomous self, she makes a claim for a radical definition of democracy, one that maximizes the possibilities of collective political action.

As their status as political commentators rose, Walker and Jordan were frequently invited to weigh in on international political issues, including the Middle East, Nicaragua, and South Africa. Walker, who had written of the joy that she and her husband had felt at the Israeli victory in the 1967 war, shifted her allegiance to the Palestinians. Jordan aligned herself with the Sandinistas as well as with the Palestinians. Even within progressive communities, their views were controversial; some of them were censored. In the introduction to *On Call*, Jordan asked her readers to consider which of the essays they were reading had been published and which had not. Several of the pro-Palestinian pieces were published for the first time in the volume. Jordan called her inability to place them earlier censorship. As the anti-apartheid struggle intensified, she and Walker were fierce in their support of the African National Congress and fiercely opposed to the policies of the Reagan administration. Along with political controversies, the authors' personal travels occasioned reflections on what might be termed transnational belonging. Repeatedly, they asked who constituted the "we" to which they belonged: What was the relationship as African American women to other people of African descent and to the women who made up the majority of the world's populations? How did one measure the privilege of U.S. citizenship? How did one take responsibility for the power of the United States in world affairs? For Jordan and Walker, these questions unfolded on a more intimate level than they had for Baldwin, in part because where he had traveled mainly to Europe, they traveled mainly in the Americas, Africa, and Asia. In their essays, they con-fronted a gap not so much between them and intellectuals from other nations in the metropole, as between themselves and the women and men who were their guides and maids in the former colonies. The identification with the communities of the oppressed proved to be far more complicated than slo-gans and bumper stickers. The open-ended form of the essay, which allowed for complication and nuance, created a space in which these questions could be addressed.

"Report from the Bahamas" starts off as Jordan's account of a beach vaca-tion she took over an Easter weekend and ends as one of her most probing analyses of race, class, and gender in the formation of community. The im-ages it foregrounds would be familiar to any North American who has trav-eled to the Caribbean; they are also images whose meaning most tourists cast aside lest they disturb the pleasure that is the goal of their travel. But the essay seeks to do more than discomfit tourists. Indeed, in the introduction to *On Call*, Jordan comments acidly on the decision of *Ms.* magazine to publish the piece in its "travel and leisure" section.[41] The essay's purpose is to consider instead the ways in which class fractures community among people of the same race, race fractures community among people of the same class, and gender fractures community among people who seek common cause. Jordan writes with a keen awareness of the difficulties in suturing the fractures, at home as much as abroad, but with an eye to ways that healing can begin.

The essay's initial image is from a brochure for the Sheraton British Colo-nial Hotel, where Jordan stays; it shows a smiling middle-aged black man in a waiter's tuxedo holding a tray of cocktails standing in the sea with the water ten inches above his ankles. What Jordan reads as his overweening eagerness to serve is as discomfiting as the history of the Bahamas printed in the wel-come packet Jordan finds in her room. It denies the experience inscribed even in the hotel's name. Black people are totally absent from an account that begins with Columbus, and continues with Tories who escaped the Ameri-can Revolution and finally Confederate blockade runners who used the is-lands as a base. The concurrent visibility and invisibility of black people in a place where they are the majority of the population is vexing. However, Jordan immediately acknowledges her own position: compared to the waiter, she is a rich woman. As she participates in the activities of the weekend, especially the haggling at the market, her consciousness of race is displaced by her con-sciousness of class. Albeit aware of her own financial limitations, she is cogni-zant of the difference in magnitude between her circumstance and those of the Bahamian vendors: "They risk not eating. I risk going broke on my first vacation afternoon."⁴² That difference creates an impassable barrier. Jordan does not know the names of the market women, but the woman who cleans her room leaves a card introducing herself as "Olive the Maid." When she tries to imagine a conversation with this woman, Jordan cannot. Her privilege gets in the way. She concedes the contradiction of being politically progressive and a client of a multinational corporation. But she has chosen the hotel out of concern for her personal safety as a woman traveling alone. She recognizes that her political values—individual rights, freedom, and desire—would be meaningless to Olive, who might well inquire, "Whose rights? Whose freedom? Whose desire?" In her characteristically blunt manner, Jordan comments, "And why should she give a shit about mine unless I do something, for real, about hers?" (41).

The essay shifts to the novel that Jordan is reading, *The Bread Givers* by Anzia Yezierska, whose poor Jewish heroine is striving to figure out a destiny beyond that which her gender, class, and ethnicity have foreordained. Jordan thinks that this heroine and Olive have more in common than she has with either of them. But it is not that simple, for the student who has given Jordan the novel has done so because he sees parallels between the novel's use of Yiddish and Jordan's "knowledge" and "love" of Black English. The connections and disconnections multiply. The middle-class student does not rely on government loans as Jordan's son does. A class divide separates student and professor. Another student, middle-aged and middle-class, expresses her envy of Jordan, whose life, she presumes, has purpose in ways that the student lacks. Jordan cannot be grateful for the discrimination that gives rise to this purpose. In her U.S. workplace, Jordan has a class advantage—she holds a privileged position as a professor—but unlike her status in the Bahamas, she holds a class disadvantage, because she is less well off financially than many of her students.

The essay pivots next to the fact that it is Good Friday, and those whose job it is to wait on Jordan clearly would prefer to observe the holy day. In the hotel sandwich shop, a recording of the hymn "The Old Rugged Cross" is playing. In a manner that is characteristic of the essay, Jordan's mind goes back in time to the Good Fridays of her youth. She remembers the devotion with which her own West Indian family observed the day. With the memory come tears, but her server looks on with a silence that Jordan understands: "She is no fool. This is a job that she needs" (45). As she prepares to catch her flight home, Jordan draws the first conclusion in her "report." She decides that "the usual race and class concepts of connection, or gender assumptions of unity" do not work in real life (46). Connections grow out of need. "It is not only who you are, in other words, but what we can do for each other that will determine the connection" (47). The essay might have ended there, but Jordan is after more than platitudes. She continues by recounting an experience that dramatizes the kind of reciprocity she has in mind.

One of the students in her contemporary women's poetry class, Sokutu, a black South African woman who is the victim of domestic abuse, comes to Jordan for help. The situation is dire: the emaciated woman is in need of medical attention as well as a safe haven. The usually self-assured Jordan is not sure what to do. Distressed that a couple who have escaped apartheid together are now the source of each other's pain, she calls every number in the campus directory that might offer a plausible source of assistance. The answer comes from Cathy, an Irish woman who is a supporter of the Irish Republican Army, and who identifies the husband's alcoholism as the problem; she has witnessed the damage alcoholism wrought in her parents' marriage. The women bond. As Jordan watches them walking away, she feels that "it was not who they were but what they both know and what they were both preparing to do about what they know that was going to make them both free at last" (49). Those bonds of connection, forged in personal vulnerability and honesty, are what identity politics miss. They are harder to forge, but more likely to endure.

Unfortunately, to my mind, the essay does not end here. The reader realizes, belatedly, that the meeting of Sokutu and Cathy has occurred sometime earlier. In the present the author is on a flight home from the Bahamas. Surrounded by strangers, she contemplates the connections she "must make" between herself and her fellow passengers (49). But these connections feel as abstract as the encounter between the two named women is concrete. The power of the bond between Sokutu and Cathy derives from its particularity. The gesture toward the universal is, by contrast, both unpersuasive and discouraging. How many individual encounters spurred by shared vulnerabilities and honest understandings, then facilitated by the intervention of an impassioned third party (like Jordan in this instance), would be required to create the ideal community that would transcend the divisions that separate us all?

Walker envisions such a connection in "My Father's Country Is the Poor," where she remembers that even as a teenager she believed her "*job* . . . was to begin to see other peoples not as strangers but as kin" (emphasis in the original).[43] An early opportunity to act on that belief was a trip to the 1962 World Youth Peace Festival in Helsinki (among the women who sponsored her trip was Coretta Scott King). Walker was enthralled by the performance of the

Cuban delegation that led the audience out of the hall and danced through the streets. When she read Fidel Castro's manifesto *History Will Absolve Me*, she "recognized the essence of a struggle already familiar to me" (201). She places the Cuban leader alongside the pantheon of black American heroes. These experiences seeded a desire to visit Cuba, but due to restrictions imposed by the U.S. State Department, she did not do so until the 1970s, when she traveled with a group of African American artists. The major part of the essay describes what she terms "fragments" of that experience, "offered with an acute awareness that my view of Cuba is neither definitive nor complete" (203). To be sure, this stance reflects her quite palpable understanding that the subject is a minefield; several times in the piece she anticipates objections to her views and directly addresses those who would disagree with her. But the posture is also conducive to the work of the essayist.

More than Jordan's explicitly titled "Report from the Bahamas," "My Father's Country Is the Poor" is a piece of reportage. Walker recounts her travels around the island nation: interviewing exiled Black Panther leader Huey Newton, visiting historic sites, and meeting with Cuban writers, filmmakers, and musicians. She reflects on the legitimacy of revolutionary violence, which she continues to question. But she celebrates the availability of medical care and education. While she acknowledges the harshness of Cuban life, she contends "that a hard life shared equally by all is preferable to a life of ease and plenty enjoyed by a few" (203). She observes residual sexism, queries the fate of political prisoners, and ponders the implications of the erasure of racial identity: she and her companions are *black* Americans; whether black or white, those they meet are *Cubans*. Interposed among Walker's observations are commentaries on homophobia and religious persecution as well as official dicta on marriage and family. But the doubts that these observations and commentaries raise are overcome by what she perceives as her "own bias," that is, "to think almost entirely of the gains of the formerly dispossessed" (221).[44]

The exemplar of these gains is Pablo Diaz, an official guide and griot of the revolution. He and Walker cannot communicate, since they do not speak a common language, but he so resembles Walker's recently deceased father that she claims him as kin. Their "relationship" takes place almost wholly in Walker's mind. In the end, it allows her to reconcile with the father from whom she was long estranged. Diaz has achieved the stature in his society denied to Walker's father in the United States, where, despite his aptitude for mathematics and storytelling, he lived out his life in desperate poverty. Denied the rights of citizenship, Willie Lee Walker has belonged only to "the country of the poor." By contrast, Diaz has risen above "the anonymity" of poverty and achieved the status of "official historian." In Walker's words, "he has fought his way to the other side of existence" (214), the side that this artist daughter inhabits.

As Walker travels through Cuba, she dreams about her father. A recurrent scene is one in which he stands, hat in hand, by the side of a road. As the scene comes into focus, she recognizes it as the moment she boards the bus for college and literally and figuratively leaves her father behind. They would never close the distance that in that moment opened between them. Against the backdrop of revolution, the estranged daughter vents her rage: "This separation, which neither of us wanted, is what poverty engenders. It is what injustice means" (216). The life she imagines for Diaz as a man who enjoys a relationship of mutual respect with his children facilitates her reconciliation with her own parent. Much like her encounter with Hurston in "Looking for Zora," this reconciliation transpires in the realm of the spirit. It takes place, that is, beyond critical questioning. Still, I cannot help but wonder about Pablo Diaz and what his children might think about the use to which the African American writer put their father.

Claiming strangers as kin poses ethical challenges. Despite the evident admiration that Walker expresses toward Diaz, she invests him with a history that serves a meaningful purpose for her, but not for him. Inevitably, one questions the extent to which Walker partakes of the literary convention analyzed by scholar Mary Sue Pratt in *Imperial Eyes: Travel Writing and Transculturation*, for example, wherein the Western traveler discovers herself through her interaction with the "Other." In my view, Walker's elevation of Diaz earns her at least the benefit of the doubt. Moreover, to a certain degree, any essayist necessarily appropriates the experience of the person she writes about. But the stakes are higher when the essayist is an avowed political progressive writing about people who have less cultural and political capital than she. For African American writers, the privilege may derive from class, nationality, and in some cases gender, instead of race. Whatever its source, it matters. After all, the unnamed postal worker in Baldwin's "To Be Baptized," Olive in "Report from the Bahamas," and Pablo Diaz in "My Father's Country Is the Poor" do not have access to media in which they can tell their versions of the story or appropriate the essayist's experience in order to work out a truth for themselves. Their relationship to the writer is, by definition, unequal. The writer's obligation then is to represent his or her own position vis-à-vis these figures candidly, to note, as Walker does, that hers is not the story of Pablo Diaz but rather her own. Jordan's more explicitly political essays required a more rigorous approach. Fearless in her determination to ally herself with revolutionaries who, unlike the Cubans, are in the midst of armed struggle, she is always mindful that no matter how fierce her quarrel with U.S. foreign policy, she remains an American. She is clear about her positionality: "Compared to anybody in Nicaragua, I am fat, I am safe, and I am rich."[45] Perhaps it is this candor that earns the trust of the Sandinistas.

In "Nicaragua: Why I Had to Go There," Jordan writes as a witness. A lifelong student of revolution, she wants to see the real thing. At the beginning of the essay, in the manner of Baldwin, she ventures a prophecy: "the end of the 20th century will finally belong to the majority."[46] Her prophecy has hardly been fulfilled, but the essay's value is its unflinching account of the sacrifices the struggle necessitates. For Jordan, Nicaragua is David to the U.S. Goliath, and she is determined to put her "life, as well as [her], words on the line" in its behalf (67). She champions the Sandinistas, who had overthrown the dictatorship of the Somoza family to assume control of a Central American nation the size of Iowa, with a population of 2.7 million people.[47]

Three decades later, it is impossible to comprehend how Nicaragua could ever have posed a threat to the United States. In her essay, Jordan deploys demographic facts as well as a heavy dose of irony to drive home the conflict's imbalance. Not only is Nicaragua's population tiny, it is geographically dispersed and impoverished. It is also racially diverse. This last fact comes as a surprise even to the poet, who reads her work to audiences in predominantly black and English-speaking communities on the Atlantic Coast. Not surprising, but shocking nonetheless, is the pervasive poverty. Reflecting on the interior of the homes she visits, Jordan observes: "Nowhere in the South, nowhere in Jamaica or Puerto Rico, nowhere have I seen anything like this combination of no shoes and no floor, inside apparently half-deserted, but utterly organized space" (67–68). The emptiness sparks an allegorical turn in which "eagles" fly over the globe and looking down at half-deserted land, assume no one lives there. They then appropriate resources for themselves. Having no gold or oil, Nicaragua seems unlikely prey—except for the example her people have set by deposing the U.S.-backed dictator and seizing their freedom.

Jordan recaps the history of U.S. interventions in Nicaragua across the twentieth century, but at its heart the essay records her singular journey. She remarks literacy projects, health initiatives, and laws mandating equal pay for equal work for women. Most dramatically she observes a wholly armed population: women as well as men, children and the aged. Passages in the essay seem transcribed from her travel diary: "It's indescribably hot, easily 115 degrees" (71).

Despite the hospitality, affection, and gratitude with which people treat her, Jordan admits her discomfort; the heat, fatigue, lack of drinking water, and terror wear her down. Hers is "a journey of harrowing hopscotch" (72). Jordan's confession of her fear elevates the courage of the Nicaraguans she encounters, though at least one of them, a poet and painter named June Beer, confides her uncertainty about the future. This June, too, is a woman of a certain age. Young people harbor no doubts about the ultimate victory. Their confidence, born of what Jordan defines as self-love, as well as their bravery, throws the challenge back to Jordan.

Coming from "the land of Goliath," she understands what the young Sandinistas are up against. She recognizes that they are no match for U.S. military might; were it to be unleashed, the revolutionaries would be crushed. Moreover, she feels certain that Ronald Reagan—"the cowboy"—would be more than willing to order it done. It becomes the responsibility of enlightened Americans (perhaps the relatively conscious whites and blacks, as Baldwin would describe them) to use their power to thwart the power of the state. Performing her own jeremiad, Jordan poses a series of questions that are intended to provoke action. The last lines of the essay dare black Americans to recognize their own power, which is so much greater than that of the Sandinistas, and use it on behalf of these worthy allies: *When will we seize the world around us with our freedom?* (75, emphasis in the original). What differentiates "Why I Had to Go to Nicaragua" from the political propaganda of the day is its first-person witness. Jordan succeeds in putting her life as well as her words on the line. In the process, she wins the respect of her readers, then and now.

Of course, the war with Nicaragua, like other crises to which Jordan and Walker responded so urgently, has passed into history. Few readers will remember the details of the Miami riots, or the military incursion into Lebanon, or the Nicaraguan revolution. Even the anti-apartheid struggle, about which both Jordan and Walker wrote extensively, is historical for readers who have come of age in the twenty-first century. Nevertheless, the essays they published exemplify one of the major tenets of this book. Writers are drawn to the genre of the essay precisely because it can be deployed in times of crisis. The immediacy of the situation and the compactness of the form suit each other. The timeliness of the intervention means necessarily that the writing will not speak in the same way to those who encounter it after the crisis has passed. But the words can still resonate. Even as the faces of the people and places change, the theme remains the same: injustice anywhere is a threat to justice everywhere. People of conscience are obligated to make common cause with oppressed people who seek the self determination that they themselves enjoy. For both Walker and Jordan, the catalyst for the struggle for self-determination is self-love. Their experience growing up as poor black women in a society that denigrated the poor, the black, and the female taught them how far out of reach self-love could be. But it was precious, because it was the foundation on which social and political change as well as personal liberation depended. The essays that explore the writers' achievement of self-love are among their most enduring.

In "Beauty: When the Other Dancer Is the Self," written at the height of the clamor surrounding the publication of *The Color Purple*, Walker confronts her own lack of self-love, its causes, and its consequences. The essay's structure mimics the novel's, with Walker making her own stylized diary entries. Set partly in the rural South, it also echoes the novel's much celebrated vernacular. But the language of the essay is more various: it incorporates contemporary colloquial speech and nineteenth-century literary diction. That is to say, it gathers together the threads of Walker's reading as well as of her memories. Writing retrospectively, from a position of significant privilege, Walker fashions a persona that is empathetic in large measure because of her ability to capture the vulnerability of her girlhood self and her capacity to laugh at herself as both a child and an adult. She dares to take seriously a subject that society at large—read, men—consider trivial and that women who hope to be taken seriously avoid. In so doing, she gives readers permission to admit their own insecurities and then offers one model for overcoming them.

The essay opens one summer day in 1947 with the story of the young Alice hoping to be taken to the county fair with her father, who has use of the car he drives for his employer and landlord. Alice is sure that of the eight children in the family, he will choose her, because she is the prettiest. The landlord, Miss Mey, is identified as "a rich old white lady," whose character is crystallized in Walker's memory of the time that the woman had offered to pay her mother 35 cents to clean her house, wash her clothes, and rake up piles of magnolia leaves. The last reference nicely captures the genteel veneer of exploitation in the South.[48] The essay's second entry is Easter Sunday 1950, when the fancily dressed six-year-old impresses church members by giving one of the longest speeches on the program. She further conveys her exceptional intelligence to her readers by quoting the simpler speech she had given when she was two. She knows that it is her "spirit, bordering on sassiness (womanishness), they secretly applaud. 'That girl's a little *mess*,' they whisper to each other, pleased" (362).

Like a similar moment in Maya Angelou's *I Know Why the Caged Bird Sings*, the scene shows the extent to which boldness and intelligence in young girls could win communal approval and the limitations its approval imposed. The church was the performance space, which sharply limited what could be said. If anything, adults regulated behavior more strictly in church than at home or in school. The dress code was stringent as well. Yet, as the scenes make clear, the opportunity to dress up was a source of pleasure and pride for adults and children alike. In Walker's essay, the emphasis is on the pleasure the child took in her own adornment: the dress she wore is lovingly described. Immediately thereafter, the nostalgic scene is interrupted by the first of a series of italicized statements that complicate or undermine readers' understanding of what we have just read: "*It was great fun being cute. But then, one day, it ended*" (363).

What follows is a scene in which young Alice is a tomboy playing cowboys and Indians with her brothers. This space is unregulated, but if it is freer, it is also dangerous. Her parents have bought her brothers a BB gun, and Alice, the designated Indian, is shot in the eye. The adult, feminist Walker is keenly aware of the part that gender roles play here. Hollywood biases reinforce the biases of a rural southern community that associates guns with masculinity. In part because her brothers make her promise not to tell, she does not receive medical attention for a week. By then, there is little that can be done. The doctor explains to her parents that "eyes are sympathetic . . . If one is blind, the other will likely become blind too" (364). Alice is terrified. But she confesses the ugliness of the eye—covered by white scar tissue—scares her even more than the prospect of blindness. She retreats into herself. Years later she asks her mother and sister had she changed after the "accident." They respond, "What do you mean?" A second italicized statement inscribes Walker's response to their obtuseness: "*What do I mean?*" The essay does not analyze the family's investment in forgetting; it focuses instead on Walker's need to remember.

She remembers how much she had changed and the ways in which her family tried to restore her to her former self. No longer sassy or spirited, she began to do poorly at school. A caring teacher tries to intervene, but in a moment out of *Jane Eyre*, the teacher leaves to marry an African prince. Alice prays for beauty. Circumstances force her parents to move, but they grow so concerned about her behavior that they send her back to their former community, where she lives with her grandparents. If their actions reflect admirably on her family, their forgetting seems associated with the power of nostalgia that permeates the opening scene. Walker, by contrast, refuses to forget her pain or its source. Years go by before she visits a brother in Boston who finds a surgeon who removes what she can only describe as "a glob." The transformation feels miraculous: the teenager becomes the most popular student in high school, the valedictorian and homecoming queen. Walker looks back on these achievements ambivalently and mocks the joy her younger self took in them. At the same time, she appreciates that she would not have the life she currently enjoys had her appearance not been fixed. Spirit and beauty do not exist in isolation. They depend on each other in ways that are uncomfortable—especially for a feminist—to admit. In the abstract, the interdependence need not be the case. But autobiographical essays deal in what was, or is, rather than what should be.

The essay moves to the present, a trickier place, I think, because although some of its readers would undoubtedly respond without hesitation to Walker as an adored celebrity, others might resist the invitation to sympathize with a woman markedly more privileged than they. Walker has been asked to appear on the cover of a magazine, and the editors have promised that the photograph can be as glamorous as she wishes. She hesitates. In a conversation with her lover, she acknowledges that she is concerned that people will see her disfigured eye. For the record, Walker appeared on the cover (*Ms.*, June 1982). There is nothing untoward about her appearance. But the essay is about her perceptions, not reality. She still imagines that onlookers will focus on the flaw, rather than on her *self*. Walker needs, finally, to be reconciled with herself; her young daughter facilitates the reconciliation by transforming what the mother perceives as a terrible flaw into a metaphor of power, even omniscience: "Mommy, there's a *world* in your eye" (370). Not only do the child's words assuage the mother's pain, they allow the mother to embrace the past in all of its complexity and to acknowledge the ways it has shaped the woman she has become.

The essay closes with a revision of the familiar trope of the divided self. Walker describes herself dancing alone to the music of Stevie Wonder's "As," or what she hears as "Always": "As I dance, whirling and joyous, happier than I've ever been in my life, another bright-faced dancer joins me. We dance and kiss each other and hold each other through the night. The other dancer has obviously come through all right, as I have done. She is beautiful, whole and free. And she is also me" (370). Only after "coming through," a term associated with spiritual conversion, and confronting the pain occasioned by her individual experiences and her family history, can Walker achieve self-love. Significantly, that love is figured in metaphors of dance that hearken back to Langston Hughes's "Dream Variations" ("To fling my arms wide/In some place of the sun,/To whirl and to dance/Till the white day is done") and that recur in African American literary tradition. Yet, its erotic references, along with the speaker's ease with her body and her unvarnished declaration of her own beauty, identify it with second-wave feminism. Walker is heir to the literary tradition and a definer of the social movement. Although her daughter's words inspire it, Walker's awareness of her position in these larger contexts enables her epiphany.

Jordan's "Many Rivers to Cross" opens with a shocking declaration that is stated in a subordinated clause: her mother committed suicide. That the independent clause describes her own condition at the time—she was looking for a job—introduces an essay that juxtaposes the experiences of two women. Both are in desperate straits, but the younger is determined to ward off the despair that causes the elder to take her own life. Nurturing a spirit of resolve that is rooted in self-love becomes the daughter's way of commemorating the mother's legacy. Yet doing so requires transgressing the codes of conduct that the mother upheld. Her stoicism and self-sacrifice earned her no rewards. Only by fashioning a new code and by baring family secrets, her own as well as her mother's, can the daughter ensure that she will not relive her mother's life.

The essay's events take place fifteen years before its narrative present when Jordan describes herself "as a mother without a husband, as a poet without a publisher, a free-lance journalist without assignment, a city planner without a contract."[49] By enumerating what she lacks, she renders the meaning of her achievements contingent. Consequently, she can concurrently own her social and political identities while emphasizing how little cultural capital they have accrued. Further measuring the gap between appearance and reality, Jordan paints a portrait of her marriage from the outside; her neighbors see "an ideal couple." Yet when her husband leaves for a year to attend graduate school and does not return, the neighbors do not pry. And, she adds, she does not tell them anything, perhaps because she is unsure herself of what has happened. Broke and with no place to take her son, Jordan has to depend on the kindness of her mother. Her father is unforgiving of what he sees as her "failure." But the divorce is only the visible "failure." Unknown to either parent, Jordan, had become pregnant and had an abortion, facts that both parents would consider "a terrible secret compounded by a terrible crime" (20).

After Jordan moves back into her childhood home, the women's stories intersect. Debilitated by a stroke and severely depressed, the mother is a shell of her former self, a condition that also defines the family. Always an astute observer of spatial arrangements, Jordan maps the family's quarters; in so doing she illustrates the distance among her kin. That distance is crystallized in the scene that unfolds when her frantic father wakes a sleeping Jordan and asks her to "*figure out*" if her mother is dead or alive. The telling is brilliantly paced. Father and daughter shout at and past each other; the daughter reflects on the situation, even as she moves ahead with her "mission." When she enters the mother's room, she soon realizes that the difference between life and death is not as obvious as she has assumed. (The mother's body is not cold, and her eyes are open. She appears to be trying to stand.) The rush of fear and grief aggravate Jordan's uncertainty. Ultimately the police arrive and true to their training make an easy call. When an aunt tells Jordan that the finding is suicide, she wakes her son and flees the scene. The next day when she returns, she and her father get into a physical altercation about the mother's insurance. He threatens to burn the papers rather than allow her what she is due. Jordan leaves again and spends the day of her mother's funeral in the hospital, recovering from complications of the illegal abortion she cannot disclose even to the physicians.

"Many Rivers to Cross" foregrounds two women and two secrets. Jordan's family colludes to keep the first. Initially, Jordan decides not to fabricate a story to conceal the second. In the essay, of course, she reveals both. The decision to lay them bare is connected to the understandings she comes to in the immediate aftermath of the events the essay narrates. As she lay in the hospital, she reflects, "I wanted to be strong. I never wanted to be weak again as long as I lived. I thought about my mother and her suicide and I thought about how my father could not tell whether she was dead or alive" (26). The remainder of the essay is a series of increasingly powerful declarations that play variations on the subjects of weakness and strength, life and death. For example, she declares her desire to live her life so that "people know the difference for sure between my living and my death" (26). Fifteen years after the fact, she recognizes that her mother's suicide was not singular; such painful inheritances are more common than anyone admits. Discarding the mythology of the strong black woman, Jordan acknowledges her mother's weakness.[50] She quotes Bertolt Brecht that "it takes courage to say that the good were defeated not because they were good, but because they were weak" (26). Yet, she concedes, that she is still "working for the courage" to embrace that truth. She expresses her gratitude to other women mentioned in the essay, the surrogate mother and the cousin on whom she has relied during this crisis, and from whom she continues to draw strength. They, as much as her mother, are the subject of the essay's final resolution: "I came too late to help my mother to her feet . . . . By way of everlasting thanks to all of the women who have helped me to stay alive I am working never to be late again" (26).

The last words of the song from which the title comes are "Yes, I've got many rivers to cross/And I merely survive because of my will." Jamaican reggae singer Jimmy Cliff's lyrics revise one of the key tropes in African American and African diasporic cultural expression. The trope recurs in a half-dozen spirituals, such as "Deep River," "One More River to Cross," and "Roll, Jordan, Roll," that figure death as a river crossing. But Cliff globalizes the range of reference and secularizes the sentiment: the first verse invokes the "white cliffs of Dover" and the last locates survival in the individual will. The essay reaffirms the mother's religious faith, as her fellow parishioners fill the house after her death. Wearing their Sunday best, they play out a preordained ritual. They act to contain the truth, when they squash the conflict between Jordan and her father. Even as it draws on the emptied-out language of Christianity, the essay, like the song, begins to fill in a new ethic, born out of a people's individual and collective histories. But it is left to readers to flesh it out.

The space to explore tough questions is one reason that Walker and Jordan gravitate to the essay form. Its open-ended, tentative quality allows them to think through the contentious issues that define their lives and times. They contemplate the meaning of freedom for educated, middle-class women like themselves as well as for poor, disenfranchised women in the United States and throughout the world. They advocate for their rights. They struggle against discrimination based on race, gender, and sexual identity and identify the ways in which they intersect in individual lives. They write to clear a space for themselves as artists. In their distinctive but complementary ways, they shape the art of the essay. But the art is never the only thing. Their individual lives—and the collective lives of the people whom they claim as kin—are equally important. At the height of their careers, June Jordan and Alice Walker lived out a twinned commitment to a redemptive art and politics. Their essays record their aspiration to live and write honorably.

Epilogue
Essaying in the Digital Age

The attacks of 9/11, the wars in Afghanistan and Iraq, Hurricane Katrina, the election of Barack Hussein Obama, the murders of Trayvon Martin, Michael Brown, Eric Garner, and Sandra Bland, among many others, and the subsequent movement called Black Lives Matter, the rise of a black diasporic consciousness, the legalization of same-sex marriage, the appropriation of hip hop as a commodity of global culture, and the election of Donald Trump are among the events, movements, and cultural trends that have defined life in the United States in the first decades of the twenty-first century. In part because everyone and everything is wired, events come at us faster than we can process them. If the function of the essay is to speak to moments of social and political crisis, to define aesthetic debates, and to reflect on the meaning of individual and collective identity, it is not surprising that the genre is as vital to the present as it has been in the past. Ta-Nehisi Coates, Jelani Cobb, Brittney Cooper, Roxanne Gay, Kiese Laymon, and Imani Perry are among the best known of a new generation of writers who continue to push the boundaries of the form. They are keenly conscious of the democratic eloquence of their precursors; their jeremiads reverberate with a passion reminiscent of David Walker, Frederick Douglass, and June Jordan. Their writing often enacts a vernacular process that is inflected with a hip hop beat.

Twenty-first century essayists work new variations on the subject of freedom, the subject that has preoccupied black writers for three centuries. Two of the definitions of freedom Orlando Patterson set forth—personal and civic freedom—are particularly salient. If the election of Barack Obama ushered in a new chapter in the relationship of black citizens to the nation—a fulfillment of the quest for civic freedom, that is, the capacity of adult members of a community to participate in its life and governance—the murders of black men and women by the state as well as by each other marked the extent to which personal freedom continues to be denied. For many, these attacks on black bodies constitute a condition of "unfreedom" that resonates with the earliest chapters of the history of Africans in America. As they always have, African American writers also respond to and in some cases initiate an expanded understanding of personal freedom in terms of whom they can love, where they can live, and the goals they can set for themselves at home, in the workplace, and in the world.

In "Shattering Black Flesh: Black Intellectual Writing in the Age of Ferguson," a piece that both celebrates and laments the central role now played by social media in black intellectual production, Julius Fleming writes, "What we stand in need of, in part, is more generous reading practices that enable us to discern the multiple forms of black writing unfolding in the Age of Ferguson and thus to know that our eyes and ears cannot behold the totality of this writing."[1] In this epilogue, I want first to amplify Fleming's call and then to suggest how the protocols for reading the African American essay I have set forth may suggest protocols for sifting through the multitudinous texts that proliferate daily on blogs and Twitter feeds. To begin, I would suggest identifying continuities such as the persistent engagement with the subject of freedom. Fleming himself italicizes a refrain that runs through his essay: "*I am a black intellectual. I love black people. I abhor anti-blackness. Black freedom, for me, is an urgent priority.*" Despite the fact that this piece was published in an academic journal, it is not a conventional academic article. If it were, I doubt that Fleming would incorporate such a refrain. Its presence may portend a turn in academic writing that brings it closer to the tradition of the essay, a subject to which I can only gesture here.[2]

Suffice it to say that, like the essayists discussed above, Fleming works around his subject, invites the reader to puzzle through the issue with him, and deploys the memorable anecdote to illustrate his perspective. He and his peers are keenly aware of the traditions in which they work; they employ the tropes and extend the innovations of those who came before them. At the same time, they respond to technological changes that have dramatically affected the relationship between writer and reader: no longer do readers necessarily consume the writer's words on the page. Partly as a consequence, the will to adorn is expressed differently in the digital age.

Like their precursors, African American essayists today publish in mainstream magazines such as the *Atlantic* and the *New Yorker* and in political journals like the *Nation* and the *Progressive*. But they publish online as well as in print. Readers under thirty are more likely to encounter their work on the Grio, Crunk Feminist Collective, Feminist Wire, Huffington Post, the Root, and Salon, to name a few of a myriad of websites, than on the page. Indeed, even essays published in print are often downloaded and read on computer screens or cell phones. The line between the printed word and the online word is as blurred today as the line between the printed and spoken word was two centuries ago. Bloggers constitute an especially broad universe of voices:

June Jordan's assertion that any citizen should be able to write an essay has come closer to reality than she could have imagined. The voices and ideas of many ordinary people can be heard in the marketplace of ideas that is the internet. Most bloggers have no literary aspirations, and their prose is intended for quick consumption. Periodic sentences, like those in which Baldwin took delight, are rare. Paragraphs are short and punchy, and the grammatical rule against one-sentence paragraphs does not apply. In lieu of digressive arguments, bloggers prefer to make highly distilled statements. There is merit in making online writing quotable, so it can be tweeted or uploaded to Facebook. For those who write with an intellectual or literary purpose, the challenge is be accessible without sacrificing complexity and nuance. Theirs is highly compressed writing, but as we have seen, the essay has always been a highly compressed form. In a sense, the difference between writing for print and writing online is a matter of degree rather than kind.

Ta-Nehisi Coates and Brittney Cooper, who are clearly concerned with both the "what" and the "how" of their arguments, publish prolifically both in print and online. Coates summons the authority of James Baldwin, while Cooper channels the rage that June Jordan brought to her essays on murdered young black people. Although Coates, a national correspondent for the *Atlantic*, one of the oldest and most storied magazines in the history of American publishing, enjoys a much higher level of visibility than Cooper, who is now a university professor, both make frequent media appearances and their writings circulate widely. With whiplash speed, Cooper and Coates respond to the rush of current events, and their readers turn to them for insight and guidance. I would like to close this book by considering how their writings fulfill the functions of the African American essay discussed throughout *On Freedom and the Will to Adorn*.

Ta-Nehisi Coates explicitly identifies James Baldwin's *The Fire Next Time* as a model in *Between the World and Me*, the best-selling volume in which Coates summons a troubled eloquence worthy of a new era. In a moment when it is more difficult than ever for any book, let alone a book-length essay by an African American, to attract the attention of a broad swath of the public, *Between the World and Me* broke through the din of media to position itself to be to the Black Lives Matter movement what *The Fire Next Time* was to the movement for civil rights. Coates begins his essay by defining his terms in ways that resonate not only with Baldwin but with the line of writers who preceded him.

The opening pages of his essay in four parts revisit themes that have recurred throughout this book: What is the meaning of democracy? What is the Dream? What is the definition of "people" in the American nation? Who belongs and who does not? Unlike many of his precursors, however, Coates argues that far from failing to live up to its democratic creed, Americans have been faithful to the ideas of race and white supremacy, which were woven into the warp and woof of the nation from the start. Coates takes it as a given that blacks have been excluded from national belonging because of their race. He has no hope that any new dispensation will include them. The issue at hand is the assault on black bodies. Much of the text meditates on murdered bodies—like those of Eric Garner and Tamir Rice,[3] whose deaths have been the focus of national media attention—and those that belong to Coates's friends, whose stories readers have not heard. Yet this is not a book of mourning. It does not mainly look to the past; it looks to the future, and its urgency derives from Coates's fears for his life and that of his son.

How can they save themselves in a nation in which black lives have never mattered? Coates takes his title from a poem by Richard Wright, "Between the World and Me," which is a graphic portrait of a lynched body, abandoned as if were a "thing," left for the speaker inadvertently to confront. The detritus that remains at the scene enables the speaker to recreate the lynching and to imagine himself as its victim. The poem sets the historical template for the incidents the essay highlights, notably the killing of Michael Brown, whose body was left abandoned in a street in Ferguson, Missouri. Like most people, Coates's son learned of Brown's killing through media reports, and his anguished response to the legal system's failure to indict his killers triggers this writing. The allusion to Wright's poem works in multiple ways. In addition to the vulnerability of black bodies, the allusion foretells Coates's emphasis on the flesh, the viscera. "Racism is a visceral experience," he writes, "that dislodges brains, blocks airways, rips muscles, extracts organs, cracks bones, breaks teeth" (10). Coates intends to convey the fear and pain of racism to his son less to inspire him to fight to overcome it than to equip him with the tools to survive it. Of course, Coates addresses his readers as well, and to some degree he writes, as his precursors did, to rouse them to act against the wrongs he so vividly enumerates.

Coates has invited and welcomed the comparisons readers have made between him and James Baldwin.[4] Having claimed Baldwin, Coates was claimed by Toni Morrison. Her endorsement of *Between the World and Me* began, "I've been wondering who might fill the intellectual void that plagued me after James Baldwin died. Clearly it is Ta-Nehisi Coates." Morrison, who had eulogized Baldwin by thanking him for giving her "a language to dwell in," honed in on Coates's language and deemed it "visceral, eloquent, and beautifully redemptive." She ended with the declaration, "This is required reading."[5] The blurb was a generous gesture and one that the former Random House editor knew would sell books. Interest in Baldwin had reached new heights: not only was there a crush of scholarly books and articles, an online journal titled the *James Baldwin Review*, and an award-winning documentary, *I Am Not Your Negro*, a new generation of artists and activists had reclaimed Baldwin's words and his example. After considering the ubiquity of Baldwin quotes on the Twitter feeds of Black Lives Matter activists, scholar William Maxwell offered a riposte to Morrison's encomium, "Jimmy himself has filled the void traced to his death."[6]

Nevertheless, the comparison of Coates to Baldwin was textually apt. The epistolary structure of *Between the World and Me* is clearly modeled on *The Fire Next Time*, and there are many themes in the text—the fierce critique of white supremacy, the apprehension for the next generation, the omnipresence of fear and the persistence of love in black life, the passion for books, and the reflections on the beauty and power of black culture—that connect it with Baldwin's. Coates, like Baldwin, publishes his book just shy of his fortieth birthday, a moment when he takes stock of his own life and looks ahead to the future awaiting his son. Like Baldwin, he insists on deconstructing the concept of American exceptionalism at and measures the nation's alleged moral superiority against its political realities. Unlike Baldwin, Coates assumes that his readers are no more convinced of the nation's superiority than is he. Yet Coates's concerns differ fundamentally from Baldwin's in another crucial respect: he is not concerned with matters of the spirit. Although he expresses deep love for his wife and son, his parents, and his friends, he has no expectation that love, or anything else, will set people free. Consequently, his perspective is bleaker than Baldwin's, despite, or perhaps because of, the fact that Coates might have been able to lay claim to the victories won in the struggle Baldwin and his contemporaries waged. As he recounts in his memoir *The Beautiful Struggle*, Coates is the son of a father, a former Black Panther and the founder of Black Classic Press, whose legacy is vigilance rather than victory. Instead of the hope that the civil rights movement was supposed to bequeath and that the election of Barack Obama seemed initially to renew, Coates and his generation reaped a whirlwind of violence.

In the autobiographical sections of the book, Coates takes his readers to the mean streets of Baltimore. His emphasis is not on intellectual or spiritual oppression, but on the visceral impact of racism on bodies—his own, that of the son to whom this cautionary tale is addressed, and the many black bodies who are violated, frequently by state-sponsored violence or what he insists is state-sanctioned violence. He writes about the bullies he outran, the mental maps he constructed in order to find safe passage through his neighborhood, the gun another black boy aimed at him, and his father's beatings.[7] The essay repeatedly stresses the vulnerability of his body, and his observation that adults in his community, no less than his peers, are consumed by fear. To make matters worse, these adults offer no historical perspective that would help Coates make sense of his situation. What he does learn of history does nothing to assuage his fears. Episodes of *Eyes on the Prize* seem to him to offer lessons in submission, when he seeks lessons in self-defense. For Coates, unlike Baldwin, the church is not a refuge. Indeed, the prose and poetry of the Bible do not leave a mark on his prose. Moreover, Coates is no Jeremiah; he has no interest in saving his white fellow citizens, even as he realizes that their destruction will ensure his own.

Coates describes an extended respite from the violence during his years at Howard University, or as he prefers, the Mecca, "the crossroads of the black diaspora" (40), the place where he develops an abiding appreciation for the cosmopolitanism of the black world. Students come from Africa and the Americas, the Caribbean and from all across the United States; students come from every class position and are of every color. Coates is deeply aware of the university's fabled history. As he strides across the Howard campus, Coates describes himself as "literally walking in the footsteps" of the school's illustrious alumni, including Zora Neale Hurston and Toni Morrison (41). Howard is to Coates what the church was to Baldwin, the repository of all the beauty and power of black culture, except that Baldwin lost his faith in Christianity. Coates never rejects the black cosmopolitanism he discovers at the Mecca. This is not to say that he romanticizes the education he received in the classrooms and library at Howard, as it forced him to confront the contradictions of history. For example, he recounts the story of Queen Nzinga, the sixteenth-century African ruler whose response to a Dutch ambassador's refusal to offer her a seat was to order one of her subjects to make of his body a chair. What seems initially an act of pride and defiance with regard to the European becomes on closer examination one of hubris and the exploitation of her fellow African.

However glorious or complicated the history Coates learns at Howard, it cannot protect him against the violence of the streets. After both have left the university, one of his best friends, the aptly named Prince Jones, is murdered by a police officer. Prince Jones becomes, as Coates puts it, "the superlative of all my fears. And, if he, good Christian, scion of a striving class, patron saint of the twice as good, could be forever bound, then who could not?"[8] The contradictions continue to haunt: the fact that Jones was a middle-class, college-educated success, yet was shot in the street as any poor, uneducated, unemployed black man might have been; and the fact that the police officer who killed Jones was black, as were all the local government officials for whom he worked. There is no resolution. The burden of history is inescapable, and it is the weight Coates bequeaths his son. By dint of his class privilege and the love and kindness of his parents, Coates's son enjoys "an abnormal amount of security in [his] black body" (130). This is not to say he is free. The struggle for freedom continues, and the father urges the son to enlist.

After the book was published, the *Atlantic* welcomed readers to post their responses to it online in an attempt to rekindle the relationship between Coates and his readers begun in 2008, when Coates started a blog sponsored by the magazine. Coates covered a broad array of topics in politics, history, and popular culture. He blogged about books he had read and provided links to articles he found interesting. Looking back on the years he was most active, he reflected, "blogging was a real-time, ongoing learning process." He described himself as a "manager" of the online community made up of the readers who commented on his posts, the "Horde" as its members dubbed themselves. That name notwithstanding, these readers abided by rules of civility that then governed discussions on the internet; the result was an exchange of ideas rather than the now common exchange of insults. Coates frequently commented on the comments.[9] By the time *Between the World and Me* was published, Coates was too famous and his audience too large to sustain the blogger's give and take. In July 2015, the month of the book's publication, the *Atlantic* announced that the comments section was closed, "to further encourage civil and substantive responses via email."[10]

For Coates and Cooper as for their predecessors, personal experience opens a window into the collective consciousness. The questions they ask themselves, to paraphrase Baldwin, begin to illuminate the world and become keys to the experience of others. Coates and Cooper begin their essays on President Obama with their individual sense of pride and disappointment and then elaborate on what they think his presidency means for African Americans and for the nation at large. In "The Champion Barack Obama: How Black America Talks to the White House," for example, Coates avers, "And no matter how many times I've seen it in my private life, at Howard, in my home, among my close friends, I don't ever expect to see a black man of such agile intelligence as the current president put before the American public ever again."[11] And yet, Coates sees Obama's message of "personal responsibility" that he delivered to black audiences on several occasions, one notably at a commencement address at Morehouse College, as both a misreading of history and a failure of the imagination. Across the "500-year tenure" of blacks in America, Coates insists, not one credible historian has concluded that the lack of "personal responsibility" has contributed to the oppression of black people. But black writers and leaders as far back as David Walker and Maria Stewart have returned to it again and again. Coates acknowledges that black audiences do not "boo" the president's message, because they have internalized it and not only as a result of its repetition. Rather, most black Americans are as quick as Barack Obama to lament the lost young men and women who stand idly on the corners of black communities. Coates allows both the president and his audience this moment of mourning, of catharsis, before insisting that it is not enough. Public policies, not personal responsibility, are the cause of, and the solution to, the problems confronting African Americans. Throughout this essay, Coates dramatizes the difficulty of at once admiring the "champion Barack Obama" for his historic achievement, his intellectual gifts, and his empathy with black people and criticizing him for playing into long-standing stereotypes. In a phrase, Coates encapsulates the work the essayist does: "and I struggle to get my head around all of this." Coates has continued that "struggle" in a series of brilliant essays in the *Atlantic*, and in a volume, *We Were Eight Years in Power: An American Tragedy*, published in 2017, the year after the Obama presidency ended.

In the midst of Obama's tenure, Brittney Cooper captured the frustration fueled by another historical moment that failed to live up to its promise in a piece titled, "Re-Nigging on the Promises: #Justice4Trayon." Her title riffs on the title of the book the president wrote for his 2012 reelection campaign, *The Audacity of Hope*. Aiming to speak for a community rather than just for herself, Cooper declares, "We are the post-post-Civil Rights Generation, the Hip Hop Generation. And we are tired of hope and dreams deferred."[12] She writes in response to the murder of Trayvon Martin, which was the impetus for the founding of #Black Lives Matter. According to the statement posted by Alicia Garza on the movement's website, "I created #BlackLivesMatter with Patrisse Cullors and Opal Tometi, two of my sisters, as a call to action for Black people after 17-year-old Trayvon Martin was posthumously placed on trial for his own murder and the killer, George Zimmerman, was not held accountable for the crime he committed."[13] Cooper expresses both anger and frustration at these events. As her title denotes, she reacts to what she sees as an old story with a contemporary twist. Before the colon, the title reminds readers that Martin's death and the attempt to villainize him in its aftermath is part of a continuous cycle in which black people are dehumanized and the promises of equality are broken; the hashtag after the colon specifies the setting as the twenty-first century. The counterpoint between the past and present continues with the next two paragraphs. The first reads in its entirety: "Another Black kid is dead." The second reads: "This time it's 17 year old Trayvon Martin."

Drawing on her personal history, Cooper recalls teaching reading in a middle school in Washington, D.C., where her pupils were vulnerable to systemic rejection and random violence. Casting her thoughts in the subjunctive mood, she repeats the clause, "I can't help but wonder," as she posits parallels between her students' experiences and Martin's. She marshals statistics, references critical theory, and cites historical events, as the essay widens its focus to place the death of Trayvon Martin in the context of public policy and history. To do so, it deploys a twenty-first-century mode of vernacular process.

For example, the writing includes a series of rapid-fire allusions. The references are truncated and deployed with a scabrous wit: "So come, let us reason together. (Yeah, I got Biblical, because in times like these we need a savior. Take that as literally or as figuratively as you will.)" In a preceding paragraph, Cooper pointed to the futility of applying logic to racism. The dialogue she invites her readers to join is not intended to explain or understand a situation, but rather to strategize a response. The reference to the gospel song "In Times like These" proposes and rejects the possibility of divine intervention resolving the situation. Later she repeats Du Bois's all-too-familiar question—"How does it feel to be a problem?" Her answer, like Coates's prose, is visceral: "It feels like gunshots, unheard screams and a lonely violent death." The essay shifts between invocations of gut-wrenching feelings and appeals to reason, however unlikely they are to succeed, because the latter are the only alternative to the former.

The comments sections on blogs create an interactive space that formalizes the dialogic structure of the essay. Readers posted myriad comments in response to Cooper's piece. Some praised it, others damned it. One commenter, insisting that race had nothing to do with Martin's death, wrote, "this is the most bias [*sic*] and unprofessional article i [*sic*] have read in a while." Another simply wrote, "Amen and Amen." Others asked for and received clarification of facts in the case. Unlike Coates's "Horde," some of the commenters on the Crunk Feminist Collective website felt free to express their ignorance, vitriol, racism, and misogyny, while others took care to be respectful even in their disagreements. After this article was posted, Cooper, writing under the pseudonym, "Crunktastic," engaged with her readers, rejecting or accepting their opinions, and defending her ideas. When an exchange reached stasis, she declared her unwillingness to continue, but this came after an extended back and forth.

Cooper found her voice on social media, as a founder of the Crunk Feminist Collective, a group whose mission was "to create a space of support and camaraderie for hip hop generation feminists of color, queer, and straight, (with)in the academy and without, by building a rhetorical community in which we can express our crunk feminist selves." That community was online, and initially the pieces did not carry a byline. Rather, it identified itself by race and gender. "Crunk" is a neologism coined from a contraction of "crazy" or "chronic (weed)" and "drunk." In the culture of southern hip hop where it was coined, "to get crunk was to get out of one's right mind." The collective appropriated the term to refer to a state of consciousness in which they declare themselves "drunk off the heady theory of feminism that proclaims another world is possible."[14]

In "My Brother's Keeper and the Co-Optation of Intersectionality," Cooper takes on President Obama's much-lauded initiative to help young black men and boys. She argues that the initiative leaves the struggles of black women invisible. Particularly galling is the support of some black women for the initiative. After quoting the rapper Project Pat, who pleads, "Don't Save 'Em . . . They Don't Wanna Be Saved," Cooper confides to her readers, "So let me think it through out loud with you."[15] This invitation links her to many of the essayists in this book, who, rather than proclaiming solutions, invite their readers to sort out issues along with them. The comments that readers post confirm that they welcome the opportunity to engage in dialogue.

Cooper's blogs for Salon expanded the reach of her voice without diminishing its power. "This Is America's Religion of Violence: The Impunity of Police Violence and the Destruction of Sandra Bland" reflects on the death of the young Chicago woman who died in a Texas jail cell after being arrested during a traffic stop. The widely replayed videotape showed Bland's encounter with a police officer who refused to answer her questions about the reasons she was stopped, her defiance of his order to put out the cigarette she was smoking, and his threat to "light her up" with a Taser if she did not exit the vehicle. She got out, hurling profanities, incredulous that she was being arrested for failing to signal a lane change. Three days later she was found hanged. No indictments were brought against the officer or the jailers, who insisted Bland had committed suicide. Cooper's blog post unfolds like any good essay. She frames her reflections on the case in the context of her driving south for the Christmas holidays, hearing the news reports about Bland as well as reports of singer R. Kelly's sexual assaults on underage black girls, and listening to her personal soundtrack of contemporary gospel, old school R&B, and hip hop.

Cooper's immediate circumstances are similar to Bland's, as she too is traveling alone, but hers is a familiar journey which she treasures: ". . . this drive, undertaken over several days in which I eat at some of my favorite places and visit friends, going and coming, is an annual ritual act of self-care."[16] Cooper is rightly reluctant to assume she knows much about Bland's life beyond what was reported in the news, though she knows Bland was traveling from her hometown to begin a new job in Texas, and she imagines she was happy about it. She also knows that Bland was a churchgoer and wonders whether gospel music was on her soundtrack. Although Cooper's friends insist that Bland would never have committed suicide, Cooper is unwilling to discount the possibility. She mentions the mental stress that Black Lives Matter activists are under when they are arrested, and then proffers this opinion: "I believe that Sandra Bland died from structural lack of care and active malice by those charged with her protection. Maybe no one smothered the life out of her as they did to Eric Garner. But the state stole something from her. Hope. Possibility. Safety. Maybe even her life." Cooper is careful not to state as fact what she cannot know, even as she does not hesitate to share what she feels.

One thing that Cooper does not mention and was perhaps unaware of is that Sandra Bland herself was a blogger, whose Facebook page, #SandySpeaks, opened with the greeting "Good Morning, My Beautiful Kings and Queens," offered commentary on the economic crisis facing young black people, and provided links to sites on African American history. After her death #SandySpeaks went viral and brought Bland's ideas to a wider audience than she could have reached when she was alive.[17] Ironically enough, Bland had fulfilled Jordan's imperative that all citizens should be able to engage in political debate. Yet, her participation could not save her life.

The news reports of R. Kelly and Sandra Bland come together in Cooper's blog to create a tableau of the dangers facing young black women, the assaults from within and without the black community, the hazards that jeopardize the lives of college-educated women like Bland as well as her less-educated peers. It occasions thoughts on the importance of self-care, for women like Bland and like Cooper herself. Cooper notes the importance of online communities, such as the one that had formed to censure R. Kelly, though, significantly, the personal story she tells involves real contact with family and friends. That story is the catalyst for a meditation on the costs of racism and sexism and on the ongoing struggle for justice. The writer's thoughts provoke and enable the reader's own.

Like Ta-Nehisi Coates, Brittney Cooper analyzes and responds to the forces that imperil black bodies. They both attack white supremacy and the structures of racism it produces. They both position themselves within the circle of the vulnerable. Yet, perhaps as a consequence of her religious faith, and almost certainly as a consequence of her participation in a collective movement, Cooper ends her meditation on a hopeful note: "Sandra Bland didn't make it. But she lived. She fought. For a new chapter. For possibility. For dreams. And in her name, so should we." Her conclusion resounds a chord that one hears in the writings of James Baldwin, June Jordan, and Alice Walker. In this writing at least, Cooper lays a claim to hope.

Coates, Cooper, and their peers in print and online write with an urgency that befits a people who continue to perceive themselves in crisis. The crisis is no longer the result of a binary struggle between slavery and freedom or between blacks and whites. These writers explore the fractures among African Americans along the lines of gender, class, ethnicity, and sexual preference as well as across barriers of race and nation. Whatever the issues they confront or the questions they puzzle through, they engage, directly or indirectly, the examples of writers before them who used the essay to focus attention on political controversies, to shape aesthetic debates, and to create a space for personal recollection and philosophical reflection. Now online as well as in print, the African American essay continues to do its work.

Notes

Prologue

1. Morrison and Denard, *Toni Morrison: What Moves at the Margins.*

2. In "The Best Man," his review of a biography of Gore Vidal, for example, Charles McGrath praises Vidal's accomplishments as an essayist, then adds, "But as Vidal was painfully aware, unless you're Montaigne, essays won't make your reputation." McGrath, 12.

3. The first two descriptions are from Francis Bacon, who stands second to Michel de Montaigne as the progenitor of the essay. Quoted in Klaus, *Made-Up Self*, 21. The third description is from Huxley, preface to *Collected Essays*, vii.

4. Du Bois, *Dusk of Dawn*, in *Writings*, 612.

5. Eight previously published essays became nine chapters in *The Souls of Black Folk*. "Of the Black Belt" and "The Quest for the Silver Fleece" were both derived from "The Negro as He Really Is," published in *World's Work*.

6. Montaigne, "Of Practice," in Frame, ed., *Complete Works*, 274.

7. Baldwin, introduction to *Nobody Knows My Name*, in *Collected Essays*, 136.

8. Montaigne, "Of Practice," 273.

9. Quoted in Campbell, *Talking at the Gates*, 51.

10. Montaigne, "Of Practice," 273.

11. Adorno, "The Essay as Form," 10.

12. Morrison, "James Baldwin: His Voice Remembered; Life in His Words," in Morrison and Denard, *What Moves at the Margins*, 92.

13. Ellison, introduction to *Shadow and Act*, in *Collected Essays*, 49.

14. Adorno, "The Essay as Form," 15.

15. Adorno, "The Essay as Form," 11.

16. Although scholars have recognized the importance of the essay to the African American tradition, few have studied it. Gerald Early is an exception. A gifted essayist himself, he edited the two-volume anthology *Speech and Power: The African American Essay and its Cultural Content from Polemics to Pulpit*. Perhaps in response to the generic crossings cited above, Early introduces the terms "gnomic" and "gnostic" to capture qualities inherent in some African American essays, qualities such as the epigrammatic, the clever, the esoteric, and the intellectual. To be sure, these qualities come to the fore in the 1920s, the decade in which Early argues that African American writing came of age and when writers as various as James Weldon Johnson, George P. Schuyler, and Zora Neale Hurston came under the influence of the iconic white American essayist H. L. Mencken. However, as the subtitle of Early's anthology suggests, the African American essay had broad antecedents.

By focusing on the "meditative essay," Cheryl Butler narrows the scope in her study *The Art of the Black Essay: From Meditation to Transcendence* in order to analyze essays by Du Bois, Baldwin, Walker, and Stanley Crouch in illuminating detail. I concur with her judgment that "the African American essay . . . serves as documentary evidence that reflects and

proves the psychic evolution, the attained psychic freedom of its author" (10). By emphasizing the psychic freedom of the writer, Butler highlights the ways in which the African
American essay enacts the influence of its European precursor. Important though this is, it
is only part of the story. The meditative essay is too narrow a term to encompass the tradition that I analyze here.

17. In Vinson Cunningham's estimation, all essayists in the United States are heirs to Emerson, whose "secular sermons" set the template for an insistent argumentative style. See
Cunningham, "What Makes an Essay American?"

18. Johnson, *Book of American Negro Poetry*, 9.

19. Hurston, "Characteristics of Negro Expression," 834, 835.

20. Quoted in Lopate, *Art of the Personal Essay*, xxxi.

21. Adorno argues that "the essay retains, precisely in the autonomy of its presentation,
which distinguishes it from scientific and scholarly information, traces of the communica-
tive element such information dispenses with. In the essay the satisfactions that rhetoric
tries to provide for the listener are sublimated into the idea of a happiness in freedom vis à
vis the object . . . ." "The Essay as Form," 20–21.

22. Williams, *Alchemy of Race and Rights*, 6.

23. Ellison, "Going to the Territory," *Collected Essays*, 608.

Chapter 1

1. Patterson, *Freedom, Vol. 1*, 9, 3–5. Patterson interrogates how freedom came to be the
preeminent value in the West and not in other places in the world, despite the fact that
slavery existed everywhere.

2. Morrison, *Playing in the Dark*, 37.

3. Quoted in Hartman, *Scenes of Subjection*, 62.

4. Hartman, 115.

5. Othello, "Essay on Negro Slavery," *American Museum*. According to the catalog of the
Schomburg Center, the essay was signed on May 10, 1788, and May 23, 1788. In the first Baltimore was listed as the location, and in the second the location was listed as Maryland.
Othello's dates are given as 1759–1806. The Schomburg, citing Abbe Grégoire, *De la Littéra-
ture des Nègres* (1806), identifies him as a black man.

6. Franklin and Higginbotham, *From Slavery to Freedom*, 116.

7. Coker, "A Dialogue Between a Virginian and an African Minister," 22, 6.

8. Huggins, *Black Odyssey*, 194.

9. I borrow the term from Kenneth Cmiel who cites four rhetorical categories: (1) low or
vulgar, (2) plain, (3) middle, and (4) grand. The second is characterized by refined syntax
and the absence of figures of speech, while the third is elegant, copious, and contains a
moderate number of figures. For my purposes, I am collapsing the second and third categories. See *Democratic Eloquence*, 20–21.

10. Mackey, "Other: From Noun to Verb," 59.

11. For an analysis of the influence of "the classical tradition of rhetoric and oratory" on
the essays in *Souls*, see Rampersad, *Art and Imagination of W. E. B. Du Bois*, 72–73.

12. Adorno, "The Essay as Form," 13.

13. Du Bois, *Souls of Black Folk*, 4. Subsequent references will be cited parenthetically.

14. Rampersad notes that Du Bois often quotes from the King James Bible and also "used biblical phraseology with more novel effect, as in referring to the fertile black belt of Georgia as 'the Egypt of the Confederacy.'" The question I cite is another example. *Art and Imagination*, 76.

15. In his 1845 narrative, Douglass writes of the songs, "Every tone was a testimony against slavery and a prayer to God for deliverance from chains." *Autobiographies*, 24.

16. Among the scholars who have analyzed the function of the epigraphs are Donald B. Gibson, introduction to Du Bois, *Souls of Black Folk*; Sundquist, *To Wake the Nations*; and Weheliye, *Phonographies*. See also my essay "Resounding *Souls*: Du Bois and the African American Literary Tradition" for an analysis of the epigraphs as hieroglyphs, sensual and abstract figures that stand for the voices of the folk that cannot be written or heard in the historical moment in which Du Bois wrote *Souls*. I argue that subsequent African American writers, including James Weldon Johnson, Ralph Ellison, and Toni Morrison, transcribe the sounds of the voices that remain silent in Du Bois's text.

17. Hurston, "How It Feels to Be Colored Me," 826. Subsequent references will be cited parenthetically.

18. Du Bois, *Darkwater*, 5.

19. Ellison, "Going to the Territory," *Collected Essays*, 608. Adam Bradley's reference to vernacular process in an article by Jennifer Howard, "Ralph Ellison's Endless Novel," first sparked my interest in the concept. Bradley's presentation at "Ellison at 100: A Centennial Symposium" in Oklahoma City on March 8, 2014, confirmed my sense of its utility.

20. Beginning with Houston Baker, African Americanist critics deployed the term "vernacular" differently than Ellison had. According to Baker, "the 'vernacular' in relation to human beings signals 'a slave born on his master's estate.' In expressive terms, vernacular indicates 'arts native or peculiar to a particular country or locale.'" For Baker, vernacular is a culture reference that is racialized, while for Ellison it is nationalized. See Baker, *Blues, Ideology, and Afro-American Literature*, 2, 3.

21. In *Women of the Harlem Renaissance*, I point out the gendered implications of "a fast brown," noting that the diminished sense of self "Zora" experiences in racial terms coincides with her emergent womanhood. 26.

22. "Cuba Libre" was first published in the November-December 1960 issue of *Evergreen Review* and given a Longview Award for the best essay of the year. In January 1961, it was published in pamphlet form by the Fair Play for Cuba Committee, which also published Fidel Castro's manifesto "History Will Absolve Me," along with essays by C. Wright Mills and Jean-Paul Sartre.

23. Baraka, "Cuba Libre," *LeRoi Jones/Amiri Baraka Reader*, 126. Subsequent references will be cited parenthetically. Critic and novelist Richard Gibson invited Baraka to join the trip. Gibson, who had published essays and reviews with a New Critical slant, cuts a dubious figure in African American literary history. At one point black writers, including Richard Wright, suspected Gibson of being a government informant. By 1960 his politics had taken a radical turn, and he became active in the Fair Play for Cuba Committee, a Leftist group in New York City that presumably funded the trip. For more on Gibson's career, see Jackson, *Indignant Generation*, especially 500–504.

24. Seemingly unbeknownst to Jones, *Cuba Libre* (New York: Anderson and Ritchie, 1948) is also the title of a volume of poems by Nicolás Guillén that was translated into English by Langston Hughes in collaboration with Howard University professor Ben Frederic.

25. After he became a Marxist in 1974, Amiri Baraka often used this and similar epithets to attack his political opponents. For more on his conversion from Black Nationalism to Marxism, see his essays "Toward Ideological Clarity" and "Why I Changed My Ideology."

26. Symphony Sid (Sid Torin) was a jazz disc jockey whose hipster demeanor and musical knowledge endeared him to fans and musicians alike. The Five Spot was a downtown nightclub in New York City where musicians such as Ornette Coleman, Thelonious Monk, and Cecil Taylor performed. Turhan Bey, known as the Turkish delight, was an Austrian-born actor, often described as "exotic" in his appearance and suave in his demeanor, who performed in Hollywood films from 1941 to 1953.

27. Williams, *Alchemy of Races and Rights*, 6. Subsequent references will be cited parenthetically.

28. For more on Matthews as a thinker and activist, see Brittney C. Cooper, *Beyond Respectability*, 39–43.

29. Matthews, "The Value of Race Literature," 288. Subsequent references will be cited parenthetically.

30. Logan, *Negro in American Life and Thought*, 52.

31. Richard Wright, "Blueprint for Negro Literature," 5.

32. Baldwin, "Everybody's Protest Novel," *Collected Essays*, 12.

33. Baldwin, "Autobiographical Note," *Collected Essays*, 9.

34. Ellison, "Brave Words for a Startling Occasion," *Collected Essays*, 152.

35. Ellison, "The World and the Jug," *Collected Essays*, 163.

36. Neal, "The Black Arts Movement," 257. Subsequent references will be cited parenthetically.

37. When Neal observes that the Black Artist "eschews 'protest' literature," he suggests the possibility of common ground with Baldwin and Ellison. So did his embrace of an African American cultural tradition as the foundation of a Black Aesthetic. Both of these observations anticipate his later praise of Ellison's writing in his essay. For his part, Baraka offered a stinging critique of Baldwin along with the South African writer Peter Abrahams for their investment in individuality in "Brief Reflections on Two Hot Shots," an essay reprinted in *Home*. Baraka made amends with an eloquent eulogy delivered at Baldwin's funeral in 1987.

38. Jones/Baraka, "The Changing Same," *Black Music*, 188. Subsequent references will be cited parenthetically.

39. Orval Faubus (1910–1994) was the segregationist governor of Arkansas who in 1957 tried to block the integration of Central High School in Little Rock. Black students—known as the Little Rock Nine—enrolled in the school after President Dwight Eisenhower federalized the Arkansas National Guard in order to protect them.

40. Among the long list of one-time gospel singers turned soul men are James Brown, Ray Charles, Sam Cooke, and Wilson Pickett. Baraka's description also brings to mind the character Rinehart in Ellison's *Invisible Man*, who is at once a preacher and a pimp, the ultimate confidence man who changes identities as easily as he changes his clothes.

41. Mathes, *Imagine the Sound*, 24.

42. Although the essay mentions Mahalia Jackson, Ma Rainey, Dionne Warwick, and Leslie Uggams in passing, its preponderance of praise is for male musicians. Among the essays collected in *Black Music*, only one, "Dark Lady of the Sonnets," a tribute to Billie Holiday, has a female subject.

43. Walker, "In Search of Our Mothers' Gardens," *In Search*, 234. Subsequent references will be cited parenthetically.

44. Hurston, "Characteristics of Negro Expression," 834.

Chapter 2

1. The foundational study is Dorothy Porter, *Early Negro Writing*. Other signal works include John Ernest, *Liberation Historiography*, and Frances Smith Foster, *Written by Herself*.

2. McHenry, *Forgotten Readers*, 13.

3. Harper, "The Colored People in America," *Brighter Coming Day*, 53.

4. As scholar Frances Smith Foster reminds us, slavery and the slave trade were not their only concerns. They "also worked to communicate physical and metaphysical realities and to develop their moral, spiritual, intellectual, and artistic selves. They wrote about civil rights, economic enhancement, love, and marriage." This range of subjects anticipates the topics that black essayists would explore in the twentieth century. It signals that despite the fact that as a group black Americans were perpetually in crisis politically, their lives were never one-dimensional. They wrote about all aspects of their experience. See Foster, "A Narrative of the Interesting Origins and (Somewhat) Surprising Developments of African-American Print Culture," 714–40.

5. Cornish and Russwurm, "To Our Patrons," *Freedom's Journal*.

6. Cornish and Russwurm, "To Our Patrons," *Freedom's Journal*. My discussion of the newspaper is informed by Bacon, *Freedom's Journal*, McHenry, *Forgotten Readers*, and James, *Struggles of John Brown Russwurm*. James argues that Russwurm's worldview was Pan-Africanist as well as decidedly more secular than that of Cornish.

7. McHenry, 50–57.

8. Franklin and Higginbotham, 176.

9. Peterson, *"Doers of the Word,"* 11.

10. Wills, *Lincoln At Gettysburg*, 47.

11. See Warren, *Culture of Eloquence*, passim.

12. Walker and Garnet, Preface, *Walker's Appeal and Garnet's Address to the Slaves of the United States of America*.

13. Walker, *David Walker's Appeal to the Coloured Citizens of the World*, 2. Subsequent references will be cited parenthetically.

14. Amos Gerry Beman, "Thoughts—No. III" from *The Colored American* 5 (December 1840). Quoted in Ernest, *Liberation Historiography*, 48–49.

15. According to his biographer Peter Hinks, David Walker lived in Charleston during the slave revolt led by Denmark Vesey. Hinks speculates that Walker might well have been involved in the revolt that was organized largely by leaders of the African Methodist Episcopal Church in Charleston. Walker left the city soon afterward and eventually relocated to Boston, where he opened a used clothing shop and became known for his antislavery activism and for his oratory. Hinks, *To Awaken My Afflicted Brethren*, chap. 2, chap. 3.

16. Sterling Stuckey deems David Walker "the father of black nationalist theory in America." Stuckey, *Slave Culture*, 120.

17. The Constitution, by contrast, was a provisional document that in its acceptance of slavery comprised the permanent ideal. In this regard, Walker is a key precursor of Frederick Douglass, who elaborates this point in "What to the Slave Is the Fourth of July?" which I discuss below. Both Walker and Douglass are in productive dialogue with Abraham Lincoln, who, according to Garry Wills, also held that "the Declaration of Independence was closer to being *the* founding document of the United States than the Constitution." See Wills, *Lincoln at Gettysburg*, 130.

18. Most sources cite Walker's dates as 1785–1830, but Hinks argues that he was probably born later, in 1796 or 1797. Hinks, *To Awaken My Afflicted Brethren*, 11.

19. Hinks, *To Awaken My Afflicted Brethren*, 269–79. The belief that Walker was murdered in consequence of authoring the *Appeal* is long-standing. Southern authorities made no secret of their desire to have him killed. However, according to the Boston Index of Deaths, which Hinks cites, Walker's cause of death was consumption.

20. David Walker, *Walker's Appeal*, ed. Hinks, 5. Subsequent references will be cited parenthetically.

21. Dinius, "'Look!! Look!!! At This!!!!'," 55.

22. Dinius observes, moreover, that "the manicules throughout *Walker's Appeal* also make visible one of the defining synecdoches of American racial slavery: the slave as 'hand'" and reads the manicule "as a synecdoche for Walker himself." In her estimation, "the manicules in the pamphlet—and by, extension, the pamphlet itself become Walker's and his readers' hands raised against every slaveholder to effect the manumission of all the 'colored citizens of the world.'" "'Look!! Look!!!'," 65.

23. See, for example, the cover of *Walker's Appeal and Garnet's Address to the Slaves of the United States of America*, published by James C. Winston.

24. Bercovitch, *American Jeremiad*, xi. During the voyage that brought the Puritans to New England, John Cotton and John Winthrop crafted sermons that spoke to the fears of, and instilled hope in, those who heard them. Most famously, Winthrop preached that the Puritans had been chosen to build the "city on the hill," to establish a Christian nation in the wilderness. Their failure to adhere to divine commandments would lead to their destruction. Yet, as Bercovitch emphasizes, the jeremiad captured the duality of their situation. Destruction was not inevitable: the people's fidelity to God's purpose would ensure their triumph. In this reading, the American jeremiad is the founding text of American exceptionalism. Its metaphors, themes, and symbols continue to animate writing in America from the seventeenth century to the present.

25. Quoted in Howard-Pitney, 10. The book's introduction informs my discussion more broadly.

26. Jarrett, *Representing the Race*, 29.

27. Eddie Glaude asserts that "biblical narrative, particularly Exodus, provided a large portion of the public vocabulary for African Americans of the period: the covenant, Egypt, the wilderness, and the promised land were tools in black public life that disclosed the violence, suffering, death, and hope so indicative of the African American experience. Reiterative reference to these stories helped organize a black American national public to confront the racial violence of the early nineteenth century." Glaude, *Exodus!*, 111.

28. Jefferson, *Notes on the State of Virginia*, 143.

29. Jefferson's appeal to science helped to shift the discourse around racial ideology in the early nineteenth century, which had previously been characterized by more free-floating prejudice. Historian Mia Bay charts the impact of the resulting racist ethnology as well as the response by black Americans, including David Walker. See Bay, *White Image*, chap. 1 and chap. 2, passim.

30. Given Jefferson's now well-documented affair with Sally Hemings, an enslaved black woman who was his property, this charge is perhaps better analyzed by psychologists than literary critics.

31. In the second article of the *Appeal*, Walker consolidates his *bona fides* as a "race man." He discusses Africa as a center of learning and Haiti as a site of revolution.

32. Franklin and Higginbotham, 179–83. Peter Hinks discusses the energized response of the black community to the American Colonization Society, including a mass meeting attended by more than one thousand people at Philadelphia's Bethel Church in January 1817. Hinks, *To Awaken*, 99. Anger at the ACS was also a major impetus for the Negro Convention Movement; the proceedings of these meetings were in turn a key generator of black print culture in the antebellum period.

33. Unlike twenty-first century writers, for whom a series of exclamation points requires merely holding down a key, nineteenth-century compositors had to set each character individually. Walker offered precise directions to his print setters.

34. Hinks documents the suppression of the text in the South. Recent scholarship shows how it circulated in the North. See Leavell, 679–95.

35. Maria W. Stewart, "Religion and the Pure Principles of Morality, the Sure Foundation on Which We Must Build," in Richardson, ed., *Maria W. Stewart*, 30. Subsequent references to this edition will be cited parenthetically. The essay was first published in William Lloyd Garrison's *The Liberator*, October, 8, 1831, the year after Walker's death.

36. Peterson, *"Doers of the Word,"* 60.

37. In "The Prologue" to her book of poems, Anne Bradstreet apologized for the meagerness of her talent, even as she claimed a place for herself as a writer: "From schoolboy's tongue no rhet'ric we expect,/Nor yet a sweet consort from broken strings,/Nor perfect beauty where's a main defect:/My foolish, broken, blemished Muse so sings,/And this to mend, alas, no art is able,/'Cause nature made it so irreparable," *Norton Anthology of American Literature*, 41. Stewart's apologia works similarly.

38. Peterson offers a perceptive analysis of Stewart's *Meditations*, the text that grew out of this conversion experience. *"Doers of the Word,"* 59–63.

39. Peterson, *"Doers of the Word,"* 67.

40. Elizabeth McHenry notes that Stewart had not been well received when she spoke earlier that year to the Afri-American Female Intelligence Society, a literary society in Boston. McHenry's description of the practices of a similar group, the Female Literary Association of Philadelphia, helps explain the negative response. While the group's members "functioned alternatively as producers, distributors, and consumers of texts," McHenry notes, they submitted their writing anonymously. See *Forgotten Readers*, 58–71. For an analysis of Stewart's boldness in speaking in public, see 68–78.

41. See Andrews, ed., *Sisters of the Spirit*, a volume that collects the spiritual narratives of Jarena Lee, Zilpha Elaw, and Julia Foote, women who, according to Andrews, "chose to step

outside their appointed sphere and seek a new way of defining themselves vis-à-vis the people of God and the people of the world" (14). Like Stewart's prose, their narratives blur the boundaries between the written and spoken word. However, although these women breached the protocol of their denominations by insisting on their vocation as preachers, their theology adhered to Christian orthodoxy.

42. Maria W. Stewart, "Lecture at Franklin Hall," in Richardson, ed., *Maria W. Stewart*, 45. Subsequent references will be cited parenthetically.

43. Consider the closing couplet of Wheatley's "On Being Brought from Africa to America," "Remember, *Christians*, *Negros*, black as *Cain*,/May be refin'd, and join th' angelic train."

44. It seems likely that when Stewart claimed a blood tie to white Americans, she was speaking literally. A photograph taken late in her life reveals a light-skinned woman with keen features and straight hair.

45. Maria W. Stewart, "Religion and Pure Principles," in Richardson, ed., *Maria W. Stewart*, 35.

46. An advertisement for "Religion and Pure Principles" from *The Liberator* reads: "For sale at this office, a tract addressed to the people of color, by Mrs. Maria W. Steward [*sic*], a respectable colored lady of this city. Its title is, 'Religion And The Pure Principles of Morality, The Sure Foundation On Which We Must Build.' The production is most praiseworthy, and confers great credit on the talents and piety of its author. We hope she will have many patrons. Extracts of the paper hereafter. Price 6 cents." Richardson, ed., *Maria W. Stewart*, 28.

47. Maria W. Stewart, "An Address Delivered at the African Masonic Hall, Boston, February 27, 1833," in Richardson, ed., *Maria W. Stewart*, 59.

48. Marilyn Richardson appends Maria Stewart's application for James W. Stewart's service pension in *Maria W. Stewart*, 116–17. The petition was filed in February 1879, almost fifty years after James Stewart's death. His widow had fared no better in accessing the estate he had bequeathed than she had his pension. As was the case for most free blacks, Maria Stewart was continuously denied her rights under the U.S. legal system.

49. Walker and Garnet, Preface, *Walker's Appeal and Garnet's Address to the Slaves of the United States of America*.

50. Douglass asserted that if slaves got word of Garnet's exhortations to them, insurrections would indeed occur and would be crushed. In 1843, Douglass was still affiliated with the William Lloyd Garrison wing of the abolitionist movement that was committed to the strategies of "moral suasion" and nonviolence. It rejected political action in part because it rejected the legitimacy of the U.S. Constitution, a document it viewed as fatally compromised by its acceptance of slavery. See Stuckey, *Slave Culture*, 158–59, and McFeely, *Frederick Douglass*, 95–96, 106–10.

51. Although Sterling Stuckey faults Garnet and Walker for their overall failure to appreciate the African retentions in the culture of the slaves, he argues that Garnet's "formulation of reciprocity between the living and the dead, of the return of the dead from the afterworld to resume life among the living, is so remarkably akin to the African religious vision that he might have been aware of it." Stuckey, *Slave Culture*, 135–36.

52. According to the convention's minutes, Douglass's rebuttal lasted an hour and a half, and was followed by Garnet's hour-and-a-half defense. For a summary of the exchange, see Gates and Burton, eds., *Call and Response*, 117–18.

53. William Lloyd Garrison, Preface to *Narrative of the Life of Frederick Douglass*. In Douglass, *Autobiographies*, 4.

54. James McCune Smith, Introduction to Frederick Douglass, *My Bondage and My Freedom*. 1855. In Douglass, *Autobiographies*, 128.

55. *Narrative of the Life of Frederick Douglass*, in Douglass, *Autobiographies*, 41.

56. In his introduction, David Blight notes that *The Columbian Orator* went through 23 editions and was still in use in the late nineteenth century. Since Blight's bicentennial edition was published, the book has become widely available in formats including e-books and audiobooks.

57. David Everett, "General Description of America, Extract From A Poem Spoken At Dartmouth College, on Commencement Day, 1795," in Bingham, *Columbian Orator*, 207–9.

58. Quoted in Bingham, *Columbian Orator*, xxii.

59. Quoted in Bingham, *Columbian Orator*, xxv.

60. *My Bondage and My Freedom*, in Douglass, *Autobiographies*. Subsequent references will be cited parenthetically.

61. In the same vivid language that animated his text, Douglass enumerated his charges: "We have men-stealers for ministers, women-whippers for missionaries, and cradle-plunderers for church members. The man who wields the blood-clotted cowskin during the week fills the pulpit on Sunday, and claims to be a minister of the meek and lowly Jesus." Douglass, *Narrative*, 97.

62. Quoted in McFeely, 85.

63. Meer, "Douglass as Orator and Editor," 46–48.

64. See Blassingame, Introduction to *Frederick Douglass Papers*, xxxi–xxxv.

65. David N. Johnson, *Sketches of Lynn*. 1880. Quoted in McFeely, 124–25.

66. McFeely, 173.

67. Other blacks in the nineteenth century held ceremonies, including public protest parades, on the fifth rather than the fourth of July, as forms of protest. A more mundane explanation is also possible: in 1852, the Fourth of July fell on a Sunday. See Meer, 53.

68. Douglass, "What to the Slave Is the Fourth of July?," 407. Excerpts from the speech were published as an appendix to Douglass's 1855 autobiography *My Bondage and My Freedom*. Subsequent references will be cited parenthetically.

69. Maya Angelou might have been thinking of Douglass's oration when she used the metaphors of the rock, the river, and the tree in her poem written on the occasion of President Bill Clinton's inauguration in 1992.

70. John Stauffer notes that Douglass was far more militant in an address the same year to the National Convention of the Free Soil Party. Stauffer contends that Douglass "downplayed his militancy when speaking to women." The female Anti-Slavery Society of Rochester invited him to deliver "What to the Slave Is the Fourth of July?" Stauffer, "Douglass's Self-Making and Abolition," 21.

71. William Nell, *The Liberator*, September 22, 1858. In Harper, *Brighter Coming Day*, 17. I follow editor Frances Foster's lead and refer to the author as Watkins Harper.

72. Frances Foster, Introduction to Harper, *Brighter Coming Day*, 15.

73. Letter from Frances Watkins to William Still, August 1854. In Harper, *Brighter Coming Day*, 44.

74. "Affairs in South Carolina," letter published in the *National Anti-Slavery Standard*, August 10, 1867. Harper, *Brighter Coming Day*, 124.

75. Peterson, *"Doers of the Word,"* 131.

76. Meredith McGill notes that even in its format *Poems on Miscellaneous Subjects* bears "the traces of a strong relationship to oral performances," which likewise treated a range of causes and songs. Especially in its earliest editions, the book was designed to appeal to the activist spirit of its readers. McGill, "Frances Ellen Watkins Harper and the Circuits of Abolitionist Poetry," 59.

77. Frances Smith Foster speculates that William Watkins, a frequent contributor to the *Liberator*, may also have assisted his niece's publishing efforts. Her first volume, *Forest Leaves*, was published in 1845. *Poems on Miscellaneous Subjects*, which despite its title contained prose as well as poetry, was published in 1854. Introduction to Harper, *Brighter Coming Day*, 7–8.

78. Harper, "Breathing the Air of Freedom," *Poems on Miscellaneous Subjects*, 1857 edition. In *Brighter Coming Day*, 45.

79. *Christian Recorder*, September 15, 1866. Quoted in Peterson, *"Doers of the Word,"* 132.

80. Peterson, *"Doers of the Word,"* 124.

81. See Emerson, "The Divinity School Address."

82. Peterson, 125.

83. Harper, "Christianity," *Poems on Miscellaneous Subjects*, 1857 edition. In *Brighter Coming Day*, 96–99. Foster notes that this piece may have first been published in the *Christian Recorder*.

84. Harper, "The Colored People in America," in *Brighter Coming Day*, 99–100.

85. Harper, "Could We Trace the Record of Every Human Heart," *National Anti-Slavery Standard*, May 23, 1857. In *Brighter Coming Day*, 102.

86. Harper, "We Are All Bound up Together," *Proceedings of the Eleventh Woman's Rights Convention*, May 1866. In *Brighter Coming Day*, 217–19.

87. Harper, "Almost Constantly Traveling or Speaking," letter to William Still, in *Brighter Coming Day*, 126.

88. Harper, "I am in the Sunny South," letter to William Still, in *Brighter Coming Day*, 123.

89. Harper, "A Private Meeting with the Women," in *Brighter Coming Day*, 127.

90. Harper, "Private Meeting," 128.

91. Harper, "Coloured Women of America." *Englishwoman's Review*, January 15, 1878. In *Brighter Coming Day*, 272.

Chapter 3

1. Quoted in Douglas, *Terrible Honesty*, 18.

2. Following George Stocking, George Hutchinson credits Franz Boas for pioneering explanations of human behavior in terms of culture rather than race. Boas rejected the view that a hierarchy of cultures existed. He insisted that "cultures should be understood on their own terms, as having developed within particular circumstances, with their own specific histories and standards of judgment." Hutchinson, *Harlem Renaissance in Black and White*, 66. Boas's ideas were critical to the theories of American culture and of vital importance

to African American intellectuals from Du Bois, who solicited essays by Boas for *The Crisis*, to Hurston, who was of course his student.

3. Hutchinson argues that an interracial group of intellectuals, artists, and publishers collaborated in producing the renaissance. He quotes approvingly V. F. Calverton in *Liberation of American Literature*: "It was not until the development of a national consciousness, and the consequent interest in things native, that the Negro's contributions to art were taken with seriousness." Hutchinson, *Harlem Renaissance in Black and White*, 102.

4. This perspective was pioneered by David Levering Lewis in *When Harlem Was in Vogue*, a book that continues to shape and inform my reading of the period.

5. See Du Bois, "The Negro in Art: How Shall He Be Portrayed?" in *Souls of Black Folk*.

6. Locke, ed., *New Negro*, 3. Subsequent references will be cited parenthetically. I explore the masculinist cast of "The New Negro," in *Women of the Harlem Renaissance*, 1–13.

7. Hutchinson places Locke's views in the context of American pragmatism, a philosophy that held: "only by means of freedom and development in the aesthetic realm . . . , through the growth of a truly democratic *culture*, would political freedom finally be gotten." From a literary perspective, however, the diffusiveness of Locke's argument weakens its effectiveness. Hutchinson, *Harlem Renaissance in Black and White*, 43

8. Locke, "Negro Youth Speaks," *New Negro*, 49. Subsequent references to this essay will be cited parenthetically.

9. But if Locke rejects propaganda on the grounds that it "perpetuates the position of group inferiority even in crying out against it," he takes care to distinguish his position from the tradition of art for art's sake. In the spirit of Dewey, he argues for "a deep realization of the fundamental purpose of art and of its function as a tap root of vigorous, flourishing living . . . It is the art of the people that needs to be cultivated, not the art of the coteries." Locke, "Art or Propaganda?" in Huggins, ed., *Voices from the Harlem Renaissance*, 312–13.

10. Johnson, Preface, *Book of American Negro Poetry*, 9. Subsequent references will be cited parenthetically.

11. Edwards, "Seemingly Eclipsed Window of Form: James Weldon Johnson's Prefaces," *Jazz Cadence of American Culture*, 587.

12. Locke, "The Legacy of the Ancestral Arts," *New Negro*, 266.

13. In an autobiographical note she submitted for Countee Cullen's anthology *Caroling Dusk: An Anthology of Verse by Negro Poets*, Spencer offered her artistic credo: "I write about the things I love. But have not civilized articulation for the things I hate. I proudly love being a Negro woman—it's so involved and interesting. *We* are the problem—the great national game of TABOO." Cullen, 47.

14. These aesthetic similarities reflect Locke's strong editorial hand, as was reflected in his interaction with McKay. The poet responded angrily when Locke changed the title of "The White House" to "White Houses" in order to avoid any reference to the residence of the U.S. president. McKay accused Locke of being a "dyed-in-the-wool pussy-footing professor," but he won the day. When McKay published the sonnet in his own volume, he reinstated the original title. See Cooper, *Claude McKay*, 225.

15. William Stanley Braithwaite, "The Negro in American Literature," in Locke, *New Negro*, 29. Braithwaite's survey of Negro character in American literature prefigures the work of scholar/poet Sterling Brown in the 1930s and beyond.

16. Montgomery Gregory, "The Drama of Negro Life," in Locke, *New Negro*, 153–59. Ironically, the examples Gregory cites are the work of white playwrights Edward Sheldon (*The Nigger*) and Ridgely Torrence (*Granny Maumee, The Rider of Dreams*, and *Simon the Cyrenian*). The black contributors to drama were actors: Charles Gilpin, Paul Robeson, and Eugene Corbie.

17. Jessie Fauset, "The Gift of Laughter," in Locke, *New Negro*, 161. Subsequent references will be cited parenthetically. Interestingly, the essay that Du Bois published in the *Survey Graphic* number was entitled "The Black Man Brings His Gifts," which took the form of an allegorical parable.

18. In his own essay "The Comic Side of Trouble," published in *American Magazine* in January 1918, Williams writes, "I took to studying the dialect of the American negro (sic), which to me was just as much a foreign dialect as that of the Italian." Quoted in Gerald Early, ed. *Speech and Power*, Vol. 2, 8.

19. J. A. Rogers, "Jazz at Home," in Locke, *New Negro*, 216–17.

20. See Stewart, "A Black Aesthete at Oxford."

21. Barnes, "Negro Art and America," 19. Subsequent references will be cited parenthetically.

22. The history of the making of *The New Negro* is told in Hutchinson, *Harlem Renaissance in Black and White*, and Lewis, *When Harlem Was in Vogue*.

23. Locke, "The Negro Spirituals," *New Negro*, 201, 199.

24. The stylized illustrations in *The New Negro* by the Negro artist Aaron Douglass demonstrate this influence, as do the illustrations drawn by the German Winold Reiss and the Mexican Miguel Covarubbias.

25. Schuyler, "The Negro-Art Hokum," in Huggins, ed., *Voices from the Harlem Renaissance*, 310.

26. Bode, *Mencken*, 4.

27. Richard Wright, *Black Boy*, 293.

28. Johnson quoted in Scruggs, *Sage of Harlem*, 57. Scruggs argues that Mencken shared a conviction with many black writers—there was something rotten at the core of America—and a commitment to realism as a fictional mode. While Scruggs acknowledges that Mencken often used derogatory terms to refer to black people—one of his essays on race relations was titled "A Coon Age"—he contends that Mencken's willingness to publish black writers and to intervene with publishers on their behalf made a notable contribution to the Harlem Renaissance. For example, Mencken's appeal to Alfred A. Knopf resulted in the publication of Walter White's first novel, *The Fire in the Flint*, in 1924 and the reissue of James Weldon Johnson's *The Autobiography of an Ex-Colored Man* in 1927. The latter was originally published anonymously in 1912.

29. Fiction writer and physician Rudolph Fisher was also a satirist in the Mencken mode. His 1927 essay "The Caucasian Storms Harlem" satirized the vogue of Harlem night life. Tongue in cheek, he describes his return to his old stomping ground after a five-year absence, and finding no familiar faces, he concludes, "The best of Harlem's black cabarets have changed their names and turned white." He notes the popularity of black art on Broadway, on the concert stage, and even in the galleries of the Metropolitan Museum. He captures its commercialization in the statement: "Negro stock is going up, and everybody's buying." In Huggins, *Voices from the Harlem Renaissance*, 75, 80.

30. Bode, *Mencken*, 80. Tellingly, two recent biographies are titled *Mencken: An American Iconoclast*, by Mary Rodgers, and *A Skeptic: The Life of H. L. Mencken*, by Terry Teachout.

31. Bode, *Mencken*, 4.

32. H. L. Mencken, *American Language*, 179.

33. See J. E. Lighter, ed., *Dictionary of American Slang*. Notably, "hokum" is not cited in either *Juba to Jive: A Dictionary of African American Slang* by Clarence Major or *Black Talk: Words and Phrases from the Hood to the American Corner* by Geneva Smitherman.

34. Schuyler, "Negro-Art Hokum," 312, subsequent references will be cited parenthetically. A few months later in his *Messenger* column, "Shafts and Darts" (August 1926), Schuyler posted "Ballad of Negro Artists," quoted in Williams, *George S. Schuyler*, 42. It began:

> Now old Merlin the wizard had nothing on us,
> though he conjured a castle up out of the dust;
> For with nothing but gall and a stoutness of heart,
> On this public we've foisted the New Negro Art.

35. Mencken, *American Language*, 192.

36. Lewis, *When Harlem Was in Vogue*, 108.

37. Rampersad, *Life of Langston Hughes*, vol. 1, 130.

38. Langston Hughes, "The Negro Artist and the Racial Mountain," in Huggins, ed., *Voices from the Harlem Renaissance*, 305. Subsequent references will be cited parenthetically. For Cullen's statement to a reporter, see Margaret Sperry, "Countee P. Cullen, Negro Boy Poet, Tells His Story," *Brooklyn Daily Eagle*, February 10, 1924. Quoted in Early, *My Soul's High Song*, 24.

39. The avuncular tone was a conceit: Hughes (1902–1967) was in fact only a year older than Cullen (1903–1946), and Cullen's first book, *Color* (1925), was published the year before Hughes's *The Weary Blues* (1926). The two were rivals rather than confidantes.

40. These details do not reflect Cullen's biography. His adoptive father was the pastor of Salem Methodist Church, one of the most prominent congregations in Harlem.

41. The essay was finally published as the lead essay in *Reading Black, Reading Feminist*, Gates, ed., 21–26. Ironically, when *The Florida Negro: A Federal Writer's Project Legacy*, edited by Gary McDonogh, was published, Hurston's essays were excluded. According to Pamela Bordelon, the stance that Hurston took in "On Art and Such" was one reason the original project editors omitted her work. Bordelon restores this aspect of Hurston's legacy in *Go Gator*.

42. Hurston, "On Art and Such," in *Zora Neale Hurston: Folklore, Memoirs, and Other Writings*, 905. All quotations from Hurston's essays are from this edition and will be cited parenthetically.

43. Hurston misstates Du Bois's title as "Our Sorrow Songs," an error that she might have corrected had this essay been published in her lifetime.

44. "Spirituals and Neo-Spirituals," in *Zora Neale Hurston: Folklore*, 869, 870.

45. "Folklore and Music," in *Zora Neale Hurston: Folklore*, 876. The essay was also written for *The Florida Negro* in 1938.

46. Such critics include Gates, *Signifying Monkey*, Hill, *Social Rituals and the Verbal Art*, and Holloway, *Character of the Word*.

47. Hill, *Social Rituals*, 2.

48. See, for example, James Snead, "Repetition as a Figure in Black Culture," in Gates, ed., *Black Literature and Literary Theory*, 59–79.

49. Paul Gilroy, *Black Atlantic*, 91. Carby, "Politics of Fiction," 75–76. According to Carby, Hurston's concern was both to establish the "authenticity" of folk material and to "expose" the ways in which contemporary representations undermined the aesthetics of folk culture. Writing about "Spirituals and Neo-Spirituals," Carby criticizes Hurston for privileging the culture of rural blacks over that of the increasingly urban black masses. As the reference to the New Orleans congregation suggests, Hurston was not always guilty of this, but she certainly viewed the southern black culture as the generative source of black expression throughout the United States.

50. A twenty-first century recording, "Take It to Jesus," repeats the lines "He's a heart fixer/he's a mind regulator/give it to Jesus. He's a burden bearer/he's a heavy load sharer/just give it to Jesus." Chicago Mass Choir, *Calling on You: Live*.

51. The term "gospel" for a musical genre was just coming into common usage at the time of Hurston's writing. *Gospel Pearls*, the first songbook of the National Baptist Convention, was published in 1921, the same year that gospel quartets began to record their music. By 1925, gospel singing was a regular feature of the convention. Harris, *Rise of the Gospel Blues*, 151–152.

52. Hurston, "Characteristics," 834.

53. Hurston's references point to her understanding that many cultures—including both African and European cultures—traditionally placed the highest value on the beauty of religious expression.

54. James Weldon Johnson, "The Dilemma of the Negro Author," in Early, ed., *Speech and Power*, vol. 2, 93. Subsequent references to this edition will be cited parenthetically.

55. Hurston made a similar argument in "What White Publishers Won't Print," *Zora Neale Hurston: Folklore*, 950–55.

56. Wallace Thurman, "Negro Artists and the Negro," in Early, ed., *Speech and Power*, vol. 2, 108.

Chapter 4

1. In lectures, Baldwin pointed out that for black Americans gospel songs and sermons "had less to do with the Old Testament than they had to do with our daily life." Then he repeated, "If *I* had *my way*! . . . [*Urgent whisper:*] I'd tear this building down . . . People in this country still do not know what black people are talking about." Quoted in Campbell, *Talking at the Gates*, 180.

2. Denning, "Special American Conditions," 170.

3. Baldwin, "The Discovery of What It Means," *Collected Essays*, 137.

4. Spivak, "Subaltern Studies," 214. Spivak later retracted the phrase because it had become "the union ticket for essentialism. As to what is meant by strategy, no one wondered about that." Consequently, she wrote, "as a phrase, I have given up on it." Quoted in Denius and Jonsoon, 35. In borrowing Spivak's formulation, I want to argue that Baldwin was acutely aware of the strategy he deployed when he used the language of American Exceptionalism in the 1950s and 1960s. By the 1970s, it was a concept he had given up on.

5. Baldwin, "Nobody Knows My Name," *Collected Essays*, 197.

6. See, for example, Baldwin, "Notes for a Hypothetical Novel" (1960), discussed below. The allusion is to R. W. B. Lewis, *American Adam* (1955). Other foundational works of literary criticism in American studies include Richard Chase, *The American Novel and Its Traditions* (1956), Charles Feidelson, *Symbolism in American Literature* (1953), Leslie Fielder, *Love and Death in the American Novel* (1960), and Leo Marx, *The Machine in the Garden* (1964).

7. Baldwin, "Discovery," *Collected Essays*, 139.

8. Baldwin, "Stranger in the Village," *Collected Essays*, 129.

9. Baldwin, "Notes for a Hypothetical Novel," *Collected Essays*, 228–29.

10. Adorno, "Essay as Form," 16.

11. Baldwin, Introduction to *Nobody Knows My Name* in *Collected Essays*, 136.

12. Adorno, "Essay as Form," 13.

13. Baldwin, "A Question of Identity," *Collected Essays*, 100.

14. Baldwin, "Notes of a Native Son," *Collected Essays*, 83.

15. Baldwin simplifies the truth here. As James Campbell points out, "Baldwin was well-read by the time he quit New York, not only in English and American literature but in Russian and French as well—'Baldwin had read *everything*,' said Mary McCarthy—and his reading, which had drawn him towards France in the first place, also helped prepare him for his life there. He had read Balzac, for example, who taught him a lesson about the place of French institutions, from the universality of bureaucracy to the role of the concierge; from Flaubert he learned about the play of morality and hypocrisy, and the importance of conventional behavior; Hemingway advised him about food, drink, and waiters; Henry Miller revealed the secrets of sex in districts which, once only places of legend, now became his haunts: Montmartre, Montparnasse, St-Germain-des-Prés." Campbell, *Talking at the Gates*, 51.

16. I use the term *homosexual* as shorthand for Baldwin's queer sexuality; he never used the term to refer to himself. Homosexuality was, however, a subject in his writings from the very beginning of his career. See William Spurlin, "Culture, Rhetoric and Queer Identity," in McBride, ed., *James Baldwin Now*, 103–21.

17. Originally published in 1949 in *Zero*, the same journal that published "Everybody's Protest Novel," "Preservation of Innocence" was not included in *Notes of a Native Son*. *Collected Essays*, 594–600.

18. Baldwin, "Many Thousand Gone," *Collected Essays*, 27.

19. Veeder and Griffin, *Art of Criticism*, 109.

20. Du Bois, *Souls of Black Folk*, 205; Douglass, *Narrative*, in *Autobiographies*, 24.

21. Quoted in Campbell, *Talking at the Gates*, 180.

22. Baldwin, *Fire Next Time* in *Collected Essays*, 306; Hurston, "Characteristics of Negro Expression," *Folklore, Memoirs*, 834.

23. Baldwin, "Autobiographical Notes," *Collected Essays*, 6.

24. Tóibín argues that Baldwin "used and adapted the tone of the great masters of English eloquence: Bacon, Sir Thomas Browne, Hazlitt, Emerson, and Henry James." Tóibín contends that this appropriation involved "a cast of mind that used qualification, the aside, and the further sub-clauses to suggest that truth was brittle and easily undermined." I would suggest that these writers, all of whom are essayists, model ways of expressing a skepticism that was also part and parcel of African American expressive culture. Baldwin appropriated elements of the style of the English essay, but he had in all probability already internalized

the cast of mind. I agree with Tóibín that Baldwin's "prose played with the explicit and the implicit, the bald statement and the skeptical gloss. His style could be high and grave and reflect the glittering mind; his thought was embodied beautifully in his style, as though fresh language had led him to fresh thought . . ." Tóibín, "James Baldwin: The Flesh and the Devil," 186, 188.

25. In the preface to the 1984 edition of *Notes of a Native Son*, Baldwin distinguishes inheritance from birthright.

26. Baldwin's list calls to mind the famous passage from *Souls of Black Folk*, which begins, "I sit with Shakespeare and he winces not" (90). Du Bois invokes a pantheon of Western geniuses similar to Baldwin's but to a very different effect. Du Bois was happy to take his place beside Shakespeare, confident in his assumption that Shakespeare would welcome his company. For Du Bois, high culture—or civilization, if you will—demolishes hierarchies of race, even as it creates a hierarchy of its own.

27. Olaudah Equiano offers a compelling contrast. In his 1789 narrative that depicts his kidnapping from a village in West Africa, he avers that Africans had the moral and cultural advantage in their initial encounter with the European strangers, whom he initially mistakes for cannibals. See *Interesting Narrative of the Life of Olaudah Equiano*, ch. 1.

28. Hartman, *Lose Your Mother*, 5.

29. Aimé Césaire (1913–2008), born in Martinique, was a poet and political leader. *Cahier d'un retour au pays natal* (*Return to My Native Land*, 1956) is one of the founding texts of the Négritude movement. Alioune Diop (1910–1980), who organized the congress, was born in Senegal; in 1947 he founded *Présence Africaine*, the journal that became the locus of the Négritude movement and a leading platform for anticolonialist thought. Born in Barbados, George Lamming (1927–) emigrated to Great Britain in 1950; his novels include *In the Castle of My Skin* (1953) and *Season of Adventure* (1960); *The Pleasures of Exile* (1960) is a pioneering work of Caribbean literary and cultural theory. Jean Price-Mars (1876–1969) was a diplomat and scholar of his birthplace, Haiti. Léopold Senghor (1906–2001), poet, scholar, and one of the definers of Négritude, served as president of Senegal from 1960 to 1980.

30. Horace Mann Bond was president of Atlanta University and of Lincoln University, where he directed the historical research in support of *Brown v. Board of Education of Topeka, Kansas*. Mercer Cook, scholar, translator, and diplomat, was head of the department of romance languages at Howard University. John Davis was director of the American Information Committee on Race and Caste.

31. Baldwin's essay may be usefully compared to Jessie Fauset's "Impressions of the Pan-African Congress," her account of the meetings held by black intellectuals in London, Brussels, and Paris in the aftermath of World War I. Fauset, one of the few women to participate, described the conditions in various parts of Africa and drew broad parallels between the problems of colonialism in Africa and segregation in the United States. But she was keenly aware of the differences and of the tensions they produced in an organization like the Pan-African Congress. In a statement that anticipates Baldwin, she reported, "Already we had realized that the black colonial's problem while the same intrinsically, wore on the face of it a different aspect from that of the black American." Fauset, 376.

32. Baldwin, "Encounter on the Seine: Black Meets Brown," *Collected Essays*, 89. Subsequent references will be cited parenthetically.

33. Kevin Gaines makes a complementary point in "Exile and the Private Life," when he states that "what Baldwin gained at the Sorbonne conference was an affirmation of his own individuality, his 'private life'" (176). After this experience, Baldwin's focus turned away from geopolitical struggle to "an inner cold war waged within the hearts and minds of Americans" (176). Gaines analyzes Baldwin's representation of that war in his novel *Another Country*. It is the subject of his subsequent essays as well.

34. Locke, "New Negro," *New Negro*, 7.

35. The Pan-African Congresses in which W. E. B. Du Bois played a leading role were held in 1919, 1921, 1923, and 1927; a later meeting was held in 1945. Attended by representatives from throughout the African diaspora as well as sympathetic whites, the meetings were organized with the goal of ending colonialism in Africa.

36. As Kevin Gaines points out in his article "E. Franklin Frazier's Revenge," Baldwin omits completely the speech given by Franz Fanon that indicted racism and gave an account of its historical evolution under colonialism. Fanon also referred, cautiously, to France's repressive conduct in Algeria. 511.

37. In his fiction, Baldwin represented gender relations more insightfully. Compared to his male contemporaries Saul Bellow, Ralph Ellison, Norman Mailer, and Richard Wright, Baldwin invented multidimensional female characters; Florence in *Go Tell It on the Mountain* is an example.

38. Glaude, *In a Shade of Blue*, 13.

39. Leeming, *James Baldwin*, 268–69, 273.

40. "Epilogue: Who Has Believed Our Report?" *Collected Essays*, 475.

41. In the *Debate: Baldwin v. Buckley*, Baldwin begins by declaring, "I am Jeremiah."

42. "Take Me to the Water," *Collected Essays*, 358. Subsequent references will be cited parenthetically.

43. Quoted in Baldwin and Stein, 10. Marianne DeKoven argues that Baldwin's use of pronouns in the early essays allows him "to annex his audience and persuade it to embrace his point of view." Over time, the shifting pronouns enact simultaneously the "dominant universalist and emergent particularist identity politics" that in her reading signify respectively the modern and postmodern impulses in Baldwin's texts. See *Utopia Limited*, 234–39.

44. Baldwin, "Autobiographical Notes," *Notes of a Native Son, Collected Essays*, 9.

45. A representative example of Baldwin's scathing judgment is "white Americans are probably the sickest and certainly the most dangerous people, of any color, to be found in the world today." *No Name in the Street*, 386. Although the critical reception of the book remains mixed, biographer David Leeming deems *No Name in the Street* "an original work," and he notes that most of the contemporary reviews were generally positive if not enthusiastic. Mel Watkins in the *New York Times Book Review* recognized in it "the old Baldwin ability to convey the national anguish and to see that anguish through his personal tragedy." *The Nation* and *Saturday Review*, "while upset by Baldwin's new militancy and critical of his tendency to 'skim,' recognized the essential power of the work." According to Leeming, Baldwin found some of the reviews hurtful. As some whites considered him ungrateful given the success he had achieved, black nationalists were suspicious of his more militant tone. He confided to his brother that he was "trapped . . . between the 'white fantasy' and the 'black fantasy.'" Leeming, *James Baldwin: A Biography*, 316.

46. Zabrowska, *James Baldwin's Turkish Decade*, 214.

47. Baldwin, "To Be Baptized," *Collected Essays*, 410. Another source of despair and alienation was FBI surveillance. As James Campbell documents in "I Heard It Through the Grapevine," the FBI kept Baldwin under "secret and continuous surveillance" for most of the 1960s. The agency tracked his movements across the globe, tricked friends and relatives into disclosing information, monitored his public appearances, and dug up dirt on his private life. For a facsimile of the file, see Maxwell, *James Baldwin: The FBI File*.

Chapter 5

1. The quotations are from Ralph Ellison, "Richard Wright's Blues," "Twentieth-Century Fiction and the Black Mask of Humanity," and "The Little Man at Chehaw Station," *Collected Essays*, 129, 89, 500.

2. Quoted in Rampersad, *Ralph Ellison*, 410. Marshall, Review, 83; Rampersad, 410.

3. Menand, "Liberated by Literature." Review of *Going to the Territory*.

4. John S. Wright, *Shadowing Ellison*, 7.

5. Ellison, " An Extravagance of Laughter," *Collected Essays*, 618.

6. According to Cynthia Dobbs, by "framing the scene as a comedy of manners, a matter of 'etiquette,' Ellison minimizes the terrifying implications at play." Along with a finely grained analysis of the essay, Dobbs documents its publication history. Dobbs, "Mapping Black Movement," 918.

7. Ellison, "Extravagance," 647.

8. Ellison, "Twentieth-Century Fiction," 83.

9. Historian Jacqueline Dowd Hall recounts the history of the "long civil rights movement" "that took root in the liberal and radical milieu of the 1930s, was intimately tied to the 'rise and fall of the New Deal Order,' stretched far beyond the South, was continuously and ferociously contested, and, in the 1960s and 1970s inspired a 'movement of movements' that 'de[fies] any narrative of collapse," Hall, "Long Civil Rights Movement," 1325.

10. The Ralph Ellison Papers at the Library of Congress contain multiple drafts of Ellison's editorial comments written for *Negro Quarterly*. Box 96, Folder 1.

11. Spillers, "The Little Man at Chehaw Station Today," 6–7.

12. Ellison, "What American Would Be Like Without Blacks," 578. Subsequent references to this essay will be cited parenthetically.

13. Hurston, "Characteristics of Negro Expression," 831. I have found no evidence that Ellison read Hurston's essays. But he had a low opinion of her fiction, which he deemed "calculated burlesque." Quoted in Lawrence Jackson, *Ralph Ellison*, 258.

14. Ellison, "The World and the Jug," *Collected Essays*, 159.

15. Ellison, "Little Man," *Collected Essays*, 500.

16. Ellison, "The World and the Jug," 162.

17. The line alludes to the title of a Louis Armstrong tune recorded in 1940.

18. Ellison, "The World and the Jug," 177. Emphasis added.

19. Ellison, "Going to the Territory," *Collected Essays*, 591. Subsequent references to this essay will be cited parenthetically.

20. Adorno, "Essay as Form," 51.

21. Ellison misspells Whittaker's middle name as "Chestnut," although most sources spell the name "Chesnut," which is the spelling I use throughout.

22. In "On Initiation Rites and Power," originally delivered as a lecture at West Point, Ellison described Whittaker as "a West Point man," who "somehow" did not graduate. In fact, Whittaker was court-martialed on charges of inflicting his own injuries. He was found guilty, but the verdict was overturned; he was then expelled from West Point for failing an exam. In 1995, President Bill Clinton awarded the commission that Whittaker should have received to his heirs.

23. Zora Neale Hurston opens her memoir with an impressionistic account of Florida's founding as a frontier state. *Dust Tracks*, 561–64.

24. For a synoptic discussion of the intellectual exchange between Burke and Ellison, see John Wright, *Shadowing Ellison*, 34–36, 51–52. More extended analyses can be found in Beth Eddy, *Rites of Identity*, and Bryan Crable, *Ralph Ellison and Kenneth Burke*.

25. Pease, "Ellison and Burke: The Nonsymbolizable (Trans)action," 67, 68.

26. Bradley, *Ellison in Progress*, 84.

27. Ellison, "The Little Man At Chehaw Station," 512–13.

28. Ellison, "The Charlie Christian Story," *Collected Essays*, 276. The innovative jazz guitarist was a classmate of Ellison's brother at Douglass High School.

29. While I do not want to berate Ellison for his sexism, some of which is typical for the time, I think it bears remarking. For example, he points to Redd Foxx's ability to joke about ugly white women the way he had for years joked about ugly black women as a sign of social progress. Hardly.

30. Ellison, "Living with Music," *Collected Essays*, 229. To illustrate the extent to which the jazz players regarded their music as a vocation, Ellison observes that some wore their instruments "as a priest wears the cross." In this regard, he and Baldwin echo each other in their representation of the priestly function of jazz musicians.

31. Ellison, "The Charlie Christian Story," 247.

32. "Going to the Territory" was first published in *The Carleton Miscellany*, Winter 1980. An 11-page typescript with the heading "Transcription of the Brown Address," is located in the Ralph Ellison Papers, Box 172, Folder 1 at the Library of Congress. The document includes penciled corrections, and page 4 is missing.

33. See James Alan McPherson, "Indivisible Man," for a contemporary account of Ellison's run-ins with black students on college campuses. 1970. Reprinted in Ellison, *Collected Essays*, 355–95.

34. Ellison, "The World and the Jug," 187–88.

35. See, for example, Edwards, "Ralph Ellison and the Grain of Internationalism."

36. The speech was entitled "The Little Man Behind the Stove." The title was changed when the essay was published in the *American Scholar* 47, no. 1 (Winter 1977–1978): 25–51.

37. Ellison, "The Little Man at Chehaw Station," *Collected Essays*, 490, 491. Subsequent citations to this essay will be made parenthetically.

38. Harrison left Tuskegee in 1936, the same year as Ellison, and joined the faculty at Howard University.

39. For an insightful analysis of Ellison's response to Black Power ideology in the context of his anti-Stalinism, see Purcell, "An Integrative Vernacular."

40. Purcell argues that the coal-heavers scene, which he reads as an extended allusion to Dante's *Inferno*, is the primary site of unease in the essay. I read the middle narrative as the

one that reveals the depth of Ellison's anxiety about the direction of U.S. culture and society.

41. In "Alain Locke," Ellison writes an appreciation of Locke's idea of cultural pluralism. *Collected Essays*, 441–47.

Chapter 6

1. June Jordan's books of essays include *Civil Wars, On Call: Political Essays, Technical Difficulties: African American Notes on the State of the Union, Affirmative Acts: Political Essays*, and *Some of Us Did Not Die*. Jordan also published a collection of essays in the U.K.: *Moving Towards Home*. Posthumously published collections include Russo, ed., *Life as Activism: June Jordan's Writing from the Progressive*, and Keller and Levi, eds., *We're On: A June Jordan Reader*.

2. I borrow the term "redemptive politics" from George Shulman's insightful study, *American Prophecy: Race and Redemption in American Political Culture*, ch. 1.

3. Shulman, 5. Baldwin, *Fire Next Time*, 346.

4. Bambara, *Salt Eaters*, 92.

5. Walker, "A Talk: Convocation 1972," *In Search of Our Mothers' Gardens*, 37. For more information about the writers' meeting, see White, *Alice Walker*, 200–202. Jordan predicted that Walker would become an important writer after seeing the room of her own that Walker had designed for herself in Jackson. Jordan published "Mississippi 'Black Home:' A Sweet and Bitter Bluesong" in the *New York Times Magazine*, October 11, 1970.

6. Press release for *Affirmative Acts* in Black Ink: *The Afro-American Newsletter from Doubleday* 1, no. 3 (1998): 1.

7. If Jordan's writing has been largely neglected by critics, Walker's has been scorned by some of the most influential, notably Harold Bloom in *The Western Canon* and in his casebooks on Walker's general career and on *The Color Purple* specifically. Thadious Davis suggests that scholars have taken Walker's contributions for granted. She reflects on how Walker, "an artist forged on the battleground of Mississippi during the height of civil rights activism, may have been one primary catalyst in naturalizing how so many scholars and artists approach the South today, and with that naturalizing a concomitant erasing of her very positionality in the process." *Southscapes*, 335.

8. King, "Letter from Birmingham Jail," *Why We Can't Wait*, 65. Among the many essays that Walker wrote on the civil rights movement are "Choice: A Tribute to Martin Luther King, Jr.," "Coretta King: Revisited," "Choosing to Stay at Home: Ten Years After the March on Washington," "Lulls," "Recording the Seasons," and "Silver Writes." Jordan published a children's biography of Fannie Lou Hamer as well as "The Mountain and the Man Who Was Not God: An Essay on the Life and Ideas of Dr. Martin Luther King, Jr." and "Update on Martin Luther King, Jr., and the Best of My Heart." The 1991 film "A Place of Rage," produced and directed by Pratibha Parmar, also documents the centrality of the movement to the writers' consciousnesses.

9. Jordan, *Civil Wars*, xi.

10. Walker, *In Search*, xi.

11. Walker, *In Search*, xi, emphasis in original.

12. Walker, "Zora Neale Hurston: A Cautionary Tale and a Partisan View," *In Search*, 88. This essay was originally published as the foreword to Hemenway, *Zora Neale Hurston*, xi–xx.

13. Walker would use the color red, which she attributes to the car in the photograph, in her representation of Shug Avery in *The Color Purple*. A womanist heroine, Shug enters the novel wearing a red dress.

14. Walker, "Anything We Love Can Be Saved: The Resurrection of Zora Neale Hurston and Her Work," an address delivered at the Zora Neale Hurston Festival in Eatonville, Florida, in January 1990, was the title essay of *Anything We Love Can Be Saved*, 45–50.

15. Quoted in Walker, "Looking for Zora," *In Search*, 93. Subsequent references will be cited parenthetically.

16. Tellingly, the last quotation in the essay is Hurston's oft-quoted declaration from "How It Feels to Be Colored Me," that she is not "tragically colored." The declaration informs her representation in this essay, just as it inspires the title of Walker's anthology of Hurston's writing, *I Love Myself When I Am Laughing and Then Again When I Am Looking Mean and Impressive*.

17. As if to affirm the contingent nature of her quest, Walker repeats information that has subsequently been disproved. For example, she misidentifies Eatonville as Hurston's birthplace.

18. The reference is to "Between Laughter and Tears," Wright's infamous review of *Their Eyes Were Watching God*.

19. The quoted phrases are from Hurston, "Characteristics of Negro Expression," 830.

20. *Their Eyes* ends with Janie sitting in reflection as the buried "Tea Cake came prancing around where she was . . . . Tea Cake, with the sun for a shawl. Of course he wasn't dead." Hurston, *Their Eyes*, 183. References to the ability of the living and the dead to communicate are plentiful in her writing. For example, Hurston describes as superstition the belief that "sometimes the dead are offended by acts of the living and slap the face of the living. When this happens, the head is slapped one-sided and the victim can never straighten his neck. Speak gently to ghosts, and do not abuse the children of the dead." *Mules and Men*, in *Folklore, Memoirs*, 214.

21. Hurston, "How It Feels to Be Colored Me," *Folklore, Memoirs*, 827.

22. Historian Lawrence Levine asserts that "no other mechanism in Afro-American culture was more effective than humor in exposing the absurdity of the American racial system and in releasing pent-up aggression toward it." Levine, *Black History and Black Consciousness*, 335.

23. In the thirty years since Walker published this essay, Hurston has of course become an acclaimed figure, locally as well as nationally. Since the early 1990s, the Zora! festival has been held in Eatonville biennially; a smaller event takes place in Fort Pierce, Florida.

24. Walker, *In Search*, xi. See also Collins, "'What's in a Name?' and Alexander-Floyd and Simien, "Revisiting 'What's in a Name?' Exploring the Contours of Africana Feminist Thought." For the impact of womanism on theology, see Cannon, *Katie's Canon*, and Gilkes, *If It Wasn't for the Women*.

25. Jordan, "Black People and the Law: A Tribute to William Kunstler," *On Call*, 100. See also "Inside America: 'My Perfect Soul Shall Manifest Me Rightly': An Essay on Blackfolks and the Constitution," *Technical Difficulties*, 55–63.

26. In "Transferences and Confluences: The Impact of the Black Arts Movement on the Literacies of Black Lesbian Feminism," Cheryl Clarke remembers the event differently. Jordan's fellow panelists were Acklyn Lynch, Sonia Sanchez, and Barbara Smith. When Smith

described Toni Morrison's *Sula* as a "lesbian novel," Clarke heard "a visceral collective groan resonat[e] throughout the room." According to Clarke, "the emphatic hostility astounded both Smith and Jordan," who continued to field questions after Lynch and Sanchez fled the stage. Clarke, *Days of Good Looks*, 329.

27. Jordan, "Notes of a Barnard Dropout" in *Civil Wars*, 9. Subsequent references will be cited parenthetically.

28. In her poem "Ah, Momma," Jordan develops the lyric potential of the essay's ending. The essay "Many Rivers to Cross," discussed below, narrates the events transpiring after the discovery of Millicent Jordan's suicide.

29. See Walker, "Looking to the Side, and Back," *In Search*, 319. For a discussion of the title essay, see my chapter, "In Search of Our Mothers' Gardens and Our Fathers' (Real) Estates," in *Worrying the Line*.

30. Walker, "Saving the Life that Is One's Own: The Importance of Models in the Artist's Life," *In Search*, 4. Subsequent references will be cited parenthetically.

31. Walker, "The Unglamorous but Worthwhile Duties of the Black Revolutionary Artist," *In Search*, 132. Subsequent references will be cited parenthetically.

32. Jordan, "The Essay as a Political Contemporary Form."

33. Jordan, "Civil Wars," *Civil Wars*, 179. Subsequent references will be cited parenthetically.

34. In 2011, Piven became the target of right-wing television host Glenn Beck, whose rants against her provoked death threats on Piven's life.

35. In Jordan's *Fannie Lou Hamer*, Hamer's mother is an example of resistance who was "too busy to be afraid" and willing to fight white men if they threatened her children. When Hamer stands up for the right to vote, she follows her mother's example. In *Soldier: A Poet's Childhood*, Jordan recounts the lesson she learned as a four-year-old: "A really excellent way to stop somebody from hitting you is to hit them back." Jordan, *Soldier*, 26.

36. Walker, "Lulls," *In Search*, 183. Subsequent references will be cited parenthetically.

37. Jordan, "'My Perfect Soul Shall Manifest Me Rightly,'" *Technical Difficulties*, 56.

38. Jordan, "For My American Family: A Belated Tribute to a Legacy of Gifted Intelligence and Guts," *Technical Difficulties*, 5. Subsequent references will be cited parenthetically.

39. In her memoir, Audre Lorde recounts a Fourth of July excursion to Washington, D.C., where her parents refuse to name the racism they encounter. As a girl she finds their silence bewildering. See *Zami*, 68–71.

40. Jordan, "Waking Up in the Middle of Some American Dreams," *Technical Difficulties*, 11. Subsequent references will be cited parenthetically.

41. Jordan, Introduction, *On Call*, 2. "Report from the Bahamas" was published initially in *Ms.* magazine in November 1982. Although it is not a service article of the kind that regularly appears in travel and leisure sections, "Report from the Bahamas" belongs to a tradition of travel writing that engages a broad range of topics. For that reason, Fish and Griffin include it in *Stranger in the Village*.

42. Jordan, "Report from the Bahamas," *On Call*, 39–49. Subsequent references will be cited parenthetically.

43. Walker, "My Father's Country Is the Poor," *In Search*, 201. Subsequent references will be cited parenthetically. I have also written about this essay in *Worrying the Line*, 225–28.

44. Walker returned to Cuba in 1992, a trip that is the subject of two essays in *Anything You Love*, "The Story of Why I am Here, or a Woman Connects Oppressions" and "Hugging Fidel." Despite harsh and widespread criticism of the Castro regime, even by former loyalists, Walker does not waver in her admiration of the Cuban Revolution.

45. Jordan, "The Blood Shall Be a Sign Unto You: Israel and South Africa," *On Call*, 107–16. Such candor had its cost. When Jordan extended the comparison from U.S. citizens and Nicaraguans to Israelis and Palestinians, she met bitter condemnation and censorship, from the Left as well as the mainstream.

46. Jordan, "Why I Had to Go to Nicaragua," *On Call*, 65. Subsequent references will be cited parenthetically.

47. In 1978–1979, the Sandinista National Liberation Front (FSLN) overthrew the Somoza regime that had ruled Nicaragua for almost fifty years. From 1981 to 1990, the Contras went to war against the FSLN, and the Central American nation became a flash point in the Cold War between the United States and the Soviet Union.

48. Walker, "Beauty: When the Other Dancer Is the Self," *In Search*, 361. Subsequent references will be cited parenthetically.

49. Jordan, "Many Rivers to Cross," *On Call*, 20. Subsequent references will be cited parenthetically.

50. See Harris-Perry on how the once empowering myth of the strong black woman has become a prison. *Sister Citizen*, 183–220.

Epilogue

1. Fleming "Shattering Black Flesh," 833.

2. I think for example of Saidiya Hartman, *Lose Your Mother*, which I reference in the first chapter, as well as Farah Jasmine Griffin, *Harlem Nocturne: Women Artists and Progressive Politics during World War II* in which Griffin asserts her intention to experiment with a less formal mode of scholarly writing. See also Emily Lordi, "Why Is Academic Writing So Beautiful?" which argues that writing by many black feminist scholars is both intellectually rigorous and aesthetically pleasing.

3. Eric Garner was killed on July 17, 2014, by New York City police officers who were arresting him for the "crime" of selling illegal cigarettes outside a store in the borough of Staten Island. Twelve-year-old Tamir Rice was shot on November 22, 2014, in a Cleveland park by a police officer who mistook the play gun he was holding for the real thing. Rice died the next day.

4. In a later, painstakingly eloquent account of Baldwin's influence on his writing, Coates remarks, "But all the magic I wanted was on the page. And when I looked closely, when I began to study, I did not even see magic, so much as a machinery so elegant, so wondrous, so imaginative as to seem supernatural. I am talking to young writers now. Your heroes are not mystics nor sorcerers but humans practiced at the work of typing and revising, and often agonized by it." *We Were Eight Years in Power*, 219.

5. Morrison, "Life in His Language," in Troupe, ed., *James Baldwin*, 76; back cover blurb, *Between the World and Me*.

6. Maxwell, *James Baldwin: The FBI File*, 1. For more evidence of Baldwin's influence on twenty-first-century African American essayists, see Ward, ed., *The Fire This Time*. The book

is dedicated "To Trayvon Martin and the many other black men, women, and children who have died and been denied justice for these four hundred years."

7. For a more lyrical rendering of his childhood, see Coates, *The Beautiful Struggle*.

8. Coates, *Between the World and Me*, 81. Subsequent references will be cited parenthetically.

9. See Smith, "Fear of a Black Pundit." Coates's blogs are archived online, as are many of the interviews on which he based the more formal columns he wrote for the *Atlantic*.

10. This announcement was appended to Dyson's "*Between the World and Me*: Baldwin's Heir?" a strong defense of Coates's decision to associate himself with the Baldwin legacy and the second in a series of solicited responses to the book.

11. Coates, "The Champion Barack Obama."

12. Cooper, "Re-Nigging on the Promises."

13. Quoted in Lebron, *Making of Black Lives Matter*, xi. Trayvon Martin was murdered on February 26, 2012, in Sanford, Florida, as he returned to his father's apartment. He was shot by George Zimmerman, a member of the neighborhood patrol, who claimed self-defense, despite the fact that Martin carried only candy and a soft drink.

14. Crunk Feminist Collective, Mission Statement, 2010. Reprinted in Cooper, et al., *Crunk Feminist Collection*, xvii–xviii.

15. Cooper, "My Brother's Keeper."

16. Cooper, "This Is America's Religion of Violence."

17. For more information on the life and death of Sandra Bland, see Nathan, "What Happened to Sandra Bland?"

Bibliography

Adorno, Theodor. "The Essay as Form" in *Notes to Literature*. Vol. 1. New York: Columbia University Press, 1991.

Alexander-Floyd, Nikol, and Evelyn M. Simien. "Revisiting 'What's in a Name?': Exploring the Contours of Africana Feminist Thought." Reprinted in *Still Brave: The Evolution of Black Women's Studies*, edited by Stanlie M. James, Beverly Guy-Sheftall, and Frances S. Foster, 92–114. New York: Feminist Press, 2009.

Andrews, William. *Sisters of the Spirit: Three Black Women's Autobiographies of the Nineteenth Century*. Bloomington: Indiana University Press, 1986.

Bacon, Jacqueline. *Freedom's Journal*. Lanham, MD: Lexington Books, 2007.

Baker, Houston. *Blues, Ideology, and Afro-American Literature: A Vernacular Theory*. Chicago: University of Chicago Press, 1984.

Baldwin, James. *Collected Essays*. Edited by Toni Morrison. New York: Library of America, 1998.

Baldwin, James, and Sol Stein. *Native Sons*. New York: One World Ballantine Books, 2004.

Bambara, Toni Cade. *The Salt Eaters*. New York: Random House, 1980.

Baraka, Amiri. *Black Music*. New York: William Morrow & Co., 1968.

———. *Home: Essays*. New York: William Morrow & Co., 1966.

———. *The LeRoi Jones/Amiri Baraka Reader*. Edited by William J. Harris. New York: Thunder Mouth's Press, 1991.

———. "Toward Ideological Clarity," *Black World* 24 (November 1974): 24–33, 84–95.

———. "Why I Changed My Ideology," *Black World* 24 (July 1975): 30–42.

Bay, Mia. *The White Image in the Black Mind: African-American Ideas about White People, 1830–1925*. New York: Oxford University Press, 2000.

Bay, Mia, Farah J. Griffin, Martha S. Jones, and Barbara D. Savage, eds. *Toward an Intellectual History of Black Women*. Chapel Hill: University of North Carolina Press, 2015.

Bercovitch, Sacvan. *The American Jeremiad*. Madison: University of Wisconsin Press, 1978.

Bingham, Caleb. *The Columbian Orator*. 1797. Edited by David Blight. New York: New York University, 1998.

Blassingame, John, ed. *Frederick Douglass Papers: Speeches, Debates, and Interviews*. New Haven: Yale University Press, 1979.

Bloom, Harold. *The Western Canon: The Books and Schools of the Ages*. New York: Harcourt Brace, 1994.

Bode, Carl. *Mencken*. 2nd ed. Baltimore: Johns Hopkins University Press, 1986.

Bordelon, Pamela. *Go Gator and Muddy the Water: Writings by Zora Neale Hurston for the Federal Writers Project*. New York: W. W. Norton, 1993.

Bradley, Adam. *Ellison in Progress*. New Haven: Yale University Press, 2012.

Bradstreet, Anne. "The Prologue." In *The Norton Anthology of American Literature*, edited by Robert Gottesman et al., 41. New York: W. W. Norton, 1979.

Butler, Cheryl. *The Art of the African American Essay: From Meditation to Transcendence.* New York: Routledge, 2003.

Campbell, James. "I Heard It Through the Grapevine," *Granta* 73 (2001): 151–83.

———. *Talking at the Gates: A Life of James Baldwin.* New York: Viking, 1991.

Cannon, Katie G. *Katie's Canon: Womanism and the Soul of the Black Community.* New York: Continuum, 1995.

Carby, Hazel. "The Politics of Fiction, Anthropology, and the Folk: Zora Neale Hurston." In *New Essays on "Their Eyes Were Watching God,"* edited by Michael Awkward, 71–93. New York: Cambridge University Press, 1990.

Chicago Mass Choir. *Calling On You: Live.* New Haven Records, 2001.

Clarke, Cheryl. *The Days of Good Looks: The Prose and Poetry of Cheryl Clarke, 1980–2005.* New York: Carroll & Graf, 2006.

Cmiel, Kenneth. *Democratic Eloquence: The Fight Over Popular Speech in Nineteenth-Century America.* New York: Wm. Morrow, 1990.

Coates, Ta-Nehesi. *The Beautiful Struggle: A Father, Two Sons, and an Unlikely Road to Manhood, A Memoir.* New York: Spiegel & Grau, 2009.

———. *Between the World and Me.* New York: Spiegel & Grau, 2015.

———. "The Champion Barack Obama," *The Atlantic,* January 31, 2014.

———. *We Were Eight Years in Power: An American Tragedy.* New York: One World, 2017.

Coker, Daniel. "A Dialogue Between a Virginian and an African Minister." Baltimore, 1810. Reprinted in *Negro Protest Pamphlets,* edited by Dorothy Porter. New York: Arno Press, 1969.

Collins, Patricia Hill. "'What's in a Name?' Womanism, Black Feminism and Beyond," *Black Scholar* 26, no. 1 (1996): 9–17.

Cooper, Brittney C. *Beyond Respectability: The Intellectual Thought of Race Women.* Urbana: University of Illinois Press, 2017.

———. "My Brother's Keeper and the Co-optation of Intersectionality," Crunk Feminist Collective, July 1, 2014, http://www.crunkfeministcollective.com/2014/07/01/my-brothers-keeper-the-co-optation-of-intersectionality/. Accessed April 6, 2018.

———. "Re-Nigging on the Promises: #Justice4Trayvon," Crunk Feminist Collective, March 16, 2012, http://crunkfeministcollective.com/2012/03/16. Accessed April 6, 2018.

———. "This Is America's Religion of Violence: The Impunity of Police Violence and the Destruction of Sandra Bland," Salon, http://www.salon.com, December 23, 2015. Accessed April 6, 2018.

Cooper, Brittney C., Susana M. Morris, and Robin M. Boylan, eds. *The Crunk Feminist Collection.* New York: Feminist Press, 2017.

Cooper, Wayne. *Claude McKay: Rebel Sojourner in the Harlem Renaissance.* New York: Schocken Books, 1987.

Cornish, Samuel E., and John B. Russwurm. "To Our Patrons," *Freedom's Journal,* March 16, 1827.

Crable, Bryan. *Ralph Ellison and Kenneth Burke at the Roots of Racial Divide.* Charlottesville: University of Virginia Press, 2012.

Cullen, Countee. *Caroling Dusk: An Anthology of Verse by Negro Poets.* New York: Harper, 1927.

Cunningham, Vinson. "What Makes an Essay American?" *New Yorker,* May 13, 2016.

Debate: James Baldwin vs. William F. Buckley. National Educational Television Network. February 1965. Available on YouTube, http://www.youtube.com.

Davis, Thadious. *Southscapes: Geographies of Race, Region, and Literature.* Chapel Hill: University of North Carolina Press, 2011.

Denning, Michael. "'The Special Conditions': Marxism and American Studies." In *Culture in the Age of Three Worlds.* London: Verso, 2004.

DeKoven, Marianne. *Utopia Limited: The Sixties and the Emergence of the Postmodern.* Durham, NC: Duke University Press, 2004.

Denius, Sara, and Stefan Jonsoon. "An Interview with Gayatri Chakravorty Spivak, *Boundary* 2 20, no. 2 (1993): 24–50.

Dinius, Marcy J. "'Look!! Look!!! At This!!!!': The Radical Typography of David Walker's 'Appeal.'" *PMLA* 126, no. 1 (2011): 55–72.

Dobbs, Cynthia. "Mapping Black Movement, Containing Black Laughter: Ralph Ellison's New York Essays." *American Quarterly* 68, no. 4 (2016): 907–29.

Douglas, Ann. *Terrible Honesty: Mongrel Manhattan in the 1920s.* New York: Farrar, Straus and Giroux. 1995.

Douglass, Frederick. *Autobiographies: Narrative of the Life of Frederick Douglass, an American Slave; My Bondage and My Freedom; Life and Times of Frederick Douglass.* Edited by Henry Louis Gates Jr. New York: Library of America, 1994.

———. "What to the Slave Is the Fourth of July?" 1852. Reprinted in *The Norton Anthology of African American Literature*, Vol. 1, 3rd ed., edited by Henry Louis Gates Jr. and Valerie Smith, 402–10. New York: W. W. Norton, 2014.

Du Bois, W. E. B. *Darkwater: Voices from within the Veil.* 1920. New York: Dover, 1999.

———. *Dusk of Dawn: An Essay Toward an Autobiography of a Race Concept.* 1940. In *Writings.* New York: Library of America, 1987.

———. "The Negro As He Really Is." *The World's Work*, June 2, 1901.

———. *The Souls of Black Folk.* 1903. Edited by Donald Gibson. New York: Penguin, 1989.

Du Bois, W. E. B., et al. "The Negro in Art: How Shall He Be Portrayed?" *The Crisis* 31 and 32, 1926.

Dyson, Michael Eric. "*Between the World and Me*: Baldwin's Heir?" *The Atlantic*, July 23, 2015.

Early, Gerald, ed. *My Soul's High Song: The Collected Writing of Countee Cullen.* New York: Anchor Books, 1991.

———. *Speech and Power: The African American Essay and Its Cultural Content from Polemics to Pulpit.* 2 vols. New York: Ecco Press, 1991.

Eddy, Beth. *The Rites of Identity: The Religious Naturalism and Cultural Criticism of Kenneth Burke and Ralph Ellison.* Princeton: Princeton University Press, 2003.

Edwards, Brent. *The Practice of Diaspora.* Cambridge: Harvard University Press, 2003.

———. "Ralph Ellison and the Grain of Internationalism." In *Globalizing American Studies*, edited by Brian T. Edwards and Dilip Gaonkar, 115–34. Chicago: University of Chicago Press, 2010.

———. "The Seemingly Eclipsed Window of Form: James Weldon Johnson's Prefaces." In *The Jazz Cadence of American Culture*, edited by Robert O'Meally, 580–601. New York: Columbia University Press, 1987.

Ellison, Ralph. *The Collected Essays of Ralph Ellison*. Edited by John Callahan. New York: Modern Library, 1995.

Emerson, Ralph Waldo. "The Divinity School Address." 1838. In *Nature and other Essays*. New York: Penguin, 2003.

Equiano, Olaudah. *The Interesting Narrative of the Life of Olaudah Equiano*. In *The Classic Slave Narratives*, edited by Henry Louis Gates Jr. New York: Signet Classics, 1987.

Ernest, John. *Liberation Historiography: African American Writers and the Challenge of History*. Chapel Hill: University of North Carolina Press, 2004.

Fauset, Jessie. "Impressions of the Second Pan-African Congress." *The Crisis* 23, November 1921. Reprinted in Jessie Redmon Fauset, *The Chinaberry Tree and Other Writings*, edited by Marcy Jane Knopf-Newman, 367–82. Boston: Northeastern University Press, 1995.

Fish, Cheryl, and Farah J. Griffin. *A Stranger in the Village: Two Centuries of African American Travel Writing*. Boston: Beacon Press, 1998.

Fleming, Julius, Jr. "Shattering Black Flesh: Black Intellectual Writing in the Age of Ferguson." *American Literary History* 28, no. 4 (2016): 828–34.

Foster, Frances Smith. "A Narrative of the Interesting Origins and (Somewhat) Surprising Developments of African-American Print Culture." *American Literary History* 17, no. 4 (2005): 714–40.

———. *Written by Herself: Literary Production by African American Women, 1746–1892*. Bloomington: Indiana University Press, 1995.

Frame, Donald. *The Complete Works of Michel de Montaigne*. Stanford: Stanford University Press, 1957.

Franklin, John Hope, and Elizabeth Brooks Higginbotham. *From Slavery to Freedom: A History of African Americans*. 9th ed. New York: McGraw-Hill, 2011.

Gaines, Kevin, ed. *Black Literature and Literary Theory*. New York: Methuen, 1984.

———. "E. Franklin Frazier's Revenge: Anticolonialism, Nonalignment, and Black Intellectuals' Critiques of Western Culture." *American Literary History* 17, no. 3 (2005): 506–29.

———. "Exile and the Private Life: James Baldwin, George Lamming, and the First World Congress of Negro Writers and Artists." In *James Baldwin: American and Beyond*, edited by Cora Kaplan and Bill Schwarz, 173–87. Ann Arbor: University of Michigan, 2011.

Gates, Henry Louis, Jr. *The Signifying Monkey: A Theory of Afro-American Literary Criticism*. New York: Oxford University Press, 1987.

———, ed. *Reading Black, Reading Feminist: A Critical Anthology*. New York: Meridian Books, 1990.

Gates, Henry Louis, Jr., and Jennifer Burton, eds. *Call and Response: Key Debates in African American Studies*. New York: W. W. Norton, 2011.

Gilkes, Cheryl Townsend. *If It Wasn't for the Women: Black Women's Experience and Womanist Culture in Church and Community*. Maryknoll, NY: Orbis Books, 2001.

Gilroy, Paul. *The Black Atlantic: Modernity and Double Consciousness*. Cambridge: Harvard University Press, 1993.

Glaude, Eddie. *Exodus! Religion, Race and Nation in Early Nineteenth-Century Black America*. Chicago: University of Chicago Press, 2000.

———. *In a Shade of Blue: Pragmatism and the Politics of Black America*. Chicago: University of Chicago Press, 2007.

Griffin, Farah J. *Harlem Nocturne: Women Artists and Progressive Politics during World War II*. New York: Civitas Books, 2013.

Hall, Jacqueline Dowd. "The Long Civil Rights Movement and the Political Uses of the Past." *Journal of American History* 91, no. 4 (2005): 1223–63.

Harper, Frances Ellen Watkins. *A Brighter Coming Day*. Edited by Frances Smith Foster. New York: Feminist Press, 1990.

Harris, Michael W. *The Rise of the Gospel Blues: The Music of Thomas Andrew Dorsey in the Urban Church*. New York: Oxford University Press, 1993.

Harris-Perry, Melissa. *Sister Citizen*. New Haven: Yale University Press, 2011.

Hartman, Saidiya. *Lose Your Mother: A Journey Along the Atlantic Slave Route*. New York: Farrar Strauss Giroux, 2007.

———. *Scenes of Subjection: Terror, Slavery, and Self-Making in Nineteenth-Century America*. New York: Oxford University Press, 1997.

Hemenway, Robert. *Zora Neale Hurston: A Literary Biography*. Urbana: University of Illinois Press, 1977.

Hill, Lynda. *Social Rituals and the Verbal Art of Zora Neale Hurston*. Washington, DC: Howard University Press, 1996.

Hinks, Peter P. *To Awaken My Afflicted Brethren: David Walker and the Problem of Antebellum Slave Resistance*. University Park: Pennsylvania State University, 1997.

——— ed. *David Walker's Appeal* to the Coloured Citizens of the World. 1829. University Park, PA: Pennsylvania University State Press, 2000.

Holloway, Karla. *The Character of the Word: The Texts of Zora Neale Hurston*. New York: Praeger, 1987.

Howard, Jennifer. "Ralph Ellison's Never-Ending Novel." *Chronicle of Higher Education* 56, no. 35 (2010).

Howard-Pitney, David. *The African American Jeremiad: Appeals for Justice in America*. Rev. ed. Philadelphia: Temple University Press, 2005.

Huggins, Nathan. *Black Odyssey: The African American Ordeal in Slavery*. New York: Random House, 1977.

———. *Harlem Renaissance*. New York: Oxford University Press, 1971.

———, ed. *Voices from the Harlem Renaissance*. New York: Oxford University Press, 1976.

Hughes, Langston. "The Negro Artist and the Racial Mountain." 1926. In *Voices from the Harlem Renaissance*, edited by Nathan Huggins.

Hurston, Zora Neale. "Characteristics of Negro Expression." 1934. In *Folklore, Memoir, and Other Writings*, edited by Cheryl A. Wall, 830–45. New York: Library of America, 1995.

———. *Dust Tracks on a Road*. 1942. In *Folklore, Memoir*. 557–808.

———. "How It Feels to Be Colored Me." 1928. In *Folklore, Memoir*. 826–29.

———. *Mules and Men*. 1935. In *Folklore, Memoir*. 1–267.

———. *Their Eyes Were Watching God*. 1937. New York: HarperCollins, 1990.

Hutchinson, George. *The Harlem Renaissance in Black and White*. Cambridge: Harvard University Press, 1995.

Huxley, Aldous. *The Collected Essays of Aldous Huxley*. New York: Harper & Brothers, 1958.

Jackson, Lawrence P. *The Indignant Generation: A Narrative History of African American Writers and Critics, 1934–1960*. Princeton: Princeton University Press, 2011.

———. *Ralph Ellison: The Emergence of a Genius*. New York: John Wiley, 2002.

James, Winston. *The Struggles of John B. Russwurm: The Life and Writings of a Pan-Africanist Pioneer*. New York: New York University Press, 2010.

Jarrett, Gene Allen. *Representing the Race: A New Political History of African American Literature*. New York: New York University Press, 2011.

Jefferson, Thomas. *Notes on the State of Virginia*. 1787. Edited by William Peden. Chapel Hill: University of North Carolina Press, 1955.

Johnson, James Weldon. *The Book of American Negro Poetry*. 1922, 1931. Reprint. New York: Harcourt Brace Jovanovich, 1969.

Jordan, June. *Affirmative Acts: Political Essays*. New York: Doubleday/Anchor Books, 1998.

———. *Civil Wars*. Boston: Beacon Press, 1981.

———. "The Essay as a Political Contemporary Form." The June Jordan Papers, Schlesinger Library, Radcliffe Institute, Harvard University. Box 7, Folder 14.

———. *Fannie Lou Hamer*. New York: Thomas Crowell, 1972.

———. "Mississippi 'Black Home': A Sweet and Bitter Bluesong." *New York Times Magazine* October 11, 1970.

———. *Moving Towards Home*. London: Virago Books, 1989.

———. *On Call: Political Essays*. Boston: South End Press, 1985.

———. *Soldier: A Poet's Childhood*. New York: Basic Books, 2000.

———. *Some of Us Did Not Die*. New York: Basic Books, 2002.

———. *Technical Difficulties: Notes on the State of the Union*. New York: Pantheon, 1992.

Keller, Christopher, and Jan Heller Levi, eds. *We're On: A June Jordan Reader*. Farmington, ME: Alice James Books, 2017.

King, Martin Luther, Jr. *Why We Can't Wait*. 1963. New York: Signet, 2000.

Klaus, Carl H. *The Made-Up Self: Impersonation and the Personal Essay*. Iowa City: University of Iowa Press, 2010.

Leavell, Lori. "'Not Intended Exclusively for the Slave States': Antebellum Recirculation of David Walker's 'Appeal.'" *Callaloo* 38, no. 3 (2015): 679–95.

Lebron, Christopher J. *The Making of Black Lives Matter: A Brief History of an Idea*. New York: Oxford University Press, 2017.

Leeming, David. *James Baldwin: A Biography*. New York: Henry Holt and Company, 1995.

Lewis, David Levering. *When Harlem Was in Vogue*. New York: Alfred A. Knopf, 1981.

Levine, Lawrence. *Black History and Black Consciousness*. New York: Oxford University Press, 1977.

Lighter, J. D., ed. *The Dictionary of American Slang*. New York: Random House, 1997.

Locke, Alain, ed. *The New Negro*. 1925. New York: Atheneum, 1992.

Logan, Rayford. *The Negro in American Life and Thought*. New York: Dial Press, 1954.

Lopate, Philip, ed. *The Art of the Personal Essay*. New York: Anchor Books, 1994.

Lorde, Audre. *Zami: A New Spelling of My Name, A Biomythography*. Freedom, CA: Crossing Press, 1982.

Lordi, Emily. "Why Is Academic Writing So Beautiful? Notes on Black Feminist Scholarship." *Feminist Wire*, March 4, 2014. http://www.thefeministwire.com/2014/03/academic-writing-black-feminism-krisof/. Accessed April 8, 2018.

Mackey, Nathaniel. "Other: From Noun to Verb." *Representations* 39 (Summer 1992): 51–70.

Marshall, Paule. Review of Ralph Ellison, *Shadow and Act. Mademoiselle*, June 1974, 83.

Mathes, Carter. *Imagine the Sound: Experimental African American Literature after Civil Rights.* Minneapolis: University of Minnesota Press, 2015.

Matthews, Victoria Earle. "The Value of Race Literature." 1895. Reprinted in *The New Negro: Readings on Race, Representation and African American Culture,* edited by Henry Louis Gates Jr. and Gene Andrew Jarrett, 287–97. Princeton: Princeton University Press, 2007.

Maxwell, William J., ed. *James Baldwin: The FBI File.* New York: Arcade Publishing, 2017.

McBride, Dwight, ed. *James Baldwin Now.* New York: New York University Press, 1999.

McDonogh, Gary, ed. *The Florida Negro: A Federal Writer's Project Legacy.* Jackson: University Press of Mississippi, 1993.

McFeely, Williams S. *Frederick Douglass.* New York: W. W. Norton, 1991.

McGill, Meredith. "Frances Ellen Watkins Harper and the Circuits of Abolitionist Poetry." In *Early African American Print Culture,* edited by Lara Lange-Cohen and Jordan Alexander Stein, 53–74. Philadelphia: University of Pennsylvania Press, 2017.

McGrath, Charles. "The Best Man." Review of Jay Parini, *Empire of Self: A Life of Gore Vidal. New York Times Book Review,* November 29, 2015, 12.

McHenry, Elizabeth. *Forgotten Readers: Recovering the Lost History of African American Literary Societies.* Durham, NC: Duke University Press, 2002.

Meer, Sarah. "Douglass as Orator and Editor." In *The Cambridge Companion to Frederick Douglass,* edited by Maurice Lee, 46–59. New York: Cambridge University Press, 2009.

Menand, Louis. "Liberated by Literature." Review of Ralph Ellison, *Going to the Territory. New Republic,* April 4, 1986, 40.

Mencken, H. L. *The American Language: An Inquiry into the Development of English in the United States.* 3rd ed. New York: Alfred A. Knopf, 1935.

Morgan, Edmund. *American Slavery, American Freedom.* New York: W. W. Norton, 2003.

Morrison, Toni. *Playing in the Dark.* New York: Random House, 1992.

Morrison, Toni, and Carolyn Denard. *What Moves at the Margins. Selected Nonfiction.* Jackson: University Press of Mississippi, 2008.

Moten, Fred. *In the Break: The Aesthetics of the Black Radical Tradition.* Minneapolis: University of Minnesota Press, 2003.

Nathan, Debbie. "What Happened to Sandra Bland?" *The Nation,* April 21, 2016.

Neal, Larry. "The Black Arts Movement." 1968. Reprinted in *The Black Aesthetic,* edited by Addison Gayle, 257–74. New York: Anchor Books, 1972.

———. "Ellison's Zoot Suit." *Black World.* December 1970. 31–52.

Othello. "Essay on Negro Slavery." *American Museum* 4 (1788): 412–14, 509–12.

Patterson, Orlando. *Freedom, Vol. 1: Freedom in the Making of the Western World.* New York: Basic Books, 1991.

Pease, Donald E. "Ellison and Burke: The Nonsymbolizable (Trans)action." *Boundary 2* 30, no. 2 (2003): 65–96.

Peterson, Carla L. *"Doers of the Word": African-American Women Speakers and Writers in the North: (1830–1880).* New York: Oxford University Press, 11.

Porter, Dorothy. *Early Negro Writing, 1760–1837.* Boston: Beacon Press, 1971.

Purcell, Richard. "An Integrative Vernacular: Ellison, Dante, and Social Cohesion in the Post-Civil Rights Era." *ELH* 80, no. 3 (2013): 917–44.

Rampersad, Arnold. *The Art and Imagination of W. E. B. Du Bois*. Cambridge: Harvard University Press, 1976.

———. *The Life of Langston Hughes, Volume 1: 1902–1941: I Too Sing America*. New York: Oxford University Press, 1986.

———. *Ralph Ellison, A Biography*. New York: Alfred A. Knopf, 2007.

Richardson, Marilyn, ed. *Maria W. Stewart: America's First Black Woman Political Writer*. Bloomington: Indiana University Press, 1987.

Russo, Susan, ed. *Life as Activism: June Jordan's Writing from the Progressive*. Sacramento: Litwin Books, 2014.

Schulman, George. *American Prophecy: Race and Redemption in American Political Culture*. Minneapolis: University of Minnesota Press, 2009.

Schuyler, George. "The Negro-Art Hokum." 1926. Reprinted in *Voice from the Harlem Renaissance*, edited by Nathan Huggins.

Scruggs, Charles. *The Sage of Harlem: H. L. Mencken and the Black Writers of the 1920s*. Baltimore: Johns Hopkins University Press, 1984.

Smith, Jordan Michael. "Fear of a Black Pundit." *New York Observer*, March 5, 2013.

Spillers, Hortense J. "The Little Man at Chehaw Station Today." *Boundary 2* 30, no. 2 (2003): 5–19.

Spivak, Gayatri. "Subaltern Studies: Deconstructing Historiography." In *The Spivak Reader: Selected Works by Gayatri Chakravorty Spivak*, edited by Donna Landry and Gerald MacLean, 203–235. New York: Routledge, 1996.

Spurlin, William J. "Culture, Rhetoric, and Queer Identity: James Baldwin and the Identity Politics of Race and Sexuality." In *James Baldwin Now*, edited by Dwight McBride, 103–21. New York: New York University Press, 1999.

Stauffer, John. "Douglass's Self-Making and the Culture of Abolitionism." In *The Cambridge Companion to Frederick Douglass*, edited by Maurice Lee, 13–30. New York: Cambridge University Press, 2009.

Stewart, Jeffrey. "A Black Aesthete at Oxford." *Massachusetts Review* 34, no. 3 (1993): 411–29.

Stuckey, Sterling P. *Slave Culture: Nationalist Theory and the Foundations of Black America*. New York: Oxford University Press, 1987.

Sundquist, Eric. *To Wake the Nations: Race in the Making of American Literature*. Cambridge: Harvard University Press, 1993.

Tóibín, Colm. "James Baldwin: The Flesh and the Devil." In *Love in a Dark Time and Other Explorations of Gay Lives and Literature*. New York: Scribner, 2001.

Troupe, Quincy, ed. *James Baldwin: The Legacy*. New York: Simon & Schuster, 1989.

Veeder, William, and Susan M. Griffin. *The Art of Criticism: Henry James on the Theory and the Practice of Fiction*. Chicago: University of Chicago Press, 1986.

Walker, Alice. *Anything We Love Can Be Saved: A Writer's Activism*. New York: Ballantine Books, 1998.

———. *The Color Purple*. San Diego: Harcourt Brace Jovanovich, 1982.

———, ed. *I Love Myself When I Am Laughing . . . A Zora Neale Hurston Reader*. New York: Feminist Press, 1979.

———. *In Search of Our Mothers' Gardens*. San Diego: Harcourt Brace Jovanovich, 1983.

———. *Living by the Word: Selected Writings, 1983–1987*. San Diego: Harcourt Brace Jovanovich, 1988.

———. *We Are the Ones We've Been Waiting For: Light in a Time of Darkness*. New York: The New Press, 2006.

Walker, David. *David Walker's Appeal to the Coloured Citizens of the World*. 1829–1830. Edited by Peter P. Hinks. University Park: Pennsylvania State University Press, 2000.

Walker, David, and Henry Highland Garnet. *Walker's Appeal and Garnet's Address to the Slaves of the United States of America*. Reprint. Nashville: James C. Winston Publishing Co., 1994.

Wall, Cheryl A. "Resounding *Souls*: Du Bois and the African American Literary Tradition." *Public Culture* 17, no. 2 (2005): 217–34.

———. *Women of the Harlem Renaissance*. Bloomington: Indiana University Press, 1995.

———. *Worrying the Line: Black Women Writers, Lineage, and Literary Tradition*. Chapel Hill: University of North Carolina Press, 2005.

Ward, Jesmyn, ed. *The Fire This Time: A New Generation Speaks About Race*. New York: Scribner, 2016.

Warren, James Perrin. *Culture of Eloquence: Oratory and Reform in Antebellum America*. University Park: Pennsylvania State University Press, 1999.

Weheliye, Alexander. *Phonographies: Grooves in Sonic Afro-Modernity*. Durham, NC: Duke University Press, 2005.

Wheatley, Phillis. "On Being Brought from Africa to America." 1773. Reprinted in *The Norton Anthology of African American Literature*, Vol. 1, 3rd ed., edited by Henry Louis Gates Jr. and Valerie Smith, 142–43. New York: W. W. Norton, 2014.

White, Evelyn R. *Alice Walker, A Life*. New York: W. W. Norton, 2004.

Williams, Oscar R. *George S. Schuyler: Portrait of a Black Conservative*. Knoxville: University of Tennessee Press, 2007.

Williams, Patricia. *The Alchemy of Race and Rights*. Cambridge: Harvard University Press, 1990.

Wills, Garry. *Lincoln at Gettysburg: The Words that Remade America*. New York: Simon & Schuster, 1992.

Wright, John S. *Shadowing Ellison*. Jackson: University Press of Mississippi, 2006.

Wright, Richard. "Between Laughter and Tears." *New Masses* 5 (October 1937): 22–25.

———. *Black Boy*. 1945. Reprint. New York: Harper Collins, 1993.

———. "Blueprint for Negro Literature." 1937. In *Amistad 2: Writings on Black History and Culture*, edited by John A. Williams and Charles F. Harris, 5–20. New York: Random House, 1971.

Zabrowska, Magdalena, J. *James Baldwin's Turkish Decade: Erotics of Exile*. Durham, NC: Duke University Press, 2009.

———. *Me and My House: James Baldwin's Last Decade in France*. Durham, NC: Duke University Press, 2018.

Index

abolitionism, 38–39, 54, 56, 72, 76–79
Abrahams, Peter, 232n37
ACS. *See* American Colonization Society
  (ACS)
Adams, John, 13, 57
"Address Before the Pennsylvania
  Augustine Society, An" (Saunders), 46
"Address Delivered at the African Masonic
  Hall, An" (Stewart), 56
"Address to the Slaves of the United States,
  An" (Garnet), 36–37, 40
adornment, 6
Adorno, Theodor, 3–4, 16, 29, 122–23, 161,
  230n21
Adventures of Huckleberry Finn, The
  (Twain), 19
Affirmative Acts (Jordan), 178
Afghanistan, 217
Afri-American Female Intelligence Society,
  235n40
African Americans: contributions to
  English language by, 6; essay as ideal
  medium for, 4
African Lodge of North America, 13
African Methodist Episcopal Church, 13,
  37, 77
African National Congress, 203
"Ah, Momma" (Jordan), 250n28
Alchemy of Race and Rights, The (Williams),
  8, 23–24
Aldridge, Ira, 165
Aldridge Theater, 165
Algeria, 144–45
Allen, Richard, 13, 40, 46
American Adam (Lewis), 243n6
American Colonization Society (ACS),
  51–52, 56–57, 154, 235n32
American English, 99–100

American exceptionalism, 13, 119–22,
  130–31, 137–38, 151, 221, 242n4
American Mercury (journal), 85, 98, 116
American Museum (journal), 13
American Negro Academy, 144
American Revolution, 60–61
"American Scholar, The" (Emerson), 37, 73
Anderson, Benedict, 155
Anderson, Sherwood, 152
Andrews, William, 235n41
Angelou, Maya, 211, 237n69
Another Country (Baldwin), 136
anthologies, 85
Anthology of Magazine Verse and Yearbook, 92
Anthony, Susan B., 75
Anything You Love (Walker), 251n44
Arnold, Matthew, 16
art: in 1920s, 84–85; in Alice Walker, 32–35;
  in Barnes, 95; Black Arts movement, 9,
  29–30, 172–73, 232n37; in Fauset, 93–94;
  in Hughes, 102–7; in Hurston, 107–16;
  language and, 99–100; in Locke, 89–91,
  95–97; in Schuyler, 97–98; social justice
  and, 85; in Thurman, 117–18
Atlantic (magazine), 218, 223–24
Auden, W.H., 151
audience, 116–17
"Aunt Sue's Stories" (Hughes), 102
autobiography, 53–54
Autobiography of an Ex-Colored Man
  (Johnson), 240n28
Awakening, The (Chopin), 193
Ayler, Albert, 31

Bacon, Francis, 229n3, 243n24
Baker, Houston, 84, 231n20
Baldwin, James, 1, 5, 22, 36, 118, 232n37;
  black separatism in, 139–40; Césaire and,

Baldwin, James (cont.)
133–34; civil rights movement and,
135–44; Coates and, 220–21, 251n4; Cold
War and, 120; colonialism in, 134; and
Congress of Negro-African Writers and
Artists, 129–30; culture in, 132–33;
Ellison and, 29; on essays, 2–3; FBI
surveillance of, 246n47; as fiction writer,
123; fragmentary quality in, 122; on
gospel, 242n1; homophobia and,
143–44; immediacy of, 4; in jeremiad
genre, 45–46; Lamming and, 134–35;
music and, 124–25; Neal and, 29–30; race
in, 126–27, 142, 146–47, 245n45; rage in,
128–29; sexuality of, 243n16; strategic
American exceptionalism in, 120–22,
130–31, 137–39, 242n4; in Tóibín, 243n24;
troubled eloquence of, 9; as well-read,
243n15; white supremacy in, 122, 139; will
to adorn in, 123–24; women in, 245n37;
Wright and, 27–28, 131–32
Balzac, Honoré de, 243n15
Bambara, Toni Cade, 177
Bandung conference, 129
"Baptism" (McKay), 92
Baraka, Amiri, 5, 8–9, 22–23, 30–32, 169,
231n23, 232nn25,37,40. *See also* Jones,
LeRoi
Barnes, Albert, 95
Barnes Foundation, 95
Bay, Mia, 235n29
Beautiful Struggle, The (Coates), 221
beauty, 81–82
"Beauty: When the Other Dancer Is the
Self" (Walker), 211–14
Bellow, Saul, 245n37
Bercovitch, Sacvan, 45, 234n24
Bernard, Émile, 193
"Best Man, The" (McGrath), 229n2
Between the World and Me (Coates), 1,
219–20, 223
"Between the World and Me" (Wright), 220
Bey, Turhan, 232n26
Bible, in justification of slavery, 13–14
biblical allusions, 48, 57, 60

Bill of Rights, 172
Bingham, Caleb, 63–65
Black Aesthetic, 232n37
Black Arts movement, 9, 29–30, 172–73,
232n37
"Black Arts Movement, The" (Neal), 30
Black Boy (Wright), 133
Black Classic Press, 221
Black Fire (Baraka and Neal, eds.), 9
Black Lives Matter, 9, 217, 219, 221, 224–25,
227
"Black Man Brings His Gifts, The" (Du
Bois), 240n17
black nationalism, 21, 27
Black Panthers, 146, 221
Black Power, 29–30, 139, 157, 172–73
black separatism, 139–40
Bland, Sandra, 217, 226–27
Blight, David, 65, 237n56
bloggers, 218–19, 223
Bloom, Harold, 248n7
"Blueprint for Negro Literature" (Wright),
26–27
blues, 106, 148
Blues People: Negro Music in White America
(Baraka), 30
Blyden, Edward Wilmot, 101
Boas, Franz, 238n2
Bode, Carl, 98
Bond, Horace, 130, 243n30
Bond, Julian, 130
Book of American Negro Poetry, The, 5–6, 84,
90–91
Bourne, Randolph, 85
"Brave Words for a Startling Occasion"
(Ellison), 28–29
Bradley, Adam, 164, 231n19
Bradstreet, Anne, 53, 235n37
Braithwaite, William Stanley, 92, 239n15
Brawley, Tawana, 23
Bread Givers, The (Yezierska), 205
Breaux, Zelia, 159, 164–65, 167–68
broadsides, 13
Brooks, Van Wyck, 85
Brown, James, 31–32, 232n40

Brown, Michael, 217, 220

Brown, William Wells, 5, 25

Browne, Thomas, 243n24

Brown University, 158–59

Brown v. Board of Education of Topeka, 8, 23, 150, 177, 243n30

Bumpers, Eleanor, 23

Burke, Kenneth, 150, 158, 163, 172

Burns, Anthony, 79

Butler, Cheryl, 229n16

Cahier d'un retour au pays natal (Return to My Native Land) (Césaire), 243n29

Cain, James, 28, 123

Calhoun, John, 41

Calverton, V. F., 239n3

Campbell, James, 243n15, 246n47

Carby, Hazel, 113, 242n49

Carlyle, Thomas, 16

Caroling Dusk: An Anthology of Verse by Negro Poets, 239n13

Cary, Mary Shadd, 37

Castro, Fidel, 207

"Caucasian Storms Harlem, The" (Fisher), 240n29

Césaire, Aimé, 130, 133–34, 244n29

"Champion Barack Obama, The: How Black America Talks to the White House" (Coates), 223–24

Chandler, Raymond, 123

"Change the Joke and Slip the Yoke" (Ellison), 149, 172

"Changing Same, The" (Jones), 30–32

"Characteristics of Negro Expression" (Hurston), 6, 10, 21, 34, 84, 108–10, 112–14, 155

Charles, Ray, 232n40

"Charlie Christian Story, The" (Ellison), 166

Chesnut, Mary Boykin, 161

Chesnutt, Charles, 105

Childress, Alice, 22

Chopin, Kate, 193, 202

Christian, Charlie, 165–66

"Christianity" (Watkins Harper), 82

Christian Recorder, 37, 77

churches, fraternal organizations and, 13

Cinque, Joseph, 59

civil rights movement, 9, 135–44, 150–51, 157, 179–80, 246n9, 248n8

"Civil Rights Movement, The: What Good Was It?" (Walker), 7, 177

Civil Wars (Jordan), 178, 190

"Civil Wars" (Jordan), 176, 195–98

Clarke, Cheryl, 249n26

Clay, Henry, 41, 51

Cleaver, Eldridge, 143–44

Cliff, Jimmy, 216

Cmiel, Kenneth, 8, 230n9

Coates, Ta-Nehisi, 1, 217, 219–24, 251n4, 252n10

Cobb, Jelani, 217

Cohen, Octavus, 97

Coker, Daniel, 13–14, 46, 64

Cold War, 120, 129–30

Cole, Bob, 93

Coleman, Ornette, 232n26

Coleridge-Taylor, Samuel, 101

colonialism, 131–34

Colored American, The (newspaper), 37, 40

"Colored Race in America, The" (Watkins Harper), 79

Color Purple, The (Walker), 178, 211, 248n7, 249n13

Coltrane, John, 31

Columbian Orator, The (Bingham), 63–65, 237n56

comedy, 150, 155–56

"Comic Side of Trouble, The" (Williams), 240n18

Common Sense (Paine), 13, 46

Confessions of Nat Turner (Styron), 142

Congress for Racial Equality (CORE), 136

Congress of Negro-African Writers and Artists, 129–35, 245n33

Constitution, 14, 24, 234n17

Cook, Mercer, 130, 243n30

Cooke, Sam, 232n40

"Coon Age, A" (Scruggs), 240n28

Cooper, Anna Julia, 8

Cooper, Brittney, 217, 219, 223–28

CORE. *See* Congress for Racial Equality (CORE)

Cornish, Samuel, 25, 39–40

Cotton, John, 234n24

"Could We Trace the Record of Every Human Heart" (Watkins Harper), 79

Cowper, William, 78

Cox, Ida, 167

"Creation, The" (Johnson), 90–92

Crisis, The (journal), 85, 93, 105

Crouch, Stanley, 229n16

Crummell, Alexander, 5, 58

Crunk Feminist Collective, 226

Cuba, 206–9, 251n44

Cuba Libre (Guillén), 232n24

"Cuba Libre" (Baraka), 21–23, 231nn22–23

Cullen, Countee, 85, 89, 92, 239n13, 241nn39–40

cultural freedom, 10

culture: African, 97, 236n51; American, 84–85, 238n2; in Baldwin, 127, 131; colonialism and, 133–34; in Ellison, 3–4, 148–50, 154–55, 157, 168–74; of eloquence, 41; in Hurston, 110, 112; mass, 84; oral, 16; Puritanism and, 98; in Schuyler, 101; womanism and, 181

Cunningham, Vinson, 230n17

Dante Alighieri, 247n40

Darkwater: Voices from within the Veil (Du Bois), 19

Davis, John, 130, 243n30

Davis, Thadious, 248n7

Declaration of Independence, 14, 24, 43, 49–50, 52, 67, 69, 72, 83, 172, 234n17

DeKoven, Marianne, 245n43

de Maupassant, Guy, 152

democracy, 10, 13, 121, 150, 156–57, 161, 166–67, 172, 177, 200–201, 219–20

democratic eloquence, 8, 50, 155

Denning, Michael, 120

"Dialogue Between a Virginian and an African Minister" (Coker), 13–14, 64

"Dialogue Between Master and His Slave" (Everett), 64

diaspora, 45, 245n35

Diaz, Pablo, 207–8

"Difficult Miracle of Black Poetry in America, The, or Something like a Sonnet for Phillis Wheatley" (Jordan), 179

Dinius, Marcy, 44, 234n22

Diop, Alioune, 130, 243n29

"Discovery of What It Means to Be an American, The" (Baldwin), 119, 125–26

Domingo, W. A., 86

Dostoevsky, Fyodor, 158

double consciousness, 17, 134–35

Douglas, Aaron, 102

Douglass, Frederick, 5, 15, 17, 25, 27–228, 231n15, 234n17, 236nn50,52, 237nn61,70

"Down at the Cross: Letter from a Region in My Mind" (Baldwin), 136, 138

"Drama of Negro Life, The" (Gregory), 92

"Dream Variations" (Hughes), 213

Dred Scott decision, 79

"drylongso folk," 102–3

Du Bois, W. E. B.: Ellison *vs.*, 158

Du Bois, W. E. B., 2, 4–5, 7–9, 16–19, 23, 36, 47–48, 82, 85–86, 124, 229n16, 231nn14,16; and Congress of Negro African Writers and Artists, 130–31; double consciousness in, 17, 134–35; and Pan-African Congresses, 133

Dumas, Alexandre, 26, 101

Dunbar, Paul Laurence, 105

Dvořák, Antonin, 25

Dylan, Bob, 31

Early, Gerald, 229n16

Edwards, Brent, 90

"E. Franklin Frazier's Revenge" (Gaines), 245n36

Egypt, 39, 51

Elaw, Zilpha, 54, 77, 235n41

Eliot, T. S., 152, 158, 169

Ellison, Ralph, 232n40, 245n37; American exceptionalism in, 151; Baldwin and, 28–29; Breaux and, 164–65, 167–68; civil rights movement and, 150–51; culture in, 3–4, 148–50, 154–55, 157, 168–74;

democracy in, 166–67; democratic eloquence in, 155; DuBois *vs.*, 158; as essayist, 3–4, 157–58; freedom in, 158–59; history in, 162–63; humor in, 150, 155–56, 160; Hurston and, 163–64; identity in, 149–51; jazz in, 164–67, 169, 247n30; language in, 156; as Leftist, 148–49, 172–73; literacy in, 37–38; lynching in, 163–64; Neal and, 29–30, 232n37; Page and, 159–62; race in, 150; slavery in, 149; and vernacular process, 8–9, 19, 98, 152–53, 156; Whittaker and, 161–62, 168, 247n22; women and, 247n29; women in, 175; Wright and, 161

eloquence, 16–17, 41, 50, 155, 230n9

Emerson, Ralph Waldo, 5, 37, 73, 77, 149, 152, 154, 230n17, 243n24

emotional salvation, 94

Encounter (magazine), 145

"Encounter on the Seine: Black Meets Brown" (Baldwin), 130

English language: African American contributions to, 6, 179; American, 99–100

equality, slavery and, 12

Equiano, Olaudah, 243n27

"Essay as a Political Contemporary Form, The" (Jordan), 195

"Essay as Form, The" (Adorno), 3, 29, 161

"Essay on Negro Slavery, An" (Othello), 12–13, 230n5

essays: Adorno on, 123; defined, 1; as hybrid form, 1, 123; as ideal for African American writers, 4; privacy of, 2; as responses, 1

Essence (magazine), 188

ethnography, 82

Everett, David, 64

Evers, Medgar, 141, 146

"Everybody's Protest Novel" (Baldwin), 27–28

exceptionalism, 13, 119–22, 130–31, 137–39, 151, 221, 242n4

Exodus, 234n27

"Extravagance of Laughter, An" (Ellison), 150

Fair Play for Cuba Committee, 231n23

Fannie Lou Hamer (Jordan), 250n35

Faubus, Orval, 232n39

Faulkner, William, 158

Fauset, Jessie, 4, 26, 85, 92–94, 97, 240n17, 243n31

Federal Writers Project, 107

Female Literary Association of Philadelphia, 235n40

feminism, 180–81, 188–89, 226, 249n26

Fine Clothes to the Jew (Hughes), 117

Fire!! A Quarterly Devoted to the Younger Negro Artists, 117

Fire in the Flint, The (White), 240n28

Fire Next Time, The (Baldwin), 4, 36, 122, 136–39, 141, 147, 177, 219, 221

Fisher, Rudolph, 86, 92, 98, 240n29

Fitzgerald, F. Scott, 84, 152

Fleming, Julius, 218

Florida Negro, The: A Federal Writers Project Legacy (ed. McDonogh), 241n41

folklore, 25, 27

Foote, Julia, 77, 235n41

Ford, Ford Madox, 152

Forest Leaves (Watkins), 238n77

"For My American Family: A Belated Tribute to a Legacy of Gifted Intelligence and Guts" (Jordan), 201–2

"For My People" (Walker), 32

Forten, James, 40, 46

Foster, Frances Smith, 233n4, 238n77

Foxx, Redd, 247n29

Franklin, John Hope, 40

Franklin, Shirley Fisher, 156

fraternal organizations, 13

Frazier, E. Franklin, 98, 245n36

Frederic, Ben, 232n24

freedom: in Alice Walker, 32–35; in Baraka, 30–32; as central topic, 10; civic, 11, 217; cultural, 10; in David Walker, 41–42, 49–50; in Douglass, 64–67; in Du Bois, 16–18; in Ellison, 28–29, 158–59; in Garnet, 41, 60–63; in Hurston, 18–21, 108; in Jones, 21–23, 30–32; in Neal, 29–30; oratory and, 82–83; in Patterson,

freedom: in Alice Walker (cont.)
10–11; personal, 11, 217–18; sentimentality
and, 27–28; slavery and, 10–13; sovereig-
nal, 11; United States as synonymous
with, 14; in Watkins Harper, 76–77;
whites and, 12; in Williams, 23–24; in
Wright, 26–27
Freedom (Patterson), 10
Freedom in the Making of Western Culture
(Patterson), 11
Freedom Journal, 25
Freedom's Journal (newspaper), 37, 39–40
"free-floating literacy," 37–38
Free Soil Party, 237n70
Frost, Robert, 92
Fugitive Slave Act, 79

Gaines, Kevin, 245nn33,36
Garner, Eric, 217, 220, 227, 251n3
Garnet, Henry Highland, 5, 15–16, 27–28,
36–37, 40–42, 58–63, 236nn50–236n51
Garrison, William Lloyd, 38, 68, 72, 75,
236n50
Garza, Alicia, 224
Gay, Roxanne, 217
Ghana, 129
Gibson, Donald B., 231n15
Gibson, Richard, 231n23
Gide, André, 151
"Gift of Laughter, The" (Fauset), 92–93
"Gift of the Black Tropics" (Domingo), 86
Gilpin, Charles, 94, 102
Gilroy, Paul, 113, 242n49
Glaude, Eddie, 140, 234n27
gnomic, 229n16
gnostic, 229n16
Goetz, Bernhard, 23
Going to the Territory (Ellison), 148, 154
"Going to the Territory" (Ellison), 157–61,
164–65, 167–68, 247n32
Gordon, Eugene, 98
gospel, 242n1, 242n51
Gospel Pearls (songbook), 242n51
Grant, Madison, 102
Great Migration, 85–87

Gregory, Montgomery, 92, 240n16
Griffin, Farah Jasmine, 251n2
Grimké, Angelina, 92
Grimké, Charlotte Forten, 25
Guillén, Nicolás, 232n24

Haiti, 39–40
Hall, Jacqueline Dowd, 246n9
Hamer, Fannie Lou, 178, 197, 250n35
Hamilton, Alexander, 13
Harding, Warren G., 101–2
Harlem Renaissance, 26, 84–86, 98, 105, 107
Harmon Foundation, 95
Harrison, Hazel, 164–65, 170
Hartman, Saidiya, 12, 251n2
Hayes, Roland, 116
Hazlitt, William, 196
Hemings, Sally, 235n30
Hemingway, Ernest, 151–52, 158, 243n15
Henry, Aaron, 178
Henry, Patrick, 50, 60
"Heritage" (Cullen), 92
"Hidden Name and Complex Fate"
(Ellison), 148, 151–52, 156
Higginbotham, Evelyn, 40
Hinks, Peter, 233n15, 235n32
History Will Absolve Me (Castro), 207
Hogan, Ernest, 93
hokum, 99–100
homophobia, 143–44
homosexuality, 243n16
hoodoo, 194
Howard, Jennifer, 231n19
Howard Players, 92
Howard University, 86, 92, 222–23, 243n30
Howe, Irving, 149, 168–69
Howells, William Dean, 26
"How It Feels to Be Colored Me" (Hur-
ston), 4, 18–21, 116, 155, 249n16
Hudson, Mrs. Winsom, 179
"Hugging Fidel" (Walker), 251n44
Huggins, Nathan, 14, 84
Hughes, Langston, 6, 22, 26, 84–85, 87,
89–90, 92, 102–7, 117, 213, 232n24, 241n39
Hull, Akasha, 84

humanity, slavery and, 48–49
humor, 150, 155–56, 160, 249n22
Hurricane Katrina, 217
Hurston, Zora Neale, 4–6, 9–10, 18–21, 26,
  28, 34, 36, 84–86, 92, 107–16, 229n16,
  241n41, 242nn49,53; in Alice Walker,
  181–87, 194, 249n17; Ellison and, 163–64;
  will to adorn in, 125
Hutchinson, George, 84, 238n2, 239nn3,7
hybridity, of essay form, 1, 123
Hyman, Stanley, 149

"I, Too" (Hughes), 92
I Am Not Your Negro (film), 221
identity, in Ellison, 149–51
"I Heard It Through the Grapevine"
  (Campbell), 246n47
I Know Why the Caged Bird Sings (Ange-
  lou), 211
illiteracy, 37–39, 57, 60–61
"Imagination" (Wheatley), 90
*Imperial Eyes: Travel Writing and Transcul-
  turation* (Pratt), 208
"Impressions of the Pan-African Congress"
  (Fauset), 243n31
Inferno (Dante), 247n40
In Love and Trouble: Stories of Black Women
  (Walker), 193
In Search of Our Mothers' Gardens
  (Walker), 176–78
"In Search of Our Mothers' Gardens"
  (Walker), 4, 8, 32–35, 188, 192
inversion, 15, 61
Invisible Man (Ellison), 28, 148–49, 156, 164,
  170, 172, 232n40
Iola Leroy, or the Shadows Uplifted (Watkins
  Harper), 75–76
Iraq War, 217
irony, 36

Jackson, Mahalia, 233n42
Jackson, Rebecca Cox, 187–88
Jacobs, Harriet, 5
"jagged harmony," 109–10, 186
James, Henry, 123, 125–26, 150, 156, 243n24

James Baldwin Review, 221
Jarrett, Gene, 46
jazz, 31, 105, 161, 164–67, 169, 247n30
"Jazz at Home" (Rogers), 94
"Jazzonia" (Hughes), 102
Jefferson, Thomas, 13–14, 43, 48–49, 51, 154,
  235nn29–30
jeremiad, 45–46, 180
Job (biblical figure), 141
Johnson, Charles S., 85–86
Johnson, Georgia Douglas, 92, 189
Johnson, Helene, 86
Johnson, James Weldon, 4–6, 26, 84, 86,
  90–91, 93, 98, 157, 229n16, 240n28
Johnson, Rosamund, 93
Jones, Absalom, 13, 46
Jones, LeRoi, 21–23, 30–32. *See also* Baraka,
  Amiri
Jordan, June, 5, 8, 36, 45; Alice Walker and,
  176, 178, 189–90, 192–93, 248n5;
  background of, 177; civil rights
  movement and, 179–80; democracy in,
  200–201; education in, 190–91; family in,
  201–2; feminism and, 188–89, 249n26;
  jeremiad genre and, 180; rape of, 202–3;
  on struggle, 176; titles of, 177; women in,
  179–80
Julius Caesar (Shakespeare), 68

Kallen, Horace, 85
Key, Francis Scott, 51
Killens, John, 22
King, Coretta Scott, 206
King, Martin Luther, Jr., 45, 141–42, 146, 179
Kirchwey, Freda, 102

"Lady, Lady" (Spencer), 92
Lamming, George, 130, 133–35, 243n27
Langston Hughes: American Poet (Walker),
  193
Larsen, Nella, 188
Lawson, Charles, 65–66
Laymon, Kiese, 217
Leaves of Grass (Whitman), 72
Lee, Jarena, 54, 77, 235n41

Leeming, David, 245n45
"Legacy of the Ancestral Arts, The"
    (Locke), 91, 95–96
"Letter from a Region in My Mind"
    (Baldwin), 122, 136, 138
"Letter from Birmingham Jail" (King), 179
Letters from a Man of Colour (Forten), 46
"Letter to My Nephew" (Baldwin), 1
Levine, Lawrence, 249n22
Lewis, David Levering, 84
Lewis, R. W. B., 243n6
Liberation of American Literature (Calver-
    ton), 239n3
Liberator, The (newspaper), 38, 72, 76,
    236n46, 238n77
Liberia, 51–52, 144
"Life You Save May Be Your Own, The"
    (O'Connor), 193
Lincoln, Abraham, 234n17
Lindsay, Vachel, 92
Lippman, Walter, 98
literacy, 37–39, 57, 60–61
literary criticism, 1
"Little Man at Chehaw Station, The"
    (Ellison), 164–65, 169–74, 247n40
"Living with Music" (Ellison), 166, 247n30
Locke, Alain, 5, 26, 84–92, 94–97, 132–33,
    239nn7,9,14
Logan, Rayford, 25, 85
Longfellow, Henry Wadsworth, 68
"Looking for Zora" (Walker), 183–84,
    186–87
Loos, Anita, 28
"Lord, How Come Me Here?" (spiritual),
    17
Lorde, Audre, 137, 201, 250n39
Lowell, Amy, 92
Lukács, George, 7
"Lulls" (Walker), 198–200
lyceum movement, 41
Lynch, Acklyn, 249n26
lynching, 163–64

Mackey, Nathaniel, 8, 16
magazines, 85

Mailer, Norman, 245n37
Maine Anti-Slavery Society, 76
Malcolm X, 141, 146
Malraux, André, 158
manicule, 44
Mann, Thomas, 151
"Man Thinking" (Emerson), 73
"Many Rivers to Cross" (Jordan), 214–16,
    250n28
"Many Thousands Gone" (Baldwin), 124
March on Washington (1963), 143
Marrant, John, 13
Marshall, Paule, 148, 201
Martin, Trayvon, 217, 224–25, 252n13
Marxism, 27
Mathes, Carter, 32
Matthews, Victoria Earle, 5, 25–26
Matthiessen, F. O., 120
Maxwell, William, 221
Maynard, Tony, 143, 146
McCarthy, Mary, 3, 243n15
McDonogh, Gary, 241n41
McGill, Meredith, 238n76
McGrath, Charles, 229n2
McHenry, Elizabeth, 38, 40, 235n40
McKay, Claude, 86, 89, 91–92, 101, 239n14
*Meditations from the Pen of Mrs. Maria W.
    Stewart* (Stewart), 58, 235n38
Meer, Sarah, 66
melting pot metaphor, 173–74
Melville, Herman, 84, 149, 152
Mencken, H. L., 85, 98–100, 229n16, 240n28
Messenger, The (magazine), 85, 107
Miami riots, 196–97
Micheaux, Oscar, 167
middle class, 103–4
Miller, Henry, 243n15
Miller, Kelly, 86
Mingus, Charles, 31
ministers, 15–16
Monk, Thelonious, 232n26
Monroe, James, 52
Monrovia, Liberia, 52
Montaigne, Michel de, 2–3, 229n3
Morgan, Edmund, 12

Morrison, Toni, 1, 3, 11–12, 178, 220–21, 250n26

Moses, Wilson, 45

Moton, Robert R., 86

Mott, Lucretia, 75

Moynihan, Daniel Patrick, 155

"Mrs. Stewart's Farewell Address to her Friends in the City of Boston" (Stewart), 57

Ms. (magazine), 179, 204, 250n41

Muhammad, Elijah, 123, 139

Mules and Men (Hurston), 112, 115, 183, 186

Mumford, Lewis, 120

music, 30–32, 105–6, 108–9, 113–16, 124–25, 148–49, 161, 164–66, 169–71, 242n1, 242n51, 247n30

"My Brother's Keeper and the Co-Operation of Intersectionality" (Cooper), 226

"My Dungeon Shook: Letter to My Nephew on the One Hundredth Anniversary of the Emancipation" (Baldwin), 136

"My Father's Country Is the Poor" (Walker), 206–9

NAACP. *See* National Association for the Advancement of Colored People (NAACP)

Narrative of the Life of Frederick Douglass, an American Slave (Douglass), 17, 38, 124

Nathan, George Jean, 98

Nation, The (journal), 85, 102–3, 178, 218

National Anti-Slavery Standard, The, 77

National Association for the Advancement of Colored People (NAACP), 85

National Baptist Convention, 242n51

nationalism, black, 21, 27

National Negro Convention (Buffalo, 1843), 59

National Urban League, 85

Nation of Islam, 139–40

Native Son (Wright), 27, 124

Neal, Larry, 9, 29–30, 232n37

"Necessity of a General Union Among Us, The" (Walker), 39–40

Négritude movement, 132, 243n29

"Negro Art and America" (Barnes), 95

"Negro-Art Hokum, The" (Schuyler), 97–103, 241n34

"Negro Artist and the Racial Mountain, The" (Hughes), 6, 26, 102–7

"Negro Artists and the Negro" (Thurman), 117–18

Negro Convention Movement, 40, 235n32

"Negro in American Literature, The" (Braithwaite), 92

"Negro in Art, The: How Shall He Be Portrayed?" (symposium), 85, 105

Negro Quarterly (magazine), 149

"Negro Speaks of Rivers, The" (Hughes), 92, 102

"Negro Spirituals, The" (Locke), 96

"Negro Youth Speaks" (Locke), 5, 88–90, 97

New Challenge (journal), 27

New England Anti-Slavery Society, 54

New Masses (magazine), 148

New Negro, 86–87, 90–91, 112, 117

New Negro, The (anthology), 85–86, 94

"New Negro, The" (Locke), 5, 86–88, 133

New Negro Renaissance, 27

New Republic (journal), 85, 117

Newton, Huey, 146

New World (Dvořák), 25

New Yorker (magazine), 136, 218

Nicaragua, 251n47

"Nicaragua: Why I Had to Go There" (Jordan), 209–11, 251n45

Nobody Knows My Name (Baldwin), 2–3

"Nobody Knows the Trouble I've Seen" (spiritual), 17

"No More Auction Block" (spiritual), 124–25

No Name in the Street (Baldwin), 119, 122–23, 141–47, 245n45

"Notes for a Hypothetical Novel" (Baldwin), 121–22

"Notes of a Barnard Dropout" (Jordan), 190–92

Notes of a Native Son (Baldwin), 28, 119, 123, 125, 142, 243n25
Notes on a Son and Brother (James), 123
Notes on the State of Virginia (Jefferson), 43, 48–49, 51
"Notes Toward a Black Balancing of Love and Hatred" (Jordan), 189
Not Without Laughter (Hughes), 105

Obama, Barack, 217, 223–24
obligato, 115–16
O'Connor, Flannery, 193
"Of Alexander Crummell" (Du Bois), 144
"Of Our Spiritual Strivings" (Du Bois), 4, 7, 16
"Of Practice" (Montaigne), 2
"Of the Dawn of Freedom" (DuBois), 7
"On Art and Such" (Hurston), 107–9, 241n41
On Call (Jordan), 204, 250n41
Once (Walker), 193
"On Initiation Rites and Power" (Ellison), 247n22
online publishing, 218
"On the Pleasure of Hating" (Hazlitt), 196
Opportunity (magazine), 85, 107
oral culture, 16
"oral literacy," 38
"Oration, An, Delivered Before Beta Kappa Society" (Emerson), 37
orations, 13–15
oratory: circuit of transmission for, 36–37; Douglass and, 63–75; Garnet and, 58–63; "golden age of American," 41; jeremiad genre and, 45–46; literacy and, 37–38; Protestantism and, 37; repetition and, 46–47; Stewart and, 53–58; typography and, 44–45; Unitarianism and, 77–78; Walker and, 36, 39–53; Watkins Harper and, 75–82
Othello, 12–13, 230n5
"Our Composite Ethnology" (Douglass), 66
"Our Greatest Want" (Watkins Harper), 82
Owen, Chandler, 85

Page, Inman, 159–62, 168
Paine, Thomas, 13, 46, 68
Palestinians, 203
pamphlets, 13–14
Pan-African Congresses, 133, 243n31, 245n35
Pan-Africanism, 39
Parker, Charlie, 169
Passing of the Great Race, The (Grant), 102
Patterson, Orlando, 10–11, 217, 230n1
Pennsylvania Anti-Slavery Society, 76
Perry, Imani, 217
Peterson, Carla, 40, 53–54, 76, 81
Pickett, Wilson, 232n40
Piven, Frances Fox, 196–98
Pleasures of Exile, The (Lamming), 243n29
"Po' Boy Blues" (Hughes), 90
Poems on Miscellaneous Subjects (Watkins Harper), 76, 78, 238nn76–77
Poor People's Movements: Why They Succeed, How They Fail (Piven), 197–98
"Portrait of Inman Page: A Dedication Speech" (Ellison), 159
Pound, Ezra, 152
Pratt, Mary Sue, 208
Présence Africaine (journal), 243n27
"Preservation of Innocence" (Baldwin), 123
Price-Mars, Jean, 130, 243n29
Prince Hall Masons, 13
"Princes and Powers" (Baldwin), 130–31, 135, 145
print culture, 37–38
privacy, of essays, 2
Productions of Mrs. Maria W. Stewart (Stewart), 58
Progressive, The (magazine), 179, 218
Protestantism, 15–16, 37
protest writing, 14
Purcell, Richard, 247n40
Puritanism, 98
Pushkin, Alexander, 26, 101

"Question of Identity, A" (Baldwin), 123
quilts, 33–34

race: in Baldwin, 126–27, 137, 142, 146–47, 245n45; in Coates, 220–22; in Ellison, 150; in Hurston, 20

"Race Men," 108

racial uplift, 6, 78

Rainey, Ma, 167, 233n42

Ralph Ellison Festival, 158–59

Rampersad, Arnold, 148, 231n14

Randolph, A. Philip, 85

Randolph, John, 51

Reid Lectures, 190

"Remembering Richard Wright" (Ellison), 161

"Re-Nigging on the Promises: #Justice-4Trayvon," 224–26

repetition, 46–47

"Report from the Bahamas" (Jordan), 204–6, 250n41

responses, essays as, 1

retaliatory violence, 197

Revolt Against Civilization, The (Stoddard), 102

Revolutionary Petunias (Walker), 193

Revolutionary War, 60–61

rhythm and blues, 31

Rice, Tamir, 220, 251n3

Richardson, Marilyn, 236n48

Richardson, Willis, 92

Rights of All, The (newspaper), 37, 40

R. Kelly, 227

Robeson, Paul, 94, 102

Rogers, J. A., 94, 98

Rourke, Constance, 158

Rushing, Jimmy, 165

"Russian Cathedral" (McKay), 92

Russwurm, John, 25, 39

Rustin, Bayard, 143

Salt Eaters, The (Bambara), 177

salvation, emotional, 94

Sanchez, Sonia, 249n26

Sandinistas, 203, 251n47

"Santo Domingo" (Douglass), 66

Saunders, Prince, 46

Savage, Augusta, 108

"Saving the Life That Is Your Own: The Importance of Models in the Artist's Life" (Walker), 190, 192–94

Schuyler, George P., 84, 97–102, 229n16, 241n34

Scruggs, Charles, 240n28

"Self-Made Men" (Douglass), 66

Senghor, Léopold, 130, 132, 243n29

sensuality, 137

sentimentality, 27–28, 76, 96

Sermon Preached on the 24th Day of June 1789 . . . (Marrant), 13

sexuality, 137

Shadow and Act (Ellison), 3, 28, 148, 164–66

Shakespeare, William, 68, 112

"Shattering Black Flesh: Black Intellectual Writing in the Age of Ferguson" (Fleming), 218

Shaw, George Bernard, 152

Sisters of the Spirit (Andrews, ed.), 235n41

"Slave Auction, The" (Watkins Harper), 41

"Slave Mother, The" (Watkins Harper), 41

slave rebellion, 56–57

slavery: Bible in justification of, 13–14; in David Walker, 39–53; in Douglass, 63–75; in Du Bois, 17–18; in Ellison, 149; equality and, 12; freedom and, 10–13; in Garnet, 59–63; humanity and, 48–49; in Hurston, 20; illiteracy and, 37–39, 57, 60–61

Smart Set, The (magazine), 98

Smith, Barbara, 249n26

Smith, Bessie, 102, 119

Smith, James McCune, 63

SNCC. *See* Student Nonviolent Coordinating Committee (SNCC)

social consciousness, 27

Society for the Abolition of the Slave Trade, 77

Soldier: A Poet's Childhood (Jordan), 250n35

Some of Us Did Not Die (Walker), 177

"Song for a Banjo Dance" (Hughes), 102

"Sorrow Songs, The" (Du Bois), 18

Soul on Ice (Cleaver), 143–44

Souls of Black Folk, The (Du Bois), 2, 4–5, 7–9, 16–18, 23, 82, 86, 124, 144, 156–57, 243n26

South America, 39

"Speech of an Indian Chief, of the Stockbridge Tribe to the Massachusetts Congress," 64

Spelman College, 177

Spencer, Anne, 92, 239n13

Spillers, Hortense, 154

spirituals, 17, 108–9, 113–16, 124–25, 216, 231n15

"Spirituals and Neo-Spirituals" (Hurston), 113–16, 242n49

Spivak, Gayatri, 120, 242n4

"Spunk" (Hurston), 107

Stanton, Elizabeth Cady, 75

Stauffer, John, 237n70

Stein, Gertrude, 152

Stevens, Wallace, 92

Stewart, James W., 53–58, 236n48

Stewart, Maria, 9, 15, 36, 40–41, 75, 235nn38,40, 236nn44,46,48

Still, William, 77, 81

Stocking, George, 238n2

Stoddard, Lothrop, 102

Stowe, Harriet Beecher, 27

"Stranger in the Village" (Baldwin), 3–4, 119, 126–28, 145

strategic American exceptionalism, 119, 121–22, 130–31, 137–39, 242n4

Stuckey, Sterling, 236n51

Student Nonviolent Coordinating Committee (SNCC), 139

Styron, William, 142

Sula (Morrison), 250n26

Sun Ra, 32

"Symbolism of Bert Williams, The" (Fauset), 93–94

Symphony Sid, 232n26

"Take Me to the Water" (Baldwin), 119–20, 141–43

Tanner, Henry Ossawa, 97

Taylor, Cecil, 232n26

Technical Difficulties (Jordan), 202

Tell My Horse (Hurston), 186

Their Eyes Were Watching God (Hurston), 189, 193, 249n20

"There Is a Fountain Filled with Blood" (Cowper), 78

"The Story of Why I am Here, or a Woman Connects Oppressions" (Walker), 251n44

Third Life of Grange Copeland, The (Walker), 193

"This is America's Religion of violence: The Impunity of Police Violence and the Destruction of Sandra Bland" (Cooper), 226–27

Thompson, Brooks, 108

Thoreau, Henry David, 84, 149

Thurman, Wallace, 117–18

"To Be Baptized" (Baldwin), 146, 208

Tóibín, Colm, 125, 243n24

Toomer, Jean, 89, 92

"To Our Patrons" (Cornish and Russwurm), 39

Torin, Sid, 232n26

"Triumph of Freedom, The" (Garrison), 75

"troubled eloquence," 8, 16–17, 230n9

Trump, Donald, 217

Tubman, Harriet, 200

Turgenev, Ivan, 26

Turner, Nat, 56–57, 59

Tutuola, Amos, 134

Twain, Mark, 19, 26, 84, 149, 152, 156, 165

"Twentieth Century Fiction and the Black Mask of Humanity" (Ellison), 149–50

typography, 44–45

Uggams, Leslie, 233n42

Ulanov, Barry, 191

Uncle Tom's Cabin (Stowe), 27

Underground Railroad, The (Still), 77

"Unglamorous but Worthwhile Duties of the Black Revolutionary Artist, The, or of the Black Writer Who Simply Works and Writes" (Walker), 176, 194–95

Unitarian Church, 77–78
"Uses of the Erotic, The" (Lorde), 137

"Value of Race Literature, The" (Matthews), 5, 25–26
Van Gogh, Vincent, 193
vernacular process, 8–9, 19–20, 98–99, 152–53, 156, 225, 231n20
Vesey, Denmark, 59, 233n15
Vidal, Gore, 229n2
Vietnam War, 142–43, 146
violence, retaliatory, 197
Virginia Slave Code, 12
voodoo, 194

"Waking Up in the Middle of Some American Dreams" (Jordan), 202–3
Waldrond, Eric, 92
Walker, Alice, 4, 7–8; background of, 177; civil rights movement and, 179–80, 248n8; freedom in, 32–35; Hurston in, 181–87, 194, 249n17; Jordan and, 176, 178, 189–90, 192–93, 248n5; oratory and, 36; scorn of, 248n7; titles in, 176–77; and vernacular process, 9; womanism and, 180–81; women in, 179–80; on writing, 176, 194–95
Walker, David, 5, 8, 15, 36, 39–53, 56, 68, 233n15, 234nn17,19, 235n33, 236n51
Walker, George, 93
Walker, Margaret, 32
Walker, Minnie Lou, 33
Walker, Willie Lee, 207–9
Walker's Appeal (Walker), 5, 39–53, 57, 68, 234nn19,22, 235n31
Warrick Fuller, Meta, 97
Warwick, Dionne, 233n42
Washington, George, 13, 64
Washington, Madison, 59
Was Huck Black? Mark Twain and African American Voices (Twain), 156
Watkins, William, 76, 238n77
Watkins Harper, Frances E., 15–16, 25, 36, 38–39, 41, 75–82, 238n76

"We Are All Bound Up Together" (Watkins Harper), 80
Weary Blues, The (Hughes), 102, 117
websites, 218
Webster, Daniel, 41
We Were Eight Years in Power: An American Tragedy, 224
"What to the Slave Is the Fourth of July?" (Douglass), 67–75, 234n17
"What Would America Be Like Without Blacks" (Ellison), 154–57
Wheatley, Phillis, 25, 33, 55, 90, 188
"When Sue Wears Red" (Hughes), 102
"Where Is the Love?" (Jordan), 188–90
White, Walter, 98, 240n28
"White Houses" (McKay), 92, 239n14
whites: in Baldwin, 128–29, 137, 245n45; in Ellison, 163–64; freedom and, 12; in Hughes, 103; lynching and, 163–64; in Schuyler, 100–101; in Stewart, 55; in Watkins Harper, 78–79
white supremacy, in Baldwin, 122, 139
Whitman, Walt, 72, 84, 116, 154
Whittaker, Johnson, Chesnut, 161–62, 168, 247n22
Wiley, Hugh, 97
Williams, Bert, 93–94, 240n18
Williams, Billy Dee, 146
Williams, George Washington, 25
Williams, Patricia, 8, 23–24
Williams, William Carlos, 154
William Watkins Academy for Negro Youth, 76
"will to adorn," 6, 8, 32–33, 123–25
Winthrop, John, 120, 234n24
womanism, 180–81, 187–88
women: in Alice Walker, 179–80; as artists, 33–34; in Baldwin, 245n37; in Bible, 57; in Cooper, 226; in Ellison, 175; Ellison and, 247n29; in Jordan, 179–80; in Stewart, 57
Women, Sketches of the History, Genius, Disposition, Accomplishments, Employments, Customs and Importance of the Fair Sex In All Parts of the World

Women, Sketches of the History (cont.)
  *Interspersed With Many Singular and
  Entertaining Anecdotes By a Friend of the
  Sex* (Adams), 57
Wonder, Stevie, 31
Woolf, Virginia, 33
"World and the Jug, The" (Ellison), 29, 149,
  158, 172
World War I, 84
World War II, 149

Wright, John, 148
Wright, Richard, 4–5, 26–27, 98, 123–24,
  130–32, 220, 231n23, 245n37

Yezierska, Anzia, 205
Young, Lester, 165
"Youth" (Hughes), 87

Zaborowska, Magdalena J., 143
Zimmerman, George, 252n13